TO THE ENDS OF THE EARTH

To the

ENDS OF THE EARTH

THE TRUTH BEHIND THE GLORY OF
POLAR EXPLORATION

John V. H. Dippel

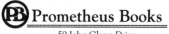 Prometheus Books

59 John Glenn Drive
Amherst, New York 14228

Inquiries should be addressed to
Prometheus Books
59 John Glenn Drive
Amherst, New York 14228
VOICE: 716–691–0133 • FAX: 716–691–0137
WWW.PROMETHEUSBOOKS.COM

22 21 20 19 18   5 4 3 2 1

Library of Congress Cataloging-in-Publication Data Pending

Printed in the United States of America

To Theo
A reader soon,
A joy forever

Author's note: All temperatures in this book are in Fahrenheit.

CONTENTS

INTRODUCTION

The test of a first-rate intelligence is the ability to hold two opposed views in the mind at the same time and still retain the ability to function.

—F. Scott Fitzgerald

Oddly enough, the first two men to lose their minds in the Antarctic were Norwegian sailors. Their names were Adam Tollefsen and Engelbret Knudsen. Likely looking for adventure, they had volunteered to go south on board the whaling ship *Belgica* in the summer of 1897. Not much is known about them. They are most remembered for the terrible thing that happened to them on that ill-fated, icebound vessel.

While the *Belgica* was trapped in Antarctic ice for thirteen months, cut off completely from the rest of the world, they both had nervous breakdowns. They eventually regained their senses, but they were never quite the same again. Knudsen had to be institutionalized after the *Belgica* returned to Europe, and he died not long afterward. Tollefsen, who had been found mumbling incoherently, wandering aimlessly on the ice, recovered and was able to return home with the rest of the crew and resume a seemingly normal life. But the Antarctic left its stamp on his mind, too.

Perhaps one should not make too much of the fact that Knudsen and Tollefsen were Norwegians. But it is strange that, coming from a Scandinavian country, they would be the most severely affected by the deprivations of Antarctic imprisonment—isolation, extremely low temperatures, months of total darkness, confinement in cramped quarters, shortages of food, immobility, boredom, lack of privacy, and fear of dying at any moment. That they suffered despite their background only indicates how inescapably stressful this ordeal on the *Belgica* was. Sailors from other countries on board also developed signs of mental illness. Even the Belgian head of the expedition—Adrien Victor Joseph de Gerlache de Gomery—fell victim to depression. Indeed, a superstitious observer might have blamed him for all that subsequently went wrong. After all, it was de Gerlache who had changed the name of this steam-powered barque when he had bought it, from *Patria* to *Belgica*—an act believed by seafarers to invariably bring bad luck. And, because of the polyglot nature of the crew he had recruited, there had been tensions from the start of the voyage south, with bad blood between the Belgian officers and the Norwegian crew members boiling over during a stop in Punta Arenas, when several of the Scandinavians had accused de Gerlache of being biased against them. But the cause of this shipboard madness ran deeper than this. The seeds for this expedition's disaster had been sown before they ever raised anchor. It stemmed from disagreements about why the *Belgica* was headed to Antarctica and what it intended to do there.

Ostensibly, the 250-ton barque was supposed to be on a scientific mission. During the recent Sixth International Geographical Congress, in London, in 1895, participating European nations had agreed that it was high time to learn more about Antarctica. This was now going to be a top priority. Expeditions would be dispatched there to study its oceans, land features, and life forms. It so happened that de Gerlache was already planning an ocean expedition, purportedly with the goal of collecting this kind of information. The ninety-eight-foot-long *Belgica* would thus be the first vessel to enter Antarctic waters solely for the purpose of increasing knowledge about this land of mystery and wonder. Its primary objectives were to reach the South Magnetic Pole and to study ocean currents and the weather. To carry out this work de Gerlache had assembled a small, international band of scientists—a Polish geologist, meteorologist, and oceanographer, a Romanian biologist and speleologist, another Pole with a background in physics and biology, and the upstate New

York physician Frederick A. Cook, who also served as anthropologist and photographer. So that they could conduct their research properly, the *Belgica* had been outfitted with what an effusive *Boston Transcript* writer described as "a splendid collection of the most modern scientific instruments."[1] With this team of scientists, as well as so much equipment and a spacious laboratory on board, there was little doubt that the expedition would make valuable contributions to better understanding this remote and little-visited region—one of the last frontiers on earth. The voyage's greatest obstacle would be encroaching ice. To avoid being caught in its steely grip, the Belgian ship was to head north to Australia after some preliminary exploration of the Antarctic Peninsula, take on new stores there, and then wait until spring before heading south again to resume its research. Wintering in the pack was out of the question. Around Antarctica stretched a vast, impenetrable girdle of ice, and the chances of surviving in it for long—without food or chance of escape—were slim to none. "No man ever wintered on the Antarctic continent, and no quadruped, like the bear and the wolf and the musk ox of the Arctic, lives in this frigid zone," pointed out one American newspaper.

But the truth was that the thirty-one-year-old de Gerlache was not steering the *Belgica* so far south in the name of science. He had a secret ambition. Instead of avoiding the ice and seeking a safe haven, he intended to plow through floes until his ship could go no farther, and then remain there through the winter, encased as in a tomb, until the ice finally cracked apart in the spring. From there he would be in an excellent position to navigate through open water and accomplish what he really wanted to do—set a new "Farthest South" record. This historic feat would make him overnight a national hero: a vessel proudly flying Belgium's tricolor flag and captained by one of its own naval officers would have eclipsed those of larger nations in approaching the bottom of the world. To make this mark, spending a winter icebound off Antarctica's coast was a small price to pay, and de Gerlache had no second thoughts about doing so. He was enthralled by the prospect of the glory that awaited him, of being the first to go where no other ever had. As he would later write, "Everything was wild, sterile and bare, and yet it was also all ours, because we had discovered it."[2]

The Belgian commander was not the only one on board with a secret agenda. Cook, a Columbia-trained physician, had joined the expedition in Rio de Janeiro at the last minute—supposedly to look after the crew's health, but, in fact, to fulfill a lifelong dream of visiting the Antarctic.[3] Exploration was his abiding passion. He had no real training as an anthropologist or keen interest in conducting scientific investigations. Roald Amundsen, the ship's first mate, was an intensely ambitious but untested explorer, who had come along to learn more about how to captain a ship and survive in the brutal polar environment. (Amundsen was the only other person on board who wanted to continue southward even if that meant wintering in the ice.) He considered science merely a necessary evil—what polar expeditions had to do in order to obtain funding.[4] Even one of the scientists on the *Belgica* had doubts about his work being worthwhile. Emil Racoviță, the well-to-do Romanian biologist who would go on to become one of the world's leading experts on cave life, amused himself during the icebound months by making cartoonish sketches of his colleagues' obsessive note-taking.[5]

In fact, the *Belgica* expedition was rent by confusion about its rationale and by internal dissension from the moment it left Antwerp. In his coat pocket de Gerlache carried no instructions from the Belgian government, which had contributed a considerable sum to help finance this voyage.[6] Nor did any of the scientists or officers have a clear idea of what their duties might be. No one at the Belgian Geographical Society had mapped out the route that the captain, Georges Lecointe, was to take. So changes of course and stops along the way were decided on the spur of the moment. Along the South American coast, the officers elected to linger and enjoy the sights. De Gerlache was so bedazzled by the fantastical icebergs they passed south of Tierra del Fuego that he paid little attention to organizational details. The officers and scientists were given so much free rein to pursue their own projects that the head scientist, Henryk Arctowski, worried the situation on board might devolve into "anarchy."[7] He had had intimations of such an outcome when shipboard discipline had broken down on several earlier occasions: one sailor had refused to leave his bunk to help prevent the *Belgica* from colliding with King Leopold's yacht in Ostende harbor; two other sailors went AWOL, got drunk, and never returned to the ship; later, the Swedish cook was let go after starting a fight in Montevideo; and another sailor was fired for refusing to help load supplies. The crew grew so volatile that Lecointe, a former artillery officer, took to carrying a pistol at all times.[8] During an extended stopover at the tip of South America, de Gerlache had to ask Chilean authorities to rein in some unruly sailors. These ugly incidents left the expedition party dangerously shorthanded and divided.[9]

Compounding this unruliness was an alarming lack of seamanship: some of the crew had never been on the open ocean before; almost all on board, starting with the captain, suffered daily from the "openly acknowledged pastime" of seasickness; an engineer was summarily put ashore on the coast of South America after he let one of the boilers run dry; the *Belgica* ran aground twice—once near the capital of Tierra del Fuego and a second time as they were gliding between icebergs in January, when the ship nearly sank; and a "misunderstood command" to the engine room caused it to slam into a berg.[10] Meanwhile, the conflicting objectives of this poorly planned voyage created more problems. De Gerlache's insistence on spending more time on Tierra del Fuego—combined with Cook's fascination with a local indigenous tribe—delayed the expedition's departure until after the New Year, increasing the odds that the *Belgica* would eventually become trapped by ice. As they continued on southward, astonishment at the strange beauty of the monstrous bergs that rose ghostlike out of the fog mixed with dread over the threat they posed. Even more disquieting was the crew's growing unease over having left their familiar world behind and entered this alien and forbidding realm—what they increasing regarded as a "place of horror and catastrophe."[11]

Cook, the most literate and observant member of the party, expressed what others were thinking when the gigantic land mass of Antarctica first rose before their eyes. "Everything about us had another-worldly appearance," he would recall. "The scenery, the life, the clouds, the atmosphere, the water—everything wore an air of mystery."[12] Every thrust forward took them that much further into the desolate unknown. Like Odysseus's crew harkening to the Sirens, they were being drawn irresistibly toward a fatal danger, with home and loved ones now "out of all possible reach for months, perhaps for years, and possibly forever." And still de Gerlache ordered Lecointe to press on, disregarding the pleas of his scientists to turn back before it was too late. He was obsessed by his own heroic image: "We seemed to be entering a different world, one where, like the heroes of Scandinavian myth, we were being subjected to supernatural trials and labours by terrifying gods. And was it not indeed a new world we were penetrating then, not to deliver some slumbering Valkyrie but to wrest a few of its jealously guarded secrets from the pristine Antarctic?"[13] But these secrets were not about to be revealed. After reaching 71.30 degrees south, on March 2, 1898, the jaunty, white-hulled barque, with its cobweb of limp rigging and impertinent little yellow smokestack, ground ignominiously to a halt, surrounded by a sheet of fresh, rapidly spreading ice, and no frantic exertions of her 35-horsepower steam engine could budge it. Now the *Belgica* was truly, as even de Gerlache had to concede, a "prisoner of the ice."[14] At the ends of the earth, the march of civilization had ground to an ignominious halt.

The party was woefully unprepared for a protracted Antarctic sojourn. De Gerlache had neglected to provide the men with winter clothing, so they had to stitch together crude coats out of wool blankets. For sustenance, they would have to depend on canned food—enough to last a year if they were prudent, but not any longer. This tasteless diet (supplemented now and then by fresh seal and penguin meat), unchanging scenery, idleness, and ever-present anxiety about the *Belgica* being crushed by the ice induced a malaise. "Little by little, the members of the Expedition became, body and soul, affected with languor," noted de Gerlache.[15] After gradually growing fainter, the sun slipped out of sight for good on May 17th, leaving the scientists, officers, and crew in utter darkness for the next two months. Deprived of light, their skin turned greenish-yellow and oily. With their rations cut, the men weakened, had constant head-aches, and could not sleep. Many came down with scurvy, but couldn't stomach the raw, greasy seal meat that would cure it. They read and reread books on navigation and lighthouses, played whist, listened to records, told stale jokes—anything to break the monotony. They ached like teen-agers for a glimpse of a woman.[16]

With no hope of liberation for months, the mood on board soured. Men withdrew into their thoughts and brooded. Cook detected a deep-ening despair: "The curtain of blackness which has fallen over the outer world of icy desolation has also descended upon the inner world of our souls. Around the tables, in the laboratory, and in the forecastle, men are sitting about sad and dejected, lost in dreams of melancholy from which, now and then, one arouses with an empty attempt at enthusiasm."[17] With all of de Gerlache's dreams of drifting closer to the pole completely dashed, all he and his crew could do was hope they could stay alive until they were set free.

As was amply illustrated by the fate of the *Belgica*, hopes that expe-ditions to the Arctic and Antarctic would demonstrate human mastery over the entire planet were all too often dashed. In fact, the history of this exploration is largely one of unmitigated frustration, disappointment, failure, and defeat, only occasionally interspersed with remarkable mile-stones such as navigating the Northwest Passage and "discovering" the two poles. One problem was the polar environment itself. Its climate, bar-renness, remoteness, and unpredictable nature defied attempts to inhabit it. But the clash between explorers and this strange world was but part of a larger conflict between expectations and reality, between ambitions and accomplishments, between actions and outcomes, that confounded the Western world in the nineteenth and early-twentieth centuries. In fact, the setbacks and disasters that explorers experienced in the polar ice fore-shadowed the disillusionment with civilization's inevitable progress that would occur decades later, as a result of naïve ideological experiments and devastating world wars.

As was the case on board the *Belgica*, some of these debilitating clashes arose from conflicting reasons for going so far north or south in the first place. Others resulted from trying to view this alien kingdom through ill-fitting and inadequate lenses and thus failing to engage it on its own terms. And still others came about because the explorers could not bring themselves to discard the values and practices that they considered supe-rior and invincible and adapt to the new demands of the Arctic and Ant-arctic. Altering this deeply ingrained outlook was particularly difficult for nineteenth-century Americans and Europeans because they adhered to a moral outlook and code of conduct that were not easily modified. The explorers were predisposed to view the world in binary terms. Everything was defined in opposition to something else: man versus Nature; "civi-lized" versus "barbaric"; Christians versus "heathens"; gentlemen versus "lower classes"; men versus women. But at the top and bottom of the world, these distinctions lost relevance or became counterproductive.

At the poles, explorers found themselves caught between what they felt they *ought* to do and what they *had* to do. Conflicts between per-sonal ambition and group well-being, between moral rectitude and self-preservation, forced them to make painful choices and then live with the consequences of their decisions. Many returned home with per-manent psychological and emotional scars. The various ways in which polar explorers reacted to the extraordinary challenges posed by condi-tions in the Arctic and Antarctic—how they wrestled with competing imperatives to survive and remain true to their convictions, and how this struggle changed them and, indirectly, the countries that had sent them there—is the subject of this book. In it, I have attempted to under-stand the explorers' responses within their historical and cultural con-texts, looking at a number of nineteenth- and early-twentieth-century expeditions to show how their experiences affected Western notions of courage, morality, conquest, progress, and human capability. Like the knights of medieval legend, polar explorers went forth into unknown territory, faced great obstacles, displayed great courage, and returned home to be greeted as heroes. But, unlike these mythical avatars, the men who went toward the poles did not come back with the same confidence and inner strength. Something precious had been left there. These explorers brought back a different outlook about what humans could achieve, and what they could not.

CHAPTER ONE

TRAILING CLOUDS OF GLORY

The steamship bearing the body of thirty-six-year-old Elisha Kent Kane arrived in New Orleans on February 23, 1857, after having been seen off in Havana—where he had succumbed to a long-weakened heart—by a solemn procession of some eight hundred Cubans, Americans, and other foreigners, led by the governor of the island. In the Louisiana port, the ship was met by a host of dignitaries, and the coffin transferred under military escort to the city hall, where it lay in state before being carried by twelve pallbearers, accompanied by members of the Masonic Order, the Sons of St. George, various civic organizations, diplomats, and elected officials, past a hushed throng of some six thousand persons, to another waiting vessel for the long and winding journey up the Mississippi and then the Ohio and on from there by train to its final stop in Philadelphia—an odyssey lasting four weeks and passing through thirteen states, making it the largest and most elaborate funeral procession the country had thus far witnessed.

Along this route "whenever it was possible the attempt was made by the people to give expression to the respect which the lofty character and ennobling services of the deceased had excited."[1] The turnout was astonishing. Clustered on the wooded riverbanks, large crowds came to stare and bow their heads reverently to the passing ship and its precious cargo. In death, as in life, the spirit of Kane remained in constant motion, ever seeking new worlds to conquer, ever fascinating. In Louisville and Cincinnati, the *Woodruff* tied up at the wharf, and thousands more—rich and poor alike—turned out downtown to pay their respects, showing how wide a range of Americans had been touched by Kane's courageous and audacious exploits.[2] Speech after speech lauded this beloved hero, who had reached places on earth never before visited by humans and survived unspeakable hardship to return to tell his tale. Flowery encomiums from all over the country hailed his 'indomitable courage, his untiring zeal, his enthusiastic love of science, and his sympathy for the suffering.'[3]

After being taken by rail to Ohio's state capital, Columbus, where so many mourners attempted to cram inside the senate chamber that half of them had to be turned way, Kane's body continued its way by train and boat eastward, on to Philadelphia. During its stopover in Baltimore, "the streets were walled with people, whilst windows, balconies and rooftops were occupied by spectators" in the largest public grieving in the city's history. Early on the morning of March 12, the day the funeral train arrived in his hometown, the streets were oddly quiet, flags hung at half-mast and black bunting adorned shop fronts and windowsills. Before noon the crowd outside Independence Hall had massed so densely that late arrivals could not get anywhere near the doors. They had to crane their necks to catch a glimpse of the entourage bearing Kane's flag-draped casket as it moved slowly atop a black-domed funeral car, drawn by six black horses, toward the soaring Corinthian columns of the Second Presbyterian Church and the nearby cemetery that was to be his final resting place. The eulogy was delivered before a hushed gathering by a fellow Mason from New York, E. W. Andrews, who spoke for over an hour, recounting the legendary feats of moral courage, scientific discovery, and sheer daring that had distinguished Kane's short but extraordinary life—from descending by rope into the crater of an active volcano in the Philippines, to saving the life of a Mexican general, to braving the subfreezing temperatures of the Arctic in search of Sir John Franklin and his men, to discovering the long-dreamed-of "Open Polar Sea"; Andrews paid fulsome homage to Kane's physical and mental energy—"a capacity for labor—a power of endurance—a resoluteness of purpose and an iron will, such as the stoutest and strongest, the Goliaths of earth, have rarely shown."[4]

Not until the death of Abraham Lincoln eight years later would there be another such national outpouring of grief. Without exaggeration, it could be said that America had lost one of its most illustrious and most admired sons—a man whose deeds and character epitomized all that the country aspired to be. But who was this young doctor from Philadelphia, of diminutive stature and frail constitution, and why had his life and death touched millions so deeply? And why is he all but forgotten today? To answer these questions, one has to go back to the era that produced Kane and understand what it longed for in its heroes.

By the middle of the nineteenth century, the United States was like a giddy teenager going through an awkward growth spurt. Over the previous decade its population had swelled by nearly 36 percent, reaching twenty-three million. The growth of factories in New England was spurring a transition from agriculture to manufacturing, with both sectors now producing roughly the same amount of income. In terms of wealth, the new nation was rapidly closing the gap with major European powers like England and Germany. Geographically, the United States had expanded westward all the way to the Pacific, gobbling up huge territories that added over a million square miles to its dominion—more than the total area of Western Europe, including Scandinavia—thus fulfilling its Manifest Destiny. But, despite all these material gains, America remained internally divided, insecure, and uncertain about its place in the world. Long-simmering tensions over slavery were coming to a head, with newly acquired Western territories turning into battlegrounds for deciding the nation's racial makeup. Whether or not the nation could remain united was now an open question: most people still used the plural form in referring to their country, as in "The United States *were* developing rapidly."[5] Diplomatically, the government had declared its right to dominate the Western Hemisphere under the Monroe Doctrine, but it had not yet promulgated a vision for dealing with the wider world. For the time being, the young republic was too self-preoccupied to do that. It was an optimistic age, but also a perilous one, as many fundamental issues had still to be resolved and there was little agreement about how to go about building the future.

The United States was by no means alone in achieving tremendous domestic progress and economic growth while, at the same time, being beset by political and international conflicts. In countries like England, France, Denmark, Holland, and Germany, industrialization had widened the gap between rich and poor and created resentment and demands for reform. In 1848, revolutions occurred in several European states, with two monarchies being overthrown and serfs freed in Austro-Hungary. The Congress of Vienna (1814) had created a durable framework for order and peace in the aftermath of the Napoleonic wars, but national rivalries and territorial ambitions persisted. As so often happens, beleaguered and unpopular governments looked for ways to divert unhappy subjects from challenging their authority by cultivating patriotism and national pride. Overseas exploration and colonization served this need well. Planting the flag on distant shores attested to a country's collective will, prowess, and courage. Foreign conquest gave military forces a chance to hone their skills and display their might. Far-flung empires raised a nation's profile and made its people feel superior. "Surplus" population— unfortunates left out of the Industrial Revolution—could be siphoned off to these faraway lands to reduce unemployment and unrest at home. Concomitantly, undeveloped corners of the world promised new raw materials, trade partners, and investment prospects. In addition, bringing "civilization" to "less advanced" peoples fulfilled a moral imperative to "enlighten" less fortunate peoples and help them advance. All this could be accomplished without risking the kind of devastating internecine war that had ravaged the Continent during the century's early decades. Thus, starting with England's opium wars in China in the 1830s, a New Imperialism informed the foreign policies of many European countries. In intent as well as in consequence, this ideology mirrored the expansionist impulse that was propelling frontiersmen, farmers, and cavalry troops over the Rocky Mountains.

For ambitious, adventuresome, and able-bodied young men, the conquering and settling of new lands brought enticing opportunities to prove themselves, make good money, widen their horizons, and escape a humdrum and often impoverished life. With their formidable navy and prosperous economy, the British had taken the lead in dispatching missions to the Far East and elsewhere.

Among the places that caught their eyes early on were the largely unexplored polar caps. These regions had fascinated Europeans as far back as the days of the ancient Greeks and the Vikings. During the more recent Age of Discovery (which commenced with Columbus's voyages to the New World), English explorers had searched in vain for a Northwest Passage that would provide a shorter commercial route to the Pacific. Sea journeys by the Italian John Cabot, Henry Hudson, William Baffin, and Martin Frobisher had probed the periphery of the Arctic and aroused popular curiosity about what might lie beyond. Some had envisioned vast (mineral) riches, others a "lost civilization" and tropical paradise at the top of the world.[6] (Leading geographers reasoned that the North Pole would be free of ice and warmer than anywhere else because the sun shone constantly there for part of the year.) Early in the nineteenth century, English fascination with this fanciful hyperborean realm was rekindled, largely thanks to the efforts of an old China Hand and colonial administrator named Sir John Barrow.

Barrow—an accomplished painter, cartographer, diplomat, and travel writer, as well as a founder of the Royal Geographical Society—had been appointed Second Secretary to the Admiralty in 1804 and happily held that position for the next forty years. Once the wars with France had ended, he realized that the Royal Navy had lost its raison d'être: hundreds of still-commissioned warships were bobbing at their moorings, their crews idle or demobilized, many of their officers forced into retirement, and the remaining ones dispirited, with no prospect of making a good career at sea.[7] (Indeed, British men-o'-war would not take part in any major battles between 1827 and 1914.) When a whaling captain reported in 1817 that Arctic waters along the coast of Greenland had been unusually free of ice the previous two years, Barrow jumped at the idea of sending ships northward to search—once again—for the fabled Northwest Passage, and perhaps even reach the North Pole. After having caught a tantalizing glimpse of the fogbound Far North from the deck of a whaler when he was only in his teens, Barrow had contracted an incurable dose of "Arctic fever."[8] Now he was convinced that the earth was entering a warming phase, and that this was thus a propitious moment for voyages into the unknown.[9] As a contemporary of his would write a few years later, Barrow hoped to revive "that bold and masculine spirit of discovery which, disdaining danger, seeks to extend the knowledge and dominion of man to the utmost limits of the globe he inhabits."[10] In the past, the British people had "derived much glory . . . from such enterprises; and it is in some sort a national duty to foster them—conducing, as they do, not merely to the extension of knowledge, but also to the life and energy of the national character." Unfortunately, the ships dispatched by the Admiralty in 1818 encountered conditions much less favorable than those they had expected. One party—with one vessel commanded by David Buchan, the other by Lieutenant John Franklin—found ice in June already clogging the waters around the island of Spitsbergen, off the northernmost coast of Norway. Buchan's ship, HMS *Dorothea*, was trapped after going only thirty miles further north. The Scottish lieutenant then gave up and headed back to England, with a frustrated Franklin reluctantly trailing along in his wake. Meanwhile, another expedition, this one led by John Ross, crept up along the eastern coast of Baffin Bay, also in search of the Northwest Passage, but had to turn back when Ross spotted what he mistakenly took to be a mountain range blocking his way. It turned out to be only a mirage.

Neither expedition had made any significant discoveries, but, thanks to Barrow's felicitous pen, their adventures were soon added to the pantheon of heroic British Arctic narratives stretching back more than two centuries. In a volume he published that very same year, *A Chronological*

History of Voyages into the Arctic Regions, Barrow reminded his readers of their illustrious seagoing tradition, noting that even these recent failures could not detract from the courage and fortitude they had exhibited in increasing knowledge about this mysterious part of the planet.[11] In so linking the legendary feats of yesteryear with the relatively modest ones of his own day, Barrow set a hagiographical tone for later books about polar explorers, encouraging his contemporaries to think of their era as more momentous than they might have felt it was—to soar in their minds and hearts higher and further, as brave seafarers were doing in Arctic waters. Much like Antonio in Shakespeare's *The Tempest*, he urged them to embrace a greater destiny by believing that "What's past is prologue."

More in love with this mystique than interested in the actual facts, a British public hungry for heroes in a dull and listless time responded to this appeal with great enthusiasm. They snatched up copies of Barrow's book and became mesmerized by the fate of polar expeditions that had set sail after Buchan's and Ross's ships. When William Edward Parry, who had accompanied Ross on his fruitless journey through Baffin Bay, returned to the Arctic the following year to "clear up the Ross fiasco," he kept a journal.[12] When he was preparing this account for publication, Parry thought about emulating Barrow and including a summary of earlier Arctic expeditions to immodestly point how his one voyage had surpassed the "repeated exertions of two centuries" in locating the likely entrance to the Northwest Passage.[13] But space limitations prevented him from doing so. Despite Parry's leaden, career officer's prose, the public was "thrilled" by his richly illustrated depiction of dodging huge icebergs, "warping" (hauling) his two ships through channels in the ice, observing dazzling auroras, groping through blinding snowstorms, and shooting walruses, polar bears, musk ox, and white whales.[14] Readers were predisposed to fill in the blanks in his account with their own vivid imaginings of what the Arctic must be like. (So were artists like the German Caspar David Friedrich, whose dramatic rendering of one of Parry's ships heeled over and crushed by massive ramparts of ice—*Das Eismeer*—was so unsettling that it went unsold until after Friedrich's death.) Evincing the same insatiable appetite, the British public devoured hundreds of newspaper articles about the ships dispatched northward by the Admiralty during the next two decades—twelve expeditions all told. Arctic devotees read whatever books they could get their hands on, went to plays, visited art exhibitions, and attended lectures, almost compulsively absorbing all the drama and romance the Far North had to offer.[15] Neither the explorers' frequent failures nor the severe deprivation they suffered could dampen this public ardor.

If anything, the descriptions of horrendous Arctic conditions only increased readers' fascination. Dealing with such an implacably hostile environment connected these explorers with a long tradition of stoic perseverance and self-sacrifice in British legend and history, going back as far as Arthurian knights and exemplified more recently by the death of Lord Nelson at Trafalgar. Polar expeditions honored a "growing belief in the Englishman's ability to survive anywhere and to triumph over any adversity through faith, scientific objectivity, and superior spirit."[16] Hardship and pain were the explorer's inseparable companions, the test of his mettle. As modern-day fables, these Arctic adventures mattered more for what they attempted than what they actually attained. For in the striving character was revealed, and character—*British* character—was what really mattered. The various reasons put forth as official justification for further exploration—charting a trade route to the East, hunting for whales, reaching the Open Polar Sea, compiling information about wind currents, temperatures, and astronomical phenomena, mapping the coastlines, attaining a new Farthest North or reaching the Pole itself—appeared to be means for achieving that greater end.[17]

The public perceived the Arctic explorer as a romantic figure who fulfilled its need for larger-than-life heroes. Regardless of whether he succeeded or failed, he was idealized. But fame brought him concrete rewards as well. His exploits were a highly marketable commodity, with booksellers lining up to offer him contracts. For example, the eminent

London publisher John Murray II forked over one thousand guineas—over $100 thousand in today's money—for the rights to print Parry's journal. (Murray had a keen eye for profitable romantic tales, having published wildly popular works by Walter Scott, Jane Austen, and Washington Irving. A few years before, his edition of Byron's *Prisoner of Chillon and Other Poems* had sold seven thousand copies in just one week.) An admiring Parliament offered Parry £5 thousand—or about $500 thousand now—in prize money if he made it as far as 110 degrees west longitude in his quest for the Northwest Passage. (Shortly after his return from this voyage, the explorer was also promoted to the rank of commander and made a Fellow of the Royal Society.) In addition to the government, there were plenty of wealthy individuals eager to bankroll Arctic explorers—newspaper editors, lecture-circuit promoters, philanthropists, and industrialists alike.

In this molding of the public hero, the man and his image often became separated. The explorer's flaws and shortcomings were overlooked. When the British government was searching for an experienced officer to head an expedition tasked with completing the mapping of the Northwest Passage in 1845, Sir John Franklin lobbied hard for this assignment: he considered it practically his birthright to take on this mission since he had already served with distinction on two previous Arctic expeditions. (Franklin was drawn back to the Far North as much by the tantalizing prize of twenty thousand guineas promised the first ship to reach the storied Polar Sea as by a desire to restore his reputation after having been fired as British governor of Van Diemen's Land—present-day Tasmania.) However, he had several glaring deficiencies. For one thing, Franklin was fifty-nine years old and had been in the Royal Navy for some forty-six years, putting him way above the normal retirement age. For another, he hadn't commanded a ship at sea in over a quarter century. Physically, Franklin did not make a reassuring impression: he was short, portly, nearly bald, and weighed over 210 pounds. His fleshy jowls sagged, and his bald pate made him look more like a retired vicar than a naval commander. His soulful gaze suggested an almost feminine sensitivity: he was wont to react squeamishly when dogs or other animals were mistreated due to the "wanton and unnecessary cruelty" of their masters.[18]

In fact, while representing the Crown in Van Diemen's Land, Franklin had passed the first law prohibiting such abuse there and had tried to reform the island's barbaric penal colony.[19] When, a few years earlier in the Arctic, his party had been attacked by a group of Inuit, Franklin had told his men not to harm them, lest that only make matters worse.[20] He would not tolerate cursing. He was so kind-hearted he could literally not kill a fly. During an ill-fated 5500-mile trek through the Canadian wilderness, when his men were nearly driven mad by swarms of sand flies biting them so fiercely that their faces had streamed with blood, the deeply religious Franklin had been observed gently blowing the "half-gorged" offending insects from his hands so he could continue taking observations, declaring with Buddhist equanimity that "the world is wide enough for both."[21] Yet he was a man who had left his first wife on her deathbed—albeit at her urging—rather than miss out on a chance to lead another overland expedition, this time to Baffin Bay. Franklin was certainly not a Lord Nelson, even if he had once served on a ship next to *Victory* at Trafalgar. (The only thing he had lost during that epic battle was some of his hearing.) Although still in reasonably good health for a man of his age, Franklin had never fully recovered from his harrowing misadventures while mapping the northern Canadian coastline some two decades before: he had fallen into an icy river and nearly drowned; his party had endured exceptionally cold weather; and they had so little to eat that they had to dig deer carcasses out of the snow and scrape putrid marrow from inside the antlers.[22] Franklin had lost eleven of his nineteen men on that trip, most as a result of starvation.[23] But none of these factors led the Admiralty to conclude he wasn't really the right man for the job. He had had Arctic experience—even it was mainly experience of disaster—and that was what counted the most. In the eyes of the public, Franklin was famous for being "the man who ate his boots"—along with lichens and rotten deerskin—and this sobriquet had earned him a great deal of admiration. When he finally returned to England from that inland expedition, he was embraced as a celebrity, promoted to captain, and elected to the Royal Society.[24] The lengthy journal Franklin had kept, detailing his travails and close calls with death, was—like William Parry's—turned into a bestselling book. Some called it "the greatest epic of all."[25] Thanks to it and detailed newspaper accounts, the British public became swept up in a "blind enthusiasm" for dramatic Arctic adventures.[26] After successfully completing a third trip to the Arctic, in September 1827, Franklin was knighted by William IV and hailed as the foremost explorer of his day. His name was on everyone's lips.

Franklin's primary purpose in 1844 was to fill in the contours of the last stretch of uncharted Canadian coastline by navigating all the way through the Northwest Passage to the Pacific. To carry out this task he was given two polar-seasoned and newly outfitted sailing vessels—*Erebus* (named, somewhat ominously, for a dark region in the Greek underworld) and *Terror* (which had fired its cannon at Fort McHenry, thus helping to inspire Francis Scott Key to write the "Star-Spangled Banner"). The two ships sailed from Greenwich on May 19, 1845, and reached Baffin Bay without incident in August. Early the next month they were spotted southwest of Greenland, sailing in warm weather, surrounded by hundreds of icebergs.[27] Other sightings were reported much further north.[28] But afterward there was no more news of *Erebus* and *Terror*. For two years there was an unsettling silence. None of the two hundred tin cylinders crew members were supposed to have thrown overboard with papers marking the ships' route were found.[29] Some observers worried, but others said there was no cause for concern: Franklin had planned to remain out of touch through the fall of 1847.[30]

But by November fears were mounting. The Admiralty announced that it was sending three parties across the Atlantic to look for the missing Franklin and his men—one, by sea, up the Bering Strait, another into Baffin Bay, and a third overland to the mouth of the Mackenzie River. But these expeditions turned up nothing. It was if *Erebus* and *Terror* and all 129 officers and men on board had vanished into the mists. The lack of any communication from Franklin, or news about his fate, grew increasingly troubling. Franklin's formidable second wife, Lady Jane, now took up his cause with the tenacity of a female bulldog. She wrote hundreds of letters—to kings, presidents, and other heads of state—begging them to help in the search for her husband. She scolded the Admiralty for dragging its feet. She pressed her case in public, displaying a panache that few women of her day possessed. With great adroitness and emotional force, she reminded political and naval leaders of their duty to the missing men, appealing to their sense of chivalry.

Touched by her plight and persistence, the American and British governments dispatched more ships to the Arctic to continue the search. Parliament announced a reward of £10 thousand for any word of the Franklin ships (and another ten thousand for discovering the Northwest Passage). The retired New York shipping magnate Henry Grinnell was so moved by her impassioned letter to President Zachary Taylor that he donated most of his fortune to finance further rescue missions. Lady Franklin herself used up almost all of her own money to finance seven voyages (and was disinherited by her father for doing so).[31] She put up a reward to whaling ships for any news of her husband. And still the search parties found no traces of *Erebus* and *Terror*. Over the ensuing dozen years, more than thirty rescue expeditions set out, from England and the United States, to find out what had happened to the missing men, in the most extensive and prolonged operation of this kind ever mounted. Governments spent some $4 million on rescue efforts (equivalent to $80 million today) between 1848 and 1854 alone.[32] At times the Arctic waters were so crowded with rescue ships that they could signal to each other with flares or balloons, and their officers exchange courtesy visits.[33]

Many people back in England—like the resolute Lady Franklin—held out hope that at least some of the officers and crew were still alive, perhaps being taken care of by local Inuit on some remote island. Unfor-

TRAILING CLOUDS OF GLORY

tunately, the would-be rescuers had only a few clues and theories about where the ships might have gone and thus where to look, and the Arctic was a vast, little-charted, and unpredictable region. Like eager Good Samaritans leaping into the surf to save a drowning person, the rescue ships themselves often became trapped in the ice and had to be rescued. All too often their quests ended in disaster. Some ships were crushed and sank. Sailors succumbed to diseases, starved, froze, and fell to their deaths at the bottom of yawning crevasses. And yet the ships kept coming, all to no avail. It wasn't until 1850—some six years after *Erebus* and *Terror* had disappeared over the horizon heading toward North America—that some traces of the lost expedition turned up. A massive mound of six hundred empty food cans, along with some sledge tracks, and three graves, was discovered on Beechey Island, west of Baffin Bay. But only in 1857, after the two crews and officers had been missing for thirteen years, did a party funded by Lady Franklin come upon more remains and a document stating that Sir John had perished in 1847, also providing more hints at the fate of the surviving members of his party. It was not the complete story, but it was enough for the British government, the British public, and even Franklin's long-suffering wife to accept there could no longer be any hope. The Franklin expedition—every last man—was dead. It was time to move on.

But what had kept the public's attention so riveted on this one lost party for so long—beyond the point where could be a realistic hope of the crew and officers still being alive? Clearly, the mystery surrounding their disappearance exercised a powerful tug on the public's imagination. Much like the fate of the aviatrix Amelia Earhart or, more recently, the Malaysian airliner that plunged without explanation into the Indian Ocean in 2015 have engrossed millions in recent times, so were people in the 1850s captivated by the puzzle of how so many men could disappear from the face of the earth. The British Empire had not suffered the loss of so many sailors since the Battle of New Orleans, in 1815. Like all who served in uniform, the Franklin party embodied the nation's pride and eminence: they had been fully expected to succeed in their quest to complete the Northwest Passage and add to their country's glorious maritime tradition. This expedition—amply supplied with food and other amenities, utilizing state-of-the-art ships sheathed in iron to protect their hulls, and equipped, for the first time, with coal-powered steam engines to barrel through the ice—was the most advanced ever to head to the Far North. Franklin and his men also had a thirty-year history of British exploration in the Arctic to draw upon. So their apparent loss came as a great shock. Instead of achieving one of the greatest feats of navigation, "the romantic and heroic idea of the British Navy in all its power overcoming Nature at her harshest had suddenly been reduced to the pathetic image of Francis Crozier [Franklin's second-in-command] leading the gaunt and diminishing remnants of a great expedition along the barren shores of an Arctic island."[34]

Furthermore, those who die so inexplicably affect us deeply because their fate touches upon our worst fears of what our own demise might be like—expiring all alone, without anyone at our side or ever knowing what has happened. Anxiety about the Franklin party's fate was intensified by the fact that their ships had literally gone off the grid, into a forbidding and unexplored part of the world, as alien in the nineteenth century as the surface of Jupiter is today. What the Arctic was actually like was one of the last great, unsolved questions about the earth's geography. This empty space on maps had been filled with wild conjecture: perhaps some "lost tribe" of humans lived there, basking on idyllic tropical isles; perhaps there were mountains filled with mineral riches; perhaps the pole was surrounded by a gigantic hole, plunging into the bowels of the earth and coming out at the other side—a theory that more than half the members of the US Senate and President John Quincy Adams had deemed worth investigating.[35] If they had reached the Open Polar Sea, the Franklin party might well have gone on to the heart of this mysterious Ultima Thule and wrested away its long-kept secrets. If so, then the missing sailors likely possessed information that would change forever how human beings thought about their planet—like the first photographs of the earth taken on the surface of the moon. Just having the courage to venture so far made the Franklin party heroic, even if they had failed to reach their goal.

Vicariously, the rest of the Western world traveled with them. One of the salient traits of this Second Age of Exploration was public curiosity about the Other—the bizarre, wild, exotic, dangerous, and unimaginable lands (and peoples) lying outside the pale of civilization that were then being visited for the first time. Because of the wide availability of newspapers and affordable books in the nineteenth century, ordinary people could closely follow what these explorers had seen and experienced. A prominent instance was James Riley's *Sufferings in Africa*—a grim tale about American merchant sailors who were shipwrecked off the coast of western Africa in 1815 and then enslaved by Arabs. This book became the first "bestseller" in America, making a lasting impression on readers such as the young Abraham Lincoln.[36] Such riveting, true-life narratives responded to a longing for adventure and escape from mundane life in the United States and Europe.

The ordinariness of the heroes did not diminish their popularity. If anything, this made them even more admirable. If Franklin had to resort to chewing on his boots, this act revealed not his desperation but his plucky resourcefulness. In fact, the term "pluck" came to signify the most admired quality of the polar explorers—especially for those who were English. It compensated for their shortcomings and mistakes. "Pluck" was also a character trait that many readers could relate to—unlike great courage or stamina. The Everyman aspect of figures like Franklin endeared them to their audiences by making them seem more plausible and abundantly human. After his exhausted party finally pitched their tents on an island in the Beaufort Sea, in far northern Canada, in mid-August of 1826, becoming only the second band of Europeans to traverse the rapids of the Mackenzie River, Franklin took out the silk Union Jack sewn for him by his recently deceased wife, the poet Eleanor Anne Porden, placed it on top of the protruding pole, and then watched silently as the wind set it aflutter. Franklin, whose brief first marriage had been something of a mismatch, wrote later in his journal that he had been nearly overcome with emotion at that moment but checked himself from letting these "natural" and "irresistible" feelings show: "I felt it was my duty to suppress them, and that I had no right, by an indulgence of my own sorrows, to cloud the animated countenances of my companions."[37] This extraordinary self-restraint, the uxorious lament for a lost wife, lying in her grave on the other side of the Atlantic, certainly must have touched the hearts of his readers. The image of Franklin as a kindly and considerate commander who always put the welfare of his men first, who read Dante's descriptions of hell for consolation around a crackling campfire, and who exemplified what Parry described as "Christian confidence in the Almighty, of the superiority of moral and religious energy over mere brute strength of body," struck a resonating chord in the minds and hearts of his countrymen.[38] He was their kind of hero.

So was William Parry, judging by how he presented himself in his books. After his ship *Hecla* had settled into its winter quarters several hundred miles to the northeast a year before, Parry had stopping keeping his diary because the days were so monotonously uneventful that there was no point in describing them. He would spare his readers a retelling of this interminable boredom—although doing so also enable him to avoid mentioning the complaints from his sailors about their inadequate winter clothing: Parry had neglected to bring along any fur-lined coats. With poor ventilation and clammy moisture inescapable below decks, the men were never able to warm up. To mollify them and enliven the long winter months, Parry mounted diversions. His second-in-command, Lieutenant Henry Parkyns Hoppner, had proposed staging monthly "masked balls," and these entertainments—performed "without licentiousness," in keeping with Parry's moral probity—had done the trick. So had plays where sailors in drag had extolled the virtue of their patiently waiting wives. So had the gay observance of all possible holidays, including Valentine's Day, when poems disavowing erotic love were read aloud, to howls of laughter. ("Cupid! Fond of unity / Our boreal community / Defies you with impunity / Your arrows and your bow."[39]) So had classes in reading and writing, as well as regular scripture readings, designed to "improve the character of a seaman, by furnishing the highest motives for increased attention to every other duty."[40] So had daily calisthenics on deck in subfreezing temperatures and putting out a newspaper. So had regular inspection and cleaning of quarters. English readers would have approved of Parry's solicitousness about his men's well-being, his improvisation, his rectitude, his discipline, his belief that hardship builds character, his confidence that Englishmen could do whatever they put their minds to, and his piety—not to mention his scoffing at the pleasures of the flesh. His less admirable traits, such as his foolish dream of sailing all the way to China before winter set in, his lack of Arctic experience, his inadequate preparation, his bad decisions, and his prudery, were kept out of the pages of his journal. Although readers could applaud what the explorers had endured, they must have put down books like Parry's with ambivalence. Boldly going where no man had gone before, for the glory of God and country, was uplifting, exciting—and a cause for patriotic pride. But these adventures exacted a heavy toll. Unlike in war, where men died bravely amid a volley of rifles, or marched home to cheering crowds, the Arctic forced would-be conquerors to submit to slow, torturous, and essentially passive suffering. Ships were caught in the ice, stuck there for years, and their crews subjected to frightful conditions over which they had no control. The pattern of becoming surrounded by ice—rendered helpless, at the mercy of unyielding elements—was repeated over and over again. The challenge for polar explorers was, in effect, to stay alive and, by showing "pluck" in the process, reveal their good character. This was a very different sort of heroism than that which the British navy had shown in defeating the French. In the icy and lifeless North, so far from home and country, Lord Nelson's rallying cries of "First gain the victory and then make the best use of it you can" or "Time is everything; five minutes make the difference between victory and defeat" bore no relevance at all.

As expeditions searching for Franklin met the same fate—more men died in the effort to find his party than had been in it—public expectations of what could be accomplished in the Far North gradually diminished. People implicitly acknowledged that Nature in this extremity was not to be conquered, only survived. Victory lay in not giving in, in not being easily defeated. Courage consisted of pushing ahead against invincible forces, not necessarily in defeating them. When Sir James Ross headed south out of Cape Town in 1841, eager to locate the South Magnetic Pole and earn his nation's applause, he came a cropper when his two ships—later to be Franklin's—came upon an ice shelf one thousand feet high and seemingly as big as all of France, which "dwarfed their ships, filled their line of vision and blocked their passage to the pole."[41] Ross then had to concede he could no sooner get past this barrier than through the cliffs of Dover. So he turned back.

Being blocked by such barriers suggested that the polar explorers were reaching a point beyond which their will, courage, and ingenuity could not take them. At its geographical extremes, the Other might still be seductively alluring, but fatally so. In attempting to press on, these modern-day adventurers were—like Icarus—vaingloriously reaching too far and thus destined to fail. The lesson recorded in their journals was a cautionary one: man was not superior to Nature. In devouring such Arctic stories, a typical English reader was at once compelled to follow these heroes as they trekked across virgin expanses of snow and made to recoil in horror at the consequences of this decision. In evoking both reactions, the polar narrative presented a new model of manliness. It subsumed defeat by elevating the effort alone to heroic stature. Hardship *did* build character, and it was this new truism that Alfred, Lord Tennyson celebrated when he was asked to write something for the memorial to Franklin in Westminster Abbey. Here Tennyson finessed the explorer's disappearance and arguably pointless death with these verses:

Not here! the white North has thy bones; and thou,
Heroic sailor-soul,
Art passing on thine happier voyage now
Toward no earthly pole.

That a sorrowful British public could find comfort in these words indicates how much the spirit of Franklin had supplanted Franklin the less-than-superman in their hearts and minds. He was not to be found, the inscription stressed, in the "frozen ice," but in the "realms of light," where his faithful widow would be reunited with him. The cult that grew up around the search for him and his men evolved from being obsessed with the rescue of 129 living officers and sailors to wishing to be united with all that Franklin stood for: his "gallantry" and his almost Christ-like "passion" in suffering as he had. As with Jesus, dying assured the explorer's passage to a better world. In their longing to connect with a dead Franklin through a few of his "relics," his devotees showed that the English romantic temper was still alive and well. Keats had captured this mood deftly in his "Ode to a Nightingale," written in the spring of 1819. In it the poet confesses he has been "half in love with easeful Death," tempted by a desire "to leave the world unseen, / And with thee fade away into the forest dim," to "Fade far away, dissolve, and quite forget . . . The weariness, the fever, and the fret / Here, where men sit and hear each other groan." This concept of suffering and death as apotheosis would increasingly take hold of the English psyche, as visions of raising the Union Jack on sun-spangled shores gave way to ones of the frozen corpses of Robert Scott and his last two companions sprawled inside a tent in the Antarctic barrens.

However, the sanguine, nationalistic temper of the nineteenth century demanded that this tendency to bow down before "gallant losers" be held in check.[42] This was, after all, an age of fierce competition among the nations of Western Europe, with each bent upon staking its claim to dominance. Social Darwinism was a self-fulfilling prophecy, akin to the Protestant ethic: nations "proved" their preordained superiority by their actions on the world stage just as Christians demonstrated that they belonged to God's "elect" by amassing wealth and power. In both contexts, individual character was the wellspring of national exceptionalism. Men—and it was only they, not women, who then counted—attested to the collective vitality and might of a people by passing tests of courage and forbearance. In a time when wars were few and far between, the conquest of new seas and lands provided the best chance for them to demonstrate masculine virtue and be acclaimed for doing so.

So ambitious young Englishmen sensed this opportunity and seized it. Robert Scott was not the first or the last naval officer to realize that being the first to reach one of the poles would assure his promotion and successful military career. Older men at the top encouraged this kind of thinking. Chief among them, Clements Markham, a former midshipman and long-time president of the Royal Geographical Society, summoned the ghost of King Alfred to exhort a new generation of naval officers to honor their seagoing heritage by planting the Union Jack at the top of the world: "To the people of this country it should have a peculiar charm; for maritime and especially Arctic enterprise, runs, like a bright silver thread, through the history of the English nation, lighting up its darkest and most discreditable periods; and even giving cause for just pride, at times when all other contemporary events would be sources only of shame and regret."[43] For this reason, intrepid explorers like John Franklin, William Parry, James Ross, Elisha Kent Kane, Fridtjof Nansen, Roald Amundsen, Charles Hall, Adolphus W. Greely, Adrien de Gerlache, Robert Peary, Frederick Cook, Ernest Shackleton, and Robert Scott took on larger-than-life importance. The adulation they received was mirrored by the American fascination with Elisha Kent Kane, and his glorification when he died so prematurely. On their success or failure much more was riding than personal ambition and vanity. The flags they carried in their knapsacks would mark the steady advance of nations toward their destinies.

Thus it was essential that the men departing for the Arctic and Antarctic be seen as heroes, regardless of whatever human imperfections they might possess. That was why "moral character" was the trait most desired in the men who volunteered by the thousands to go on these expeditions.[44] Entrusted with the lives of their crews, as well as the hopes of their countrymen, leaders needed to have this quality in abundance and maintain their poise and good judgment under duress. They had to command respect and obedience, as well as admiration. They had to help their men adapt to prolonged isolation and hardship.[45] They had to make split-second decisions that would decide the fate of the expedition. They had to look after the well-being of their men, show empathy, preserve order, and uphold some semblance of normalcy. They had to personify self-denial, calm forbearance, competence, and confidence. They had to keep their own fears and doubts to themselves and make light of near disasters, as when Ernest Shackleton danced a waltz with Frank Worsley on the deck of the *Endurance* after their ship had been nipped by floating ice off the Antarctic coast.[46] If any in their parties showed signs of cowardice, they had to be weeded out before this "disease" could infect the others—as Lieutenant George Back had done on the shore of Lake Winnipeg, when a Canadian *voyageur* forester had revealed his "unmanly" and "pusillanimous weakness" by predicting they were all going to starve to death.[47] And, perhaps most importantly of all, leaders had to persist—until it was impossible to go on. Only then would they have to let go of their dreams and turn back, as Franklin had had to do reluctantly in August 1826, with winter coming on early in northern Canada, with his men crippled by legs raw, red, and grotesquely swollen from wading through near-freezing water, and with little hope of finding food or firewood anywhere nearby.[48] If a leader lacked these crucial traits, the other officers, the scientists, and the ordinary sailors and soldiers would lose faith. They would become disaffected and plot rebellion. They would turn sullen, lapse into despair, and even go mad. Then they would all be lost.

Only truly exceptional men could pass all these tests of polar leadership. Most fell short. Men who had the audacity—or foolhardiness—to leave their homes and families and go off on voyages lasting years in places where survival was doubtful at best were not perfect beings when they set out, and they became less so as time went on and conditions grew dire. Just as the huzzahs of thousands of well-wishers soon faded away, so did their self-confidence dissipate on board an icebound ship or adrift on a floe. The stresses and strains of living in close quarters for so long made crews irritable and despondent. Personal animosities intensified. Expedition leaders became frustrated by the agonizingly slow progress in reaching their goals. Responsible for the men under their command, they were also obligated to the governments and private benefactors who had paid for their voyages. Furthermore, they bore the heavy weight of public expectations on their shoulders. Commanders like Franklin felt pressure to become greater men than they actually were. Expedition leaders had self-serving reasons for living up to such an exalted image, as well. Many of them were monumental egotists, whose entire lives had been dedicated to attaining fame and glory through exploration. When Roald Amundsen succeeded in sailing all the way through the Northwest Passage in 1906 he was fulfilling the "long, long dreams of his youth."[49] Doggedly fanatical in his twenty-year quest to reach the North Pole, Robert Peary regarded accomplishing this feat as his "final bid for immortality."

Undoubtedly, having such unrelenting drive was the *sine qua non* of polar success. Unyielding determination could sustain some men through frightful ordeals so that they could set a new Farthest North record where others had to turn back. But intense focus and drive alone were not enough to achieve these triumphs. Explorers first had to pull off the equally daunting tasks of planning, organizing, equipping, supplying, and manning their expeditions—a huge logistical challenge. But before taking that on, they had to raise the funds to pay for their journey. That was even more of a headache. Polar trips were very expensive. For example, in drawing up a proposal for a trans-Antarctic land expedition in 1913, Ernest Shackleton estimated the entire enterprise would cost roughly £50 thousand—equal to £3.8 million, or $5.6 million in today's money. Perennially short of cash, Shackleton could only come up with this amount by attracting a donor who wanted to associate his name with this "last great Polar journey that can be made."[50] (Ultimately, a Scottish jute manufacturer named James Caird agreed to underwrite the expedition—gaining lasting renown when the twenty-three-foot lifeboat named for him brought Shackleton and five of his men safely across the treacherous southern Atlantic to South Georgia Island.) Unless their governments were willing to foot the bill, or they found such a generous private benefactor, polar explorers had to spend considerable time and energy raising money. In essence, they had to market themselves as worthwhile investments. So they had to engage in two kinds of campaigns at the same time—to set new geographical records *and* to capture the world's attention. The second was just as important as the first because projecting a positive, compelling image was vital to selling the books and giving the lectures that paid for their future expeditions.

To advertise their exploits, explorers often found willing partners in organizations like England's Royal Geographical Society (where Clements Markham almost singlehandedly made heroes out of naval officers like Robert Scott) and in newspaper owners, who promoted death-defying voyages to bolster sales. Foremost among the latter was the eccentric and scandal-ridden publisher of the *New York Herald*, James Gordon Bennett Jr., one of the wealthiest men in New York City. It was he who, having taken over this newspaper from his father when he was only in his mid-twenties, had devised a scheme to send a mild-mannered correspondent named Henry Morton Stanley halfway around the world to "find" the missionary David Livingstone in "darkest Africa." Bennett's penchant for headline-grabbing escapades carried over to his bizarre personal life: he reportedly hired editors only if one of his beloved Pomeranians showed a fondness for them, breakfasted exclusively on plover eggs, and once showed up drunk at his fiancée's family mansion and urinated in the fireplace.[51]

Looking for "new worlds to conquer," or, rather, new worlds to cash in on, the eccentric Bennett agreed in 1879 to pay for a naval expedition seeking a sea route to the North Pole, led by a dashing Annapolis graduate from New York City, George Washington De Long.[52] This thirty-five-year-old lieutenant had shown a flair for the outlandish by, among other things, riding a horse in the Lisbon circus just to win a bet. De Long—who as a boy had become enamored of naval heroes like Admiral David ("Damn the torpedoes!") Farragut and Frederick Marryat—had impressed Bennett with his courage during a previous voyage to Greenland, when the young officer had rammed an ironclad steam launch through two-foot-thick ice while trying to locate the missing crew of another ship, the *Polaris*.[53] This episode had given De Long a bad case of "Arctic fever," and—after skeptical navy brass had turned him down—he made a successful pitch to Bennett to finance a "dash" to the pole by ship through the usually ice-blocked Bering Strait. The *Herald* then drummed up interest in this long-shot expedition through a series of hyperbolic articles trumpeting this expedition as "the event of the century"—America's chance to be the first nation to reach this long-elusive goal.[54]

Cockily arrayed on the deck of the small, three-masted, and heavily laden USS *Jeannette*, De Long and his civilian party of thirty-two had sailed out of San Francisco Bay past a huge throng of well-wishers waving their hats and cheering them on as if they were newlyweds embarking on their honeymoon. To make sure the *Herald* kept readers abreast of their progress, Bennett had arranged for his paper's science editor, an Irishman named Jerome J. Collins, to tag along, take photographs, and send back periodic reports. But these were never written, for the *Jeannette* became trapped in the ice early in September and then, after drifting aimlessly for nearly two years, was crushed by ice and ignominiously sank. Collins was among the twenty men, including De Long, who starved to death in the Siberian tundra while making a desperate attempt to reach safety.

In dying, De Long—like other polar explorers before and since, including his countryman Elisha Kane—ascended to mythical status in the eyes of his admiring fellow Americans. Here was a daring young commander, full of promise, striving to bring lasting glory to his country. After his death, De Long was memorialized as a courageous leader, "superabundant in joyousness and activity" in emergencies, possessed with a "magnetic power which made him singularly successful in dealing with men and in carrying out the purposes which he conceived"; as an exemplary figure who kept his men in "excellent health and spirits" and sustained their morale on board ship by ordering them to carry out their daily chores with military precision.[55] Even in the worst of situations, the crew had gladly and without becoming "disheartened" put their faith in him. De Long "belonged to the men who have cared for great things, not to bring themselves honor, but because doing great things could alone satisfy their natures, and he entered upon the work before him with a single-minded earnestness, and a brave trust in God." Despite the unrelieved tedium of their long shipboard imprisonment and the crew's mounting despair, he had clung to his naïve belief that "all will come out right" in the end. Throughout the nineteenth century and beyond, this sort of glorification of polar explorers was commonplace. In the words of one Canadian literary scholar, "The explorer in charge of such a noble undertaking took on the sheen of heroism, joining the cadre of what [one historian] terms the 'secular hagiography' of Arctic heroes."[56]

Such was the sanitized public perception of Arctic and Antarctic explorers that girded their adventures. The explorers themselves contributed to this image-making by the stories they told, the books they wrote, and the one-dimensional personae they helped to construct. Shackleton, for instance, shrewdly chose to name his ship *Endurance*, adopting his family motto of *Fortitudine Vincimus*—"by endurance we conquer." As a result, for all time his name and this manly virtue will remain inseparable. But these stories and images omitted much. The flaws, weaknesses, miscalculations, indecisiveness, selfish motives, self-aggrandizing, and blunders of expedition leaders were concealed to make them appear singularly heroic. For example, the fact that, during one of his Canadian expeditions, Franklin had not laid down caches of food, had brought along ineffectual shotguns instead of hunting rifles, and as a result had to rely on natives for food; that he had had no prior trekking experience and therefore frequently lost his way through the wilderness; and that when his situation was practically hopeless he looked to God and not his own ingenuity to save him and his men—all of these deficiencies were ignored so that the world could see him as a "gallant" and tragic martyr.[57]

In an age lacking in warfare and military conquest, polar explorers filled a void. Even if their quests were largely symbolic, the public did not care. The heroic spirit they exhibited was the same as the soldiers', and this was what people in Europe and the United States badly needed to celebrate. Yet, beneath the surface, the disparity between heroic image and cowardly, self-serving deeds continued to grow. As more and more expeditions failed to achieve their aims, as more and more ships were stuck in the ice, as more and more lives were lost, this incongruity would become increasingly difficult to conceal. Either the sordid reality of polar exploration would have to be revealed, or the concept of heroism altered to reflect the unprecedented challenges explorers were facing at the top of the world. In any event, the old definitions of "fame" and "glory" would have to go.

CHAPTER TWO

HAIL THE CONQUERED HERO!

In the spring of 1880, Arthur Conan Doyle was in the midst of his medical studies at the storied University of Edinburgh when he got wind of an unusual opportunity. A local Greenland-bound whaling ship—one of the last still in operation, portentously named *Hope*—was badly in need of a physician, as the one that had been recruited, a fellow student of his, had abruptly bowed out. Without a moment's hesitation, Doyle agreed to interrupt his training and sign on.[1] This may have appeared to be a snap decision, but it actually reflected a well-developed contrarian streak in his character. Raised in a strict Catholic family and educated by the Jesuits, Doyle had recently left the Church and become an agnostic. His urge to escape from organized religion and his starchy Scottish upbringing was a manifestation of a rebellious spirit that had been fomenting inside him for some time.

Doyle's longing to move away from his roots had been spurred by reading books by his fellow Scot Winwood Reade—a well-to-do historian and explorer who in his youth had flunked out of Oxford and then impulsively sailed for Africa to do exciting things like look for the source of the Nile and then write about his exploits. He would make sense out of the "Dark Continent" as no European had ever done. Along the way he would reinvent himself, free of the stifling influences of British civilization, religion, and materialism.[2] Reade did turn his travels into a series of extremely popular books, starting with *The African Sketch-Book* (1873). At his young and impressionable age, Doyle could easily imagine himself having similar adventures in the frozen North and retelling them in print as a second career. Already in medical school he had tried his hand at writing short stories.

As it turned out, there was little to keep a doctor busy on the SS *Hope*, and so Doyle spent most of the next seven months conversing with the grizzled captain, one John Gray III, who—because of his position and Victorian class proprieties—had to remain aloof from the crew and, as a result, was desperately in need of someone to talk to. A well-read and curious young doctor could certainly enliven the evenings. So the two of them would dine in Gray's cabin and converse about subjects ranging from Mary Shelley's *Frankenstein* to the likelihood of war with Russia, while the steam-powered *Hope* basked in the eerie, perpetual light of the Arctic summer.[3] While Doyle enjoyed this sojourn at sea and—as he had hoped—wrote about it after he got home, the dark and unsettling aspect of his extended stay in this alien part of the world also left a lasting impression on his imagination. He had sensed the "melancholy" and feeling of helplessness that arose when the *Hope* came close to being stuck in the ice. But it was the strange plight of the skipper—how he endured such loneliness for so long, month after month—that haunted him most.

A few years after his return to Scotland, Doyle published a story entitled "The Captain of the *Pole-Star*." It was a ghost story, clearly inspired by his stay off the coast of Greenland (and possibly by Melville's *Moby-Dick*). It told of a whaler surrounded by ice, unable to get near its prey, with food supplies running low, its crew restless and homesick, and its captain maniacally bent, like Ahab, about finishing the job he'd come to do. Suspended in limbo, the sailors on the *Pole-Star* begin to hear strange "plaintive cries and screams" astern. Two of them insist they have seen a ghostlike figure dressed in white, scurrying across the ice field. Growing fearful, their shipmates want to turn the ship around and head back, but the captain—Craigie—refuses to do so. Instead he "spends the greater part of the day at the crow's nest, sweeping the horizon with his glass." The men are convinced he has gone mad and plot to put him in irons. The captain's obsession with finding whales only intensifies as the *Pole-*

Star becomes firmly encircled by solid ice and caught in its death-like embrace: "No lapping of the waves now, no cries of seagulls or straining of sails, but one deep universal silence in which the murmurs of the seamen, and the creak of their boots upon the white shining deck, seem discordant and out of place." Then the captain, too, falls under the spell of this apparition. After catching a better glimpse, he tells the men that this is no ghost, but a real woman. He paces up and down the deck like a caged animal, unable to shake himself of this obsession, which has "brought out all his latent lunacy in an exaggerated form." When the crew realizes the ship can now break free, Craigie will not listen: he hears only the siren call of the sprite. After staring into the mist one day, he cries out "Coming lass, coming," jumps over the side of the ship, and races off. When the men go out to look for him, they find the captain dead, lying face down encased in ice, with snow in the shape of a woman whirling around him, and a "bright smile upon his blue pinched features." After he is buried at sea, the rest of the men return home, their captain's secret concealed with him deep beneath the sea.[4]

While Doyle's melodramatic portrayal of a sea captain driven insane by his inability to fulfill his ambitions is fictional, it does speak to what he sensed during his voyage with the whaler *Hope*—namely, how a widening gulf between hopes and intransigent reality could torment the soul. At the perilous and unpredictable poles, madness always hovered on the horizon, waiting for its moment to move in. It did so when this mental tension grew overpowering. Then anyone could succumb. A commander was particularly vulnerable to becoming unstable because—like Ahab—he was deeply committed to achieving his goal. He carried great responsibility, at a great personal cost. The captain was also the one person on whom all the other lives depended: if he broke down the entire crew would be endangered. Symbolically, his going mad implied the breakdown of reason and control. This was the risk inherent in testing the limits of human capabilities, far outside the pale of civilization. That is why literary treatment of the "commander gone amok"—first developed by Melville—resonated so powerfully. Ostensibly, leaders like John Franklin, Elisha Kent Kane, and George De Long were exploring the far reaches of the Arctic wastes to advance science, human curiosity, commercial interests, or territorial aspirations, but at heart they were also furthering their own ambitions. They had the most to gain, and the most to lose. Because of their position, they were also a law unto themselves. But commanders had to disguise such naked ambition, as Victorian mores required. The public would not admire a leader who spoke openly about his selfish motives. Their real reasons for going toward the polar caps could only be discerned by what they did once they got there. Being in charge of an Arctic or Antarctic expedition called for an exceptionally strong ego, able to dismiss these inconsistencies between words and deeds. Otherwise, like Doyle's Captain Craigie, they would go mad.

When the Franklin party did not reemerge from the Arctic long after they were supposed to, the fate of "so many good, gallant, and brave men" became a national obsession:[5] newspapers bemoaned their fate, governments organized rescue missions, and dozens of prominent figures stepped forward offering to lead them. But all too often these volunteers were more interested in making a name for themselves than in finding Sir John Franklin or any of his companions. Some came up with truly harebrained schemes for doing so. A man named Shepherd wrote to the Admiralty proposing that he be given a ship to sail northward laden with explosives so that he could blow the ice to smithereens and thus reach the presumably beset English vessels, *Erebus* and *Terror*.[6] A onetime actor and novice aeronaut, George Gale, offered to soar over the Arctic ice pack in a balloon to locate the missing men.[7] (Turned down, he would plunge to his death less than a year later, at Bordeaux.) More experienced Arctic hands like the seventy-three-year-old John Ross also volunteered to lead search parties. Lady Franklin encouraged others to join the rescue effort in haste, without waiting for official backing.[8] Although her interest was clearly selfless, those she implored to join the hunt for the missing sailors were not always so high-minded. Tellingly, as was revealed in their journals, many search-party leaders made only perfunctory attempts to discover traces of the Franklin party before turning their attention to finding new routes that might lead to the Open Polar Sea. One such adventurer was Robert Randolph Carter, a twenty-four-year-old Virginia blueblood and recent Annapolis graduate who would later gain notoriety as a Confederate blockade runner.

In 1850 Carter signed on as first officer and navigator on the aptly named *Rescue*, an American brig purchased and retrofitted for Arctic service by shipping tycoon Henry Grinnell, who was sparing no expense to relieve Lady Franklin's distress.[9] Manned by navy crews and officers, this small brig and a larger companion vessel, *Advance*, were instructed to pick up where the unsuccessful British search had left off. Carter went along on this voyage not out of any compassion for his fellow seamen but because he wanted to play a role in discovering the Northwest Passage—still tantalizing to Arctic mariners long after its commercial potential had evaporated—and the so-called "Polynia," or polar sea, which was believed to lie just north of it. Looking for Franklin gave him, and, more generally, the US Navy, an excuse to join this wider exploration: Americans were now eager to become "players" in a growing Arctic territorial competition. Carter had been warned by his friends against going (as months on a cramped ship under spartan conditions would not suit him well), but this chance to share in an "achievement most glorious that the annals of the earth could record" was not to be forsworn.[10]

However, Carter soon became "heartily disgusted" by the "discomforts and vexations" on board and spent most of his time on watch taking potshots at gulls and pining for his fiancée. There was no sign of open sea to the north and west, where the *Rescue*'s captain, Samuel Griffin, had hoped to find it. The two American ships never got clear of ice in Lancaster Sound, located to the north of Baffin Island. Seasick and homesick, Carter made no mention of John Franklin in his journal until *Rescue* happened upon some British ships that had located three graves of Franklin's men. Even then, all Carter could think of was getting home as soon as possible.[11] In his indifference he was only reflecting what Edwin De Haven, the commanding officer of the *Advance*, had made clear when the two American vessels had arrived in the Arctic: Franklin was *not* their priority; finding the Northwest Passage was.[12] Published accounts of British voyages in search of the Franklin party similarly pay lip service to the official rationale, but they also reveal that their real purpose was to discover new routes and territory.[13]

Like Carter, Elisha Kent Kane had joined this first Grinnell-funded expedition, as its chief medical officer, scientist, and historian, for the sheer love of adventure—and the fame and fortune that would ensue. After he made it back to the States in 1851, Kane gave a series of lectures at the Smithsonian to win congressional backing for another Arctic expedition. At the podium he waxed eloquent about leading a party all the way to the polar sea to find Franklin, because the fate of the missing explorer was what his audience cared about. He kept quiet about what he really wanted to do—plant his foot farther north than any human had done before. Employing this same altruistic pitch, he persuaded Grinnell to again outfit the ice-tested *Advance*, and on May 30, 1853, the Philadelphia doctor strode confidently up a gangplank in New York harbor to set sail on his second trip to the Arctic, this time as commander—a position he had never before held. Friction between Kane's agenda and that of his motley crew—a "mish-mash of seasoned sailors, family friends, green volunteers, and the sweepings of New York's docks"[14]—became apparent soon after the *Advance* reached Smith Sound, in far northern Canada, that September. At first, Kane told his men that they would have to return home as the ship had been badly damaged by collisions with ice floes. But then he changed his mind: the party would stay for the winter so that he could use this outpost as a jumping-off point for sledge journeys further north once the weather had improved. The men howled in dismay, but to no avail. That spring, six men from the ship plodded some two hundred miles north across a Greenland glacier, through a "freezing purgatory," until they reached the coast at Rensselaer Bay. There they beheld not the open, navigable sea Kane had expected but a "wilderness of ice and barren rocks" stretching to the northern horizon. Despite this bitter disappointment, Kane could claim some credit for this party's having attained a new Farthest North record of 82.30 degrees before, close to death, they had to turn back. Hallucinating, chanting, cursing, and waving their arms wildly, the men managed to stave off pain and cold and kept going, sleeping for twenty-seven nights on the ice without a fire to warm them, until they made it back to the snow-shrouded *Advance*.[15]

A fluent and dramatic storyteller, Kane turned this escapade and his subsequent ordeal in Greenland into the kind of book publishers drool over—a phenomenal, richly illustrated page-turner entitled *Arctic Explorations*. During its first year in print some sixty thousand copies were sold.[16] Between its covers Americans found the hero they had been longing for—a frail, skinny young man with tremendous spunk and an unquenchable spirit, who had survived horrific Arctic conditions solely by dint of his willpower and refusal to quit. Once, when men on a sledging excursion fell ill and could not go on any further, Kane and a sailor named William Godfrey struck out for camp on their own to bring back food and water—an incredible journey that the Philadelphia doctor described thusly:

> I cannot tell how long it took us to make the nine miles, for we were in a strange sort of stupor, and had little apprehension of time. . . . We kept ourselves awake by imposing on each other a continued articulation of words; they must have been incoherent enough. I recall these hours as among the most wretched I have ever gone through: we were neither of us in our right senses, and retained a very confused recollection of what preceded our arrival at the tent. We both of us, however, recall a bear, who walked leisurely before us and tore up as he went a jumper . . . into shreds and rolled it into a ball, but never offered to interfere with our progress. I remember this, and with it a confused sentiment that our tent and buffalo-robes might probably share the same fate. Godfrey . . . had a better eye than myself; and, looking some miles ahead, he could see that our tent was undergoing the same unceremo-

nious treatment. I thought I saw it too, but we were so drunken with cold that we strode on steadily and, for aught I know, without quickening our pace.[17]

This was, indeed, a gripping tale, vividly conveying Kane's physical pain, life-threatening danger (the polar bear), and his exhausted and disoriented state of mind. A reader could imagine being there and feeling what Kane had, drawn into this strange environment to a degree that previous polar narratives, written mostly by naval officers with little literary flair, had not been able to do. It is easy to see how a book like this could transform a relatively inexperienced explorer, with only a modest record of accomplishment, into "Dr. Kane of the Arctic Seas"—a larger-than-life figure embodying the storied American tradition of indomitable individual struggle against a hostile Nature—a Daniel Boone for the Industrial Age. Kane was also portrayed as a global Man of Science, in the mold of the famed German naturalist Alexander von Humboldt, braving the polar snows to extend human knowledge.[18] This popular image was, in fact, a carefully calculated creation: Kane invariably spent his polar nights hunkered down in a wind-lashed tent, scribbling in his journal with his eye keenly focused on eventual publication. Back in Philadelphia, his younger brother, Tom, advanced this goal by convincing magazines and newspapers to run excerpts from Elisha's accounts, with riveting headings such as "A Storm among the Bergs." It was small wonder that the American public became more fascinated by this remote and mysterious region than ever before.[19]

But this bond with the explorer was built on a false premise. The persona Kane forged for himself was just that—a forgery. Its connection with reality was tenuous and, at times, nonexistent. In his writings, Kane exaggerated his accomplishments like a politician courting votes, not as a scientist objectively describing what he had actually seen and done. Inconvenient truths were kept out. As a general rule, Arctic and Antarctic explorers could get away with this deception because their adventures took place thousands of miles away, under conditions where hard facts were difficult to establish. On top of that, expedition leaders—or their financial backers—usually exercised exclusive control over what was published about their trips. But in the case of Kane's second Arctic expedition this was not the case. William Godfrey, the man who had tramped with Kane through deep snow and howling winds to rescue their comrades, had a tale of his own to tell, and a compelling reason for doing so. He and Kane had clashed several times during their stay in Greenland—most dramatically when the fiercely independent Yankee sailor had left the ice-bound *Advance* without permission, and Kane had threatened to shoot him as a mutineer. When Kane's book came out, Godfrey was incensed to find himself branded a "bad fellow" and his commander justifying an attempt to kill him simply because he had disobeyed an order. In the doctor's book, Godfrey also found many statements he considered false or misleading and vowed to set the record straight. In his own book, which came out a few months after Kane's death, Godfrey pointed out that, among other things, the doctor had gotten his facts wrong in describing the incident with the polar bear. The two men hadn't been delirious, only Kane; there was no bear: that was "a creation of the doctor's fancy"; and they both hadn't stumbled back to the tent, only Godfrey, who was carrying an incoherent and helpless Kane.[20]

Exactly whose version of these events was more accurate is impossible to say, but there is no doubt that Elisha Kent Kane had a penchant for self-promotion (aided and abetted by his ambitious father and younger sibling Tom back in Philadelphia). Dramatically embellishing his accomplishments would ensure that his fame spread and his books sold. (Godfrey would go so far as to accuse Kane's brother of orchestrating an elaborate funeral in order to do just that.[21]) Frequently, in his lectures and books, Kane presented himself as the leader he wanted to be, an idealized projection.[22] Whether or not he fell so much in love with this image that he could not see there was a difference between it and the person he really was we cannot know for sure. In any event, the self-absorbed and self-aggrandizing Kane could lord over this world he had created, with his own words virtually unchallenged, like an imperial monarch who brooked no naysayers. In his narratives, Kane achieved the unity and consistency that was missing in his actions. With the stroke of his pen, failures could be turned into triumphs and mistakes construed as events beyond his control.

In the undefined white expanses at the polar caps, amid wildly swirling snow and curtains of fog, what really happened remained, ultimately, subjective. One could easily convince himself that things had happened, which hadn't, and deny what had really taken place. Thus, men like Frederick Cook and Robert Peary could go on arguing until they died about which of them had first reached the North Pole. Character was supposed to be the arbiter of truth, but—like the sextant and the chronometer at high latitudes—it was not always reliable. Any explorer could be tempted to distort the truth for his own benefit. The British public may have wagged their fingers at Roald Amundsen for concealing his intent to make for the South Pole instead of heading northward in 1910, but their own heroes were not faultless in this regard: Scott and Shackleton squabbled like petulant schoolboys over who had the "right" to use McMurdo Sound as a base of operations, and Scott was not exactly "honorable" in purportedly encouraging the crippled and dying "poor soldier" Lawrence Oates to swallow a morphine pill so that the others could go on ahead faster without him.[23] On the other hand, character in an existential vacuum—devoid of the gritty alloy of real-life experience—was a volatile and dangerous substance. The romantic British notion that superior moral fiber alone was sufficient to sustain days of manhauling eight-hundred-pound sledges up the steep slope of a glacier would prove, time and again, to be disastrous. ("Gentlemen don't practice," was Scott's credo, although—in truth—one he didn't always abide by.[24])

In the end, deciding who was telling the truth—whose claim was plausible, Cook's or Perry's?—was left up to public opinion: it wasn't something that could be definitively proven or disproven. At the poles, belief was irrefutable. By adroitly cultivating a good public relations campaign and sticking to one's story, the shrewd explorer could turn legend into fact, failure into triumph (or, as in Scott's case, into martyrdom), and thus avoid the madness that could easily result when desires and the unyielding realities of the polar world collided. Of course, to be a prisoner of one's delusions is another form of insanity, but someone like Elisha Kent Kane probably never stayed awake late at night wrestling with demons. His chronic indifference to truth was not a liability but a means of empowerment.

That said, not all leaders of polar expeditions were possessed by the Old Testament megalomania of an Ahab, able to compel men, as under a spell, to do their bidding unquestioningly. Nor did all of them have the ability to hold unpleasant facts at bay indefinitely. To have their way, they had to engage with both their crews and the strange, protean world in which they found themselves. But in this regard, there were some cultural differences: the British class system and military tradition kept men and officers strictly separated—eating in different messes and performing different duties, whereas Americans and Scandinavians tended to deal with one another as equals. In these egalitarian environments, the men in charge were more subject to close scrutiny and criticism. They had to earn respect and uphold their leadership by making the right decisions. Otherwise, when things went wrong, they would get the blame. Open conflict with subordinates could threaten their status and undermine an entire expedition. So democratic-minded commanders had more reason to feel insecure and fear they would lose control.

For instance, on the *Jeannette*, Lieutenant De Long and the journalist-cum-meteorologist Jerome Collins could not stomach each either from the start. The Irishman's constant punning got on the commander's nerves. He had not wanted to bring a scientist along, saw no point in keeping weather records, and didn't think much of Collins's credentials.[25] When the *Herald* reporter asked if he could try out the electric lights Thomas Edison had given the expedition to brighten the Arctic winter, De Long denied him permission, saying he worried that the men would be disappointed if they didn't work. (As it turned out, the lights weren't turned on because it would have taken too much precious coal to keep them glowing.[26]) Collins felt he was being treated like an "accessory," since De Long pointedly assigned scientific tasks to others. After the *Jeannette* became stuck in the ice and started heeling over, tensions between the two men erupted into the open. De Long was then frustrated that his dream of reaching the Open Polar Sea had come to naught so prematurely. So when Collins flatly refused to take part in the crew's morning physical exercises, De Long accused him of disregarding a direct order and threatened severe consequences.

Meanwhile, battered by ice floes, the ship was taking on water at the rate of sixty gallons a minute, and the lieutenant's inexperienced crew was growing apprehensive. After looking at their faces and thinking of his own state of mind, De Long wrote in his journal that being so immobilized strained "man's temper or physical endurance" more than any other experience.[27] On Christmas Day the men ate a wordless breakfast, with "with memories accumulating in the silence." By mid-February, the once sanguine commander had to confess that "All our hoped-for explorations and perhaps discoveries . . . seem slipping away from us." When De Long and his fellow officers stood watch at night they had nothing to say to each other. Still unable to move forward at the end of June 1880, he had to admit to himself that the Open Polar Sea was "a delusion and a snare." Like Doyle's fictional captain of the *Pole-Star*, De Long could not accept that ice had prevented him from achieving his objective at only 77.19 degrees north latitude, still some seven hundred miles from the pole. The voyage he had envisioned through the Bering Strait had begun with high hopes but now would be consigned to the world's "dreary wastebasket."

Coal was fast running out, and so was their time on the doomed ship. Living day after day with the fear that at any moment the hull could be smashed and the *Jeannette* sink, the men became morose; they withdrew into tight cliques and muttered their grievances out of earshot of the others. (Each group had its "pet" dog, and when these famine-crazed creatures lunged at each other, snapping, going for the jugular, these canine struggles seemingly acted out the crew's repressed hostility.[28]) Collins was more direct, dashing off a note to De Long complaining about his "contemptuous disregard" for the journalist's feelings and accusing him of not showing proper respect. De Long's response was to relieve Collins of all meteorological duties. It was as if this grating of nerves on board was mirroring the grinding and groaning of the ice against the sides of the ship, creating ever greater pressure. De Long tried to keep up discipline and daily routines so as to remind the men of their connection to the "normal" world they had left behind, but this did little to stop morale from breaking down. Life on the imprisoned *Jeannette* was turning into a form of psychological torture none of them had foreseen. What they were discovering on this voyage was not new territory, but their own inner selves. As Hampton Sides has put it in his book on the De Long expedition, "If they had not really gone anywhere, they had journeyed into regions of the psyche where few men had ever been, interior spaces that brought out aspects of themselves they'd never known existed."[29] De Long came to feel closer to his men in this increasingly desperate situation, but he also found out there was a plot brewing to take over the ship and relieve him of command. Crew members were agitated over the growing likelihood of having to abandon the ship and strike out for safety across a frozen sea. Late on the night of June 12, with the hull splintering and water pouring in, De Long finally gave the order to unload provisions and equipment and take to the ice. After they had hurriedly set up a temporary camp several hundred yards from the rapidly sinking *Jeannette*, De Long tried once more to look on the bright side, jotting in his journal, "All cheerful, with plenty to eat and wear."[30] (He neglected to mention that many of the men were doubled over with cramps caused by having eaten lead-contaminated food.[31]) Whether he really believed what he had written or was only trying to make himself believe it cannot be determined. What is clear from De Long's journal is that he oscillated, in a manic-depressive manner, between unrealistic hopes and frank despair, between candid acknowledgement of his desperate predicament and longings to have his wife, Emma, at his side so that they could gaze up at the beautiful Arctic night sky together.[32] One moment, De Long would affirm his motto of "Hope On, Hope Ever," and the next lapse into a lachrymose lament like this:

> There can be no greater wear and tear on a man's mind and patience than this life in the pack. . . . The absolute monotony; the unchanging round of hours; the awakening to the same things and the same conditions that one saw just before losing one's self in sleep; the same faces; the same dogs; the same ice; the same conviction that to-morrow will be exactly the same as to-day, if not more disagreeable; the absolute impotence to do anything, to go anywhere, or to change one's situation an iota.[33]

Time and again, he would push such bleak thoughts away and grasp at another straw. One marker of this was his frequent use of the word "cheerful," as if this served as a verbal talisman to ward off disaster, or keep him oblivious of it. (Soon after the coal heaver Nelse Iverson had tipped him off about the intended mutiny, De Long was dumbfounded to hear from the surgeon on board, James Ambler, that this man was "trembling on the border of insanity," incoherent and hysterical: the lieutenant had always found Iverson " bright and cheerful."[34] De Long's poor eyesight cannot excuse this obtuseness.) De Long evoked this bromide one final time in the Siberian wilderness, 120 days after leaving the *Jeannette*, with men dying daily around him, and the survivors reduced to chewing on deerskin scraps: "All hands weak and feeble, but cheerful. God help us."[35]

The apparent divide in De Long's grasp of reality was not unique to him, but rather representative of a larger, cultural dichotomy. Nineteenth-century European and American decorum dictated that thoughts and feelings remain private. Middle-class and upper-class men ventured into the public arena wearing a well-fitting mask and interacted with others through it. What we today might regard as hypocrisy was, in their day, behaving properly. One had to be true to more than one's own self. Their other responsibility was to live up to expectations, regardless of what the extenuating circumstances might be. For polar explorers, this was an especially trying duty: their moral convictions warred against the life-or-death exigencies they faced. They could not survive in this unforgiving realm without, at times, violating their values, and yet if they disregarded these principles they would betray their code of honor and self-respect. It was a terrible choice they had to make. For expedition leaders, who were supposed to set an example for the other men, it was soul wrenching.

For some of them, like Robert Scott, the solution lay in retreating inward, keeping their own counsel, and turning challenges like crossing a glacier with almost no food or fuel left into tests of courage and perseverance. Passing these was the essence of manliness. As a commander, Scott was famously introspective, diffident, and secretive—formal and reserved to a fault. He signed off on his instructions to the heads of his Antarctic sledge parties with "Wishing you all success, Robt. Scott, Captain." (In sticking to proprieties, he resembled the Norwegian explorer Fridtjof Nansen, who had trekked for nine months across the frozen Arctic Ocean accompanied by a young coal stoker named Hjalmar Johansen before he felt comfortable enough to propose switching to the informal *Du* form in speaking to each other.[36]) Scott was also self-contained, melancholic, and unobtrusive, perhaps because of his modest family circumstances:[37] he lacked upper-class savoir faire and confidence about his social status.[38] He was also a bit of a dreamer, content to lose himself in poetry and other kinds of escape from the world around him. Since the age of thirteen, Scott had been in the Royal Navy, and over these many years the man and his identity as an officer had merged. He was not one to cultivate intimacy with his peers or underlings or bare his chest to them. Uncertain about how to proceed in the unfamiliar wasteland of Antarctica, Scott would periodically withdraw to his quarters, brood for a while, and then return to summarily announce his plans to his companions.

This standoffishness was compounded by a sentimental streak—preventing him at times from making sound, pragmatic decisions. Scott's affection for animals, for example, clouded his judgments about how to use them effectively. He became so attached to the dogs dragging their sledges that he would not allow Oates to kill them for food. In his dealings with his men, Scott was also inclined to let highly subjective assessments prevail over practical considerations. When he chose companions for his 1901 *Discovery* expedition, he picked—almost to a man—persons without any polar experience. In preparing for his disastrous 1910 expedition to Antarctica, he selected team members largely on his assessment of their characters (of which he was a poor judge) and overlooked significant shortcomings, such as Apsley Cherry-Garrard's nearsightedness. He allowed a dog handler named Cecil Meares to pick out the Siberian ponies for his trek to the South Pole even though the fun-loving Irishman had no knowledge about these animals and ended up buying ones that were weak and sickly. He allowed Edward Wilson, Cherry-Garrard, and "Birdie" Bowers to undertake an excursion across the Ross Ice Shelf in the middle of the Antarctic winter to retrieve some Emperor penguin eggs—an ill-conceived side trip that rapidly devolved into the "worst journey in the world," weakening the health of the men he needed to have in good shape for the final march south. He left behind the person most skilled in operating motor sledges because his second-in-command, Lieutenant "Teddy" Evans was not comfortable having such a higher-ranking officer come along.[39] None of these fateful decisions had anything to with "bad luck"—which Scott would blame for his failure to reach the pole ahead of Amundsen.

Good leaders must be dreamers in imagining grand destinies, but to turn these dreams into reality they have to be hard-nosed, clear-sighted persons who listen to advice, learn from experience, and adapt in the face of unforeseen circumstances. Scott's fatal flaw was his inability to focus exclusively on the most efficient means of carrying out his mission, and for this he paid a high price. His "madness" lay in believing that the human spirit alone could triumph over the natural world. But this was not the only reason why so many expedition leaders met with disaster at the ends of the earth. Many were simply overwhelmed by the physical and psychological barriers they faced. At the poles, failure was not just a possibility; it was what could be expected. During the mid-nineteenth century, of the dozens of ships that sailed forth looking for traces of the missing Franklin expedition, almost none of them succeeded in finding anything. (It was not until 2014 that one of Franklin's two vessels was discovered, largely intact, on the bottom of Victoria Strait. The other, *Terror*, was located two and a half years later, some distance to the south.) As was noted earlier, many of these "rescue" missions ran into serious trouble: ships were caught in the ice and sank; men suffered from scurvy, starvation, and extreme cold, and many of them died. Being imprisoned in the Arctic, with dwindling supplies of food and coal, living in cramped quarters with no guarantee of ever returning home, exacted a heavy toll. Because expedition leaders had no one in whom they could confide or from whom they could get advice, pressures on them intensified when the situation on board deteriorated. Few bore up well under this strain. Their relationships with their crews grew tense and volatile. Personality conflicts led to backstabbing, open dissension, defiance of authority, and even revolt. In this way, a leader's weaknesses undermined the esprit and resolve of the entire party.

Such conflicts were more apt to arise when the party was diverse in its make up or motives. As happened on the *Belgica*, competing objectives—geographical conquest versus scientific discovery, for example—could breed contempt and animosity. Fearful for their lives, men formed "tribal" bonds with those like them and turned their backs on the others. Estrangement could fragment a crew. During the ship's long stay in the Antarctic pack, curses in Polish, Norwegian, Flemish, French, Romanian, Russian, and English had peppered the dank quarters below deck and amplified feelings of alienation. On another multinational voyage to Antarctica, the British-financed sealer *Southern Cross* duly flew the

Union Jack even though all but two in the party were Norwegian. The captain, a half-Norwegian, half-British ex-schoolmaster named Carsten Borchgrevink, clashed with the scientists on board even before leaving England, when he made them each sign a piece of paper granting him exclusive rights to publish their findings. Borchgrevink further angered these men by reaming them out for returning late to the ship during a stopover in Madeira. Anxious to be accepted as a peer, he claimed to be a scientist, although he had not been trained as one. (Borchgrevink had revealed his true reason for sailing south when he had leapt overboard during a previous, 1895 Antarctic expedition so that he could become the first person to set foot on that continent.[40]) After some of the scientists questioned his authority, an irate Borchgrevink accused them of fomenting mutiny. When the *Southern Cross* departed for New Zealand in March 1899, ten men stayed behind at Cape Adare—becoming the first to winter on the Antarctic continent. This small band soon grew even more cantankerous. Borchgrevink outraged the Belgian-born astronomer Louis Bernacchi by telling him to stop taking magnetic readings and photograph a seal instead. Repeatedly, Borchgrevink lashed out at the others to conceal his own feelings of inadequacy. As T. H. Baughman has summed up in his book on the *Southern Cross* expedition, the neophyte captain "never succeeded in establishing his moral right to lead."[41] This critical ability—which Ernest Shackleton would exemplify during his 1914–1917 *Endurance* expedition—could spell the difference between success and disaster.[42]

To some extent, a strong ego and vanity were essential traits for someone wishing to lead a polar expedition, but these qualities could also destroy the fragile bonds that kept crews focused on their mission and made their sacrifices seem worthwhile. If a leader was driven solely by selfish ambitions, his authority would always be suspect. This is what William Godfrey had concluded about Elisha Kent Kane after he had saved the latter's life in northern Greenland and Kane had then altered the facts in his book in order to glorify his own heroism. Likewise, the well-liked and much admired Frederick Cook, who had shown such solicitous concern for the health of his fellow crew members as physician on the *Belgica*, later revealed a dark and self-serving side of his character when he made up a story of having climbed to the top of Mount McKinley and went on to claim, without offering any proof, that he had reached the North Pole ahead of Peary.[43] Even a highly respected Norwegian explorer like Fridtjof Nansen had lost much of his crew's respect when he abruptly announced he was abandoning them on the icebound *Fram* to proceed on foot to the North Pole—a decision that has been justly called "one of the most foolhardy in the history of polar exploration."[44] Up until that point Nansen had professed his only Arctic interest was scientific.[45]

One of the most egregious examples of pernicious leadership was that of First Lieutenant Adolphus Washington Greely. Born in Newburyport, Massachusetts, descendant of an old New England family and the son of a shoemaker, Greely had volunteered for the Union Army as a seventeen-year-old, taken part in bloody battles like Antietam, been wounded twice, and then worked his way up the ranks from private to brevet major by the time the war ended. (By the time he finally retired, in 1908, Greely had attained the rank of general, making him the first American soldier to rise from the lowest rank to that level.) A few years later, as a lieutenant in the Signal Corps, he had volunteered and been selected to lead a military party to Greenland in the fall of 1881 aboard the steamer *Proteus*, as part of a coordinated international effort to collect scientific data about the Arctic region. Having never served at sea before, let alone been to the Far North, Greely was an odd choice for this assignment. Most likely it was his experience as an infantry officer during and after the Civil War, as well as his knowledge of meteorology, that earned him command over these soldiers. (None of them had ever been to the Arctic either: their previous service was in the cavalry on the Great Plains.) Maintaining discipline was absolutely essential during a protracted stay far from civilization, and Greely's Civil War and frontier service suggested that he could manage well under these circumstances.[46]

Surprisingly, the *Proteus* found open water all the way to Ellesmere Island, off the northwestern coast of Greenland (in a bay named for Lady Franklin), and the men unloaded their 350 tons of supplies just as winter was closing in. Working day and night, the twenty-five soldiers and officers hammered together a poorly insulated, three-room building and makeshift observatories at this site some six hundred miles south of the pole—making it the northernmost inhabited spot on the planet. They named it "Fort Conger," in honor of the Republican US senator from Michigan who had sponsored a bill to fund the expedition. Forging a cohesive, mutually supportive unit would turn out to be much more daunting. There had already been considerable friction en route: some of the enlisted men had balked at being ordered to clean a rifle belonging to one of the lieutenants. In apparent retaliation, Greely had made them submit to bare-chested physical exams—something the soldiers found humiliating.[47] Another source of discord was the civilian surgeon, Octave Pavy—a native of New Orleans, Paris-educated, worldly wise, and veteran of one previous voyage to the Arctic—who had joined the party in southern Greenland. (The War Department had relaxed its regulations so that he could take part in this military mission.) Henry Independence Clay, a grandson of the famed Kentucky lawmaker, had put aside his own political career to sign up for the *Proteus* voyage. After wintering together in the Arctic, he and Pavy were scarcely on speaking terms.[48] Rather than jeopardize the men's health by depriving them of a doctor who had "shown a marked disposition to extreme measures" if Clay stayed on, the latter announced that he was leaving on the soon-to-depart *Proteus*, in the interests of "harmony."[49]

The second-in-command, Lieutenant William Kislingbury, suffering from depression brought on by the recent death of his second wife, declared his unhappiness with Greely's strict regulations and asked to be relieved of his duties. He intended to go back on the ship, too, but it sailed while he was busy with paperwork, so he was stuck at Fort Conger, stripped of all official duties, and reduced to performing housekeeping chores—trapped in a bizarre limbo. With the long polar night almost upon them, and the men now crammed into their new quarters, completely cut off from the outside world, other petty grievances soon poisoned the claustrophobic atmosphere. Chiefly these involved Greely and Pavy: the doctor bridled under Greely's martinet-like regimen. After items such as overcoats, mittens, axes, and tent poles were lost or damaged during the unloading of the *Proteus*, or on subsequent excursions, the lieutenant convened formal boards of inquiry to determine who was responsible (and thus avoid having to pay for this government property himself).[50] He reprimanded two lieutenants for sleeping late and missing breakfast. He also antagonized the enlisted men by telling them they had to do the officers' laundry. (They refused.) The men shivered in temperatures so low that kerosene for the lamps had to be thawed out before it could be used. Once one of their puppies ran outside and froze so fast in its tracks that they had to take an axe to chip it free.[51] All of them suffered from the demoralizing darkness, which was to persist for another five months. They stopped eating and showed signs of "gloom, irritation, and depression" as the days dragged on. They argued over inane questions such as which city had the better fire department, New York or Chicago. To keep the talk civil, an "Anti-Swearing Society" imposed fines for cursing. The soldiers found it hard to sleep. Their skin took on a ghastly greenish hue. Their hold on reality grew tenuous. One December morning, an Inuit in their party, Jens, decided that he was going to walk back to his home in Greenland—some one thousand miles away—or die trying, and he had to be tracked down in the snow and coaxed back.[52] He was not the only one to temporarily lose his reason. A private, William Whisler, became delirious from staying outside for a long spell and went "out of his head" for several hours after returning to the fort.[53] As soon as the sun returned, in March, Greely insisted on sending out sledge parties to reconnoiter and lay the groundwork for spring explorations. The men suffered terribly during these excursions, sleeping for days on end in bags that stiffened as hard as iron in temperatures falling as low as minus 48 degrees and becoming badly frostbitten. Greely's obsession with setting new records turned some men against him, even though he promised each a reward of nine hundred dollars if they reached a "northing surpassing any ever before attained."[54] On May 13, 1882, a party led by Sergeant David Brainard did just that, trekking to a headland located at 83.23.8 degrees north and thus ending a nearly three-century-old British polar monopoly by surpassing, by four miles, that country's previous Farthest North.

This ecstatic triumph quickly gave way to more discontent, and then despair, as the expected resupply ship failed to materialize, and the Lake Franklin Bay party had to brace itself for a second winter on drastically reduced rations. Greely and Pavy sparred over this decision, and others in the party chafed under the lieutenant's tight control—forbidding them, for example, from going more than five hundred yards from the ship without first getting his permission. (This restriction was imposed, he said, because of the risk of polar bear attacks.) Sergeant David Linn, who was wont to mutter the incantation "United we stand, divided we fall," took umbrage at this policy, and Greely promptly reduced him in rank for making "disrespectful" remarks. Some men complained about having to attend Sunday services, during which Greely intoned passages from the Book of Psalms, sounding like the prophet Jeremiah. He, in turn, laid into Kislingbury for "fraternizing" with the enlisted men by playing cards with them.[55] Worried about another ship not being able to reach them, Greely mulled over a long-shot scheme to navigate through the ice in small boats when spring arrived to reach a depot believed to exist at Cape Sabine, some 250 miles to the south. (His orders from Washington had dictated this course of action in case no relief vessel made it to Fort Conger.) The men thought he was crazy to think of leaving their safe and relatively comfortable outpost for the hazards of the open sea, but Greely would not be deterred. Pavy told him flatly that this risky and foolish undertaking was likely to end "disastrously." Another breach of discipline occurred that July, when Pavy announced that, with his one-year contract now up, he had no intention of renewing it. When asked to turn over his private diary and other papers, he refused, insisting that he was no longer under Greely's command and therefore didn't have to comply with his demands. Greely then had the doctor temporarily placed under arrest.

After giving up all hope of a ship arriving that summer, a despondent band of soldiers departed the fort on August 9, 1883, in their five boats. Brainard nailed the door shut, leaving twenty-one dogs and two pups inside, along with overturned barrels of blubber, pork, and bread to feed on, but there was little hope of their surviving very long.[56] Only one sergeant on board had any navigational experience, and Greely was completely out of his element. He spent long stretches sulking inside his sleeping bag on the floorboards. Intermittently, the lieutenant barked orders, dismaying the others with his poorly thought-out plan to abandon the boats and drift southward on an ice floe. (Pavy thought the lieutenant should be relieved of his command for this "suicidal" proposal, and three of the men secretly plotted to take over command, but then changed their minds when they realized they had no one who could replace Greely. Brainard scribbled just one word in his diary—"Madness."[57]) The breakdown in order continued when the engineer, Sergeant William Cross, who was chronically drunk—this time on stolen fuel alcohol—ran the launch aground and then uttered "insolent" words. Greely wanted to punish him, too, but no one else knew how to keep the engine running.

Two weeks out, the ice closed in on them like a pack of white wolves, and Greely's party had no choice but to take to a floe. Miraculously, after having drifted at the mercy of erratic currents for fifty-one days, they came ashore on the rocky, barren coast near Cape Sabine. The men had to find shelter in a hastily built stone hut—a place they named Camp Clay—for a third winter, with starvation looming: musk ox and other wild animals were nowhere to be found. Nor could they locate any of the expected food caches. They had to settle for moldy dog biscuit, supplemented by a small stash of meat, dried potatoes, and pickles they had unearthed nearby, left years before by British mariners. To make meager these supplies last as long as possible, Greely cut back their rations to one-fifth of the normal five thousand calories per day needed in the Arctic. Slowly, on this meager diet, the men weakened, burrowed deeper into their shared sleeping bags, and waited to die. With their food nearly exhausted, the emaciated soldiers argued and traded blows over scraps. By mid-March 1884, their rations were down to eleven ounces of pemmican and bread a day. To appease their empty stomachs, they chewed on candle wax and the soles of their boots. They fantasized about sumptuous feasts. Indifferent to discipline, a few of them responded to Greely's commands with "insolent" language and refused to do work like shoveling snow or cooking breakfast. Ever worried about maintaining his control, Greely vowed to shoot anyone who tried to wrest it away. When the enlisted men refused to obey one of his commands, he made one of them crawl outside and stay there until he showed more respect. Once the lieutenant became so enraged at Pavy that he came close to grabbing a rifle and dispatching him.[58] A German-born private, Charles Buck Henry, who had a history of thievery, stole some precious bacon, and the lieutenant ordered him shot in June to discourage others from doing this. (Henry was not the only soldier to take more than his share of provisions: the diary kept by Sergeant Brainard records several instances of others pilfering and hoarding provisions. The private may have been singled out for extreme punishment because his thefts were the most frequent and egregious and because he was not an American.[59]) Day after day, Greely's efforts to stop his men from undermining his authority, surrendering their last vestiges of humanity, and turning into "brutes" warred against their steady physical decline. It was a struggle of mind against matter—the commander's insistence on upholding standards versus their bodies' failing. As Brainard wrote in his diary, "The constant gnawing of hunger almost drives us mad."[60] By May, with other soldiers making out their wills, he conceded there was "nothing else to do but die like men and soldiers."[61]

In bunches—five in April, four in May—they lapsed into unconsciousness and died, some babbling like babies or calling for their mothers,

others completely silent as if sleeping. Too heavy to be carried outside, some bodies were left on the hut floor, turning it into an impromptu morgue—or a vision of hell as conceived by Hieronymus Bosch. By the time a rescue party reached Littleton Island by ship on June 22, 1884, only seven of the original twenty-five men were still alive, and they only barely so. Starvation, extreme cold, bullets, and the frigid Arctic waters had claimed the rest. Greely was one of those who had survived the winter—testimony to his iron constitution. And, indeed, his life was far from over. Adolphus Washington Greely would live for another half a century, to the age of ninety-one, finally dying of a blood clot in his leg at Walter Reed Hospital in 1935. He would then be buried with full military honors in Arlington National Cemetery next to his faithful wife, Henrietta, mourned as an illustrious hero, the grand old man among American polar explorers, and a recipient of the Congressional Medal of Honor.

Like Elisha Kent Kane before him, Greely was a man who stubbornly imposed his will on those he commanded—and by sheer perseverance etched his name in the history books. Both gained heroic stature not so much because of what they had achieved but because of what they had managed to endure. Without his infamous ordeal at Cape Sabine, Greely would have gradually faded into obscurity, just as Kane would have without the engrossing tales of almost incredible ordeals and survival he had written. Around both men, too, grew up a legend that was larger than life and often at odds with the facts. (Their shortcomings were largely overlooked or forgotten, although rumors that Greely's men had resorted to cannibalism tarnished his image for years.) The exploits of these two explorers—like those of Franklin and Scott—fueled a nineteenth-century hunger to sanctify suffering, a need for secular Christ figures whose sacrifices endowed life with a higher purpose. The hunger for self-glorification that had taken hold of both these explorers and driven them to go to such lengths—manipulating others to follow—had no place in this apotheosis, and so it, too, was kept out of the record. It was the legend that needed to be printed, not the truth.

A personal note: one day, in the course of doing research for this book in the stacks of Columbia University's Butler Library, I pulled a copy of Greely's 1885 memoir, *Three Years of Arctic Service*, off a shelf and gently opened it. Tucked inside the front cover was a letter—an old letter judging by the crisp feel and yellowish tint of the paper. I unfolded it and found to my great surprise that this was an original letter, written by Greely toward the end of his life to Bassett Jones, a frozen-food magnate and bibliophile with a passion for polar books. Somehow this letter had been left inside this volume—part of Jones's collection, purchased by Columbia for its rare-book collection—which had never been properly shelved. Reading it that afternoon, I was transported back into a bygone era, and into the mind of an elderly, but still defiant and willful Adolphus Greely. He denied having earned any money from giving lectures on his Arctic exploits, even though he had had six children to support on a modest army salary. He had likewise not deigned to ask his friends for loans, even though it had taken two decades for the American Geographical Society to acknowledge the significance of what he had accomplished in the Greenland wilderness. Furthermore, the crusty old brigadier went on, "I am proud that nothing claimed in *Three Years of Arctic Service* has ever been disputed." But it was in his final sentences that Greely really tipped his hand, thinking no doubt that at this point in his life, and in this letter, he had nothing more to hide: "However," he concluded, "I have what no single man can give or take away—FAME. In my 88th year the people are proud of me, judging from their letters."[62]

Chapter Three

BY NATURE POSSESSED

Fittingly, Captain James Cook's first encounter with Antarctica in 1774 contained all the elements that later explorers would associate with this mysterious continent—indistinct shape, massive size, frightful cold, sudden danger, seductive allure, and grandiose metaphor. As on later expeditions, there was even a dog involved. For several years, Cook had been roaming the South Pacific in search of the fabled *Terra Australis*—a gigantic land mass believed by the ancient Greeks to exist somewhere in these largely unexplored waters. The year before, his HMS *Resolute* had crossed the Antarctic Circle for the first time in recorded history, navigating cautiously between huge icebergs and floating chunks of ice, until, further slowed by heavy mist and snow, the vessel once again turned northward. In December, Cook had resumed his dogged quest, again heading south, his way again blocked by large "ice islands" and a curtain of fog. But in late January 1774 a favorable wind and calm seas bore the *Resolute* up close to a large ice mass, and Cook sent out two boats to bring back samples. It was so cold that cascading snow stiffened the rigging, and the sails hardened like "boards or plates of metal." On the morning of the 30th, the clouds congregated ahead of them were an unusual snowy white, indicating an ice field lay ahead, and they made for it.

As they approached, they could see that the ice stretched in either direction out of sight. Over this amorphous white mass, the sun's rays rose like a curtain of pale, flickering flame. In the distance, Cook and his men counted as many as ninety-seven icy peaks, which rose so high they disappeared in the clouds. Around the edge of this sheer shelf, a mile or so in width, floated a phalanx of ice floes, jammed so closely together that they threatened to crush like an eggshell any vessel that dared to come any closer. So Cook prudently ordered the *Resolute* to reverse course and make for safer climes.[1] And the dog? Well, it so happened that the tireless, globe-circling captain soon afterward suffered acute pain from gallbladder stones and had to be put to bed for several days. The only food he could keep down was fresh meat, and the only source of that was one of the dogs on board—the darling of Cook's polymath Scottish naturalist, Johann Reinhold Forster. The animal involuntarily obliged, thus becoming the first in a long line of canines to be sacrificed in the Antarctic for the good of their hungry masters.

So began the modern era's fascination with the Seventh Continent—a place unlike any other on earth, fraught with perils but as irresistible to explorers as the Sirens' call was to Odysseus's crew. Perhaps most enchanting was its staggeringly expansive landscape. For Europeans from outside Scandinavia, these soaring, jagged, dazzlingly white icebergs were truly an amazing spectacle. Without comparison in their experience, the bizarre shapes defied description. Explorers felt as if they had landed on another planet: everything was that strange and overwhelming. In their written accounts, early voyagers like Cook groped for the right words to describe what they had seen.[2] But they were poorly prepared to do so, for the English language of their day was ill-equipped to adequately capture such grandeur. Furthermore, they were seafarers used to dealing with familiar facts and concrete problems, not disposed to reflect upon natural wonders and ultimate mysteries. The largely unschooled Cook conceded as much in his history of this South Seas voyage, in which he cautioned readers not to expect "ornament" from his prose, only "candour" and "fidelity" to the truth—that is, a catalog of information, compiled by a "plain man" who was simply doing his duty. His choice of words typified an eighteenth-century preference for depicting Nature in objective, neutral terms, rather than reacting to it with romantic embellishment. For Cook and his contemporaries, ice was simply ice, not something sublime or a "vehicle and revelation of vital energy."[3] Their polar surroundings were not some richly evocative realm where the physical and metaphysical merged, but merely a series of obstacles to be avoided.

So when Cook and his men came upon a mass of ice the size of the largest cathedral in the British Empire, his first reaction was not to stare spellbound but to ask his men to scrape off some snow so that he might have a closer look at it. Ice floes he labelled "floating rocks," while apologizing for this pedestrian metaphor.[4] Cook's plain style was unwittingly imitated more than a century later by the first man who would claim (erroneously) to have been the first to set foot on the Antarctic continent, Carsten Borchgrevink. His eagerness to record this feat far surpassed any wish to depict it memorably.[5] He, too, stuck to the plain facts, thus recalling the events leading up to this historic event: "Very little drift-ice was to be seen towards the south-west of the bay and in the immediate vicinity of the actual cape. A strong tidal wave passed near the cape north-westwards toward the western side of Robertson Bay."[6] A wind-hollowed sweep of snow bank he saw as a "kind of fence" near a "sort of gallery" next to a mountain. The mist that draped his vessel like a shroud inspired no romantic reveries: it merely prevented Borchgrevink from observing the moons of Jupiter. At the top of the world, John Franklin had likewise not made any effort to capture in glowing phrases the astonishing panorama that was sprawled across the Western horizon when he and his thoroughly drenched and exhausted band reached the upper falls of the Mackenzie in late August of 1825, noting only that the refracted light from the sun transformed these dwarfing mountains into the "most extraordinary shapes."[7] William Parry, whose ship *Hecla* was trapped by Arctic ice and steadily encroaching darkness at about the same time—becoming the first vessel to winter this far north—welcomed a dazzling aurora borealis one November afternoon as an interruption of shipboard tedium, but failed to say what made this heavenly sight so "remarkable."[8] Readers simply had to accept that Parry had witnessed a natural marvel they would never have a chance to see—and that words could never capture, like the dark side of the moon.

Most polar explorers of the eighteenth and nineteenth centuries were so bent on moving quickly ahead—going further than anyone else before them and discovering new land—that the extraordinary terrain they came upon held little intrinsic interest for them. Struggling just to stay alive at temperatures well below zero, with gales whipping across snow-encrusted decks and crews weakened by scurvy and rations almost gone, ship captains had no time to admire the dazzling natural beauty around them. Strangers in a strange land, they first saw what they had to see and then what their preconceptions allowed them to take in.[9] Often these first impressions were misleading: things did not always turn out to be what they had appeared to be. A mountain peak estimated to be ten miles away might actually be much closer, and ghostly human figures approaching through the mist prove to be only mirages. With few books on the poles available in the early nineteenth century, commanding officers like Cook, Franklin, and Parry were as poorly prepared mentally for the Arctic and Antarctic as their woolen naval jackets and sterling silver knives engraved with family crests were appropriate for the environment. To make sense of this bizarre, intimating realm, explorers needed a new frame of reference, a new vocabulary, and a new sensibility.

In the early part of the nineteenth century, several such frameworks were available to them. The most common was religious. Almost all Europeans and Americans believed that the world was created and guided by the omniscient and benign hand of a Christian God. The natural world was his creation, and its unity, diversity, and beauty expressed his limitless power and wisdom. Humans could not fully understand the Almighty's plan, as their reasoning ability was insufficient for this task. The best they could do was to explore and study the world around them for evidence of it. Accurate measurement and classification of natural phenomena could help reveal the underlying scheme. As children of the Enlightenment, Western explorers brought with them a belief that the world was "an orderly and perfect place where everything fit neatly into the Great Chain of Being."[10] Expeditions to the poles could witness God's glory in a pristine state, untainted by civilization or the passage of time. Goethe, for instance, considered glaciers to be prehistoric evidence of divine handiwork, offering insights into how the oceans and continents were formed.[11] In its purity, the polar realm was closer to God. Most early Arctic explorers who traveled far north or south trusted that Providence would watch over them there. Faith provided them both a way of understanding this ice kingdom and protection against its perils. During Sunday services on the North-Pole-bound *Hecla* in 1827, a deeply devout William Parry was wont to utter this prayer:

> Oh, Eternal Lord God, who alone spreadest out the heavens and rulest the raging sea . . . we thy unworthy servants humble desire to go forth in this, our enterprize . . . save us in every danger . . . help us to overcome every obstacle and grant . . . that having faithfully performed our duty to our country, we may return in safety, health, and honor to enjoy the blessings of the Lord, with the fruits of our labours . . . [We offer thanks for Your] gracious and fatherly protection . . Keep us from all evil, lead us aright in the way which Thou seest to be the best for us . . . be our guide, our guard, and our Almighty Friend.[12]

The stunning beauty beheld by polar explorers somewhat compensated for the hardship they had to face in voyaging so far into this untrammeled domain. It seemed to attest that God had left his mark on this remote part of the world, and thus confirmed his omnipresence. When the land party led by Lieutenant George Back was trekking toward the mouth of the Great Fish River, at the edge of Canadian territory, in 1833, they emerged from thick woods and swarms of mosquitoes to behold below them a "sylvan landscape . . . in all the wild luxuriance of its summer clothing."[13] As Back wrote in his journal, "Even the most jaded of the party . . . seemed to forget his weariness, and halted involuntarily with his burden, to gaze for a moment, with a sort of wondering admiration, on a spectacle so novel and magnificent." Such occasional glimpses of a tranquil, Wordsworthian landscape temporarily lifted the spirits of these

Englishmen, worn down by storms, rapids, and diminishing supplies, exhausted from endless river portages, and dispirited by the prospect of many more "horrors" ahead. Shortly after being bitten so badly by black clouds of sand flies that their faces swelled beyond recognition, driving them "almost to madness," Back would offer up thanks to the Almighty "for the mercies which had been already vouchsafed to us." Confidence in their success was renewed by such moments of prayerful communion.

Explorers could sense that a higher, spiritual power was operating in Nature. American polar novice Charles F. Hall, setting out on the whaler *George Henry* to look for the Franklin party in the spring of 1860, suffered through twelve straight days of seasickness and then a ferocious gale but still managed to discern through his afflictions the awesome power of God at work: "It seemed to me as if no one could . . . appreciate the beauty, the grandeur, the greatness of God's creation but in experiencing a storm at sea."[14] Half a century later, Edward ("Uncle Bill") Wilson, a saintly Anglican to his fingertips, would take up his watercolor brushes to sketch the Antarctic terrain for the benefit of future explorers, but also to convey his sheer delight at this enchanting manifestation of the divine. As one British historian has observed, Wilson "worshipped God by observing the natural world, in the tradition of Turner and Ruskin."[15] Looking up at a clear midnight sky in the Antarctic pack made him feel closer to his maker than he had at any other place on the planet.[16] When expeditions narrowly escaped disaster, such as happened in January 1910 to the crew of the French three-masted barque *Pourquoi-Pas?*, this was attributed to divine grace. After his vessel had slipped unscathed between icebergs to open water off an Antarctic peninsula, the leader, Jean-Baptiste Charcot, likened this good fortune to a resurrection: "All of a sudden before me the black gulf turns brilliant and golden, dazzling with light, adding to the fantastic strangeness of the scene, but giving the impression of an entry into paradise after leaving hell."[17]

Even without such overtones, the beauty of the polar regions could still be deeply inspiring and salubrious. After the flowering of English romanticism early in the nineteenth century, many explorers began to see this world more poetically than predecessors like Captain Cook had. Instead of recording only facts, they dwelled upon the emotional impact of what they had seen. This literary temper offered explorers a way of creatively imagining the polar environment. Apsley Cherry-Garrard, Wilson's companion on Robert Scott's 1910 expedition to Antarctica, evoked the continent's beauty with nuanced, almost painterly language. From the rolling deck of the *Terra Nova* Cherry-Garrard, a twenty-four-year-old newcomer to these choppy waters, looked up in amazement at the heavenly spectacle that was taking place before his eyes: "The northern sky was gloriously rosy and reflected in the calm sea between the ice, which varied from burnished copper to salmon pink; bergs and packs to the north had a pale greenish hue with deep purple shadows, the sky shaded to saffron and pale green."[18] Half a century earlier, the multihued Arctic sky had cast a similar spell over British naval surgeon Alexander Armstrong, sailing on HMS *Investigator* with hopes of locating Sir John Franklin: "the sunset was peculiarly beautiful, tinting the western horizon with colours no effort of art could pourtray [*sic*]—the most brilliant scarlet and crimson, stratified on a rich neutral ground, formed by a harmonious blending of all the elementary colours of the rainbow, a picture of pure Arctic scenery, stillness and beauty, which cast an auspicious halo around this new land."[19] Sometimes words failed to do justice to the effect of these almost surreal sights, but that did not stop explorers from trying to capture it. Traveling for the first time north, also in search of Franklin, Elisha Kane reacted to the first icebergs he saw with this somewhat overwrought language: "There was something about them so slumberous and so pure, so massive yet so evanescent, so majestic in their cheerless beauty, without, after all, any of the salient points which give character to description, that they almost seemed to me the material for a dream, rather than things to be definitely painted in words."[20] For introspective men like Wilson and Cherry, the protean nature of the polar realm acted as a springboard for quiet contemplation. A Cambridge-educated zoologist, Wilson spent hours aloft in the crow's nest of *Discovery* scanning the vast horizon and finding in this splendid Antarctic isolation "a peace which passes all understanding."[21] Similarly, the turn-of-the-century English alpinist and Arctic explorer Martin Conway felt himself drawn out of himself into a primal union with Nature as he gazed down on a setting sun and fog-shrouded slopes from high atop a snow saddle in Spitsbergen, Norway:

> At such times Nature gathers a man into herself, transforming his self-consciousness into a consciousness of her. All the forms and colours of the landscape sink into his heart like the expression of a great personality, whereof he himself is a portion. Ceasing to think, while Nature addresses him through every sense, he receives direct impressions from her. In this kind of *nirvana* the passage of time is forgotten, and as near an approach to bliss is experiences as this world is capable of supplying.[22]

The pleasure derived from being directly in touch with the natural world, unsullied by human footprints, grew greater toward the end of the nineteenth century, as Western Europe and the United States were evolving into industrialized, urban societies. Longing to go back to a simpler way of life heightened the appeal of journeys to the Arctic and Antarctic: there, English Romantics like Scott could travel back in time and experience a more elemental and seemingly more vital existence than what they had previously known. The frequency with which explorers used the word "pure" to describe what they saw suggests what they valued most when they were so far from the civilized world. As polar travel writer Sara Wheeler has written of Scott, "The Antarctic possessed a virginity in his mind that provided an alternative to the spoiled and messy world."[23] The psychic impact of this exposure was often more memorable than the physical challenges they had overcome. Ernest Shackleton, justly admired for his ability to lead men out of seemingly unsurmountable predicaments, was keenly aware of how the Antarctic had changed him inwardly as well as outwardly. He conceived of the continent more as a mental and emotional construct than as an actual, physical place, and it was for the unique feelings it aroused in him that he longed for it. During his Farthest South sledge journey, in December 1902, Shackleton scribbled these verses, which were later published (anonymously) under the title "L'Envoi," in the shipboard *South Polar Times*:

> With regret we shall close the story, yet ever in thought go back ...
> Though the grip of the frost may be cruel, and relentless its icy hold,
> Yet it knit our hearts together in that darkness stern and cold.[24]

For Cherry, too, "the response of the spirit" was what mattered in the long run.[25] In the frozen wastes, one came close to death, experienced something life-changing—and was born again in a higher form.

Many explorers found glimpses of divine grandeur in the vivid displays of celestial fireworks near the poles—streaking comets, astonishingly vivid stars and planets, multi-tinted solar halos, blinding moonlight, rainbow-hued auroras, bursting meteor showers. Elisha Kane observed these marvels from his spartan winter outpost near the Arctic Circle:

> ... the last days of January you have the magnificent chance, at noon, of seeing the tops of the high mountains, surrounding the fiord in the color of purple extending with every day more and more over the snows of the highland, and descending gradually until his beams are reflected from the fiord and the frozen fields of ice. The dark season is not felt, oppressively, except when combined with unsteady and stormy weather, a hazy atmosphere and a fall of snow. With a clear atmosphere and good weather the inhabitants miss at no time 2 or 3 hours of daylight for going out of doors and seeking substinence [*sic*] of the ice or the sea.... On clear days, you see at noon, besides the light of the sun in the South, a gloriously colored atmosphere at the North, or, the opposite sides of the heavens appear like a more or less intense red light in the form of an arc, which forms the limits between the lowest dark-blue part, darkened by the earth, and the uppermost part of the heavens brightened by the sun.[26]

For Kane and others, these awe-inspiring signs of God's presence helped to sustain them through their darkest hours. In the depths of a particularly miserable Greenland winter in 1855, hunkered down below decks on the *Advance*, reduced to eating the "overlooked godsend" of a frozen bear's head (raw) and jelly made from boiling its claws, and with many of his men bedridden due to scurvy, Kane took heart from the first glimmers of light returning after fifty-two days of total darkness. He experienced an almost pagan exuberance as the amount of sunshine increased each day, until finally the full orb of the sun rose above the horizon, vindicating his faith in Providence. Like a man possessed by angels Kane ran across the ice toward it, his arms flung wide, shouting to the "Great Author of Light," as he would have greeted Christ arising from the grave.[27] Indeed, the disappearance and miraculous return of the sun at this high latitude seemed to reenact the Easter story of death and resurrection, culminating with the same rapture. The sharp elemental contrasts of the polar cycle—unending light yielding slowly to blackness and then back again to light—touched their souls.

Even if these natural phenomena did not conjure up a sense of the divine, they still left an indelible impression. At the polar caps Nature seemed to have pulled out all the stops, far exceeding—in scale, dramatic energy, and color—what Europeans and Americans were familiar with. Peering through veils of fog and snow into this secretive kingdom, officers and ordinary sailors alike felt that they were entering a truly otherworldly realm. Its strangeness led them to see it as surreal and magical. In 1850, William Parker Snow, an English writer based in New-York, convinced Lady Franklin he had had a vision showing him where her missing husband was to be found and abruptly booked passage on the *Prince Albert*, bound for Greenland, so that he could prove he was right. Off its coast, his ship ran into a blinding snowstorm, transmuting the view ahead into a fantastical vision: "At times, these mountains were enveloped in a thick haze; then again looming through, and presenting the most curious and fantastic forms, pyramids upon pyramids displaying their sides to view. The valleys . . . appeared to be filled with snow and . . . seemed to convey the idea of our being in an icy and barren region. It was more like a misty picture produced upon the stage of a theatre than a semblance of reality."[28] The Australian scientist Louis Bernacchi had sailed with Borchgrevink on the *Southern Cross*, intent on wintering for the first time in Antarctica. Soon he found his attention drawn away from the magnetic field he was supposed to be measuring to the glorious scene that greeted him every day: "In all Nature's realm there are few sights more impressive than a vast field of magnificent glittering ice-floes on a beautifully calm morning with the deep blue Antarctic sky overhead. Lonesome, and unspeakably desolate it is, but with a character and a fascination all its own."[29]

As much as they tried to make sense of these sights, the explorers still could not find appropriate words for them: this continuing failure paralleled their inability to conquer this icebound kingdom with ships and sledges. So Nature was doubly victorious. The best most of them could do was fall back on inadequate metaphors and analogies, just as they would rely on inadequate clothing, tools, and know-how as they bored deeper into the unknown. They used classical and literary allusions to evoke what had no parallel. In his account of the first Henry Grinnell-financed search for Franklin and his men, Kane frequently leaned heavily on this sort of hyperbolic analogy. The first iceberg they ran across was "twice as large as Girard College" (a boarding school in Philadelphia co-founded by his father).[30] It reminded him of a "great marble monolith, only awaiting the chisel to stand out in peristyle and pediment a floating Parthenon." On another occasion the horizon "resembled an extended plain, covered with the debris of ruined cities" like ones in ancient Egypt and Greece. When his ship entered Barrow Strait (which separated Canada from Greenland) in early June the crew were dismayed to find it still blocked by ice three feet thick. "Sometimes," Kane wrote, "a hummock is as complete a jumble of confused tables as if Titans had been emptying rubbish carts of marble upon the floes." The descriptive accounts written by other polar explorers are larded with references to icebergs as castles, monasteries, cathedrals, and the like. So linking them to earlier, much-admired eras in human history lent a grandiose gloss to the strange apparitions that swam into their ken.

Clements Markham, the leading British advocate for Arctic exploration in the nineteenth century, set an example with his descriptions of the first icebergs he had seen when, as a young midshipman, he had taken part in the search for Franklin: "But it is when a line of icebergs is refracted on the horizon that the polar scenery is converted into a veritable fairy land. Some are raised up into lofty pillars. Again a whole chain of them will assume the appearance of a long bridge or aqueduct, and as quickly change into a succession of beautiful palaces and temples of dazzling whiteness, metamorphosed by the fantastic wand of Nature."[31] In like manner, William H. Gilder, a Union veteran wounded during the defense of Cemetery Ridge, drew upon classical as well as more contemporary parallels to recount his reaction to icebergs during an 1878 overland expedition looking for relics of the Franklin party: "one appeared like a huge circus tent, with an adjoining side-show booth"; another was "a most perfect representation of a cottage by the sea, with gables toward the observer, and chimneys rising at proper intervals along the roofs." On the ship's opposite side, "a huge monster presented a vast amphitheatre, with innumerable columns sparkling in the sunlight and dazzling the spectator with their intense brilliancy." One of these "monsters of the deep" was a "perfect counterpart of Newstead Abbey."[32]

In part, these melodramatic comparisons bespoke the Romantic sensibility of the mid-nineteenth century. From this perspective, Nature was infused with intimations of lurking danger and terror. Explorers' imaginations were primed by their literary readings to perceive the polar environment as threatening as well as enchantingly beautiful. And, indeed, danger was ever present: ice could suddenly crack open and swallow a sailor or encase a ship for years; a polar bear could shred a man's face with one swipe of his claws. Like Gothic novels and poems, Arctic and Antarctic expeditions juxtaposed an unsettling reality with visions of decayed splendor. What, under other circumstances, might lessen fears—say, a well-fortified castle or columned facade—only increased them because these images of past civilizations were laden with a sense of foreboding and doom.[33]

This Gothic temper had been made immensely popular by the young Mary Shelley—herself a voyager into new and unfamiliar territory, needing to gain a foothold in it. Fleeing a repressive England with her poet lover for the warmth and openness of the Continent in 1814, she had instead found an unseasonal chill—first, in the deep snow and ice during their coach's journey south through France, and then in the Swiss Alps; later, in the self-contained egoism of Percy Shelley. These atmospherics were given voice in the tale she composed on the shore of Lake Geneva two years later—*Frankenstein*. This story presented not only an emotionally cold man of science and his lonely "monstrous" creation, desperate for love, but also a frozen, lifeless Arctic landscape echoing the life-denying sterility of Victor Frankenstein. In Mary Shelley's narrative, Nature was the very antithesis of the benign, consoling presence imagined by Wordsworth—in which humankind could find a sheltering peace and security. In Shelley's visionary North, no such respite was afforded: one ventured into its sterile wastes at one's own peril—and could easily perish there. As more and more expeditions headed to the Arctic looking for the fabled Northwest Passage, for John Franklin, or for the ever-elusive North Pole, their previous faith in human invincibility, divine protection, and Nature's submissiveness was sorely tested. Their attempts to impose their wills on this impassive environment proved futile. Rather than yield, the polar world rebuffed these intruders, cut them off, rendered them immobile and impotent, and thus made evident its superior power. The would-be conquerors were defeated. When the young aspiring naturalist Joseph Hooker happened upon an erupting Mount Erebus near Antarctica in 1840, he found this sight "so surpassing everything that can be conceived and so heightened by the consciousness that we had penetrated to regions far beyond what had been deemed practicable before, that it caused a feeling of awe to steal over us at the contemplation of our comparatively utter insignificance and helplessness."[34] Bitterly disappointed, resigned to never reaching the Open Polar Sea with the *Jeannette* four decades later, George De Long could only watch helplessly as the ice grew thicker around his trapped vessel at the start of their second Arctic winter and concede that this "icy waste will go on surging to and fro until the last trump [*sic*] blows." The immense emptiness of the black sky over him, with its "majestic and awful silence," only reinforced the fact that he and his men were at the mercy of forces far greater than humans could command, making it painfully clear "how trifling and insignificant he [man] is in comparison with such grand works in nature."[35]

However, the explorers did not give up their quests easily. Theirs was a struggle as ancient as Adam and Eve's defiance of God in the Garden of Eden—a refusal to submit, no matter what the consequences. That was why a "Do it now" leader like De Long jotted down Horace's motto *Nil desperandum* ("Never despair") so frequently in his journal; why futile Franklin search parties set out with other Latin mantras flapping on their sledges, trudging stoically off like troops on maneuvers; why having eight of his toes amputated as a result of frostbite did not stop Robert Peary from going for the North Pole ten years later; why Robert Scott and Ernest Shackleton embraced the lines Tennyson had given to Ulysses: "To strive, to seek / To find / And not to yield." They all believed the human spirit could prevail. Their unshakable resolve was their last battering ram against an unyielding Nature. If it could not bring them victory, it would at least help them survive.

Early in the age of polar exploration, commanders had come to realize that the greatest threat to a party's well-being was having nothing to do for months at a time, particularly once the sun had dipped below the horizon, curtailing sledge excursions into the surrounding territory. Monotony and boredom sapped morale and made crews despondent. For military men, order and discipline were the keys to endurance: rituals like morning calisthenics on deck or wind sprints around the ship preserved a patina of normalcy in an exceedingly abnormal existence, kept the men fit, busy, and under control. *Mens sana in corpore sano.* Following a daily schedule also reinforced the notion that ship life near the poles could be as routine and predictable as in the Mediterranean. Doing the same things at the same times reminded crews that human-imposed patterns could be maintained where the diurnal rhythm of night and day no longer demarcated the passage of time. On board the *Hecla*, William Parry quickly instituted just such an inflexible schedule: all hands were awakened at 5:45 a.m.; after dressing, they scrubbed the deck with stones and sand until eight, when breakfast was served; afterward, inspections were held on the quarterdeck; the sailors went for a walk on shore until noon, whenever the weather was fair: otherwise, they ran on the decks; in the late afternoon, the men once again cleaned the decks and stood inspection; it was only after supper that they were permitted "free time" to play cards, read books, or make music; lamps were turned out promptly at 9 p.m.

But an unvarying schedule only compounded the ennui and tedium of being stuck in the ice. So wise commanders sought to enliven shipboard life by mounting frivolous entertainments—musical performances, theatrical skits, and masquerades. Even a pious William Parry recognized the need for light-hearted diversions on the *Hecla* during the winter of 1819: "I had dread [*sic*] the want of employment as one of the worst evils that was likely to befal [*sic*] us."[36] To boost morale, he had the men put on a raucous and lavishly costumed staging of David Garrick's farce *Miss in Her Teens*—a production that occupied the crew for some weeks and created the comic relief he had hoped for. But such a distraction had only an ephemeral benefit. Idleness was a chronic problem, and thus had to be constantly warded off, like scurvy. So festive meals and celebrations for all manner of holidays were regularly held to punctuate the otherwise uneventful weeks and months.

The civilian "scientists" (a term that was not then in use) who accompanied polar expeditions had other tasks to carry out, which did help them pass the time. But their daily work had more intrinsic value than the sailors': they were observing, measuring, and recording environmental conditions and collecting samples of polar animals, plants, fish, and minerals to add to human knowledge. Their routines were seen as a way of understanding and thereby subjugating Nature. Being beset by ice did not stop them from carrying out this work. The scientists could continue to believe that they were fulfilling a central purpose of Arctic and Antarctic exploration—namely, to show that the "civilizing" impact of Western civilization was unstoppable, sustainable even under the most adverse of conditions.[37] Unlike the passive oneness with the natural world extolled by Romantic poets, these midcentury "naturalists" sought to wrest away its secrets for humanity's benefit—a rational probing that Wordsworth, for one, found reprehensible:

> Sweet is the lore which Nature brings;
> Our meddling intellect
> Mis-shapes the beauteous forms of things:—
> We murder to dissect.[38]

Literally this was the case near the poles, with penguins, seals, polar bears, walruses, and birds routinely stabbed or shot to death so that they could be more carefully studied. Most explorers were not sentimentalists, easily upset by killing other creatures, but in this innocent environment, violent assault on trusting and unsuspecting animals could seem cruel and barbaric, as when frolicking polar bear cubs were shot at point-blank range. During the *Southern Cross* expedition, Louis Bernacchi was appalled at the carnage he saw take place one day: to him, it seemed "truly a horrible intrusion slaughtering those harmless seals sleeping upon the ice under the peaceful silence of the blue Atlantic sky and dyeing the dazzling immaculate white of the ice-floe with glaring crimson pools of blood."[39] Still, this had to go on. Explorers might aspire to set new Farthest North records and enjoy occasional spiritual communion with the polar world, but their quotidian job was to serve science, and science was a stern taskmaster. To honor the mandate of the governments and patrons who had paid for them to go there, expeditions faithfully amassed knowledge about the climate, terrain, marine life, atmospheric pressure, water depth and currents, magnetism, and celestial bodies. This mission gained stature in the wake of an 1895 international conference that committed the major European powers to just such a scientific purpose. Nationalism also elevated the role of scientists: their discoveries were considered as prestigious and valuable as geographical conquest in enhancing their countries' stature. Scientists could also become national heroes.

"Taming" Nature by breaching its defenses and fathoming its mysteries gave proof of the limitless capabilities of humanity. As his fellow Norwegian Nansen would say of Roald Amundsen's bid to "discover" the South Pole, this was to be a "victory of human mind over the dominion and powers of Nature; a deed that lifts us above the grey monotony of daily life; a view over shining plains with lofty mountains against the cold blue sky, and lands covered by ice sheets of inconceivable extent; a vision of long vanished glacial times; the triumph of living over the stiffened realm of death. There is a ring of steeled purposeful human will—through icy frosts, snowstorms and death."[40] From a scientific point of view, knowledge about the Arctic and Antarctic could also advance commercial objectives. Learning about how sea currents flowed and when ice melted could benefit fishing and mining interests, if not improve trade with the other side of the world. The largely unexplored polar regions were regarded as one big laboratory, full of many precious secrets. For this reason, polar-bound vessels carried in their holds sophisticated instruments for gauging everything from the speed of the Arctic wind to the positions of the magnetic poles. Icebound parties set up makeshift observatories near their vessels and went to great pains to accurately record measurements—under appalling conditions, and with what strikes us today as an obsessional and unnecessary diligence. This devotion to data collecting bespeaks a nineteenth-century belief in the importance of numbers as ends in themselves. This notion grew out of the scientific positivism developed by the French philosopher Auguste Comte, who argued that genuine knowledge could only be found in the "minute particulars" of sensory experience.[41] In 1834 the Statistical Society of London—a trailblazer in its field—had been established to further this purpose by gathering "all facts illustrative of the present condition and prospects of society, especially as it exists in the British Dominions."[42] This organization declined to interpret any of the reams of figures it compiled, lest it become entangled in social-policy issues. The facts could speak for themselves. Subsequently, an enormous amount of information was compiled by numerous bodies on a host of social, economic, demographic, geographical, and scientific topics, but a lack of number-crunching tools and causal theories prevented much sense being made of these masses of figures. Still, such analytical limitations did not lead the polar explorers—or, at least, the scientists in their parties—to question the importance of what they were measuring and sampling. On the contrary, the absence of any higher rationale made performing these scientific tasks as thoroughly as possible even more important.

So they pursued this goal with tremendous dedication and diligence. When William Parry set out on the *Hecla* in 1819, accompanied by HMS *Griper*, to look for the Northwest Passage, he brought along two astronomical clocks, eleven chronometers, one transit instrument, one portable observatory, one repeating circle, two dipping needles, one instrument for "magnetic force," one variation transit, one variation needle, four compasses, one dip vector, four barometers, two altitude instruments, one "theodolite," two anglometers," one circular protractor, three artificial horizons, one hydrometer, one water bottle, fourteen thermometers, and two electrometers.[43] As the two Royal Navy vessels probed the Arctic coastline, officers made daily recordings of such meteorological data as air temperature, surface water temperature, barometric pressure, and wind direction, as well as of longitudinal and latitudinal positions (confirming that the latter did not correlate with changes in temperature), the dipping of a magnetic needle, compass bearings, and more arcane phenomena such as how much the weight of various woods changed after being submerged for various periods of time. All of this information was diligently transcribed in tables published in the appendix of Parry's journal, as if they summarized the justification for his two-year-long journey (although becoming the first ship to reach 110 degrees west longitude was what earned him and his crew a parliamentary prize of £5 thousand).

Such painstaking record-keeping was a hallmark of polar explorations during the nineteenth and early twentieth centuries, even though it entailed great personal hardship and risk. For example, during the two winters that George Back and his men spent at Fort Reliance on Great Slave Lake, they maintained a strict schedule for measuring the temperature—with four outdoor thermometers—hourly, from six in the morning to midnight. In the middle of the night, when outdoor temperatures reached minus seventy degrees, the ink in Back's pen froze inside their primitive quarters. All game fled from the surrounding wilderness, forcing his party to subsist on fish and putrid meat scraps given them by local indigenous peoples.[44] And this party's suffering on behalf of science seemed like a minor inconvenience compared to what Elisha Kane and his men had to put up with when they wintered on Littleton Island in 1853–54. In total darkness, and with many of them bedridden with scurvy, they still succeeded in observing an eclipse of Saturn and then of Mars and attempted to carry out magnetic observations in a shack that was "an icehouse of the coldest imaginable description"—made more inhospitable by the lack of insulating snow. This shed was located some one hundred yards from their vessel, and one of the four officers had to trudge there and back twice a day, without any light to illuminate the path, to record temperature, currents, wind direction, and barometric pressure. In mid-January the temperature inside fell to 99 degrees below the freezing point of water, turning ether and other gases into solids. Observing the movements of the stars and planets had to be done outside, where it was even colder—as low as minus 75 degrees.[45]

Marooned for the second time a few years later, near Prince Regent

Inlet—still some one thousand miles from the North Pole—Royal Navy Captain Francis Leopold McClintock and his fellow officers on the *Fox* rigged up a line on poles connecting the ship to their magnetic observatory and stumbled out there religiously in equally frigid temperatures, prevented only once by a howling "north-wester."[46] The self-discipline and perseverance shown in carrying out these tasks under such conditions is perhaps more impressive than anything else these explorers accomplished because they did this not for personal glory but for science. Like Cherry-Garrard and his two companions, who nearly died hauling a sledge sixty miles to Cape Crozier in the middle of the Antarctic winter to grab a few penguin eggs from a rookery, these "science-heroes" lent new meaning to the word "courage." Accomplishing the work of science meant a lot to these explorers—if only for the satisfaction of having finished a job they had set out to do, no matter what the obstacles were.[47] Cherry would later justify this grueling trek by contending that "Exploration is the physical expression of the Intellectual Passion."[48]

All these efforts to quantify Nature revealed an underlying fear of the Unknown—what lay outside the bounds of human settlement and experience. More than any other places on the planet, the polar caps—featureless and practically devoid of life, gigantic in scale, unpredictable in movement, insensible to human actions and needs—presented intractable challenges. They called into question belief in steady, inevitable progress ending with the "subduing" of the entire planet. If these icy expanses did not admit the explorer's encroaching footsteps, if their frozen seas did not part before the ironclad bows of ships, if flags could not be raised at the poles, then humanity would have to acknowledge having reached the limits of its power. If its dominion over the earth could not be complete, then man's place in the universe would have to be rethought. Thus much more was riding on the fate of those elegant, tall-masted ships disappearing over the horizon to fading cheers than merely the setting of new geographical records and the discovering of new lands. The cheers were for the human race.

CHAPTER FOUR

"LA BELLE DAME SANS MERCI"

Quaker raised in modest circumstances in rural Pennsylvania during the 1840s, Isaac Israel Hayes early on set his sights on broadening his horizons. He received a rigorous education at the local Friends school and did so well there that he became an instructor before graduating. Medicine was a career well suited to his outsized ambitions, and Hayes breezed through a three-year course of study at the University of Pennsylvania in only two years, eager to leverage this professional credential to pursue bigger adventures. John Franklin and his men had vanished into the Arctic mists while he was still a schoolboy, and more Americans had since become fascinated by the North Pole and its mysteries. In late 1852, Elisha Kent Kane was preparing to lead the second expedition underwritten by retired shipping merchant Henry Grinnell to hunt for signs of the missing Englishmen, and he was much in need of a surgeon for this party (the position held by Kane on his first voyage north). The twenty-one-year-old Hayes offered his services to the already famous explorer in a letter the following January. Kane—another Penn man and fellow Philadelphian—probably saw in the forthright Hayes a younger, less polished version of himself and immediately signed him on, even though Hayes had not yet earned his medical degree and had never been outside the United States. Still, Kane reasoned, his training in botany and geology would come in useful, and, if Hayes needed help dealing with the crew's health problems he could give him a hand.[1]

Things did not get off to a good start that spring. A nautical "green-horn," Hayes was violently sick in the heavy seas they ran into on the way to St. John's, Newfoundland, and wasn't of much help to anyone. Then, unexpectedly for that time of year—it was only August 20th—the *Advance* became hemmed in by ice off Littleton Island, near the western coast of Greenland. Worse, the ship's anchor line broke, and it started to drift dangerously close to several large floes, smashing its jib boom against one of them. Hayes, who had never experienced such a menacing environment, was terrified: he feared "the tossing, grinding, surging, of the broken, crushed and crumbling masses . . . riding on the billows" would splinter the hull at any moment.[2] Totally at the mercy of strong currents, the *Advance* smacked into one floe, her bow driving up onto the ice and finally coming to a grinding halt. Then the stern was lifted up out of the water by another huge ice block, leaving the brig high and dry like a beached whale. So stranded, the ship was unable to get free—a major blow for Kane, who had hoped to navigate another hundred miles farther north before having to stop for the winter.

After this close call, Hayes took to the volatile polar world with boyish wonderment and delight. At first, he spent a few days on shore, hunting for game with another crew member. But what they found one evening was far more riveting—a glacier, "a sloping wall of pure whiteness," which, "apparently boundless, stretched away toward the unknown east. It was the great mer de glace of the arctic [*sic*] continent."[3] As the two men moved cautiously toward this mesmerizing mass, now shrouded in darkness, a "brilliant meteor fell before us, and by its reflection up the glassy surface beneath, greatly heightened the effect of the scene; while loud reports, like distant thunder or the booming of artillery, broke at intervals from the heart of the frozen sea." Hayes's enchantment with natural splendors inconceivable back in his Pennsylvania hometown is equally obvious in how he later described the landscape around the Danish outpost of Godhavn: "Never had my eyes beheld or my mind contemplated such unalloyed beauty as this little Eden was clothed in."[4]

Like many Arctic newcomers, Hayes was overwhelmed by the magnificence and scale of its natural features. Safe on land, out of danger, he could admire them more dispassionately, with a discerning eye—much as a museum *habitué* will pause to admire a colossal landscape by Frederic Church or William Turner.[5] Indeed, Hayes possessed the trained eye and talent of an artist, having purportedly once studied with Church.[6] (Hayes would illustrate his book about his second Arctic expedition—*The Open Polar Sea*—with his own highly dramatized drawings.) So, by temperament as well as by training, he was highly susceptible to the ever-changing spectacle that greeted his eyes. His wonderment did not abate during his two stays in the North, despite the many harrowing experiences he had there. In fact, Hayes's ability to transmute what he was seeing into something more uplifting and comforting helped him survive these trials and tribulations. Imagination could keep horror and disaster at bay. Sent out to locate a lead to open water later that winter, he and several companions had to give up after they climbed a cliff and saw only ice stretching to the horizon in all directions: "All our bright dreams of succor and safety seemed to be ending," Hayes lamented.[7] Determined not to return to the *Advance* empty-handed, this small party continued along the coast by sea, hoping to find some Inuit outposts with food or reach the Danish settlement at Upernavik. But quickly their small boats became blocked by ice, and they feared they might have to spend the winter trapped there—far from their ship, holed up in a makeshift stone hut, forced to subsist on rock lichen, and with only buffalo robes to keep them from freezing to death.

Faith that Providence would look after them helped sustain Hayes and his motley party ("a German astronomer, a Baltimore seaman, a Pennsylvania farmer, a Greenland cooper, a Hull sailor, an East River boatsman, an Irish patriot, and a Philadelphia student of medicine"), but so did Hayes's positive responsiveness to his surroundings. He perceived the sea to be a "fertile plain, with walls, hedges and sunny fields. . . . Clusters of little hummocks suggested herds of cattle and flocks of sheep. Larger masses were converted into trees; and a long bank of snow, whose vertical wall threw a dark shadow on the plain, was the margin of a dense forest. Farther away, a pinnacled berg became a church with spire and belfry;

another wore the appearance of a ruined castle; while still farther to the southwest, where the stream seemed to discharge itself into the oceans, stood a giant fort, under whose bristling guns lay a fleet of stately ships."[8] On his return voyage to the Arctic, this time as an expedition leader planning to push on to the pole, Hayes reacted to the mountainous coast of Greenland emerging out of the fog as if he had miraculously entered some Nordic fairyland, its magical spell transfixing him

> as if we had been drawn by some unseen hand into a land of enchantment, rather than that we had come of our own free will into a region of stern realities, in pursuit of stern purposes—as if the elves of the North had, in sportive playfulness, thrown a veil about our eyes, and enticed us to the very "seat eternal of the gods." Here was the Valhalla of the sturdy Vikings; here the city of the sun-god Freyer,—Alfheim, with its elfin caves,—and Glitner, with its walls of gold and roofs of silver, and Gimle, more brilliant than the sun,—the home of the happy; there, piercing the clouds, was Himiniborg, the Celestial Mount, where the bridge of the gods touches Heaven. It would be difficult to imagine a scene more solemnly impressive than that which was disclosed to us by the sudden change in the clouded atmosphere.[9]

In his diary, Hayes added that no other sight in the Arctic had moved him as much: "The bergs had wholly lost their chilly aspect, and, glittering in the blaze of the brilliant heavens, seemed, in the distance, like masses of burnished metal, or solid flame."[10] Some resembled blocks of marble—one the Coliseum, half submerged under a "line of blood-red waters. . . . Nothing indeed but the pencil of the artist could depict the wonderful richness of this sparking fragment of Nature."

This ability to poetically gloss over reality kept Hayes from succumbing to despair—or madness. Earlier Arctic and Antarctic explorers had trusted in a higher, spiritual power to watch over them. They believed that the earth was governed by an omnipotent divine being, who had created it for the good of the human race. Nature's unpredictability, occasional violence, and even disasters at sea did not shake this faith. Even in the Arctic, God ruled. Standing on the deck of a ship approaching the misty outline of the Antarctic continent, explorers felt his presence acutely. Entering this pristine world, it seemed them that they had traveled back in time to the Dawn of Creation. Here was still the Garden of Eden—marvelous and enchanting and untouched by human hand. Now they were completing their God-given destiny by conquering the last frontier.

The poles were supposed to become the grand stage on which humankind would display its unrivalled stamina, character, resourcefulness, and intelligence by subduing this last bastion of unsubjugated Nature. This would complete its dominance over the earth. In more optimistic times, ambitious men and nations had turned their eyes northward and southward, welling with visions of being the first to reach these blank spots on the map, filled with a "capacity for wonder and . . . desire for challenge."[11] There, astride this alien ice, personal dreams for glory would be immortalized as testimony to the human spirit, or, more modestly, as Barry Lopez has argued, fulfill "the hope that one's own life will not have been lived for nothing."[12]

But, over the years, explorers came to see the polar world in increasingly negative terms. In their eyes, a Nature that had first appeared as staggeringly beautiful and inviting slowly morphed into an obstructing, indifferent object, and finally into a malevolent force bent on destroying them. This change sprang from a larger shift in cultural attitudes, brought about by Darwin and midcentury thinkers who did not see the natural world as aligned with any benevolent spiritual presence. Centuries-old assumptions about God's ongoing involvement with a world he had created were gradually giving way to skepticism about any such higher guidance. Natural forces appeared to operate according to their own laws. This less sanguine outlook was succinctly articulated in Tennyson's 1850 poem *In Memoriam A. H. H.*, in which he referred to Nature as "red in tooth and claw." Toward the end of life, polar explorers no longer arrived in ships as emissaries of empire but as witnesses to their species' failure to exercise its control over the planet.

As the young Parisian explorer Joseph René Bellot, who had joined the search for Franklin and then tragically disappeared through a cleft in the ice in the summer of 1853, wrote about this loss of security, "Moral nature seems to have abdicated, and nothing remains but a chaos without a purpose."[13] Estrangement from the polar environment deepened the explorers' feelings of isolation and helplessness. The kingdom they had expected to rule over stubbornly refused to surrender. Even Isaac Hayes— after he and his party had managed to get back to the icebound *Advance* and from there reach the outpost of Upernavik—could not look back on what he had suffered in trying to find the Open Polar Sea without admitting that he had just been plain lucky to return alive. Nature had been arrayed against him, but he had prevailed. The popular image of the Arctic as hostile—not some twinkling fairyland—had been accurate. All one could expect there were "Vast seas covered with masses of ice rushing to and fro, threatening to crush the most skilful navigator—towering bergs ready to overwhelm him—dangerous land-journeys—cold, piercing to the very sources of life—savage beasts, and scarcely less savage men—isolation, disease, famine, and slow death."[14]

Remote, inaccessible, and inhospitable lands still appealed so much because they demanded nothing less than supreme human effort—physical as well mental.[15] The "irritatingly and uncharacteristically uncooperative" polar region, with its "unfamiliar rhythms" of relentless light followed by relentless darkness and solid ice giving way overnight to wildly marauding floes, was like no other place on the planet.[16] Nature in this extreme guise took on more symbolic importance as Western Europe and the United States entered into an era of relative peace after the end of the American Civil War. The poles became an alternative arena for international competition, where bands of courageous young men could be tested to the limit, and where only the fittest would succeed and thus attest to their superiority. But men were drawn to the ends of the earth for a variety of reasons. The uniqueness of the ice kingdom was one of them. It possessed an otherworldly quality not found anywhere else. Restless souls like Ernest Shackleton and Robert Scott could revel there in a majesty and purity that satisfied their yearnings for a place without definition or constraints. As Scott's sister Grace would later write of her martyred brother, he responded to "the call of the vast empty spaces; silence; the beauty of untrodden snow; liberal of thought and action; the wonder of the snow and seeming infinitude of its uninhabited regions whose secrets man had not then pierced, and the hoped-for conquest of raging elements."[17]

Regardless of their motives (and these were really known only to themselves), explorers arrived brimming with confidence and with an aura of invincibility about them—a blithe, almost childish arrogance that was both a prerequisite for going to the poles and a fatal flaw in their ability to come back alive. While crews relied on cockiness and blind faith, their leaders put their trust in good planning. Men in charge of expeditions assayed their chances as generals surveyed a battlefield, learning as much as they could about circumstances on the ground before deploying their troops. Armed with the best knowledge—they thought—they could harness Nature to their purposes. They took note of temperatures, wind speed and direction, water currents, ice and snow conditions, and features of coastlines and interior terrain. Voyages and sledge journeys near the poles were planned with this information firmly in mind. Sound theories about how best to glide through ice-clogged waters and attain a new Farthest North arose from such detailed assessments of the environment.

But they did not always get it right. Nature did not always cooperate with their plans. Disasters could not be avoided. Early in the nineteenth century, several prominent Arctic explorers, including William Parry and John Franklin, had pegged their hopes of sailing through the Northwest Passage to the fabled Open Polar Sea on what was known about favorable currents and ice-free waters in the Bering Strait. (A brief spell of milder weather misled them about what they might expect.) Even though numerous attempts to traverse this narrow channel between Alaska and

Russia had failed, some subsequent explorers continued to believe it was the best route to take.[18] The crushing of the *Jeannette* in Siberian ice in June of 1881 finally laid this theory to rest. But new strategies soon emerged to supplant this debunked one. The canny Norwegian explorer Nansen—who also happened to be an experienced oceanographer—concocted a scheme for getting close to the North Pole by allowing his ship, the *Fram*, to drift on an ice floe, borne with the east-to-west current that was thought to be prevailing in Arctic waters. Ignoring many raised eyebrows from his contemporaries, Nansen set out in 1893 from the northern tip of his native country to test this notion. For a while, the currents cooperated. But then, hemmed in by dense pack ice, the *Fram* could only meander desultorily westward along the Siberian coast for three years without getting any farther north than 85.55 degrees. Calculating that it would take him another five years to reach the pole this way, Nansen decided to abandon the ship with a single companion to see if they could make better progress on foot, over the ice. In the end they did set a new latitude record—twenty-two miles beyond where the *Fram* would eventually arrive by drifting.

Repeated rebuffs by the elements caused explorers to reconsider their view of the polar world as a manifestation of God and as theirs to possess. Centuries of frustration, with so many grinding to a halt in intractable ice, with the explorers' hopes crushed as ignominiously as the hulls of their ships, and with so many lives lost, altered perceptions of what could be realistically accomplished. Explorers' relationship with Nature became acrimonious. In fact, failure after failure to push back the Arctic and Antarctic frontiers foreshadowed the costly, disastrous, and ultimately pointless battles of World War I, when charges across No Man's Land killed thousands and brought little or no gains. (Shackleton implicitly recognized this connection between the two life-and-death struggles by dedicating his book on his wartime *Endurance* expedition to "My comrades, who fell in the white warfare of the South and on the red fields of France and Flanders.")

From the outset, dying and exploring went hand in hand at the top of the world: the toll was grim. Franklin's party was not the first to die in this harsh, unforgiving realm: it was only the one with the single most casualties. In 1777, some 350 British seamen whose whaling vessels had become icebound off the coast of Greenland set out to find a safe haven: only 140 of them made it to land. Half a century later, a dozen ships were likewise beset, and half sank to the bottom squeezed in the ice's relentless grip, with most of the crew on board two vessels drowning.[19] The honor roll of the dead grew longer and longer, and still the ships kept coming. It is not at all surprising that these clashes between man and the elements soon came to be viewed as hopeless warfare. Only here the enemy was the battleground itself. Nature was anthropomorphized into a malevolent force determined to thwart any human inroads. The French explorer Jean-Baptiste Charcot described ice battering the keel of his ship, the *Pourquoi-Pas?*, near Wandel Island on the Antarctic Peninsula as if it were an infantry attack: "Happily there is no damage done, but it is with difficulty that we drive off the aggressor with poles."[20] The American Anthony Fiala—awarded the Medal of Honor for heroism during the Spanish-American War—entitled his account of commanding a 1903–1905 Arctic expedition *Fighting the Polar Ice*. In it, he described the north wind as an "active enemy" that stopped his party from moving forward as tenaciously as a line of riflemen. (His crew included several former cavalrymen.) Fiala, who had gone north with the intent of fulfilling God's command to Adam that he "subdue the earth," considered his polar assignment a military operation, emulating Nansen's "splendid march" toward the pole. Blocked from reaching his planned winter quarters by the worst ice that seasoned sealers had seen in years, Fiala had his ship, the *America*, reverse engines, retreat a thousand yards, and then charge the pack with its engines at full throttle, but to no avail. Caught in a fierce storm off the Franz Joseph Archipelago, the *America* was pinioned by floes and met the same fate that had befallen so many vessels: it broke apart and soon disappeared beneath the ice, taking with it most of their provisions and coal. Fiala led most of his men southward to safety, but he came away from this Arctic misadventure with a sobering sense of human limitations in the face of such natural resistance. The proud American spirit of John Paul Jones—"I have not yet begun to fight"—was badly bent, if not broken, by experiences like these.[21]

Once thought to be a primordial paradise, the polar world now seemed to more closely resemble a torture chamber, like Dante's ninth circle of hell, where traitors were stuck for eternity. The battering ice, the relentless cold, and even the flesh-eating animals were fiendishly arrayed against those who dared to venture there. To some, it appeared that a sly, evil intelligence lay in wait to "repel the explorers who would invade the secret places it guards."[22] Fearful of being marooned any longer in the Arctic with his band of "scurvy-riddled, broken-down men" in 1854, Elisha Kane saw it that way: winter had it in for them. "We are," he would later write, "ten men in a casemate, with all our energies concentrated against the enemy outside."[23] Hayes, beset by heavy Greenland snow during the winter of 1860–1861, could only curse the frigid weather as "the torment of my life and the enemy of my plans. . . . the veriest [*sic*] flirt that ever owned Dame Nature for a mother."[24]

For other explorers, darkness was the most dreaded foe: prolonged lack of light caused them to lose their grasp on reality and their imaginations to conjure up perils worse than those they actually faced. Once the sun had vanished below the horizon in early November 1880, George De Long sensed how its disappearance made the men with him on the paralyzed *Jeannette* more fearful: ". . . the horrible yelling and screeching of the ice, and its piling up around us and squeezing and crushing, make darkness a more terrible enemy than the cold."[25] He worried most about his first officer, Lieutenant Charles Danenhower, who had experienced spells of mental instability in the past and was thus more prone to what the writer Hampton Sides has termed the "melancholy of the polar darkness, the claustrophobic dread that could set in while one was living under conditions of near imprisonment."[26] Because of how it preyed on the mind, "the whole Arctic experience was a perfect incubator for insanity." Perpetual blackness—an extreme form of what is now known as "seasonal affective disorder"—confounded the explorers' sense of time and space, leaving them disoriented and subject to depression—what Kane termed "constant and oppressing gloom"[27]—as well as diseases like scurvy and mishaps like falling into a crevasse. The absence of sunlight for months was a deeply demoralizing aspect of polar life, against which human will power and ingenuity were virtually helpless. Darkness was a kind of living death. It frustrated human expectations about the rhythms of life and left the crews irritable and disoriented. Even a sanguine adventurer like Isaac Hayes was not immune from this malaise: "The grandeur of Nature ceases to give delight to the dulled sympathies. . . . The dark and dreary solitude oppresses the understanding; the desolation which everywhere reigns haunts the imagination; the silence—dark, dreary, and profound—becomes a terror."[28] Craving for light reduced human beings to a primal level of existence. From it there was no escape. All they could do was shriek with joy like little children on Christmas morning when the sun finally returned.

So, too, was the balance of power between man and beast overturned in this elemental environment. Even armed with rifles, explorers were not always confident that they were the predator and not the prey. Polar bears stalked them, as they hunted these monstrous creatures. The "poor bruin" that Lieutenant George Back had lamented having to shoot for scientific purposes while HMS *Terror* was caught in Arctic pack ice in the fall of 1836; the marauding white hulks that officers would take potshots at so that could bring back their hides as gifts for their wives—this exotic animal could turn in an instant into a crazed, bare-fanged, roaring killer, unstoppable by half a dozen bullets.[29] This elemental struggle between bear and explorer grew more desperate as the human invaders pressed closer to the poles, where food was scarce and ravenous bears dug up long-buried caches in a wild frenzy, raided tents, boarded ships, slashed dogs, and pursued human scent in the snow with the single-minded ferocity of the starving. Under these dire circumstances, the line between man and beast became blurred, and the ultimate winner in this Hobbesian struggle could not be confidently predicted. This disconcerting role reversal was dramatically captured in Edwin Henry Landseer's 1864 painting *Man Proposes, God Disposes*, which depicts polar bears gnawing lasciviously on human ribs and blood-red sails amidst the strewn wreckage of a ship—hinting at the likely fate of the lost Franklin expedition.

If all these predators—bears, walruses, orcas—had not existed near the poles, explorers might have been safer, but much more alone. While they were grim adversaries, man and beast at least afforded each other a kind of grotesque companionship. This peculiar bond was especially important in a region that was otherwise completely barren. To be in sight of another species—even a murderous one—was to remain part of a larger living presence. But the brutal winter at the top and bottom of the world was inimical to many other creatures, and one of the saddest occasions for explorers facing long months of darkness and cold was watching the remaining migratory birds silently flap their way southward—the last nonhuman "companions" (aside from fish) they were apt to see until spring. This exodus could start as early as the beginning of October, not long after the first snowflakes and frost dusted the explorers' huts. This departure, as sobering and depressing as the vanishing sun, severed an elemental tie: now the men were truly alone. Conversely, the return of these animals and birds was cause for rejoicing—here was a sign that life was being renewed. Thus, Elisha Kane would hail the first dovekies spotted over Baffin Bay as "welcome visitors" and stay his hand from reaching for his rifle.[30] At times, explorers closely identified with these other living beings—thinking of them as fellow voyagers and survivors. Observing flocks of ducks, geese, black guillemots, and auks pass overhead, Kane could not help but sense that they, too, were "seeking the mysterious north" and wonder, "What is there at this unreached pole to attract and sustain such hordes?"[31] For centuries, birds had assumed a richly symbolic significance for mariners. Superstition held that a storm petrel—the smallest species of seabird—protected ships from storms, and if a sailor were to kill one it would spell disaster. (Isaac Hayes wrote a story about just such an incident, telling of a seaman who shot and wounded a petrel and who could then only redeem himself by nursing it back to health.[32])

For carefree company, explorers turned to the dogs that traveled with them across the seas, toiled tirelessly and loyally on the ice, and suffered silently and stoically by their side. They admired their distinctive personalities and traits and mourned their deaths. British explorers tended to be the most affectionate toward these canine companions: Scott was notorious for projecting human emotions onto his dogs and could not bring himself to kill them for food. When they were all gone, explorers felt keen pangs of loneliness. This sense of abandonment could also arise when other creatures went away. Sailing as a naturalist with the *Erebus* to Antarctica in 1839, Joseph Dalton Hooker—a man without any religious convictions—had happily sketched penguins and other marine life under sail, and he was dismayed when these creatures disappeared when his ship came upon an erupting volcano: "This was a sight so surpassing everything that can be conceived and so heightened by the consciousness that we had penetrated to regions far beyond what had been deemed practicable before, that it caused a feeling of awe to steal over us at the contemplation of our comparatively utter insignificance and helplessness."[33]

Antagonism between humankind and Nature was acutely felt in the polar regions, but, by the 1860s, explorers reaching other remote corners of the planet experienced it there as well. In the heart of Africa, Henry Morton Stanley—the intrepid Welsh journalist (and veteran of both the Union and Confederate armies) dispatched in 1869 to locate the missing missionary David Livingstone—soon came to recognize that "Nature herself in her most savage manifestations . . . [was] an unceasing and ever-vigilant enemy."[34] Not giving up in the face of such hostility was a hallmark of his character, but not all adventurers had the same unshakable confidence that the devout Stanley did. Without such faith, would-be conquerors came to accept that often all that stood between them and disaster was sheer luck—the last-minute change of course an errant ice floe barreling toward their ship might take, or how soon winter arrived. Having almost no knowledge of the ice-clogged waters they were exploring or of what obstacles might lie ahead made the first polar excursions truly frightening undertakings. As Jeannette Mirsky wrote in her 1934 book *To the Arctic!* "Men were as fearful of the dangers of the Arctic as they were of the terrors of hell."[35] Neither realm offered them much hope of salvation. And the further the explorers advanced, the greater the hazards they faced and the greater the chances of their dying. But still they were drawn there by a fatal, ineluctable attraction, by an "emotional intangible" that defies understanding in our age of more complex, carefully calculated risk-taking. Theirs was a quest like those of medieval knights (whose sagas resonated in Victorian England and inspired explorers like Robert Scott) in search of the Holy Grail.[36]

An alluring seductress leading men on to their doom was a motif introduced in medieval ballads and then revived during the Romantic era to dramatize the hold of the unattainable on the human imagination. The recurring theme of "death and the maiden" linked sex and death and revealed a male anxiety over assertive female sexuality. But the same nexus of emotions could also be projected onto a "virgin" landscape, its mists concealing lurking dangers. Conquering it also required a treacherous dance with death. The English poet John Keats's immortalizing of "la belle dame sans merci" ("the beautiful lady without pity") in his 1819 ballad by the same name made the parallel explicit—and uncannily relevant to the polar explorers who would set out after it first appeared in print. Keats places his nameless knight-errant in a dreary setting that men like John Franklin would have found familiar:

> O what can ail thee, knight-at-arms,
> Alone and palely loitering?
> The sedge has withered from the lake,
> And no birds sing.

O what can ail thee, knight-at-arms,
so haggard and so woe-begone?
The squirrel's granary is full,
and the harvest's done.

The damsel he has met in the meadow is beautiful, and the knight
has paid homage to her by weaving flowers through her hair and around
her wrists, but "her eyes were wild"—a telltale sign of danger. Despite his
attempts to "tame" her through love, it is the knight who is "lulled" to sleep,
only to dream of finding himself in the company of lost, noble souls:

I saw pale kings and princes too,
Pale warriors, death-pale were they all;
They cried—"La Belle Dame sans Merci
Hath thee in thrall!"
I saw their starved lips in the gloam,
With horrid warning gapèd wide,
And I awoke and found me here,
On the cold hill's side.

For a celebrated Romantic like Keats, "La Belle Dame" was a cautionary tale—a warning flag on the path to total infatuation. It might
have served the explorers well to heed the poet's implicit advice, but
in their treks to the poles there were no such markers along the way—
nothing to slow the explorer's stride but his own mounting fatigue and
despair. Thus, the march continued, in spite of setbacks, disappoint-
ments, agonies, defeats, retreats, and deaths—in spite of a gnawing awareness that the odds were so stacked against these intemperate trespassers
that they were bound to fail in this bid to assail Mother Nature in her
most jealously guarded lair.

In fact, the more the explorers advanced, the more defiant Nature
became. There was no long lost paradise at the end of their journeys, no
tropical waters gently lapping palm trees at the poles, as men like George

De Long and Elisha Kane had once believed (and, as we now know, had actually existed there some fifty-five million years ago), only more snow and ice to greet them. At its geographical extremes, the earth offered no rewards for those strong or lucky enough to get that far. It simply was what it was. The dreams of explorers about finding God in the snowy outlines ahead, of extracting deeper meaning from the ice kingdom, of charting new routes across the globe, of discovering vast riches, and unlocking great secrets—all these ambitions fell away in the end, and all that was left was the conquest itself. All that could be accomplished was to make a symbolic statement by raising a flag in a blinding swirl of snow, on a spot no one was likely ever to see again. The explorers—and their entranced followers—could not admit this to themselves. Instead, they transformed an absurd quest into something greater—a triumph of the human will. But in doing so, they created a chasm between the reality of their so-often-futile efforts and how these deeds would be celebrated. As in war, the image and the facts of polar heroism made for strange bedfellows. These contradictions weighed heavily on the explorers' minds. It was hard for some not to feel, in the agony of the moment, that the ultimate goal was not really worth it. It really *was* insane to go on. But this they could not admit either. Too much was invested in them—like Keats's anonymous knight—to drop out of the race. And so they teetered toward another kind of insanity—living with contradictions but pretending they did not exist.

In the history of polar exploration no expedition better illustrates the foolish notion that the human mind could best Nature than the British Antarctic Expedition of 1910–1913, led by Robert Falcon Scott. The fact that this *Terra Nova* trip to the South Pole was plagued by ill-conceived plans and egregious blunders from start to finish was often overlooked in posterity's eagerness to embrace Scott and his men as gallant "martyrs" in an ennobling cause—as victims of "bad luck" whose "pluck" otherwise would have gotten them to the pole and guided them back safe and sound. In the popular telling of their tale, Nature comes across as an irascible bully, rudely butting in and spoiling what would otherwise have been a splendid display of manliness and grace under pressure. But the truth is less kind to the Final Five, who were desperately trying to reach Hut Point before their food and energy ran out. And the truth also is that, toward the end, it became apparent to Scott and at least some of his companions that they had been living a lie. Mind was not mightier than matter. Nature was uncaring and unforgiving. They had overestimated their fortitude. The Antarctic did not respect this. They were going to die.

Here, it should be noted, Edward Wilson stands apart, with his unwavering faith in God's plan—even if that entailed freezing to death in this unyielding wasteland. This belief had enabled him to respond to Antarctica with the same feeling of awe that the first travelers to the continent had experienced. When the *Terra Nova* arrived on the coast, "Uncle Bill," its resident artist, recorded in his journal:

> Now and again one hears a penguin cry out in the stillness near at hand or far away, and then perhaps he appears in his dress tail coat and white waistcoat suddenly upon an ice-floe from the water . . . crying out in his amazement as he comes from time to time, but only intensifying the wonderful stillness and beauty of the whole fairylike scene as the golden glaring sun in the South just touches the horizon and begins again to rise gradually without ever having set at all. We have now broad daylight night and day, but the beauty of the day with its lovely blues and greens amongst the bergs and ice-floes is eclipsed altogether by the marvellous beauty of the midnight, when white ice becomes deepest purple and golden rose and the sky is lemon green without a cloud. No scene in the whole world was ever more beautiful than a clear midnight in the pack.[37]

We have every reason to think that this gentle soul—this throwback to a simpler and more naïve age—would have written with the same unabashed affection as he was dying, if he had had the strength to do so.

Scott is faulted today for a series of mistakes he made—opting to rely on ponies instead of dogs, allowing himself to be distracted by scientific pursuits (like collecting ancient rocks) instead of focusing monomaniacally on reaching the pole, hiding his intentions from the other men, and so forth. But his greatest blunder lay in not recognizing Nature for what it was and thinking he could somehow defeat it by refusing to admit unpleasant facts—the way a poker player with poor cards will try to bluff his way to the pile of chips. Scott wagered his life—and those of his companions—on his being able to outwit an Antarctic environment he knew little about, and he lost this bet badly. Still, at the end, with time and hope rapidly running out, he seems to have come around to admitting the folly of his approach to life and to letting reality set in. Scott may have gone south as the quintessential romantic hero, but, like the corrupted ivory trader Kurtz in Joseph Conrad's *Heart of Darkness*, he eventually perceived the world in sharp relief, without illusions—as a place rampant with "horror." Before he breathed his last, Scott had become a twentieth-century existentialist—a man all alone against the indifferent elements.

Some of Scott's contemporaries—products of a skeptical, post-Victorian era—looked at the world with a cold, unsentimental gaze. For them, the ice kingdom was a battlefield that had to be negotiated warily, as one must tiptoe past a sleeping polar bear—or trigger a savage, unprovoked attack at any moment. Ernest Shackleton—who, more than any other polar leader, understood human psychology and realized that survival in the Antarctic depended on his men knowing how much he cared for them—was also astute in sizing up Nature.[38] Sailing in April 1916 with five others from Elephant Island to South Georgia Island through some of the most treacherous seas on the planet, in a twenty-three-foot-long peapod named the *James Caird*, Shackleton acknowledged, during a lull in the gale that had thwarted their progress for two days, that their lifeboat was but a "tiny speck in the vast vista of the sea—the ocean that is . . . pitiless always to weakness."[39] The next day, as if to prove Shackleton's point, the *Caird* was struck by a gigantic wave and nearly swamped, tossed about like "a cork in breaking surf."[40] Above them, albatrosses looked down with "hard, bright eyes," taking an "impersonal interest in our struggle to keep afloat amid the battering seas."[41] Shackleton's highly experienced New Zealand navigator, Frank Worsley, less frightened by such storms than his landlubber "Boss," got his own lesson in terror and human insignificance on the gale-wracked slopes of South Georgia several days later, when the unbridled power of Nature was unleashed on them like an army run amuck:

> The hell that reigns up there in heavy storms, the glee of the west gale fiends, the thunderous hate of the grim nor'wester, the pitiless evil snarl of the easterly gales, and the shrieks and howls of the southerly blizzards with ever oncoming battalions of quick-firing hail squalls, followed by snow squalls, blind a man or take away his senses. The wind fiends, thrown hissing, snarling, reverberating from crag to crag, from peak to precipice, hurtle revengefully on to the ice sheets, and clawing, biting, gouging, tear out great chunks and lumps of ice to hurl them volcanically aloft in cloud dust of ice and snow.[42]

In the case of a youthful explorer with a dry sense of humor like Apsley Cherry-Garrard (a self-proclaimed idealist whose favorite writer was Kipling, and who would look back on polar exploration wryly as "at once the cleanest and most isolated way of having a bad time which has been devised"[43]) a "strong urge to conquer the dreadful forces of nature"[44] may have induced him to sign up for Scott's last expedition in 1910, and to concur that its mission was to "go forward and do our best for the honour of the country without fear or panic."[45] But his unalloyed optimism, reverence for the "utmost peace and beauty" of the Antarctic coastline, and selfless dedication to "pure science" (with no thought given to "personal gain") could not withstand the "horror" of their nineteen-day trek in the Antarctic winter to Cape Crozier in search of a few penguin eggs.[46] In total darkness, with temperatures so low (minus 75.8 degrees) that his clothes froze stiff as steel sheets within fifteen seconds of putting them on in the morning, Cherry, "Uncle Bill" Wilson, and "Birdie" Bowers plodded on, knowing that "it was folly to go forward," but unable to turn back—caught in an Edwardian moral straitjacket as constricting as their ice-caked garments. As they neared the cape, the Great Ice Barrier rose up like a curtain and "seemed to cast a spell of cold immensity, vague, ponderous, a breeding-place of wind and drift and darkness." Like someone who had just entered the Gates of Hell, Cherry let out an uncharacteristic *cri de coeur* anticipating Scott's at the pole: "God! what a place!" On the way back, it was even worse: one night, beaten into submission by the "indescribable fury and roar" of a great wind that ripped away their tent, Cherry closed his eyes and prepared to die, giving up all pretense of playing the hero. In the darkness, "Birdie" somehow succeeded in locating the shredded canvas and propping it up so that they had enough shelter to make it through that night. The rest of the way back was just a blur in Cherry's memory. Afterward, he could not pretend it had been "anything but a ghastly journey."[47]

And more suffering was still to come. In November 1911, Cherry set out with Scott and fourteen other compatriots, still hoping to beat Amundsen to the pole. But at the base of the Beardmore Glacier, he was sent back by Scott, assigned the mundane task of bringing food for the returning polar party to a cache known as the One Ton Depot, located not far from their base camp on Cape Evans. He arrived there on March 3rd and waited a week for the five men who had gone on ahead to arrive. Then, because of exceptionally cold daytime temperatures, Cherry decided not to go out and look for the overdue party and instead returned to the *Terra Nova* hut. It was a fateful decision—one that would haunt Cherry for the rest of his life (he died in 1959)—because Scott, Wilson, and Bowers ended up freezing to death only eleven miles from One Ton Depot—easily within a day's march. Perhaps to assuage his guilt, perhaps to keep faith with his dead comrades, Cherry refused to repudiate the idealism that had brought him and the others so far and then cost them so much. At the end of *The Worst Journey in the World*, Cherry reminds his readers that the English may be a nation of shopkeepers, but the brave souls who trudged through Antarctic snows had a nobler lineage, stronger nerves, and a higher calling. A "desire for knowledge" set them apart and made them heroic.[48] In his mind, this may have been true, but the world at large remembers Scott's old-fashioned manhauling team mainly for its tragic shortcomings—arriving second at the South Pole and then dying on the way back. Cherry's tribute has the ring of a speaker looking back over his shoulder with moist eyes, recalling for his audience a glorious past when feats they might now—in light of World War I—consider wasteful and inexplicable had meant a great deal. If history be the judge, then these martyred Englishmen cannot escape an ironic reappraisal: their assault on the world's last remaining unconquered geographical marker strikes us today as the last, futile gasp of a dying age, innocent of the blood that was about to be shed in its name on the fields of France, and the tarnish that this holocaust would bring to once-noble words like "duty," "honor," and "country."

Scott himself would die with at least some of his innocence intact. He could not have known that his sacrifice would be used as inspiration for young men to put on British Army uniforms and march off lockstep toward the Western front to the strains of the "Colonel Bogey March." Nor could he have foreseen the hundreds of thousands of soldiers being blown to pieces in the trenches or mowed down by machine-gun fire in their own quixotic effort to carry forward the Union Jack, defy the odds, seize new territory, and thus attest to their own heroism. How he would have reacted to these events—had he lived—is, of course, impossible to say. Scott was a complicated person, a very private and secretive man who wrote eloquently and left behind a moving testimonial to his unsuccessful quest, but also someone who used language to camouflage what he really thought. But one senses that he may have had an inkling of what lay ahead for the generation of patriotic young men who imitated his example—because he had already had a peek himself. His awareness of the limits on his will imposed by Nature—barriers he could not possibly transcend—appears here and there in the journal entries he made during the final weeks of his life.

When Scott, Oates, Wilson, Bowers, and Edgar Evans finally reached the pole, on January 17, 1912, only to find the Norwegians' flag and flagstick protruding—like a sword plunged into their hearts—from the lopsided tent they had erected there five weeks before, the British explorers were understandably crushed. After crossing some eight hundred miles of Antarctic ice in two-and-a-half-months, after battling through deep snow and being battered by storms, they had made this final push on the brink of exhaustion, believing the prize was still theirs for the taking. But the names of the five Norwegians, scribbled on a piece of paper inside their tent, spelled out defeat—perhaps the most sardonic greeting card ever written. Scott, who, a month earlier, had still counted on his luck and just days before written with schoolboyish ardor of the men building castles in their minds—à la Thoreau—now that the pole was within grasp (only about eighty miles away), let out a Conradian wail of anguish in his journal as the truth sank in—"Great God! this is an awful place and terrible enough for us to have labored to it without the reward of priority."[49] When this raw reaction of Scott's later came to light in print, Cherry-Garrard, devout keeper of the flame, refused to read it as a "cry of despair" (over coming in second?), only as Scott's conceding the "ghastly facts"[50]: they *were* frostbitten, snow-blind, and incapacitated mentally as well as physically, and this was not a cheerful spot. But the expression on his face (along with the drooping Union Jack behind him), captured in a commemorative photograph of the five taken on January 18th—the disconsolate look of a man who has just been told his wife and children have been found murdered—reveals much more about Scott's state of mind. Here is a man who has drunk deeply from the bitter well of disappointment, and still has to go on. The journey back was just as long as the one to the pole, and infinitely more pointless.

If Scott's real adversary was not really the Norwegians, but Nature—and his naïve approach to it—one needs to look back over the course of his life to see how he had formed this outlook and how, ultimately, it did him in. Ironically, for a man remembered for two trailblazing treks into the heart of Antarctica, Scott spent remarkably little of his forty-three-plus years on the earth's surface. At the age of twelve, after a carefree and somewhat dreamy childhood, he was packed off (per his father's orders) to a naval preparatory school to study for his officer exams, and after passing them and donning a midshipman's uniform, he remained for almost all of his adult life on, or near, ships. (In this odd deficiency he was the inverse of Shackleton, who had no previous experience steering a small sailboat or scaling snowy cliffs—the two miraculous accomplishments that would earn him immortality.) Out of inclination (having been a melancholy and insecure boy) or lack of opportunity, a reserved, slight, and physically delicate Scott was inclined to look inward and distance himself from events as well as from the people around him. He reportedly had a scandalous love affair when he was in his early twenties and thereafter shied away from the fair sex until he was thirty-eight, a famous explorer, and—like a character out of Jane Austen—badly in need of a wife.[51] (In part because of his prolonged absences at sea, two years would elapse before Scott and the free-spirited and sophisticated sculptress Kathleen Bruce, ten years his junior, would marry.)

Before traveling to Antarctica for the first time, in 1901, Scott visited Norway and trained for a while under conditions similar to what he expected to face at the bottom of the earth. But, aside from this limited exposure to a quasi-polar environment, Scott came south for the first time largely unprepared for Antarctica. He did gain considerable experience— and fame—for going (with Shackleton and Wilson) further south than any previous explorers, coming within 530 miles of the South Pole at the end of December 1902. However, his *Discovery* expedition was hampered by its unfamiliarity with skiing and dog handling. Scott took these inadequacies as vindication of his own preference for manhauling. He subsequently returned to Norway to try out the motorized sledges he felt could supplement manpower in covering the 1,766 miles from Hut Point to the South Pole and back—the equivalent of going on foot from New York City to Chicago. (His advocacy of these largely untested vehicles with tank-like treads again shows his poor judgement: Scott wrote a memorandum suggesting that even though they could only cover two miles in an hour, these machines were a "practical" option.[52] He did not consider how well their engines would hold up in extreme cold, or on soft and uneven ice. One of these gas-powered vehicles fell through the ice during unloading in Antarctica and was lost; another broke down just a few miles from the Southern Party's starting point. The remaining two failed to perform as expected and played no part in the trek toward the pole.)

Scott could easily be confounded by the unexpected. On the voyage south, when the *Terra Nova* had to constantly dodge erratic pack ice, he became frustrated, exclaiming "What an exasperating game this is!" In spite of his long naval career, Scott was at a loss about how to navigate through this veritable minefield: he had never seen anything so "formidable." The ensuing twenty-day delay at sea he attributed to "sheer bad luck." While taking supplies ashore at Cape Evans on January 8, 1912, he and his party were temporarily cut off from the three-masted *Discovery* by shifting ice—a near-calamity that caught him off guard. Even with the help of a university-trained meteorologist, George Simpson, Scott was flummoxed by the volatile Antarctic weather. When it turned unfavorable, he would attribute this—again—to his bad luck. (At one point, confounded by powerful wind gusts that hardened the snow underfoot, Scott noted with resigned irony how this demonstrated "the balance of nature whereby one evil is eliminated by the excess of another."[53]) The Manchurian ponies he had counted on to carry much of their equipment had suffered terribly during the extended ocean journey. Once on unfamiliar ice, they struggled to keep their footing, and then, famished and worn out, they started to die off. None of these outcomes Scott had anticipated. Only "Titus" Oates, a former cavalry officer, had done so, pronouncing these "knock-kneed" and old animals on first sight "the greatest lot of crocks I have ever seen."[54]

Like other polar explorers before and after him, Scott soon learned how this fickle climate could defeat even the best laid of plans. Earlier on, he had projected his own stolid personality onto the silent Antarctic expanse, as a way of comprehending and coming to terms with it. In the course of the *Discovery* expedition, he and the others had found that to "go out on a still winter evening to appreciate total silence, as if on a dead planet, was a profound experience."[55] But, as a career naval officer accustomed to being in charge and adhering to well-established rules, Scott was constitutionally ill suited to cope with an environment that was so uncertain, mercurial, and uncontrollable. He had never experienced the utter chaos of war to shatter his faith in an ordered existence, and so he found Antarctica baffling, like a country where he couldn't speak the language, didn't know his way around, and couldn't relate to what was going on. As his recent biographer, David Crane, has well expressed it, here was "nothing he could predict, nothing that behaved as he wanted or expected it to, or prayed that it would. . . . It was the bewildering contrast of appearance and reality that baffled Scott's imagination, the co-existence of beauty and danger in so extreme a form."[56]

His realizing that he was—borrowing Shackleton's nautical simile—merely a cork bobbing on the surface of the sea must have shaken Scott to the very core of his being. For he had no overarching trust in an all-knowing God, or in an afterlife, as his dear companion Wilson did—no belief other than in his own abilities to solve problems by examining them closely and thinking them through.[57] And here he was confronted by enormous problems for which there did not appear to be any solutions. Reaching that conclusion left him helpless, with no other resources to fall back on except his stub of a pencil and a blank sheet. And so Scott kept writing, to the very end, his words conveying his final wishes to a far distant world where he no longer belonged, and in which he no longer believed. Yet he still wanted to. Two weeks after the indomitable ex-soldier Oates—suffering from an old war wound, scurvy, and frost-bite—had murmured, "I am going outside, and may be some time," and then staggered shoeless out of the tent and disappeared into a blizzard, on March 17, 1912, a morning when the temperature outside was minus forty degrees, Scott scrawled a last, somewhat maudlin letter ("To my widow") to Kathleen asking her to make their three-year-old son Peter "interested in natural history if you can—it is better than games," adding, as if cover all the bases, "Try and make him believe in a God; it is comforting."[58]

CHAPTER FIVE

KEEPING THE BRUTES AT BAY

When fifty-nine-year-old Sir John Franklin sailed out of the Thames estuary on May 19, 1845, on board HMS *Erebus*—bound first for Greenland and then for parts unknown—he was traveling in grand style, as befitted a senior Royal Navy captain, knighted decades before for his discoveries in the Canadian Arctic. At that moment, he was arguably England's most admired living hero, the descendant of a long line of country gentlemen, and, most recently, the Crown's emissary to Tasmania. To maintain his standard of living, Franklin had taken along silverware engraved with his family crest, cut-glass wine goblets, and exquisite china plates for the dinners he intended to host nightly for several of his officers. On these occasions they would arrive wearing dark-blue woolen frock coats, adorned with gold lace buttons, and sup by candlelight on mock turtle soup, cured Westphalian ham, calves' heads, pickled tripe, macaroni, canned vegetables, and Double Gloucester cheese, while sipping fine claret, polishing off the meal with chocolates or biscuits slathered with raspberry jam. Afterward the officers would adjourn to the ship's twelve-hundred-volume library to read a few chapters of *The Vicar of Wakefield* or browse through an earlier explorer's journal over cigars before listening to a tune cranked out on the hand organ Franklin had brought along to enliven evenings at sea. This elaborate display of food, drink, and entertainment was, in the words of one of his biographers, "the ultimate expression of Franklin's idea that you could take everything with you."[1] As commander of this naval expedition, he was determined to show his officers and men that they could exist in the Arctic as comfortably as at home.

Franklin stocked *Erebus* and its companion coastal bombardment (or "bomb") vessel *Terror* sumptuously, cramming "every hole and corner" below decks with provisions at their last port of call on the western coast of Greenland before the two ships steered north, into the ice, where no additional food or fuel would be available.[2] Onboard supplies included an estimated thirty tons of flour, eight tons of beef, two tons of chocolate, and the same amount of lemon juice. He had several other reasons for providing so amply for his officers and men. On his first trip into the subfreezing Canadian wild a quarter century before, Franklin had nearly starved to death. The "man who ate his boots" was not about to repeat that ordeal. Nor did he want to see any of his men waste away to skin and bones on spoonfuls of pemmican, dying slowly and horribly before his eyes as had happened back then. His party had been caught out in the open by an early, punishing winter, and then not found the dried meat promised by local French voyageurs waiting for them at Fort Enterprise. Despite these near disasters, Franklin still trusted in his luck—something they had badly needed on that misbegotten, underfunded, and inept expedition, when he and a few companions had unwisely set out into the snow-covered forest even though not one of them had ever hiked, hunted, or camped before. (They were, after all, *navy* officers.) Brushing aside warnings from local Inuit, Franklin had relied solely on his (unreliable) compass and chronometer to guide them to the Great Slave Lake, and that and other poor decisions (along with some bad luck and unreliable indigenous peoples) had cost them dearly: eleven of his nineteen men never made it back to England.

When he was planning this 1845 voyage to find the missing link in the fabled Northwest Passage, Franklin still had overweening confidence that he—as a seasoned commander—possessed the character, judgment, and Arctic experience needed to make this expedition successful. Having retrofitted his two sailing vessels with auxiliary, 20-horsepower steam engines (from railroad locomotives), covered the sturdy, double-planked oak hulls with iron sheathing, installed a warm-air heating system, recruited a complement of highly regarded officers, and stocked the ships with at least three-years-worth of food gave Franklin more reason to believe all would go well. (He anticipated having to spend only one winter in the ice.) His were the best outfitted ships in the Royal Navy. He also had faith in his God to sustain him. As his contemporary William Parry once observed, Franklin displayed a "Christian confidence in the Almighty, of the superiority of moral and religious energy over mere brute strength of body."[3]

There were also important psychological benefits from making life on *Erebus* and *Terror* as comfortable as possible. Remaining so far north for years put the crew under great mental and emotional stress. Feeling bored, isolated, lonely, and forgotten would eat away at their resolve. With nothing to do for months at a time they would become introspective and depressed. The men would miss their wives, families, and friends dearly as the months turned into years, and their separation grew from being one of great geographical distance to an existential divide: the explorers' world was so different and inconceivable to loved ones in England that they would become deeply estranged. Letters—handed over to a passing ship headed home—were a tenuous lifeline, not much to count on. (On at least one voyage, carrier pigeons had been brought along to carry notes across the Atlantic, but the birds had refused to leave the ship.[4]) To ward off loneliness, many men had talismans from home—a wife's likeness, a child's lock of hair—and put these precious relics on display in their cramped and spartan quarters below decks. Lavish celebrations, replete with multicourse banquets, abundant alcohol, raucous toasts, bawdy songs, and crossdressing dances—aimed to break the monotony and remind the marooned mariners that life could still be fun. Usually Christmas was the high point of the year. At midcentury, the commander of HMS *Investigator*, Captain Robert McClure, marked this holiday, as well as his recent discovery of the Northwest Passage, with a feast of musk ox and mincemeat, accompanied by "many a dainty dish" from his ancestral Scotland. The men conjured up their families by guessing when they would be attending church services and having dinner. A year later, still stuck in the ice, McClure used the occasion of their second Christmas celebration on the ship to heap praise upon his long-suffering crew, who had remained in good spirits notwithstanding. Several of his petty officers—perhaps emboldened by rum—declared they had never spent a happier holiday, with "a feeling of more perfect unanimity and good-will."[5] A few years later, some of Elisha Kane's party, sequestered for their second winter on the *Advance*—riddled with scurvy, surviving on chunks of frozen seal and walrus meat given them by Inuit fishermen, their morale at a low point after an accidental fire had destroyed their store room—somehow pulled themselves together for Christmas dinner, meager as it was (pork and beans) and, as Kane would recall, "forgot our discomforts in the blessings which adhered to us still; and when we thought of the long road ahead of us, we thought of it hopefully."[6] The men clinked glasses and toasted their absent friends and laughed uproariously at stale jokes, although Kane had to admit they might have just been putting on a good face, in order to temporarily stop thinking about their bleak situation. Making a navy ship feel like a home helped dull the crew's awareness of being cut off and forgotten. Furthermore, keeping up "civilized" appearances on board kept crews mindful of the superior moral principles these expeditions exemplified.

Some have argued that how Franklin's ships were outfitted and how their crews behaved in the frozen Arctic expressed his "cultural arrogance."[7] It is true that he considered his expedition to be representative of a British civilization that towered above all others. His vessels and their men were expected to illustrate this superiority by how well they managed under extraordinarily demanding conditions. The men on board *Erebus* and *Terror* carried out the same time-honored protocols and daily routines on the high seas that they observed while tied up at the Portsmouth Dockyard. Therefore, Franklin wanted his voyage into the Arctic to honor this decorum. The dress dinners, player-piano concerts, evening lectures, Sunday scriptural readings, and elaborately staged festivities proved that sailing beyond the civilized world did not mean they had to leave its trap-pings behind. No matter what the circumstances, English gentlemen, military or civilian, were expected to dress and behave in accordance with their station in life. Most celebrated for upholding his upper-class stan-dards while traveling was the young Lord Byron, who, when he departed for the Continent with his good friend John Hobhouse and his personal valet in 1809, brought along four large and three small trunks, three beds with bedding, two bedsteads, four English saddles, and a large quantity of linen. ("We could not have done well with less," Hobhouse protested.[8])

The British military was as class conscious as any other social institu-tion, if not more so: the distinctions between officers and enlisted men or sailors paralleled those separating aristocratic "gentlemen" from lesser males. They were, in effect, two categories of men—each with strictly defined standards for breeding, education, manners, cultivation, and social behavior, as well as character.[9] On ships of the Royal Navy, this translated into two spheres of living. Officers and ordinary seamen had separate and different responsibilities, slept in separate quarters, ate in separate rooms, and enjoyed separate social activities. (In 1819, a starchy William Parry had made these class divisions seem self-evident: "It is scarcely necessary to add, that the evening occupations of the officers were of a more rational kind than those which engaged the attention of the men."[10]) Segregation was deemed essential for efficient functioning, but also for upholding the social hierarchy. However, under certain circum-stances, sticking to such rules could seem ridiculous and detrimental to overall well-being. For example, because naval officers were exempt from performing physical labor, this left the exhausting work of hauling boats across the ice to enlisted men, impeding their progress. Even more bizarre was the isolation of ranks maintained when primitive living conditions seemed to call for more informality. In 1912, Scott's so-called Northern Party, consisting of three officers and three enlisted men, was forced to seek refuge for half a year inside a tiny snow cave, near a granite outcropping they whimsically dubbed "Inexpressible Island." After they had finished digging it out, the officer in charge, Lieutenant Victor Campbell, drew a line with the sole of his boot to demarcate the sailors' underground quarters from those of the three officers (the "quarterdeck"). Although each section was within earshot of the other, the two groups agreed that what was said on one side of the line would not be "heard" on the other. But the sordid realities of their confinement made a farce out of such artificial partitioning. Said the party's surgeon, George Levick, "You cannot watch one of your naval officers vomiting, shitting on himself, and wetting his sleeping bag and hold him in quite the same awe and esteem."[11]

Such class hierarchies were part and parcel of a broader notion of human inequality. Throughout the nineteenth century and well into the twentieth, "advanced" Western nations believed they stood ahead of all other peoples in a Darwinian struggle to dominate the planet. London's enormous Crystal Palace (more than a third of a mile long), erected in 1851 to commemorate England's scientific and geographical progress during the Industrial Age, was a secular cathedral to the "Progress Goddess" that had brought the nation great wealth and power and made it the envy of the world. In outlining his vision for the international exhibit to be held in this palace, Prince Albert praised man's recent achievements in "approaching a more complete fulfillment of that great and sacred mission which he has to perform in this world . . . to discover the laws by which the Almighty governs his creations, and . . . to conquer Nature to his use."[12] A major obligation of "advanced" nations like England was to bring their "enlightened" ways to "primitive" people living in distant, "backward" corners of the earth. Explorers served as the advance party, introducing Christianity along with modern technology, while gathering information about the earth's resources, climate, and geography. Contact with "natives" confirmed the Euro-American belief that their societies were far ahead of the rest. Whereas theirs were undeniably "modern," the others remained "savage." Innate racial differences had given the British (and other Europeans) a character and intellect that these lesser humans could not match. These other races had little to offer "modern man" other than the satisfaction of affirming his superiority. Darwin's *On the Origin of Species* was fittingly on many explorers' reading lists. Fridtjof Nansen made a nightly habit of reading from it as he was readying for a trek to the North Pole in 1895. A few years later, Edward Wilson would read aloud from Darwin's ground-breaking opus to Scott and Shackleton while they were stuck in their Antarctic tent, waiting for the weather to improve before they could move further toward the South Pole. During their subsequent 1912 expedition, both Wilson and Scott found that *Origin* made for good bedtime reading.

By and large, early European explorers probing the Arctic frontier adopted a condescending attitude toward the native peoples they met there. They manifested the prejudices and stereotypes of their day. And they were received as higher beings. The sudden appearance of oddly dressed white men, in tall, three-masted sailing vessels laden with cannon, rifles, telescopes, buttons, brass kettles, needles, and other marvels, duly impressed and even intimidated the Inuit natives, who reasoned these newcomers must be gods. But, for their part, commanders like Parry and Sir John Ross perceived only "the savage" incarnate. Ross, the son of an Anglican priest, spent four winters living near Inuit settlements but all that time kept his distance, as if fearing some kind of contamination. The casual morals of the Inuit—who were more than eager to share their "wives" with these newcomers (in exchange for jackets or knives)—appalled him. After some of his crew members still went ahead and had sex with some of these women, he called them "disgusting brutes."[13] After Parry invited several Inuit to board his ship off the coast of Baffin Bay to trade, he was pleasantly surprised that his curious visitors evinced a "respectful decency" (they did not try to steal anything, as Inuit were wont to do) and "less of that intolerable filth by which these people are so generally distinguished." While friendly toward the Inuit and admiring of their igloos, warm deerskin and fur clothing, intelligence, and kindness shown their children, Parry could not helping regarding them as practically subhuman: "In the situation and circumstances in which the

Esquimaux [*sic*] of North Greenland are placed, there is much to excite compassion for the low state to which human nature appears to be there reduced; a state in few respects superior to that of the bear or the seal."[14] After returning several times to the Arctic, Parry adopted a more balanced view: although the Inuit people may have lacked some "higher virtues" of other savages, they were also free of their "blackest vices."[15]

Because they were "heathens," ignorant of Christianity, indigenous peoples of the Far North were considered hopelessly deficient in moral character. A few Danish missionaries were trying patiently to convert Inuit, but most explorers thought this a waste of time. What was more important was that their English guests not "lapse" into their primitive ways. The kindly Franklin felt pity for the Inuit and treated them like children: he showered them with trinkets in return for food or to win their good will. (Attempted thefts by some Inuit later made him change his mind about their trustworthiness.) Other explorers were simply appalled by their manners, hygiene, and appearance. George Back was dismayed that some Inuit women were willing to barter away their children for "a few needles."[16] Most came to the conclusion that these natives were unreliable and dishonest: they could not be counted on to keep their word. At best, Englishmen and Americans regarded these inhabitants of the Arctic as exotic oddities. Watching some of them dance at a Danish outpost in Greenland, William Godfrey, a member of Elisha Kane's midcentury expedition, declared them "the most extravagantly burlesqued specimens of humanity that were ever produced in Nature's workshop."[17]

Negative preconceptions prevented these early Western emissaries from appreciating the good sides of the Inuit, let alone learning from them. The idea that these "savages" in furs had anything to teach white Europeans was laughable—as absurd as expecting a child to teach a man how to hunt or sail a ship. So British crews kept wearing their wool naval jackets and flannel pants, even though it was obvious that the Inuit were staying comfortably warm inside their parkas. (To be fair, it should be noted that the English were not alone in refusing to adapt their military garb to different environments. When Napoleon's troops arrived in Egypt in the middle of the summer of 1798, they were wearing similarly inappropriate woolen uniforms. Ordered to march in them—and without canteens—for six days across the desert from Alexandria to Cairo, thousands of them died from heat exhaustion and dehydration.) The explorers also didn't try to harness dogs to pull their sledges or to build igloos. They disdained sleeping bags and considered snowshoes a poor substitute for sturdy leather boots. Gradually, however, these new arrivals to the Arctic came to admire how well the Inuit and other indigenous peoples coped with their harsh environment and actually adapted some of their ways. Over time, familiarity bred more than contempt. During his first excursion through northern Canada, Sir John Franklin became curious about the locals' lore and made efforts to learn more about it. His surgeon and naturalist, Richardson, may have labeled the Cree a "vain, fickle, improvident and indolent race," but he was willing to excuse their deficiencies as caused by their materially and spiritually impoverished circumstances: "the moral character of a hunter is acted upon by the nature of the land he inhabits, the abundance or scarcity of food, and, we may add, his means of access to spirituous liquors," he noted.[18] Richardson realized that judging the Cree by Western standards was patently unfair: "It may be proper to bear in mind also, that we are about to draw the character of a people whose only rule of conduct is public opinion, and to try them by a morality founded on divine revelation, the only standard that can be referred to by those who have been educated in a land to which the blessings of the Gospel have been extended."

As more and more expeditions came to know Inuit and other indigenous tribes better, the explorers' opinions grew more differentiated. Condescension toward these "lower races" gave way to grudging admiration of their skills, knowledge, and personal traits. That native hunters had kept Franklin and members of his party alive during the bitter winters of 1820 and 1821 by bringing them game (even if they were not reliable in doing so), made the Englishmen realize how dependent they were on local help:

they were not particular good hunters. (In a change of heart, Franklin's men took to wearing fur caps as well as leather gloves and pants during the extremely cold Canadian winter of 1825–1826.[19]) By midcentury British and American explorers were describing Inuit and other indigenous peoples in more favorable terms—and beginning to adapt their ways more widely. Pragmatic-minded Americans were the first to have a change of heart. In his first dealings with Inuit, on the Crown Prince Islands, Elisha Kane had been repelled by their filth and squalor.[20] But his disdain did not long stop him from trying on their vastly superior footwear. After returning to Greenland in 1853, and finding himself beset on the *Advance*, Kane had visited a nearby Inuit settlement and been impressed by their well-insulated stone huts. Afterward, his men had protected their shipboard quarters against wintry blasts by likewise stuffing moss and turf on the inside walls of the hull.[21] Wrote Kane, "My resolve was to practice on the lessons we had learned from the Eskimos. I had studied them carefully, and determined that their form of habitations and their peculiarities of diet . . . were the safest and best to which the necessity of our circumstances invited us."[22] While wary of becoming too much like these "savages," he had to admit that some of their ways were worth adopting.[23]

Kane's enormously popular books persuaded some other explorers—eager to learn how to survive in the Arctic—to also learn from the Inuit. (The fact that Franklin and 128 of his fellow Englishmen had presumably died of starvation while nearby Inuit continued to survive had not been lost on them.) Before his first northern expedition, Charles Francis Hall—a Cincinnati newspaper publisher who had become obsessed with the Arctic—read all the explorers' written accounts he could get his hands on, including Kane's, and when he joined the search for Franklin in 1860 he announced that he intended to "go native" when he reached the Far North. Hall told a reporter from the *New York Times* that he was prepared to eat "cheerfully" seal blubber and meat, along with standard explorer fare of pemmican (canned dried meat mixed with fat—a diet borrowed from the Cree). He also said he planned to "identify himself in a measure with the Esquimaux"—a startling admission for an American in that racially charged era.[24]

In need of a sailing master familiar with Arctic waters, Hall chose Sidney O. Budington, a whaler who also happened to be fluent in the Inuit language and sparked Hall's interest in it. Believing they knew details about the fate of the Franklin party, the devoutly Christian newcomer to the Arctic spent three years living with the Inuit, gaining their trust, and observing and mastering many of their skills. To Hall, the Inuit were not "savages," but honest, solicitous, good-natured human beings—"glorious good fellows," who had been badly maligned by previous explorers. He encountered many of them who had already embraced Christianity and translated the Lord's Prayer into their language to encourage more conversions. Hall was convinced his efforts would succeed: "Plant among them a colony of men and women having right-minded principles, and, after some patient toil, glorious fruits must follow."[25] Intermarriage with Danish immigrants would hasten the Inuit's cultural and religious development. Hall was fulsome in his praise of these natives: their women were attractive and exquisitely adorned, their villages "beautiful," their customs more genuinely freedom loving than those back in the United States. He even admired their penchant for swallowing raw whale meat whole and drinking seal blood. At times, Hall sounded like a religious convert. Once, during a sledge journey, he ate some putrid whale meat even his Inuit companions could not stomach.[26] After sleeping for forty-two consecutive nights in an igloo, he found life back on his ship too comfortable and was unable to sleep there.[27] In short, the man from Cincinnati was besotted.[28] Hall was essentially a Christian humanist, who saw in all people and in all places the handiwork of the Almighty and felt his all-encompassing faith could unite them. He was also a pioneer of modern anthropology, taking the position that "One has to make up his mind, if he would live among that people, to submit to their customs, and be entirely one of them."[29]

Hall's willingness to go to great lengths to enter into Inuit society and absorb its lessons marked a radical change in how American and European explorers thought about distant, "backward" regions of the world and the people who inhabited them. Before Hall's day, Western explorers had generally remained aloof from them. Inuit and other indigenous peoples stood so low on the evolutionary ladder that no self-respecting European or American officer would want to associate with them any more than he would wish to dine with his servants, dance with his slaves, or share a cigar with his wife. Hall's change in attitude called the Great Chain of Being into question. Readers of his books began to wonder if their assumptions about other peoples were really valid. Perhaps no one race had a monopoly on knowledge and skill: perhaps these were only relative advantages, grounded in particular circumstances. Using a sextant to plot a course or knowing how to operate a steam engine might be important skills for getting to the Far North, but they were of little use when trying to survive there. There the Inuit was the wise master, and the explorer only an ignorant and helpless fool.

This relativistic outlook was most readily adopted in those Western nations where social stratification was not deeply entrenched, where individualism was valued, and, where there was little or no imperialistic history—namely, in the United States and Scandinavia. Like Hall, the Norwegian explorer Nansen lived with Greenland Inuit for one winter, learning their language and survival skills, and this sojourn made him appreciate how these "hardy children of Nature" had triumphed over the polar environment, thanks to their "ingenious implements" and hunting prowess. Echoing Jean-Jacques Rousseau's notion of the "noble savage," Nansen concluded that the coming of the white race and its "civilizing" imperative had brought ruin to the Inuit, causing them to sink "lower and lower" under the "iron heel" of these Western invaders.[30] By preaching Christianity, some explorers and missionaries had discredited the myths and legends that had explained the past to Inuit for thousands of years. It would have been wiser, Nansen wrote, never to have introduced a Western belief system that was so strange and bewildering to them.[31] In making statements like this, a renowned figure like Nansen was tapping into a growing disillusionment with modern, industrialized European society. Confidence that the future was always going to be better—a belief symbolized by London's Crystal Palace—was no longer as strong as it had been at midcentury. The loss of community, intimacy, individuality, freedom, and independence was now keenly felt. The Inuit and other less "advanced" peoples seemed to be holdovers from a simpler age, and getting to know them fueled a nostalgic longing to return to it.

This turnaround in Western attitudes toward "primitive" Arctic peoples reached a high with the arrival of a twenty-seven-year-old Canadian anthropologist named Vilhjalmur Stefansson (born William Stephenson) in 1906. Of Icelandic extraction, Stefansson had done graduate work and taught at Harvard after earning a bachelor's degree at the University of Iowa. He was recruited as a scientist for the Anglo-American Polar Expedition, to study various tribes on the northern Canadian and Alaskan coastline. During his stay in that Arctic region, Stefansson became fascinated stories of a race of "Blond Eskimos"—believed to be descendants of intermarriage between early Scandinavian voyagers from Iceland and native women. After a brief interlude, Stefansson returned to the Arctic, this time as head of an expedition sponsored by the American Museum of Natural History, to locate and learn more about Inuit bands that some thought were living on remote islands in the Beaufort Sea. Upon reaching the delta of the Mackenzie River, where it emptied into the Arctic Sea, he was delighted by the warm reception given him by Inuit he had gotten to know a few years before. For these natives he had only the highest praise. "Under their communistic system of living, the Eskimos have developed the social virtues to a higher degree than we have; they are therefore people easy to live with," he would later write in *My Life with the Eskimo*.[32] Stefansson was also delighted to learn of the wholesale conversion of Inuit in this part of Canada to Christianity, as well as their appetite for imported Western foodstuffs, such as flour and canned meats and vegetables. These developments suggested to him that the Inuit were far more educable and capable of "advancing" than other Native American peoples.

Stefansson expressed this Pollyannaish view of the Inuit and his confidence that "a white man can live on the country wherever an Eskimo can do so"[33] in his later, 1921 book, *The Friendly Arctic*—the product of five years spent mapping previously unexplored territory in northern Canada. Here he argued that lush grasslands, moderate temperatures, and abundant game could be found close to the North Pole, and thus humans could survive there as well; months without sunlight did not make this impossible. In Stefansson's view, the Arctic was not a place to be dreaded, as predecessors like Parry and Ross had reported. And the people who thrived in this challenging environment—the Inuit—were to be envied. Their lives were not, in fact, "wretched," but contented and carefree, with plenty of "wholesome" food readily available to them. Although they wore skins, ate raw meat, and resembled "cave men," the Inuit were, according to Stefansson, "the kindliest, friendliest, gentlest people, whose equals are difficult to find in any grade of our own civilization."[34]

Scandinavian visitors like Stefansson envisioned the Far North as an outpost of their ancestral homelands and its people as kindred spirits. This connection generated a positive response to this hitherto little regarded part of the world. But explorers from other countries remained unpersuaded. They did not feel at home in the frozen expanses above the Arctic Circle, among a strange people with such strange ways. They did not have a long history of hunting for seals or living in perpetual snow. Nor could they easily discard their own cultural habits, even if these did prove to be woefully inadequate there. Unlike Hall, Stefansson, Nansen, and Amundsen, these explorers refrained from fraternizing with the locals. They wanted to preserve the line between them and "the Other." Their organizational structure encouraged this separation. Military parties were less willing to adapt in the Arctic than civilian ones. As a result, they tended to have more disastrous outcomes. A 2005 study by a business professor at the University of Washington examined the fate of some ninety-two polar expeditions between 1818 and 1909 and found that privately (less-well) funded, civilian parties fared better than ones made up of men in uniform. While nearly half of the men on government-sponsored expeditions suffered from scurvy, only thirteen percent of those on private expeditions did. Nearly nine percent of crew members on government ships died, compared with just six percent on civilian-financed voyages. Private expeditions lost 0.24 ships out of an average fleet size of 1.15, whereas government-backed fleets averaged 0.53 ships sunk or destroyed out of 1.63 deployed.[35] The author of this survey concluded that "poor leadership structures, slow adaptation to new information, and perverse incentives" were harmful to the military expeditions. Their structures of command, rigid routines, and lower pay scales did not serve this group well. (Private funding and military organization were not always mutually exclusive: for instance, on the *Jeannette* expedition of 1879, financing came from the newspaper publisher James Gordon Bennett Jr., but the officers and crew were naval personnel.)

The British paid the highest price for sticking to their military ways. Having ruled the seas for centuries, the illustrious Royal Navy had set what the maritime historian John Maxtone-Graham has termed an "imperishable example . . . of courage, improvisation, and skill for others to follow."[36] But, over time, tradition and success became a straitjacket, particularly under polar conditions. Just because James Cook had rounded the Pacific wearing tight wool pants in the 1770s did not mean that this garb would be appropriate for all future British explorers in the northern Arctic or Antarctic. (In fact, these pants caused the men's legs to sweat and moisture to freeze on them.) Likewise, William Parry's faith in "bluejackets on foot" made little sense when it came to hauling thousand-pound sledges over nearly vertical ice hummocks. It took him three voyages in quest of the Northwest Passage to admit that his crew's wool clothing was not keeping them very warm.[37] As late as the 1880s, military expeditions like Adolphus Greely's to northern Greenland were still unwilling to switch to furs and skins.[38] Once sailors and soldiers had to abandon sinking ships and make their way over the ice, the orderliness of life on deck tended to break down. Many such parties lost their cohesiveness and their bearings. Lieutenant Adolphus Greely had carefully chosen experienced soldiers and officers for his Lady Franklin Bay Expedition, believing that the loyalty, obedience, and group solidarity they had learned on the Western frontier would stand them in good stead in the Far North. But, faced with baffling new challenges for which they were not at all prepared—long-term isolation and the prospect of starvation—some of them lost all self-control and turned on each other.

Then as now, the mindset and manner of a military leader was decision-oriented. Taking his own counsel, he weighed options, reached decisions, gave orders, and expected them to be carried out without question. He relied mainly on his past experiences, his judgment, and his hunches to make the right choices. A commander was not supposed to doubt or second guess himself. But in the Arctic and Antarctic unforeseen circumstances could turn his decisions into disastrous mistakes. In the polar world, the unexpected was what had to be expected, and expedition leaders had to be prepared to change their course of action. But such flexibility did not come easily to officers who had spent their careers following well-established protocols. During the second half of the nineteenth century, and well into the twentieth, heads of British expeditions could not escape the long shadow of Clements Markham, whose notions of the Arctic and how to deal with it had been set fast back in the 1850s, when he was a young midshipman. (Scott, handpicked by Markham for the dash to the pole, had made sure one of his mentor's books found its place in the hastily thrown-together *Terra Nova* shipboard library some sixty years later.[39]) In his old age, Markham was obsessed with making sure the British conquered Antarctica first, convinced that accomplishing this feat would revitalize his country's heroic spirit and attest to "its manhood and superiority to a slightly disbelieving world."[40] Sticking to an old-fashioned, but arduous method like "manhauling" was essential: the greater the hardship overcome, the greater the triumph. To his way of thinking, using dogs in Antarctica would be cheating—and unmanly. (In 1904 Scott would similarly write that using dogs "robs sledge-travelling of much of its glory.... In my mind no journey ever made with dogs can approach the height of that fine conception which is reached when a party of men go forth to face hardships, dangers, and difficulties with their own unaided efforts."[41]) Markham's determination to have a British naval officer lead the Antarctic expeditions caused him to give short shrift to amply qualified candidates. For example, he brushed off an offer from William Speirs Bruce—a fervent Scottish nationalist and a naturalist considered the finest polar scientist of his day—to accompany Scott on the 1901 *Discovery* expedition for fear of Bruce's usurping Scott's (English) leadership role.[42] (Scott knew no science and had had no prior Antarctic experience.)

This British inclination to regard polar exploration and conquest as exemplifying certain ideals discouraged experiential learning on the fly. Setting aside time to practice skiing (as Scott at first refused to do) or studying the mistakes of other parties (as Amundsen did almost religiously) was not a high priority.[43] Generally speaking, British explorers remained incurious about the people they encountered and did not bother to learn their languages. This reluctance to reach out only widened the gap between them and the native peoples like the Inuit, deepening suspicions that they were deceitful, thieving, and untrustworthy. Too often uncooperative reality was kept out of sight, like an unruly child whose cries were best ignored for the sake of strengthening its character. Although Markham had anticipated British explorers acquiring a store of knowledge about these races in order to better understand human evolution, in practice most English explorers did not bother to do this.[44] Early arrivals like Parry had not taken the time to query Inuit he had come into contact with. Sir John Richardson, a naturalist, was the only member of Franklin's overland parties to pick up some of their language and on later British expeditions to the Arctic, very few officers or sailors attempted to converse with the locals in their own tongue. By contrast, Americans such as Isaac Hayes, Charles Hall, Sidney Budington, and—later—Frederick Cook, Robert Peary, and his African American companion Matthew Henson were able to communicate with them, as were Norwegians like Nansen, Amundsen, and Stefansson.

Expedition leaders as varied as Franklin, Kane, De Long, Hall, Greely, Shackleton, and Scott felt that the inner qualities they and their men possessed would make the difference in this icy kingdom. Character was not something that could be taught, let alone learned from Native Americans and Inuit. Among expedition members it was valued far above physical strength and youth. As Elisha Kane wrote to his benefactor Henry Grinnell when he was putting together a team to hunt for signs of the Franklin party in the spring of 1852, "I am convinced that the plan proposed by me could be carried out, without feeling the absence of an artificial discipline. All that is needed is a crew of proper moral material, controlled by prudence and decision, and made aware beforehand of what they had to endure."[45] The problem was that it was not easy to discern moral fiber in the course of a fifteen-minute interview, or to predict how it would hold up under great and prolonged stress. On shifting and treacherous polar ice, situations arose that baffled the moral compass because there was no precedent for dealing with them. Furthermore, surviving and "doing the right thing" could be at odds. On the fringes of the world, this lesson was learned time and again, and not only at the poles. The newspaperman Henry Morton Stanley went off to unmapped Africa with a keen moral sense firmly in mind, even though he himself was not wholly free of sin. (In New Orleans Stanley had frequented a brothel but then denounced the whores "wicked" because of how they had touched him.) He believed in the superiority of the white race as strongly as he believed in his Christian God. His conscience was clear about the mission later entrusted to him—to spread his religion throughout this "dark" continent. Like Livingstone before him, he was motivated by a vision. In the words of a German biographer, "his breast was animated by an heroic ideal, for whose realisation he was ready to make any sacrifice."[46] But

Stanley, the English conquistador, committed horrible crimes during his crusade. In fact, he killed more Africans than any other explorer, before or since, all in the name of bringing spiritual enlightenment and the blessings of Western civilization. For the "nigger" people he met and treated brutally during this quest he showed not the slightest interest, dismissing both their religion and ancient culture as lacking in any redeeming value. Toward the end of his life, Stanley repudiated what he and others of his generation had done in the name of "progress" and even developed a hankering for some of the "barbarism" that he had tried to destroy. He had by then soured on his ideal of "civilization," having seen how it had relied on the sword to do its bidding.

Moral confusion and contradiction seemed to dog nineteenth- and twentieth-century Western explorers wherever they went. Extending their countries' power and building an empire was a messy, ugly business and scruples only got in the way. Racist thinking made some lives less valuable than others, and killing natives seemed like a minor transgression in this "civilizing" process. Occasionally, however, the moral lines would become blurred and explorers would be forced to act toward their own men in a way that violated the principles they were supposed to exemplify: they behaved like the "barbarians" they looked down upon. Some of Franklin's men faced this paradox early in 1821, when poor planning and the unexpectedly early onset of winter had forced them to take refuge at Fort Enterprise, on the shore of a lake in northern Canada, with almost nothing to eat. To survive, they had to depend on a young Iroquois named Michel Teroahoute to kill game. One day Michel showed up bearing some strange-tasting meat he claimed came from a wolf, but the Englishmen suspected this was actually human flesh: two French-Canadians in their party had recently disappeared. Faced with this accusation, Michel threatened to stop hunting and gathering firewood—a virtual death sentence for the others.

This tense situation came to a head when the men inside the fort heard a shot, and their leader, the naturalist Richardson, ran outside to discover a young midshipman and talented artist named Robert Hood lying dead in the snow with a bullet hole in his head. Michel, who was already on the scene, insisted that Hood, who had been near death from lack of food, had committed suicide. But Richardson was certain that Michel, who was also desperate for something to eat, had murdered him: the bullet had entered through the back of Hood's skull. Although Richardson had previously described the Iroquois youth as an "instrument" of God, sent there to save the Englishmen, he now saw Michel as an imminent threat, unrestrained as he was by any "belief in the divine truths of Christianity."[47] To prevent him from taking another life, Richardson waited for Michel to return carrying firewood, and then shot him point-blank in the forehead. He showed no qualms in committing the very same crime for which the young Iroquois had stood accused. Later, after they had managed to survive this horrible winter and return to civilization, Richardson and the others declined to say how they had found enough food to live without Michel's help. There were rumors that they had resorted to cannibalism—broken the same taboo that they had accused him of violating. But there would be no investigation into these allegations: no one in England wanted to know that these intrepid explorers had sunk so low in order to save their lives. So the full story of their miraculous survival was never told.

When they ventured into the perilous polar realms, European and American explorers had confidence that their superior religious faith, knowledge, skills, and character would see them through. By adhering to civilized norms under the most trying circumstances, they would show that they were indomitable. Demonstrating this exceptionality was as important as setting foot on untrodden territory. Largely for this reason, many explorers did not stoop to make use of the "primitive" methods honed by Arctic peoples over the centuries but, instead, stubbornly clung to the customs and way of thinking that they were conditioned to believe were best—social rules, organizational structures, clothing, types of food and shelter, and means of travel. Most of these would turn out to be disastrously ill suited to polar survival. Only some explorers (mainly Scandinavian and American ones) came to realize that they had to change and "go native" in order to come back alive. For the rest, doing so would have been a defeat—recognition that they did not enjoy a monopoly on wisdom and know-how they had long taken for granted.

Before, during, and after the modern era of polar exploration, the most horrifying crime one could commit was cannibalism. It was so abhorrent as to be unspeakable. Thus, when reports trickled back to England that some of John Franklin's men had resorted to eating each other's flesh to stay alive, the public flatly refused to believe them. It would take a long while for the British public to accept that sailors and officers of the Royal Navy could have done so. By then, the lines between "civilized" and "uncivilized" peoples had begun to blur, and notions of morally acceptable behavior had become more fluid than what William Parry or Franklin himself would ever have countenanced.

CHAPTER SIX

DOG EAT DOG, MAN EAT DOG, MAN EAT MAN

As the ice closed in around them, the crew of the small, onetime herring sloop *Gjøa* reluctantly made preparations to spend the winter where they were—trapped in the Arctic ice south of King William Island. Roald Amundsen's lifelong dream of being the first to traverse the Northwest Passage would have to wait until spring. They hastily covered the old sailing vessel with canvas—just in time, as frost would be coating it in the morning. The Eskimo dogs on board, which had fought incessantly and taxed the nerves of the six-man Scandinavian party, finally had a chance to stretch their legs, and they made the most of it, yapping and racing around the slippery deck like incorrigible children on a school recess. Many of the dogs had died during the voyage up the Greenland coast earlier in 1903—victims of some mysterious malady that had first rendered them lethargic, then paralyzed their limbs, and finally killed them, as they lay inert and stiff in their cramped quarters. As soon as one died, the other starving dogs tore it apart and gulped down every last scrap of bloody meat. The men shot numerous reindeer and ptarmigan—Amundsen hoping these additional stores would see them through the barren Arctic winter and help them avoid the fate of the much larger Franklin party, which had perished half a century earlier in these waters after running out of food. Wisely, the men skinned the deer and made undergarments from their hides, to stave off the cold. But the dogs had no concept of the future, no way of imagining beyond the moment and their frenzied need for food. There was still not enough to go around, and so they kept dying.

One day a bitch named Silla gave birth to a litter, and as the slick, eyeless pups twitched and whimpered in a snowdrift near the ship, the other dogs, growling menacingly, pounced on them like an angry mob and devoured them all in a few seconds. Struggling to her feet, Silla staggered back toward the *Gjøa*, and then stopped, quivering for a moment, until the last pup slid out of her. Before the other dogs could approach, the new mother—a cross between a Norwegian elkhound and an Eskimo husky, born a few years before on Nansen's *Fram*—hesitated only a second before thrusting her neck forward and swallowing the pup whole.[1] The crew could only watch in stunned disbelief. Before their eyes, life's most sacred and instinctual bond—a mother's attachment to her young—had been broken. Survival was all that had mattered to these huskies. At core, Nature was pitiless and cruel. This was not a moral universe.

Of course, dogs were mere brutes, without conscience or compassion, driven by a will to live that was intensified by frantic desperation as death was closing in. Unleashed and unwatched, they would turn on the weakest one and eat it. Newborn pups were unexpected snacks. Adolphus Greely had seen this happen during his party's stay in Discovery Bay, when three litters of pups had been born in rapid succession, and another bitch had managed to kill one of them before some of the men had dragged her away. A soldier had to stand guard over the remaining pups. Leaving any of the adult dogs unattended was an invitation to attack. Not long after the sun had slid below the horizon, in November, several of them died, and the rest of the pack quickly ate them.[2] The crew did all they could to keep the dogs alive as long as they were still healthy and useful. But they also had to keep an eye out for other threats. Sometimes polar bears would pick up the scent of dogs or humans and saunter close to a ship looking for a meal, and the men would have to yell and fire their rifles to drive the bears away. Other times the huskies would go tearing off in mad pursuit and end up getting the worst of their encounter, returning slashed and limping. Dogs were the explorers' best friends, but it was a friendship of necessity: without them to drag the sledges over rough snow and ice, the men could not get very far. So they watched over the dogs with keen interest, like mothers, attune to the slightest changes in their moods and health. If one became sick or was badly injured, there was little the men could do but pet it and try to feed it, and then, afterward, mourn its loss in silence.

Nansen had been so taken by the strength of huskies belonging to some Russian traders his party had met in Siberia that he had brought thirty-four of them with him on the *Fram*. He had done this after calculating their practical value to him: there would be enough on board to enable him to reach the pole should the vessel become frozen solid. But these Siberian dogs did not take to shipboard life and fought like demons, killing one and exasperating their new owner. Still, Nansen soon came to pity these "wretched" creatures, so removed from their element on the high seas. When one puppy was caught in the axle of a mill, its howls were "heartrending," and he was greatly relieved to learn it had not been badly harmed. The dogs had a particularly tough time during their first winter. They snarled and snapped at each other. Several died from the cold. If they were left on the ice overnight, they would fight to the death. One morning three of the dogs had disappeared, forcing several of the crew members to bundle up and go out in the subfreezing air to look for them. They came upon one dog being gnawed by a polar bear—which they promptly shot—but got there too late to save this husky. Two other half-eaten carcasses lay nearby, stiff and hard as bricks. One of these dogs had taken a disliking to the boiler stoker Hjalmar Johansen and barked and bared its teeth whenever he came near, but instead of feeling glad that it was now dead, he told Nansen he regretted that they hadn't had a chance to "make it up."

In December, another hungry bear climbed onto the snow-covered ship and made off with two more dogs. When spring returned to the Arctic in 1894, an increasingly impatient Nansen placed all of his dwindling hopes of being the first man to reach the North Pole on the huskies' well-being, but then several pups mysteriously went "mad" and died. When he and Johansen finally set out, nearly a year later, they took along twenty-eight huskies, panting in harness, tongues lolling, dragging three four-hundred-pound sledges on skis over the uneven hummocks. Nansen had decided to undertake this overland journey with so many dogs—all of those on board save for a few puppies—for one reason: they would eventually become the only available food for the other animals—and, perhaps, for the two men themselves. He and Johansen could not count on shooting seals or walruses along the way. When they started out, the two Norwegians got by on cans of pemmican, bread, chocolate, bacon, cake, and eighty-six pounds of butter. They had enough provisions to last a hundred days, but the dogs had biscuits for only thirty. After hauling for many days, the dogs became exhausted, stopped in their tracks, chewed on their traces, and had to be prodded with poles to go on. The biscuits were soon used up, and so the two men had to start culling the pack. Killing the first one was very unpleasant: Nansen admitted this was the most "disagreeable work" he had to perform. He had to hold it from behind and slit its throat with a knife. At first the other huskies only sniffed curiously at the steaming chunks of bone and meat flung on the snow near them and then stalked off, but after a few more days of laboring in harness most of them overcame their scruples and ate this now-hardened flesh.

The going was agonizingly slow and taxing, with ice ridges rising up ahead as much as thirty feet. The remaining dogs were spent, their whitened tongues dragging, and the explorers had to kill some more off to keep the others alive. Nansen now hated this slaughter more than ever: he and Johansen had become close to them during their long trek. Like bank robbers with hostages in tow, they had gotten to know their different personalities and think of them as fellow sufferers rather than as captive beasts at their mercy, destined to be eaten, despite all their hard work and loyalty. Killing these uncomplaining and unsuspecting creatures was a "horrible affair."[3] By mid-May only a dozen of them were still left. They were mostly skin and bone. Gaunt and tottering on their blood-stained and shredded paws, they could barely haul the sledges a few feet forward without having to stop and pant. The men themselves were running out of food, down to two ounces of bread and two of pemmican per day. At one point they killed a dog and made porridge out of its blood. In order to save ammunition, the two men tried to stab some of the remaining animals, but this task was now so repellent that they gave up and tried to strangle one instead. But they were too weak to finish the job. By now Nansen had given up on his dream of getting to the pole, and they were making a beeline westward, hoping to reach Spitsbergen before their supplies were completely gone. In mid-June, after one hundred days on the Arctic ice, the two Norwegians had only three dogs left to share their misery, trudging endlessly and wordlessly through the summer slush. They cut the animals' rations to a bare minimum, just enough to keep them from refusing to move. On July 24, 1895, Nansen and Johansen finally spotted land on the distant horizon and were ecstatic to realize their ordeal was nearly over. The remaining trio of dogs staggered on, oblivious, like drunken sailors. For several days, they had nothing to feed them now but then a few seabirds appeared, and they were able to shoot one out of the sky and share this bounty. Their dwindling band kept going.

On August 3rd, while paddling between floes in a kayak, Johansen was attacked by a bear and knocked over. He grabbed the surprised animal by the throat and pulled away. Hearing his cry, Nansen grabbed a rifle out of his kayak, got a good bead on it, and killed the animal with a single shot to the head. Twelve days later, the Norwegians put their boots on dry land for the first time in two years. They were so thrilled that they jumped from one granite boulder to the next like mountain goats, just to feel solid rock under foot again. They raised a wrinkled Norwegian flag. They had no idea where they were, but that didn't matter. They were back on Mother Earth. But they were now also completely alone: on the edge of the ice, where they had lashed together their kayaks and put up a mast and a sheet to sail the rest of the way to shore, they had shot the last dogs and eaten them.[4]

The relationship between men and dogs at the poles was complex and fluid. One man's meat could be another man's pet. Sometimes it was based on emotions, at other times on a practiced indifference. Attitudes could change with circumstances. Culture could also influence them: The Inuit treated their dogs—well, like dogs—and considered puppy stew a delicacy. Many Americans and Europeans, on the other hand, were used to thinking of border collies back home as members of the family. This was particularly so for British explorers, who were loath to think of their beloved pets as beasts of burden, let alone as meals on paws. (Partially because of this sensibility, dogs had not been taken to Antarctica until Borchgrevink brought seventy of them on the *Southern Cross* in 1898. Even after this expedition, some British parties continued to see "man-hauling" as the true test of stamina and looked on dog-drawn sledges as a form of cheating.) Scott's paternal affection for the dogs he had reluctantly decided to take with him on his 1912 trek to the South Pole may have been extreme, but it was not that exceptional. In his journal, Scott expressed regret that his dogs were the "main sufferers" when the weather worsened. When one, named Mukaka, was inadvertently run over and dragged by a sledge while the men were unloading supplies at Hut Point, Scott took special interest in the welfare of this "poor little beast" that was no longer of any use to him, in the same way that a frontline commander might inquire about a gravely wounded soldier in his unit.[5] After several others had fallen into a crevasse, he insisted on being the one to be lowered down by rope to rescue them. During the long months spent in total darkness, explorers grew sentimentally attached to their canine companions and openly showed this affection. One can even say that having dogs living with them so intimately for so long humanized the explorers, allowing them to express their emotions more fully than could happen in their "civilized" world, where masculine codes discouraged such openness. Some of them would play with their favorites— even dance them with them to maudlin tunes played on an accordion.[6] Expedition members gave them names that captured their distinguishing traits or features ("Devil," "Girly," "Little Bear," "Foxy," "Ginger Bitch," "Slippery Neck," "The Pimp," and "Grandmother") or connected them with illustrious figures ("Franklin," "John Bull," "Scott," "Shackleton," "Bismarck," "Caruso," "Nansen," "Osman," "Peary," "Cook," "Pavlova," "Shakespeare"). Men tried to protect their dogs and save those they were most fond until the bitter end. Even a pragmatic person like Amundsen developed a soft spot for his huskies. (He claimed he could read their characters by looking into their eyes and selected dogs based on this visual assessment of how well they would stand up to the demands of polar trekking.[7]) While the *Fram* was sailing to Antarctica in 1910, the Norwegian divided up responsibility for looking after the dogs among the crew members, to assure that each animal would be sufficiently "pampered" and in good shape for the dash south. When he and his party met Scott and his men in McMurdo Sound, Amundsen took pride in showing the stunned Englishmen how fast and how well his dogs ran in harness, making clear the advantage this would give his team.[8]

When supplies ran low, a beloved pet dog was quickly dispatched, as Nansen and Johansen had been forced to do. For some men, the slaughtering came easily. For others, it was fraught with moral qualms, guilt, or squeamishness. Despite his generally utilitarian philosophy, Amundsen became so attached to his dogs that he would turn up the flame in his Primus stove so that he didn't have to hear the shot when one of them was killed.[9] When he was traveling with Borchgrevink on a sledge journey toward the South Pole, Louis Bernacchi was distraught at having drawn the task of slaying one of their weaker dogs: "As I approached the doomed animal, it lifted its wise grave face and regarded me with the dignity of a sea-god and I felt but little inclined to slay such a rational-looking creature."[10] Overcoming this resistance, Bernacchi took another step forward and drove his Bowie knife into the dog's heart.

Even some explorers who did not bond with their dogs—or consider them useful—turned up their noses at the thought of actually eating one. It simply wasn't a proper thing to do. (Animals could be held to the same high moral standard. A sensitive soul like Robert Scott was so revolted by the "horrid" sight of puppies eating their own excrement on the deck of *Discovery* that he summarily shot them.[11]) Remaining a civilized person meant drawing certain lines and honoring them, no matter what circumstances arose. Behaving like an animal ultimately turned one into that animal, and that was simply inexcusable. But for some explorers, such inflexible rules did not apply under the exigencies of the Arctic and Antarctic. During a mapping expedition into the Antarctic interior in December 1912, the Yorkshire-born, Australian geologist Douglas Mawson and his two companions were running out of food—for them as well as their dogs—and energy. When one of the two other men—a twenty-five-year-old lieutenant in the Royal Fusiliers by the name of Belgrave Edward Sutton Ninnis—fell to his death in a deep crevasse, their situation became dire. Almost all their remaining food, their main tent, tools, and six of the dogs, had vanished into the abyss with Ninnis and his sledge. And they were still roughly 320 miles from the base camp.

With the few dogs left running out of stamina, Mawson and Xavier Mertz, a Swiss law-school graduate, dog handler, and expert skier, decided they would have to kill one of the six animals for food. Unaware that the liver of dogs (as well as polar bears) was highly toxic, they saved this "delicacy" for themselves, but eating it only made them weaker. When the last dog, Ginger, perished when the two survivors were scrambling down the face of Ninnis Glacier, they cut up her carcass and boiled her head, gulping down the meat inside her skull, eyes, and brain, as well as her paws—even as they were still lamenting the loss of this loyal beast. Because of their inadequate diet, skin was now peeling off both men's bodies, and frostbite setting in. Rapidly losing both his strength and his mental balance, Mertz, bit off the fleshy tip of one finger to show that it was frozen. Mawson tried to feed him some biscuit, but Mertz couldn't manage to swallow any of it. So thoroughly chilled that he could not move, suffering from delirium, he slipped into a coma inside the tent and died in the early morning of January 8, 1913.

Summoning the little energy he had left, Mawson staggered on, his skin falling off in strips—the exposed raw flesh causing him excruciating pain with each step. He restricted his daily diet to two biscuits and two sticks of chocolate for the twenty days he estimated it would take him to make it back. Each night when he removed his boots, the soles of his feet came off with them. Mawson had to reattach these calloused flaps in the morning with bandages and lanolin and plod on. Once the geologist fell into a crevasse some fourteen feet deep, but somehow pulled himself out and kept going. With Mertz's jacket stitched into a makeshift sail and held over his head, strong tailwinds propelled him forward, and by the sheerest fluke Mawson stumbled upon a cairn containing a bag of food that had recently been left at the spot, only about twenty miles from the coast. After holing up there for a few days, gorging on biscuits and chocolate, he pressed ahead until he finally came into sight of the hut on a cove where he and his two companions had started out nearly three months before. Spotting this haggard apparition approaching him, the first person to emerge from the shelter stared back with confusion and disbelief, his expression silently communicating the question *Which one are you?*[12] At this point Mawson weighed only one hundred pounds—half what he had when he had left. That he was still alive was unfathomable.

In the years that followed, admiration for Mawson's incredible feat of endurance became sullied by doubts that his story—the only surviving account of this journey—told the whole truth. Some speculated that the explorer could not have trekked so far on the meager rations he had described in his book: he must have had some other source of food. There were even suggestions that Mawson had resorted to eating human flesh—sawing off chunks of Mertz's corpse with a knife and cooking them over his Primus, as he had done with Ginger's head.[13] But no one could know for sure if this had actually happened. Posterity was left to ponder if Mawson was, in fact, an exemplary heroic figure, a despicable monster—or a little bit of both.[14]

In Mawson's day, revulsion at cannibalism was still deeply entrenched in the Western moral consciousness. It was associated with the savage stage of human evolution, which modern-day Europeans and Americans looked back on with horror. According to myth, the ancient Egyptians had regularly eaten human flesh until the time of Osiris, who had introduced organized religion and a system of laws. But the practice had persisted in some parts of the world, among primitive tribes, up to modern times. These were detailed in Sir James George Frazer's magisterial, cross-cultural study of folklore and religion, *The Golden Bough*, first published in 1890. Here Frazer recounted the eyewitness accounts of missionaries and explorers who had seen human beings being torn apart by teeth and eaten as part of grotesque religious rituals carried out by native peoples in the Americas.[15] During the Age of Exploration, Western voyagers had observed acts of cannibalism in many remote, exotic places, and these gruesome scenes had helped to justify their conquest and subjugation. Influential works like *The Golden Bough* further legitimized this colonization. However, in drawing a dividing line between these "savage" practices and those of "civilized" peoples, Frazer neglected to remind his readers that "medicinal" cannibalism had widely practiced in Europe and North America as late as the seventeenth century. Furthermore, this consuming of the body continued—at least symbolically—in in the form of wafers during Holy Communion. Since cannibalism was believed to be confined to distant times and places, "enlightened" Europeans and Americans could not easily admit that it could take place among them. Maintaining this belief was essential to preserving their cultural superiority.

However, the experiences of crews who sailed across the oceans forced a reassessment of this comforting illusion: sailors drifting in lifeboats or shipwrecked on Pacific islands without food often had only one way to stay alive—to eat each other. An early recorded instance of Western cannibalism took place after the American cargo vessel *Peggy* was dismasted and disabled during an Atlantic storm on its way back to New York in the fall of 1765. After having consumed all other edible items on board—including tobacco, pigeons, barnacles, and the ship's cat—the men drew lots to see which one would be sacrificed for the sake of the others. In what was apparently a rigged lottery, the captain's African American slave drew the shortest straw and was immediately shot. Eating his raw liver caused some to go "mad," and this dissuaded the others from eating more of his body. The *Peggy* survivors were finally rescued by a passing ship after more than four months in their rudderless vessel. In other cases, African American crew members were similarly singled out, no doubt because racist thinking made their being murdered more palatable. (As a rule, officers were the last to be carved up.[16]) On whaleboats from the sunken *Essex* in the Pacific, starving crew members ate the bodies of African American sailors, although they had apparently died of natural causes.[17]

When news of these incidents leaked out, the public was shocked, but forgiving. They could excuse cannibalism in such extreme situations (it was known euphemistically as the "custom of the sea"), and few sailors were ever prosecuted for it.[18] Still, the taboo was upheld. Western seafarers were not supposed to succumb to this self-preserving instinct: it was preferable for them to starve to death. Public distaste was well described in Edgar Allan Poe's 1838 novella, *The Narrative of Arthur Gordon Pym of Nantucket*. In this macabre tale of a seagoing odyssey gone awry, the four survivors of the wrecked *Grampus* draw straws, and the one with the shortest is stabbed to death, his blood drunk, and most of his body eaten by the others. Poe describes this act with a certain degree of acceptance: the sailors had no choice. But not all men could be so easily forgiven. Those who belonged to a higher class—that is, a ship's captain and his officers—were supposed to abide by the credo "Death before dishonor." Otherwise, they would sink to the level of beasts, as graphically depicted in Landseer's painting, *Man Proposes, God Disposes*. Here the artist implies that by overreaching and venturing far beyond the pale of civilization, human beings have gone where their moral and physical powers are not supreme: near the poles, the law of brute survival prevails. The implicit choice depicted in this work was that explorers either had to become like the beasts or be devoured by them.

Since neither option was acceptable for officers of the Royal Navy, the only way of avoiding these two possible outcomes was to pretend they didn't exist—much the way these same officers with polished brass buttons on their coats would deny lusting after a comely, sexually available Inuit woman they might run across on the coast of Greenland.[19] For a long time, people back home in England preferred not to hear about such base impulses—let alone find out that they were acted upon. But these unpleasant facts were hard to keep hidden, especially once public fascination with polar explorers intensified. Prurient curiosity to find out what really had taken place on these voyages then clashed with a reluctance to expose odious realities. In the end, curiosity won out: newspaper readers enthralled by polar expeditions wanted more than one-dimensional, hagiographical accounts of their heroes' adventures. They wanted the truth, salacious as that might be. What had once been inappropriate to read about or even imagine became so compelling that the whole story eventually had to emerge. This change in sensibility came in the wake of the mysterious disappearance of the Franklin party and the later, shocking discovery of what had happened to some of its members. By vanishing so inexplicably, the "man who ate his boots"—the amiable, kindly commander who could not bring himself to kill a fly—became a tragic figure. His whereabouts and fate obsessed his nation, much as the disappearance of Amelia Earhart would her fellow Americans nearly a century later.

Although many of those who sailed off to locate the missing Franklin did so primarily out of personal ambition—to set new geographical records—concern for his party was genuine and widespread: Americans and Europeans alike longed for some sign of life and for years nurtured hopes that the crews would be found alive—or, at least, that some telling "relics" would turn up. The fact that the "gallant navigator's" quest to navigate the Northwest Passage now seemed quixotic did not stop millions from celebrating Franklin as a national hero. For, whatever his purpose, he was carrying England's proud seagoing tradition into uncharted Arctic waters. Some felt that the longer the sailors were not heard from, the greater the likelihood that they had achieved some historic break-through—perhaps sailing across the Open Polar Sea all the way to Japan. At time passed, and no trace was found, interest in the Franklin expedition remained intense. The discovery of three graves on Beechey Island in August 1850, by members of the First Grinnell Expedition, only heightened it. In fact, preoccupation with the lost expedition was so strong that in March 1854 the Admiralty had to declare Franklin and his men dead in order to divert the nation's attention from them to an impending war with Russia. An indignant Lady Franklin showed her disdain for this decision by donning pink and green mourning garb.[20]

Later that year, John Rae, a forty-one-year-old Scottish physician and explorer, was mapping the Arctic coastline along the Boothia Peninsula, approximately seventy degrees north of the equator, when he came upon a group of Inuit who had some stunning news: while hunting seals four years earlier, they had encountered a party of approximately forty white men, dragging a boat over the ice southward, where they hoped to find deer. These men were almost completely out of food. Using signs, the leader communicated that their ships had been crushed in the ice. Not long afterward, the same group of Inuit had happened upon the bodies of thirty of these sailors, all apparently starved to death. Many of their bodies showed signs of having been cut up, with knife marks visible on some bones. In cooking pots nearby was the residue of what appeared to be human flesh. From these disturbing signs, Rae had deduced that the white men had "been driven to the last dread alternative" to stay alive.[21] He was also shown and purchased a number of items unmistakably belonging to the Franklin expedition—engraved silverware, a compass box, part of an engraved gold watch, two certificate boxes marked with initials, a monogrammed knife handle, and a similarly marked piece of vest.[22] These proved beyond any doubt that the bodies discovered by the Inuit were those of crew members of the *Erebus* and *Terror*. In its desire to bring this mystery to a close, the Admiralty released Rae's findings in October 1854, concluding that the entire party had perished, but without going into details about how: top naval officials did not want to delve deeper into indications of cannibalism.[23] However, Rae's veiled reference was sufficient to create a sensation. The London *Times* published a front-page article quoting from his official report, and this provoked a collective shudder of dismay in England—followed by loud condemnation of what Rae had dared to say. Newspapers, prominent public figures like Wilkie Collins and Charles Dickens, top Admiralty officials, and—most vociferously—Lady Franklin denounced the stories told by the Inuit, who were dismissed as "savages" and liars.[24] How could their word be trusted? How could an exemplary English gentleman like Sir John Franklin possibly have done what they claimed? (At that point, it was not clear that he had died several years before.) A book published in 1855 (by a surgeon who had taken part in the search for Franklin) pointed out that Rae's allegation had been "wholly rejected" in the press.[25] At the same time, many wondered aloud how English sailors and their officers could have failed to find food while the "primitive" Inuit had succeeded in doing so. Perhaps there had been foul play. Dickens asserted as much in a series of articles in his magazine *Household Words*. The novelist theorized that the English sailors had actually been "set upon and slain by the Esquimaux themselves," since they were a "gross handful of uncivilised people, with a domesticity of blood and blubber." He fiercely defended the moral character of Franklin's party, writing that it was inconceivable that they "would or could in any extremity of hunger, alleviate that pains of starvation by this horrible means."[26] Some who did accept Rae's version of the facts regretted that the doomed crew had not simply starved to death: that would have been the right thing for them to do.

Rae stubbornly stuck to his story and defended the integrity and honesty of his Inuit informers. In private, many eminent explorers agreed with his findings, but they kept quiet in public. Rae was shunned, denounced as "power hungry," and his reputation ruined. Instead of being applauded for having finally discovered the last unmarked section of the Northwest Passage (as apparently he—and not Franklin—had done), his name and his deeds were largely written out of the history books. It would take nearly a century and a half, until 1997, when more human bones with knife cuts on them were found on King William Island, for Rae's account of the Franklin party's demise to be vindicated.[27]

Despite the discovery of one of Franklin's ships—*Erebus*—in the waters north of this island in 2014, and of *Terror* over two years later some distance to the south, the full story of what happened to this party may never be told. (The location of *Terror* does indicate that it had reached the "missing gap" in the Northwest Passage and thus deserves the credit for this navigational breakthrough.) Toxicological analysis of the discovered bones in the 1980s revealed a high lead content, which suggested that at least some crew members had been poisoned by eating from contaminated tin cans, but more recent studies have disputed this. Disease and starvation likely took most lives. As for Franklin himself, the finding of a piece of paper by an English search party led by Captain Francis L. McClintock in 1859 established that he had died as early as 1847—long before the party had begun to run out of food—or committed cannibalism. Thus he had been spared the horrors that later befell his men: as McClintock diplomatically put it to in a letter to Lady Franklin, her husband had not been "harassed by either want of success or foreboding of evil."[28] His reputation as an honorable English officer could thus remain intact. Franklin would be remembered for having been forced to eat his boots, but nothing worse than that. His exoneration made the scandal about knife-scarred bones easier to absorb.

For years after these remains had been found, the desperate steps taken by members of the Franklin party acted as a cautionary tale for any subsequent explorers who might find themselves in similar straits. If these Englishmen *had* committed cannibalism, that still did not make that act morally permissible for anyone else. The taboo was upheld. At least that was what those returning from the poles professed. When some men belonging to Charles Hall's 1871–1872 *Polaris* expedition became separated from their ship and were marooned on an ice floe, the man nominally in charge, navigator George Tyson, feared that some Germans in this group—lacking in "self-control, bravery, or endurance"—might attempt to seize control and then shoot the two Inuit accompanying them—for food. "God forbid," Tyson scribbled in his journal, "that any of this company should be tempted to such a crime! If it is God's will that we should die by starvation, let us die like men, not like brutes, tearing each other to pieces."[29] Killing several seals helped stave off starvation and any test of Tyson's resolve. After drifting on the floe for 197 days, over some fifteen hundred miles, this emaciated band was spotted by a sealer and brought to safety.

But nineteenth-century polar exploration did not fully escape the specter of cannibalism. The second most infamous instance occurred during the Lady Franklin Bay Expedition, when Adolphus Greely and his men took refuge in a hut on Cape Sabine at the beginning of winter in 1883. With supplies running low and men already dying from starvation, Greely had zealously protected their storehouse, and when one soldier—a German immigrant named Charles Henry—was caught stealing stolen shrimp from the common pot, he was promptly shot. The surviving men grew weaker and weaker, with only one of them—Sergeant Brainard—still able to crawl out of his sleeping bag: he would put out nets to catch tiny shrimp and bring these back to the others. When a rescue party finally reached the hut toward the end of June, only seven men were still alive, and they barely so. But more than by the grotesque condition of these survivors, the rescuers were appalled by what else they found on this barren, wintry site: the body of Lieutenant Frederick Kislingbury, who had died earlier in the month, showed signs of having been stripped of some flesh. The nearby remains of a private named Wheeler, who had died more recently, also appeared to have been cut up. Autopsies of several bodies dug up near the tent and taken back to the States later revealed they, too, had been cannibalized.[30] The army tried to keep this information under wraps, but it leaked out. In August 1884, *The World* ran a lurid story under the banner headline "Eating Dead Comrades."[31] Like the British public three decades before, Americans were aghast at this news: their first reaction was to exculpate Greely's soldiers. An 1884 article in the *Medical Journal* contended that persons deprived of adequate nutrition for a long period of time regressed mentally, "lapsing into a stage where brute instincts and brute appetites predominate." In this "state of positive frenzy or insanity," they could not be held accountable for their actions.[32] The best way to prevent such "revolting" behavior was to stop sending men into the Arctic wastes. A fierce debate ensued about whether or not polar expeditions should continue, given this hazard. The English explorer George Nares argued that extending geographical boundaries was like war: men were expected to die for the greater good.[33] But the Lady Franklin Bay party was never exculpated. Dogged by accusations of cannibalism under his command, Greely denied any knowledge of any such acts and continued to serve in the Signal Corps for another two decades, retiring as a brigadier general in 1908. A quarter century later he was given the Medal of Honor. But a whiff of scandal never left him.

Mention of cannibalism was kept out of accounts of polar expeditions for decades, deemed incompatible with the image of courageous, self-sacrificing heroes that the public wanted to read. This was particularly so in England, where "tragic" but noble failures were preferred to tawdry successes. For example, in his 1910 homage to the *Heroes of the Polar Age*, J. Kennedy MacLean did not mention members of the Franklin party resorting to eating fellow crew members. Instead, he glossed over the expedition's final stages thusly: "Grim, indeed, is the tragedy that was at length revealed—the wary imprisonment amid the ice during the long winters of endless darkness and the short summers of unfailing light, the hope of relief that never came, the merciful passing away of the gallant old commander before the final catastrophe with its relentless doom fell upon his brave men."[34] For, when Kennedy was writing, the "heroic age" of polar exploration was in full swing, with giants like Ernest Shackleton and Robert F. Scott boldly striding across the Antarctic continent in search of greater glory—for themselves and their country. Thus the time was not propitious for any revelations about a dark, morally reprehensible aspect of their adventures.

Still, the stain on the Franklin party lingered—a grim, ghostly reminder that all that transpired at the poles was not as admirable and uplifting as the carefully edited memoirs and polished stone monuments would have people believe. Even though the fate of some crew members of *Terror* and *Erebus* was rarely discussed, it could not be erased from public consciousness. Since cannibalism had been practiced on this expedition, it could happen again: it was not limited to "primitive" tribes; it was part of human reality. The awareness that members of the Royal Navy had committed such deeds affected how many people in England and elsewhere thought of themselves—not as advanced human beings, but akin to those who had lived centuries before them. John Rae had been one of the first to grasp this link between primordial past and progressive present, between the poor and the well-bred. As a recent biographer of his has pointed out, the Scottish doctor "simply did not believe that Royal Navy officers and sailors, no matter how well-educated, how devoutly Christian, were superior to all other human beings and so exempt, under extreme conditions, from normal behaviour. The Arctic had taught him otherwise."[35]

The lessons about human nature gleaned at the ends of the earth were sobering and startling. They cast aspersions on the romantic temperament, as Rae's report had. What explorers might have to do in life-and-death situations became an accepted part of human existence, for better or for worse. Explorers may have accomplished amazing deeds and demonstrated incredible courage and fortitude, but they had done so, at times, at a horrendous cost—in lives and to their own image. As the polar historian Beau Riffenburgh has put it, the gruesome fate of members of the Franklin party had "eliminated the sublimity" surrounding their adventure.[36] To conquer the poles called for stretching the limits of what humans were capable of, but this was not always something to be proud of. The paradox was all too apparent: the pursuit of greatness by means of exploration could entail the loss of something even more precious—the mantle of godliness in which "civilized" man liked to wrap himself. Just as Adam and Eve had had to defy God and bite the apple of knowledge so that they could go forth and rule the earth, so did modern humans have to abandon their righteous high ground to complete the task of subduing Nature.

There were other, practical consequences of the Franklin disaster. The great loss of life—the most ever on a single polar expedition—caused many to oppose future voyages to the Arctic, certainly any involving large groups of men. The Admiralty, for one, became disinclined to send out more parties, fearful of another blot on its reputation. After the search for traces of Franklin's party was over, England essentially ceded hegemony in the Far North to the United States and the Scandinavian countries. The inability of ships to penetrate Arctic pack ice made overland expeditions to reach the pole seem more promising, and in this new race to the top, the seagoing British were literally out of their element, even if they had chosen to compete. Secondly, the fact that so many men on *Terror* and *Erebus* had apparently starved to death focused attention on the matter of provisions: large crews required tremendous amounts of food, and transporting so much weight over long distances could slow an expedition's advance and increase the likelihood of being caught in the ice. Furthermore, dependence on supplies brought all the way from Europe or the United States meant that expeditions were doomed if these stores ran out, as had happened on the Franklin voyage. For these reasons, when he was planning to navigate the Northwest Passage in 1903, Amundsen decided to take only six other men on the *Gjøa* with him and to emulate the Inuit people by living off the land as much as possible—if and when his five-year-supply of canned goods ran out. Other explorers, such as Nansen, similarly sought to solve the food problem by slaughtering seals and polar bears on their way toward the North Pole. Unlike many of their British navy predecessors, who—being sailors—were generally poor marksmen and had to rely on native hunters, they counted on their expertise with rifles. Realizing there would be no game available during the

Arctic winter, northbound expeditions often laid down a chain of food caches—a practice Franklin had dismissed as "an absurdity."[37]

The Franklin tragedy taught explorers the wisdom of adopting local customs and living like Arctic peoples as much as possible. But there were dangers, too, in "going native." One had to be careful not to commit criminal acts—a gross betrayal of the civilizing rationale that had brought Europeans and North Americans to these icy frontiers in the first place. The lingering shame and revulsion surrounding the Franklin party called for expiation, a reaffirming of the differences separating savages from Christians. Starvation could never fully justify what these sailors had done, nor could it ever do so in the future. So the best solution to the quandary the Franklin party had faced was to never end up in that kind of situation again. Jumping ahead in time half a century, we can see in Robert Scott's approach to his race to the South Pole this continuing need to preserve standards of decency no matter what happened. Cannibalism was never part of his vocabulary, and it is highly unlikely that he or any of the other gentlemen on the Southern Party would have ever entertained that option. Throughout his naval career, Scott had adhered slavishly to all rules and regulations, his actions guided—as a recent biographer has summed up—by "Conformity, obedience, centralisation, abstract reasoning, unthinking bravery, chivalric idealism, unswerving duty in the narrowest sense of the word."[38] When, as a young cadet, he had first heard about the fate of the Franklin party, Scott must have been appalled. He must have vowed that this would never happen when he was in command, the sheer barbarity of these acts viscerally abhorrent to a sensitive officer who pitied the plight of his stumbling ponies on the *Terra Nova* so much he lay sleepless in bed worrying about them, and who later felt "awful" when two of these animals had to be killed with pickaxes.[39]

As Scott, Bowers, Oates, Evans, and Wilson grew weaker and weaker, lifting their ice-smothered boots one agonizing step after another during their dispirited and dismal return from the pole, making it back was not their sole preoccupation—*how* they would do so mattered as much. As it became apparent that they were not destined to survive, how they would face death became paramount. This was evident in their refusal to abandon Oates—"The Soldier" who had scoffed at surrendering as a twenty-one-year-old army officer in the Second Boer War—who was then incapacitated by gangrene and frostbite, so that the rest of them could get back sooner. (Still, Scott did grouse that Titus was a "terrible hindrance" and had Wilson distribute opium tablets so that Oates could choose to end his suffering.[40]) In his journal Scott could not help but congratulate himself and the others for lingering, recording with a schoolboy's unabashed pride, "I take this opportunity of saying that we have stuck to our sick companions to the last."[41] Doing the right thing was what motivated Oates to take the unilateral decision to slip outside and disappear into the snow with this Etonian understatement: "I am just going outside and may be some time."[42] And it was plain to see inside the snow-carpeted, half-collapsed tent, where Cherry-Garrard and the other searchers found the bodies of Scott, Wilson, and Bowers eight months later—not scarred with knife cuts, or befouled by shreds of flesh lying beside them, or disgraced by blood-stained knives still clasped in their yellowed fingers, but serenely, miraculously, almost virginally intact, already welcomed into immortality—the frozen Scott lying face up in the middle, the flaps of his sleeping bag thrust apart, his coat wide open, as if inviting surrender to the death that he must have welcomed at the end—an end without disgrace, as he would wish it remembered. With these final, heartbreaking gestures, which would be immortalized in the hearts of millions, the stain of John Franklin's men had finally been expunged. The honor of England had been restored.

CHAPTER SEVEN

MORE NOBLE THAN THE "GREED FOR DISCOVERY"

Karl Weyprecht was an unlikely pioneer of polar science. Born in the picturesque, landlocked Hessian city of Michelstadt, Germany, in 1838, he enlisted as a cadet in the Austrian Navy at the age of seventeen, hoping to make a career at sea. Within a few years he saw limited action in the Austro-Sardinian War and then served in the Mediterranean under the command of Admiral Wilhelm von Tegetthoff, a towering figure in his country's military. Weyprecht seemed destined to rise through the ranks to help Austria achieve greater prominence in the eyes of the world. But in July 1865 he happened to attend a lecture in Frankfurt that changed the direction of his short life—and of polar exploration. This took place during an inaugural gathering of German geographers. The man giving the talk was August Petermann, his country's leading light in this emerging field—a man obsessed by the mysterious disappearance of the Franklin party and a staunch believer in the existence of the Open Polar Sea, which the missing English sailors had been trying to reach. The forty-two-year-old Petermann spoke at length with compelling enthusiasm about this supposedly navigable body of water at the top of the world, making a case for Germany to dispatch ships explore it. Like many other geographers, Petermann was convinced that the warm waters borne northward by the Gulf Stream eventually pooled in the Arctic and thereby created a temperate girdle around the North Pole. Because of its high salt content, this expanse of water never froze over.[1] Access to this unexplored sea thus could be of great military, commercial, and scientific importance, and Petermann wanted his country to take the lead in capitalizing on these opportunities. With Germany recently unified, the moment was now opportune for it to assume a more active role in exploring this part of the world. He proposed that a vessel be outfitted and sent north as soon as possible.

Weyprecht was enthralled by this idea. After the lecture, he spoke with Petermann, and the headstrong and impatient cartographer impulsively asked the young navy lieutenant if he would be willing to lead this proposed "reconnaissance voyage." Weyprecht just as unhesitatingly agreed. But the Austro-Prussian War then broke out, and the attention of Germans and their leaders turned away from the Arctic. Weyprecht served with distinction and was decorated for the courage displayed in assuming command of his ship during the Battle of Lissa, in the Adriatic, after its captain had been decapitated by a shell. Once this conflict had ended, he resumed his peacetime career. But Weyprecht's dream of being a polar explorer did not go away. In January of 1868, he and Petermann met again, in Croatia, to discuss the voyage they had been planning. This time, however, it was his health that got in Weyprecht's way: he had contracted a chronic, debilitating fever while on duty in Mexico, and this forced him to take a leave of absence. Still, his passion for going to the Far North would not die. Finally, in June 1872, after a successful preliminary cruise during which he was delighted to find warm, ice-free water near Siberia, Weyprecht sailed from Bremerhaven, in northern Germany, as captain of the three-masted schooner *Tegetthoff*, with the goal of navigating the entire Northeast Passage—which ran north of Norway and Russia—and then going on from there to reach the Polar Sea, if not the pole itself. His ship didn't get very far, as these waters turned out to be clogged by ice. As far as he and his crew could see, there was no Open Polar Sea ahead of them. During the two winters the vessel drifted helplessly, Weyprecht and the Austro-Hungarian expedition's land leader, Julius von Payer, did discover a mountainous archipelago in the Barents

Sea, which they named Franz Josef Land in honor of the reigning Austrian monarch. But, in terms of his declared objective, the voyage was a deflating failure.

By not getting anywhere near the North Pole and by showing that Petermann's theory about a warm polar sea was dead wrong, this voyage effectively ended the sprawling Austro-Hungarian Empire's bid to be an Arctic power. On top of this, the *Tegetthoff* was split apart by ice pressure and had to be abandoned. Weyprecht and his men dragged three small boats, weighing four thousand pounds each, on sledges over the ice for three months before they reached open water, where they were eventually spotted and picked up by two passing Russian whalers. Despite all these setbacks, Weyprecht was welcomed home as a great national hero and awarded a gold medal by England's Royal Geographical Society.[2] But then, somewhat mysteriously, he had a complete change of mind, denouncing the obsession with discovery for its own sake that he had advocated for years. He now spoke out in favor of another rationale for going toward the poles—the scientific knowledge to be acquired there. Having seen firsthand how much time and money were wasted when countries carried out similar explorations on their own, Weyprecht proposed that they now collaborate in gathering data about the Arctic and Antarctic regions.

In suggesting this, Weyprecht was out of step with his time—scientifically as well as politically. He first broached this idea during a speech before the Vienna Academy of Sciences in January 1875—just a few years after the end of the Franco-Prussian War, a conflict that had humiliated the French, emboldened the Germans, upset the balance of power on the Continent, and sowed the seeds for World War I four decades later. This was hardly a propitious time to call for international cooperation. If anything, national rivalries were intensifying as Europe's major powers were busy carving out colonial empires in Africa and Asia. Science, too, was caught up in this chauvinistic fervor. Some looked at discoveries about the natural world as a worthy substitute for war—a way to "flex imperial muscle" and show superiority without bloodshed.[3] Even Weyprecht himself had argued as much in seeking funds for his North Polar exploration: wasn't Austria—an empire several hundred years old—the equal of an upstart Germany? Why, then, should it not compete with the Prussians in demonstrating its "scientific" prowess? (In the parlance of his day, "science" meant practical knowledge about natural phenomena, put to use to improve the world.) In reporting on his polar discoveries to a whipped-up gathering of scientists in Vienna, Weyprecht had declared: "Gentlemen! This year for the first time we have hoisted the flag in the Arctic region, and will bring to life again the faint hopes of finally reaching the pole! The Austrians have . . . successfully entered the contest."[4]

Whatever had changed Weyprecht's mind, his call for international scientific cooperation found a receptive audience in that hall and almost overnight revolutionized the rationale for sending government-sponsored expeditions toward the poles. European meteorologists bought the Austrian officer's argument that persisting in an "international steeplechase" to plant a flag a few miles further north or south was exceedingly costly and yielded little of value.[5] They also concurred that only acquiring more information about this remote realm, and sharing it for the good of all, made this exploratory pursuit worthwhile. As Weyprecht outlined his vision, comprehensive magnetic, weather-related, and astronomical data could be amassed by teams from different countries based at permanent outposts forming a ring around the North Pole and in Antarctica. Encountering remarkably little resistance, these scientists convinced their governments to finance the setting up of these on-site laboratories.[6] By 1881, seven nations—Austria, Denmark, Sweden, Norway, Russia, the Netherlands, and the United States—had agreed to participate in this first international polar collaboration. (Adolphus Greely's disastrous Lady Franklin Bay Expedition would be the American contingent.) Sadly, Weyprecht died in March of that year—a victim of tuberculosis—before any of these stations were set up.[7]

Among the nations of Europe, scientific cooperation was not a new concept. As far back as the mid-eighteenth century, astronomers from several countries had worked together to observe the transits of Mercury and Venus. This effort had spurred many more such international ventures.[8] Throughout the Victorian era, this working together had extended to many fields, including meteorology, botany, and geology, driven by a common desire to increase human knowledge—and sustain economic progress—for mutual benefit. In 1829, the Prussian naturalist Alexander von Humboldt had proposed that scientists from many nations pool their resources to study magnetism and the weather near the Arctic Circle. Prince Albert had given a royal blessing to this "great and sacred mission" of revealing the laws of Nature at the opening of London's Crystal Palace, in 1851.[9] International congresses of scientists met periodically to share their findings and set standards. During earlier expeditions to the Arctic and Antarctic, science had taken a backseat to territorial discovery and conquest. But now this pragmatic, commercially based focus gave top priority to the collecting of data on topography, temperatures, sea currents, magnetic fields, and marine life. Since they were now risking their lives for the betterment of humankind, these so-called "missionaries of science" were hailed as heroes—much like the fictional Indiana Jones in our day—supplanting those explorers who had gone north and south on quixotic, self-serving adventures.[10]

This growing curiosity about the polar world was part and parcel of a broad scientific effort to identify, codify, and understand little-known regions of the planet and their life-forms. This had started in the eighteenth century, with naturalists like Joseph Banks and Mungo Park, and reached its apogee with Darwin's voyage to the Galapagos in the 1830s. (In the United States, President Thomas Jefferson had promoted this kind of investigation by tasking Lewis and Clark with gathering specimens on their way to the Pacific.) At the top of the world, such achievements compensated for the repeated failure of mariners to locate the Northwest Passage or reach the North Pole—including the Franklin disaster. After his party disappeared, exploration "for its own sake" lost much of its allure, and "the hope and need and romance of reaching the East" faded away.[11] "Explorer-adventurers" became "explorer-observers."[12] Donors and sponsors of expeditions felt that important scientific findings gave them a good return on their investments. Organizations like England's Royal Geographical Society were now reluctant to sink money into a "record-chasing dash to the pole or more adventure travel." By the mid-1860s, even an ardent admirer of polar heroism such as Clements Markham had come around to believing that the symbolic triumph of reaching ninety degrees north by itself was not enough to justify more high-risk expeditions.[13] Mapping uncharted territory was now considered much more important than setting foot on it.

Several early nineteenth-century explorers had already put considerable emphasis on learning about the polar environment. While a young officer in the Imperial Russian Navy, the Baltic-German cartographer Fabian Gottlieb Thaddeus von Bellingshausen had taken part in that country's first round-the-world voyage in 1803–1806 and then, just over a dozen years later, led an expedition south that became the first to clearly see (unlike Cook) the Antarctic continent. Hoping to interest his adopted country in the economic potential of this scarcely visited region, Bellingshausen brought hundreds of specimens of plant and animal life, as well as minerals, back to his ship, even though it had been inadequately outfitted for proper scientific study.[14] But in this aspiration he was to be sorely disappointed, as the items he had brought back gathered dust on museum shelves for decades. In Bellingshausen's day most governments still regarded Antarctica as an empty, frozen wasteland, of no practical value. However, the British Admiralty did send along naturalists on the expeditions it sponsored, as part of a concerted bid to render the unknown world comprehensible, and with this knowledge conquer it. In the Arctic tundra, the Scottish surgeon John Richardson accompanied Lieutenant John Franklin expressly for the purpose of compiling samples of plants and rocks as he and his men explored far northern Canada in the 1820s. While mainly eager to trace the route of the elusive Northwest

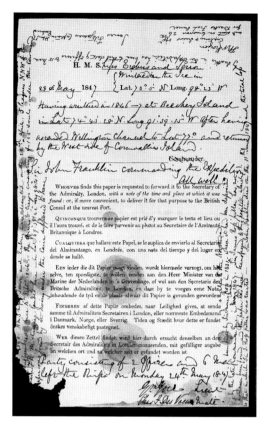

This last written communication ever found from the doomed Franklin expedition revealed that Sir John Franklin himself had died the year before (in 1847) but gave no clue about the fate of the surviving officers and men, thus keeping alive faint hopes that they might have survived. Photo by John Powles Cheyne, British Franklin Search Expedition.

The body of native son Elisha Kent Kane lying in Independence Hall, Philadelphia, in 1857. Kane's two-week-long funeral procession from New Orleans drew tens of thousands of mourners, giving powerful witness to the nation's fascination with polar adventurers. "The Death Watch"; engraving by DeWitt Clinton Baxter.

Because of his undaunted optimism, Lt. George De Long continued to press on northward after his ship, the Jeannette, *became icebound in the Arctic in 1881. When the vessel began to sink, his party had to abandon it and make a desperate attempt to reach land, but all perished on the way.* Crew of Jeannette dragging boat over ice, 1881; engraving by George T. Andrew.

In order to maintain discipline with their food running out at their Arctic outpost in 1884, Lieutenant Adolphus Greely imposed severe punishments for those who broke the rules. When twenty-eight-year-old private Charles Henry, a German immigrant, was caught stealing shrimp and showed "neither fear nor contrition," Greely promptly had him shot. Greely order for Pvt. Henry's execution, 1884.

Of the twenty-one officers and men who had accompanied Greely (seated, center) to Lady Franklin Bay in 1881, only five eventually returned with him. While hailed as heroes when they arrived at Portsmouth, New Hampshire, rumors of cannibalism dogged them for the rest of their lives. This disastrous outcome made the American public and government wary of sending other expeditions to the Far North. Survivors of the Greely Expedition; photo by A. W. Anderson.

Fridtjof Nansen (center) and his companions observing a solar eclipse beside their ship Fram in 1894. Although Nansen had a doctoral degree in zoology, his professed interest in exploring the Arctic for scientific purposes masked his real ambition of becoming the first person to reach the North Pole. National Library of Norway.

With Frederick Cook and Robert Peary making rival, unsubstantiated claims to have reached the North Pole first, the winner of this race was largely decided in the court of public opinion, with Cook gaining an initial advantage thanks to sensational headlines like this one. The Chicago Daily News hails Cook's reaching the North Pole.

His single-minded focus on getting to the pole first, undistracted by scientific objectives, gave Roald Amundsen a clear edge over his British rival Scott. The Norwegian also treated his men as his equals and thus avoided the resentment and bickering that plagued the British expedition on its way south in 1911. Amundsen photographing at the South Pole.

A poor planner, wont to remain aloof from his men, Robert Scott achieved his greatest triumph in the written record he left behind—journals that glossed over his shortcomings and idealized the companions who finally reached the South Pole with him in 1912. Robert Scott writing in his journal; photo by Herbert George Ponting.

The final page from Scott's journal, written March 29, 1912: "We shall stick it out to the end, but we are getting weaker, of course, and the end cannot be far. It seems a pity, but I do not think I can write more. R. Scott. For God's sake look after our people." British Library.

Scott's reluctance to disappoint his friend Edward Wilson led him to allow members of his Southern Party—Wilson, "Birdie" Bowers, and Apsley Cherry-Garrard—to venture forth into the appallingly cold Antarctic winter to retrieve some Emperor penguin eggs. This ordeal left the three explorers exhausted and not in the best shape for the trek to the pole. Cape Crozier party returns; photo by Herbert George Ponting.

Like so many explorers before him, Ernest Shackleton (right) found that the frigid polar environment presented insurmountable barriers. His plan to bring ashore supplies for a proposed trans-Antarctic land expedition collapsed when the Endurance *became beset in the Weddell Sea in February 1915. The vessel drifted and was slowly crushed by ice, until it sank the following fall, forcing Shackleton and his men to undertake their incredible sea voyage to South Georgia Island.* Wreck of the Endurance; photo by Frank Hurley.

While he was less wedded to "manhauling" than his contemporary Robert Scott, Ernest Shackleton found he had to resort to such back-breaking measures when the Endurance became stuck in Antarctic ice in 1915. These harsh realities confounded the romantic temper and self-confidence that many British explorers brought with them to the poles. Shackleton's crew hauling the James Caird; photo by Frank Hurley.

Shackleton realized that in order to survive extreme conditions at the poles, he and his men had to form unbreakable bonds, trusting that each would stand by the others to the end. Even when he and five others had to leave the rest of his party behind on Elephant Island in April 1916, members of the Endurance party never lost this faith in each other. Waving goodbye to the Caird on Elephant Island; photo by Frank Hurley.

Admiral Richard E. Byrd unilaterally decided to spend half a year all by himself in the interior of Antarctica during the winter of 1934, but this complete isolation nearly drove him mad. He had to be rescued after five months, and was never completely the same again. US Navy, National Science Foundation.

Passage, Franklin was proud of the fact that his nation's expeditions proceeded "not from any prospect of immediate benefit to herself, but from a steady view to the acquirement of useful knowledge, and the extension of the bounds of science."[15] His former companion George Back adopted the same philosophy when he was searching for the missing John Ross a decade later: adding to scientific understanding was a major reason why his sovereign had sent him there.[16] So Back dutifully made magnetic readings and other scientific measurements as he followed fur trading paths leading to the post where Ross had disappeared.

During much of the nineteenth century the accurate and exhaustive compiling of data was the chief purpose of science. Spurred by the South American discoveries and the writings of the influential Humboldt, this approach derived from the belief that all natural phenomena were interrelated: by carefully observing and collating the "minute particulars" of what was observed and examined, a sense of underlying order would emerge, ultimately revealing God's plan for the universe. Thus, naturalists who went into the wilderness after Humboldt kept meticulous, precise, and detailed records of all the animals, plants, fish, birds, and reptiles, as well as inorganic forms (minerals and fossils) they happened upon. In carrying out this often tedious, exhausting, and at times dangerous work, these men of science (the term "scientist" did not come into use until the 1830s) were seen as courageous pioneers. Their notebooks were filled with long lists of numbers added to humanity's relentless quest for truth: "measuring the world, measuring men, and measuring empire" defined this new heroism.[17] Because the conditions and life-forms found in the Arctic and Antarctic were so greatly different from those that existed elsewhere, information from these regions was especially treasured: it would add crucial missing pieces to an immense earthly jigsaw puzzle then still being completed. "Mapping" the planet was the nineteenth century's great scientific challenge—a task that, as long as it remained unfinished, was—in the words of the 8th Duke of Argyll—"a reproach upon the enterprise, civilisation, and condition of knowledge of the human race."[18]

This elevation of science made it obligatory that meteorologists, geologists, oceanographers, and naturalists have a prominent role in expeditions reaching for the poles. More than merely compilers of facts about currents, channels, ice movement, and temperatures, they were representatives of a noble, civilizing imperative. Exploiting the public's admiration for this new type of hero, some explorers wrapped themselves in the mantle of science and thus added more luster to their image. None better personified this penchant than Elisha Kent Kane. As a student at the University of Virginia in the late 1830s, he had studied natural science and become fascinated by this nascent field. At medical school he went on to conduct seminal research on a film or coating present in female urine that was a sign of pregnancy, receiving international recognition for this discovery before he had even earned his degree.[19] While subsequently traveling across the Pacific, Kane kept extensive notebooks describing in great detail what he had seen and done. This habit sharpened his observational skills, which he would later put to good use in the Arctic.

As chief medical officer and scientist on the *Advance*, during the 1850–1851 Grinnell-funded "crusade in search for a lost comrade"—John Franklin—Kane took advantage of his ship's being icebound in Lancaster Sound to study ice formation, local geology, and weather conditions, although he was handicapped by having had just one day to procure the requisite equipment before his ship had sailed from New York. (He also found time during this Canadian interlude to shoot and skin a polar bear over eight feet long.) In writing afterward about this abortive voyage, Kane made a point of stressing how much he had devoted his time to making observations—at the expense of looking for traces of the vanished Franklin party. (He went so far as to imply that the latter endeavor had not really been worth the bother: "For myself, looking only at the facts, and carefully discarding every deduction that might be prompted by sympathy rather than reason, my journal reminds me that I did not see in these signs the evidence of a lost party.") But his descriptions (and sketches) of natural phenomena were laden with romantic rhapsodies about the beauty of the Arctic world and its strange creatures: a huge iceberg looked like a "great marble monolith, only awaiting the chisel to stand out in peristyle and pediment a floating Parthenon"; walruses— or, as he preferred to call them, "marine pachyderm"—were described as "grim-looking monsters," reminding him of the "stage hobgoblins, something venerable and semi-Egyptian withal."[20]

These were not the words of a naturalist or medical doctor, but of a would-be Lord Byron or Shelley, exalting the world around him as the backdrop for an exotic, heroic adventure, with himself front and center. Kane was not writing to inform his readers, but to sweep them away. In fact, he, his younger brother Thomas, and their father—a Philadelphia judge—had decided to produce a book that would make him famous, building on the notoriety Elisha had already acquired by going on this Arctic expedition and then enduring a winter's imprisonment in Baffin Bay.[21] As the three of them had foreseen, the book's combination of melodrama and scientific dedication was wildly popular, and almost overnight Kane became the prototype for the dashing American scientist defying death in his relentless quest for knowledge.

When Kane returned to the Far North a few years later, ostensibly to resume searching for the Franklin party, his scientific zeal was even more apparent. Settling in for winter off the coast of Greenland in 1853, Kane and his men set up two observatories on the ice—one for magnetic readings, the other for studying the weather. Even after temperatures dipped as low as 75 degrees below zero that February, they kept up their routine of leaving the ship several times a day to take readings. Astronomical calculations had to be made outdoors—in spite of frozen fingers, snow-encrusted eyes, and chattering teeth. The igloo used for measuring the magnetic field was, in Kane's typically hyperbolic language, "an ice-house of the coldest imaginable description." Two men at a time would go out there clad in sealskin trousers, reindeer jacket, dogskin cap, and walrus boots, to sit on top of a wooden box and record the movements of a magnetometer at precise, six-minute intervals. This process went on uninterrupted for twenty-four hours a day—yielding several hundred readings each week. Since there was a small stove burning inside the igloo, the real challenge was getting to and back from this makeshift observatory, with only a small lantern and pole to point the way through the otherwise total darkness.[22] When Kane's hefty, two-volume account of this expedition was published, it contained eighteen appendices, not only summarizing the various overland journeys Kane's party had made, as well as the plants collected along the way, but also containing extensive tables on temperature, atmospheric pressure, wind speed, and magnetism that he and his companions had compiled. (Details about magnetic fields near the poles were then considered important in understanding the underlying physics and helping ships navigate by compass.[23]) Publishing such lengthy findings—as was the custom for polar explorers back then—was intended to showcase this scientific "payoff" from explorations.

Kane's second book was a phenomenal bestseller: some sixty thousand copies were sold the year it came out, and as many as three million persons would ultimately read about his bone-chilling adventures in the Greenland ice, with presumably far fewer checking the scientific tables at the back.[24] More than any previous account of polar expedition, Kane's dramatic tale satisfied Americans' longing for a bold, fearless masculine figure who could triumph over a hostile Nature by blazing new paths into the wilderness, at a time when Western expansion and Manifest Destiny were dominant national preoccupations. The unparalleled appeal and commercial success of Kane's books made them models for future explorers hoping to make a name for themselves—and a fortune— from their exploits. The public's notion of a scientist was central to this heroic image, and so carrying out science-related tasks became a *sine qua non* on subsequent voyages and sledge journeys. The audacity and perseverance needed to perform this dangerous work was seen as equivalent to what was required to set a new Farthest North. Indeed, scientific "victories" could make up for geographical "defeats." It was the demonstration of courage, gumption, and character that counted, and Kane embodied those qualities in spades, even if his territorial conquests were less than spectacular.

Piggybacking scientific experiments onto an Arctic voyage also guaranteed that backers would not be totally disappointed if no new territory was discovered. Thus, when Francis McClintock sailed from Aberdeen, Scotland, in command of the *Fox* in July of 1857, hoping to bring an anguished Lady Jane Franklin some closure by finding relics of her husband, he also took along £50 worth of equipment provided by the Royal Geographical Society to enable him learn more about the North Magnetic Pole.[25] (McClintock was also supposed to look for proof that Franklin had actually discovered the Northwest Passage; finding this would ease the pain of the lives presumed lost and give his widow added reason for being proud of him.) In retrospect, Franklin was also acclaimed for his "scientific" accomplishments, although these had not been his primary mission: Lady Franklin arranged for a marble tablet to be placed on Disko Island, off the western coast of Greenland, in memory of "Franklin, Crozier, Fitzjames, / and all their Gallant Brother Officers and Faithful Companions who have suffered and perished / in the cause of science and / the service of their country."[26]

Increasingly, scientific discoveries were valued as affirmation of national stature and prowess. Accordingly, many explorers in the second half of the century took them seriously. A notable example is the Scottish-Canadian oceanographer Sir John Murray, who first traveled to the Arctic in 1868, when he was in his late twenties, scooping up exotic marine creatures and plumbing the bottom of the waters his ship passed through. In the course of a subsequent voyage, on board the *Challenger*, Murray collected some four thousand previously unknown species and published his descriptions of them in a massive, fifty-volume set. During this circumnavigation of the earth, he also laid the foundation for modern oceanography, by measuring the depth, temperature, and terrain of the sea floor. For a man of science like Murray, gathering such data had intrinsic scientific merit, but it also brought prestige to the nation whose scientists did this work.[27] In a November 1893 speech before the Royal Geographical Society, in which he called for more Antarctic expeditions, Murray would rhetorically ask, "Is the last great piece of maritime exploration on the surface of our earth to be undertaken by Britons, or is to be left to those who may be destined to succeed or supplant us on the ocean? That is a question this generation must answer."[28] At a time when curiosity about the unknown dovetailed with nationalism, this argument resonated with his London audience. Because governments were often footing the bills, the information brought back from polar expeditions was supposed to further national ambitions: amassing new facts was akin to acquiring new colonies. Both kinds of conquests bolstered a country's prestige and increased its power on the world stage. In the words of one historian of Germany's polar expeditions, knowledge acquired in the Arctic deepened the "steadily expanding link between science and the state and the gradual absorption of scientific exploration in the political aims of the state."[29]

Adjusting to this new rationale, explorers who really only cared about setting a new Farthest North began to emphasize the scientific importance of their proposed expeditions. Often the need to attract funding made this virtue a necessary. Charles Hall, for instance, had to make his case for underwriting an 1871 voyage toward the North Pole on these grounds, despite the fact that he was largely uneducated and had no real interest in science.[30] To obtain the $50 thousand Congress eventually appropriated for this expedition, Hall reluctantly agreed to accept on the *Polaris* a team of German scientists, who ended up opposing Hall's geographical ambitions and rebelling against his leadership.[31] Likewise, Lieutenant George De Long regarded himself first and foremost as a pioneering explorer and tolerated scientific work on his ill-fated *Jeannette* only to satisfy the US Navy—under whose auspices he was sailing.[32] He, too, frequently clashed with the two civilian scientists he had been compelled to take with him.[33] Expedition backers like the Royal Geographical Society stressed the need to make accurate observations and keep detailed records, insisting that explorers be trained in the use of equipment such as sextants and barometers.

During the First International Polar Year (1882–1883), science took center stage more than ever before. This was due, in large part, to a tacit acceptance among the nations interested in the Arctic and Antarctic that the human costs of continuing to pursue new geographical "firsts" were simply too high. (It has been estimated that, between 1770 and 1918, approximately one of every two polar explorers perished on expeditions.[34]) Furthermore, the commercial advantages once believed to be derived from navigating the Northwest Passage had not materialized, after centuries of unsuccessful attempts to trace this route in its entirety. While some explorers, like Hall, clung to the dream of reaching the North Pole, other, less grandiose goals seemed more attainable, and so more energy and resources were invested in achieving them. The idea of establishing stations around the poles, to conduct meteorological, astronomical, and geophysical observations, fit well into this more realistic approach. By making science its focus, the International Polar Year turned the mundane tasks of measuring and recording data into a noble endeavor for the seven-hundred-odd men from eleven countries who would be participating in this effort.

The twenty-five-man American party, known as the Lady Franklin Bay Expedition (for its location some six hundred miles from the North Pole, along the northern Greenland coast), and commanded by Lieutenant Adolphus W. Greely of the US Army Signal Corps, set about its scientific mission starting in the late summer of 1881 with military doggedness and discipline. By so honoring this commitment, they were demonstrating how seriously the United States took science—a sign that it was on a par with the major European powers. Before the Arctic winter arrived at their Fort Conger base camp, and before the last rays of the sun disappeared, soldiers and scientists took turns going regularly out to their observatories to write down the temperature, wind speed, barometric pressure, tidal rise and fall, movement of the stars, and tilt of the magnetometer—filling notebooks with thousands of notations.[35] (Only in the depths of winter did their record-keeping become more lax.[36]) Greely's small band also jotted down descriptions of the aurora and other cosmic phenomena, gathered marine, mammalian, plant, bird, and fossil specimens, and made anthropological observations about Inuit who lived near the fort.[37] These Civil War veterans stuck to their routines in spite of the intense cold, their increasingly depressed and irritable mood, and the risks involved. After no relief ships had reached them, and with supplies running low, the Greely party abandoned its lonely outpost in August 1883 and made its way south to Cape Sabine, where food caches had been left by previous voyagers. It was only at this point that the men stopped keeping meteorological records.[38] Greely had copies made of these and other findings, sealed them in water-tight tin boxes, and carried this heavy (over fifty pounds) load with him throughout this grueling, two-month-long, two-hundred-mile retreat, first by boat and then drifting on the ice. After being rescued the following June and making it back to New York, the six surviving soldiers (plus Greely) were praised for their "enlargement of scientific survey" and given promotions, despite the whispers about cannibalism that had accompanied them.[39]

The need for scientific breakthroughs and new national heroes was so great because those who had gone to the Arctic strictly because of territorial ambitions—what Charles Daly, longtime president of the American Geographical Society, had called "wild discovery"—had accomplished very little.[40] Memories of the Franklin and *Jeannette* fiascos were hard to shake. Wealthy patrons of later polar expeditions like Daly and Grinnell helped the public get over these disasters by trumpeting another kind of achievement in which they could take pride. And, by and large, the public bought into this new exploratory objective because it called for the same manly heroics they longed for. Adding to human knowledge was also another justification for territorial aggrandizement and cause for chauvinistic celebration. Just as Clements Markham was determined that newly discovered locations in the Arctic have only British names, so were many of his contemporaries eager to have only their scientists receive the credit for important scientific discoveries. Karl Weyprecht may have believed that learning more about the polar regions would benefit all of humanity, but others saw this undertaking as another form of international competition, in which there would always be winners and also-rans.

Yet some explorer-scientists toiling in the Arctic and Antarctic were indifferent to this quasi-Darwinian aspect of their research. They seemed to have taken to heart the idea that what they were responding to was a higher calling. Perhaps not coincidentally, several leading polar scientists around the turn of the century were deracinated individuals, largely devoid of patriotic fervor. Carsten Borchgrevink, for example, was a native of Oslo, who had begun his polar career in 1894, as a member of a Norwegian whaling voyage to the Arctic. But a few years later he took command of the British-financed *Southern Cross* expedition after having convinced Sir George Newnes, wealthy publisher of the *Strand Magazine*, to back him for that position (over the vehement objections of British chauvinists like Markham). In deference to Newnes, Borchgrevink brought with him five hundred tiny Union Jacks, attached to bamboo poles, so that he could visibly mark any new extensions of the British Empire his party might claim. Although in retirement he returned to Norway, his loyalties remained divided between these two countries. Likewise, Louis Bernacchi—the chief "magnetician" and meteorologist on Borchgrevink's expedition—had been born in Belgium, to Italian parents, and then, at the age of eight, moved with them to Tasmania. He took his university degree in Australia and became fully assimilated there. During the *Southern Cross* and the *Discovery* expeditions to Antarctica, Bernacchi dedicated himself to studying magnetism: he was convinced the real value of the continent lay in the scientific secrets it concealed. During World War I, he served in both the American and the British navies. Bernacchi lived the rest of his life in England and died in London in 1942. Similarly, Douglas Mawson—respected as the only true scientist on the Antarctic continent during the age of Scott and Shackleton—was a native of England who spent almost his entire life (when not at the bottom of the world) in Australia. For transnational men like these it was easier to separate "science" from "state" and advance one without having to worry about betraying the other.

But even deeply loyal subjects of the British Empire could devote themselves wholeheartedly to "pure" science. The best-known examples of such dedication were the members of Scott's two expeditions who chose to carry out projects in conflict with their quests to reach the South Pole. From the start, these two Antarctic journeys—the first undertaken by Englishmen since the days of Sir James Ross—had been riven by incongruent missions. During the planning for the 1901–1904 *Discovery* expedition, polar enthusiasts like the Royal Geographical Society's president, Markham, had opposed any distraction from traversing unexplored territory near the Ross Ice Shelf and insisted that navy men should run the show, whereas top officials at the co-sponsoring Royal Society—Britain's preeminent scientific body—argued for glacial geologist John Walter Gregory to be put in charge. In the end, Markham got his way, Scott—his protégé—was given command, and Gregory withdrew from the expedition, saying that he could not countenance scientific study being subordinated to "naval adventure."[41] Only one member of the remaining scientific team—Bernacchi—had had any prior experience in the Antarctic. Nonetheless, Scott's was instructed to give equal weight to "meteorological, oceanographic, geological, biological and physical investigations and researches" during his travels.

It was during Scott's dash to the South Pole eight years later that the tensions between scientific and territorial aspirations came to a head. Reflecting his personal inclination and his sponsors' wishes, this *Terra Nova* party sought to strike a balance between these two purposes—a fateful compromise since they proved to be detrimental to each other, especially when the English expedition discovered it was in a tight race with the Norwegians. Whereas Amundsen, "unfettered by science," could keep his gaze riveted like a laser on getting to the pole first, Scott's party was delayed going south by a commitment to collect information about the Antarctic environment. The chief scientist, Edward Wilson, in particular, took this work very seriously: he was eager to complete his study of Emperor penguins and carry out geological, magnetic, and meteorological studies, convinced that this research should be the main focus of the expedition. In a letter to his father, Wilson made his priorities crystal-clear: "No one can say that it will have only been a Pole-hunt, though that of course is a *sine qua non*. We *must* get to the Pole, but we shall get more too. . . . We want the scientific work to make the bagging of the Pole merely an item in the results."[42] He and some of the others, including Scott, saw themselves exemplifying a twentieth-century ideal of manliness that combined physical courage with scientific expertise and brains. At one point, while waiting for Wilson, Bowers, and Cherry-Garrard to return from Cape Crozier, Scott jotted in his diary: "Science cannot be served by 'dilettante' methods, but demands a mind spurred by ambition or the satisfaction of ideals."[43]

Wilson's resolve to set out into the howling Antarctic winter (something no one had dared to do before) to collect a few penguin eggs so that he could confirm an evolutionary theory tapped into the romantic side of Scott's nature: he envisioned this proposed excursion as a grand expression of the human spirit—soaring to great heights over extreme adversity for the sake of a selfless purpose.[44] What some might belittle as a foolish and dangerous side trip, Scott saw as the kind of manhood test that Clements Markham expected British naval officers to pass while they were in the Arctic and Antarctic.[45] He knew full well how much Wilson yearned to do this, for his own reasons. Before departing, one spring evening at Cape Evans, the Cambridge-educated ornithologist had presented a talk on penguins and spelled out what he hoped to learn from their eggs. His passion for this subject was infectious. Scott admired Wilson so much that turning down his request would have been like hiding a birthday present from his young son. When the trio of Wilson, Bowers, and Cherry-Garrard returned from their "worst journey in the world" five weeks later, looking more like long-trapped Welsh coal miners than English gentlemen, with three of the precious eggs nestled in a bundle,

Scott could only admire their extraordinary courage ("It makes a tale for our generation which I hope may not be lost in the telling"[46]) even if the eggs meant little to him, and even if he realized how terrible a physical toll this ordeal had taken on men he planned to take south to the pole in three months' time. (Wilson would afterward disparage their side trip to Cape Crozier as "useless" because they had had only a day in which to forage for eggs.[47])

In accomplishing this incredible feat, the three Englishmen had remained true to the devil-may-care abandonment that bound them together, like schoolboys in a rugby scrum, even in the face of death. As Scott would reflect in his journal on the eve of his departure for the pole, "We are all adventurers here, I suppose, and wild things in wild countries appeal to us as nothing else could do."[48] For Wilson and Cherry-Garrard, this "winter journey" was an act of faith—faith that someday what they accomplished would make a difference. Cherry admitted in his memoir that the immediate importance of scooping up Emperor penguin eggs under these harrowing circumstances had not been apparent to him. Still, with no thought of "personal gain," they had struggled like trusting acolytes to bring back some scientific evidence, leaving it to others to sort out what it might mean.[49]

The trip to Crozier had been simply "ghastly." Insanely cold temperatures, three-day blizzards, frozen clothes, stomach cramps, frostbite, near misses with crevasses—all these ills had plagued the three explorers like some polar parody of the Book of Job. Despite it all, Bowers kept detailed meteorological records, and they had trudged on. Having only a faintly shining Jupiter to guide their steps, their faith in this mission was literally as well as figuratively blind. It was as if they had crossed over into another realm of existence, in which pain and purpose and plausibility no longer impinged upon their consciousness: "We were quite intelligent people," Cherry wrote, "and we must all have known that we were not going to see the penguins and that it was folly to go forward. And yet with quiet perseverance, in perfect friendship, almost with gentleness those two men led on. I just did what I was told." By the time the trio—tied together with ropes in the dark in case one of them should slip into a crevasse—finally staggered into the midst of a hundred or so nesting penguins near the Great Ice Barrier—possibly the most inhospitable spot on the entire planet—their task appeared more hopeless but, at the same time, more worthwhile. Cherry now felt it was of the "utmost importance" to science that they snatch some eggs and bring them back. And that they did, wrenching away five from underneath irate but helpless parents. After the men escaped from this rookery and returned to the relative safety of a nearby ledge, they discovered that Cherry had dropped two of them along the way, and they had been lost.[50] The remaining ones would eventually find their way safely back to Cape Evans, from there, by ship to England, and then, finally in 1913, to the Natural History Museum in London, where they would remain unexamined for some twenty-one years. When this did happen, in 1934, it was determined that the eggs revealed little about penguin embryology and provided no support for the theory that birds had descended from dinosaurs.

In some ways, this "worst journey in the world" foreshadowed Scott's dash to the South Pole a few months later. In both instances, historic milestones were achieved—at great personal sacrifice and under horrific conditions. Yet both "triumphs" had ironic, deflating consequences: just as the arrival of Scott and his men at the pole *after* the Norwegians had left them deeply dispirited and then—because they died on the way back—turned them into martyrs, so did collecting penguin eggs on Cape Crozier (and then hauling them back to England) demonstrate English fortitude and "pluck," but, at the same time, the ultimate pointlessness of what they had achieved. Results like this did not encourage more efforts but sowed seeds of disenchantment. Two years after the *Terra Nova* tragedy, Shackleton's *Endurance* expedition—which was to be the last of the "Heroic Age" explorations—took place, but it, too, ended in failure, even if it was enshrined in memory as one of the greatest survival stories in human history. After it, English boots rarely touched the Antarctic continent again.[51] Future scientific work there was largely turned over to other nations.

In large part, this rapid waning of interest stemmed from disillusionment with gallantry on battlefields like the Somme, but even before World War I the apparent futility of gaining glory at the ends of the earth had soured the British public on such expeditions—much as the loss of the Franklin party had half a century before. When, in his obituary for Scott, Clements Markham saluted him as a "martyr in the cause of science," he was sadly bidding farewell not only to his protégé but also to the national mood that had elevated Scott to such a lofty stature.[52] After Scott's death, a sacrifice like his could not shake its association with pointlessness and disappointment. So tarnished by defeat, the endeavors of scientist-explorers at the poles, once deemed "heroic," no longer glittered as brightly as they once had. Three dusty penguin eggs, languishing on a London museum shelf for decades, were a fitting epitaph to this era of extravagant hopes, heroic struggles, and elusive fulfillment.

Chapter Eight

"DOWN WITH SCIENCE, SENTIMENT, AND THE FAIR SEX"

W hen thirty-two-year-old Lieutenant John C. Colwell of the US Navy reached the partially collapsed tent on rock-strewn Cape Sabine, he took out a knife and slit the canvas so he could peer inside. Probing the darkness, his eyes alighted on a scene from a charnel house. One man lay dead on his back, with glassy eyes staring into eternity. Another, motionless, but still alive, apparently had neither hands nor feet. A third, sprawled forward on his knees, as if caught crawling, stared up in disbelief, a red skullcap plastered on his head, a long, thick beard obscuring his face, his frail body sheathed in a ragged dressing gown. "Greely, is this you?" Colwell blurted out. "Yes," the man whispered, almost inaudibly. Then, after a pause, he added, in the labored rasp of someone who had not spoken in a long time, "Yes, seven of us left. Here we are, dying—like men. Did what I came to do—beat the best record."[1] Then he collapsed.

In morte, veritas. With death seemingly near, Adolphus Greely wanted to make sure the world knew what his party had managed to do—reach a new Farthest North of 83.23 degrees, besting the British mark set eight years before. This was the goal he had come to achieve, the feat that really mattered, the accomplishment that would earn him the adulation of a world that not heard from his expedition in three years. Colwell must have been taken aback as much by Greely's assertion as by the pitiful condition of these survivors of the Lady Franklin Bay Expedition he had just rescued. For the American government had not sent these soldiers so far

into the Arctic barrens—on the first federally funded polar expedition—
to strive for some dramatic territorial milestone like reaching the North
Pole.[2] Instead, as participants in the First International Polar Year, they
were supposed to collect data on the weather, magnetic field, and celestial
events from their base in far northern Greenland. But Greely had said
nothing about that. It was as if he had forgotten what he had come for.

In fact, the Greely party had not stuck to the task it had been assigned.
Quietly, and as early as their first winter on Ellesmere Island, the task of
accumulating "scientific knowledge instead of expanding mere geography
had been largely shelved."[3] Despite Greely's later protestations that scientific study had been the expedition's "main" task, his focus from the outset
had been on gaining fame as an explorer and discoverer of new lands.
(In an 1882 letter to his mother, Sergeant David Brainard had explained,
more candidly, that their purpose was "exploration and observation."[4])
The US government had tacitly approved this shift in emphasis, realizing that it needed to sell the Lady Franklin Bay mission to an American public hungry for glorious deeds. Having previously overseen the
stringing of military telegraph lines across the West, Greely had set his
sights on leading an Arctic expedition after listening to a fellow officer
(and his closest friend), William Henry Howgate, describe *his* dream of
colonizing the region around the North Pole, and then devouring all the
books by earlier explorers he could lay his hands on. Captain Howgate
had been in line to command the American contingent during the International Polar Year but had had to abruptly resign his commission after it
became known that he had embezzled several hundred thousand dollars
in government funds. Respected for his steady leadership under trying
circumstances, Greely had then been chosen by President Rutherford B.
Hayes to take Howgate's place, although he was totally lacking in Arctic
experience. Knowledgeable about meteorology and well versed in signal
technology, Greely seized at this opportunity to test these skills in the Far
North. But he also realized that lasting renown went to those who accomplished dramatic "firsts" there.

However, the Greely party was poorly manned to carry out scientific tasks. The newly appointed Secretary of War, Robert Todd Lincoln, who had not the slightest interest in Arctic exploration, had dragged his feet on authorizing the expedition, leaving Greely little time to assemble a qualified team of scientists. In fact, only half of those who joined the expedition had had any scientific training. All of the soldiers were—like Greely and his second-in-command, Second Lieutenant Frederick Kislingbury—totally unfamiliar with polar conditions. This ignorance led them to grossly overestimate what could be accomplished in a place like northern Greenland. The chief scientist and medical officer, Dr. Octave Pavy, a native of New Orleans educated in France, was the sole exception, having already taken part in two Arctic expeditions. He would have sailed on a third—the doomed *Jeannette*—if he had not been disqualified because he was a civilian.[5] Subsequently, Pavy had conducted extensive studies of the weather, as well as animal and plant life, in Greenland. He had also learned the Inuit language and became conversant with their way of life. While Pavy was highly regarded for this field work, what he really wanted to do was sail a ship to the North Pole. As early as 1872 he had proposed such a voyage by way of the Bering Strait. This plan had to be scrapped when his chief financial backer died. But Pavy's territorial ambition persisted and would distract him from doing scientific work on the Lady Franklin Bay Expedition.

The other members of Greely's scientific team were enlisted men, young and inexperienced. After they had built their quarters, Fort Conger, in the summer of 1881, they went about their duties with military precision. Sergeant Hampden S. Gardiner, whose job it was to keep records about the tides and weather, walked out onto the ice every hour to note how high the water beneath was, while being besieged mercilessly by mosquitoes. Another polar neophyte, Gardiner slipped and broke his left leg in late November while attempting to make a tidal reading. He was then laid up for three months. Sergeant Edward Israel—only twenty-three years old when he came to Greenland, having been selected for this assignment while still a student at the University of Michigan—had made a positive impression on Greely because of his meteorological and astronomical know-how, as well as his congenial temperament. He, too, showed great diligence in making hundreds of observations daily, including ten visits to a shed where he had to calculate the tilt of a magnet suspended by a silk thread. But Israel was short and had a "weak physique." After he had staying out in the open air in January—three times a day for sixteen days in a row—with the temperature hovering around minus 50 degrees, to observe the movement of a pendulum so he could gauge the pull of gravity—he developed frostbite in one foot, making further such work exceedingly painful.[6] Another sergeant, Winfield S. Jewell, hailed from New Hampshire, and apparently his chief qualification for conducting Arctic weather observations was the year he had spent in charge of the observatory on the top of Mount Washington. Scientific measurements at Fort Conger were also hampered by Greely's discovery that, because they had been short on funds and in a hurry to depart St. John's, Newfoundland, before winter ice set in, he had brought along many instruments that didn't function well in this subfreezing climate.[7]

While all these data were being carefully recorded during the early fall of 1881, Greely and several others went on sledge trips into the interior, ostensibly to reconnoiter, but also to test how well these heavy conveyances held up in deep snow, and to lay down caches for future excursions.[8] After Greely injured one of his knees, these periodic outings from the fort continued without him. After a winter's hibernation, they were resumed, with Pavy told to see how far north he could go over the frozen Polar Sea. (Greely concealed his eagerness for a "geographical success" by asking the surgeon to also look for signs of the still-missing *Jeannette*.)[9] Meanwhile, his new second-in-command, Lieutenant James Lockwood, was busy exploring the northern Greenland coast with sledges pulled by men and dog teams—a task Greely considered the "most important . . . geographical work of this expedition." In early April, Lockwood took a party of four sledges, laden with two thousand pounds of food and equipment, toward the northeast, to get information "regarding lands within the Arctic Circle." When they ran into a gale with winds up to sixty miles an hour, the party laid low in sleeping bags for two days before moving on. But even stronger winds then battered them—one gust blowing a sledge into one of the soldiers, injuring him badly. Violent storms damaged two other sledges, and they had to be abandoned. The men staggered in their drag ropes but kept going, even though it was now impossible to get any sleep when they stopped: their bags were frozen solid. The gales were relentless. Whenever the men tried to pitch a tent it was almost immediately covered by drifting snow. During one brief lull, Lockwood read aloud to the men a letter from Greely—still unable to make the trek himself—promising them a reward of nine hundred dollars or more if they set a new Farthest North record. Four days later this small party—totally exhausted and crippled by snow blindness—arrived at Cape Bryant, where the channel separating Greenland from Ellesmere Island emptied into the Arctic Sea. There they began looking for a cairn left by British explorers when they had set the highest latitude record: this was the milestone they intended to surpass.

From that spot Lockwood chose Sergeant David Brainard and an Inuit named Frederick Christiansen to accompany him out onto the rough, frozen sea. The men with the other remaining sledge were sent back to Fort Conger. After four days this threesome reached Cape Britannia—a rocky promontory guarded by glaciers—and pushed on ahead toward their ultimate destination, Cape Washington. After a ten-hour haul through heavy snow on May 13, 1882, they came upon a pyramid-shaped island jutting up out of the ice, which they named "Lockwood." After they had made camp at its northern end, Lockwood calculated they had attained the latitude of 83.23.8 degrees north—a new record. The following day, to celebrate this triumph, the two Americans scaled a two-thousand-foot-high cliff near their tent and unfurled a Stars and Stripes on its summit, as Brainard put it, "to the exhilarating northern breezes with an exultation impossible to describe."[10] For the first time in history,

Americans had gotten closer to the pole than any other human beings. It was a tremendous national success. And it was also—Adolphus Greely would feel when he got the news—money well spent.

But it would take a long time for Greely to secure the honor and fame he had so assiduously sought—over half a century, in fact. For years after he and the six other survivors of the Lady Franklin Bay Expedition returned to the States, their reputations would be tainted by reports of murder and cannibalism. These would overshadow the geographical milestone the Americans had achieved—a record that would last thirteen years, until the Norwegians Nansen and Johansen surpassed it by nearly three degrees. Then the Greely party's accomplishment would be further eclipsed by the expeditions of Robert E. Peary, whose claim to have reached the North Pole in 1909 would make him the most celebrated American polar explorer since Elisha Kent Kane. In his later years Greely would soldier on, rising to the top rank of brigadier general in the Signal Corps but never receiving the recognition he felt he deserved. Instead, he published climatological studies and helped create what would become the National Weather Bureau. He became a leading advocate for the international use of the telegraph, and in 1888 was one of the founders of the National Geographic Society. In 1906, Greely coordinated relief operations in San Francisco following the devastating earthquake there. As time passed and memories of the horrors at Cape Sabine faded, he did finally earn some acknowledgement of his Arctic service. As early as 1886 he had been awarded the Founder's Medal of the Royal Geographical Society of London. But it was not until 1922 that the American Geographical Society presented him with its Charles P. Daly Medal, for "valuable or distinguished geographical services or labors"—the first time an American organization had so honored him. Finally, at the very end of his life, on March 27, 1935, on the day Greely turned ninety-one and after embarrassment over the government's long neglect had grown too onerous, a procession of soldiers on horseback, followed by the Secretary of War in a limousine, clattered up to his Georgetown house bringing

Greely the Congressional Medal of Honor for his "life of splendid public service." (At that point he was only the fourth explorer—after Floyd Bennett, Richard Byrd, and Charles Lindbergh—to receive the nation's highest award.) When these words were read to him, Greely's eyes welled with tears, and his hand trembled visibly as he saluted the band outside serenading him with a military march. His long, long wait had finally paid off. The lasting fame he had been denied for so many years was now his.[11]

As Greely had foreseen when he set out for Ellesmere Island, this belated honor was bestowed on him not for any contributions to science, but for his party's Farthest North. The citation did not refer specifically to the Lady Franklin Bay Expedition, perhaps for fear of recalling its infamous events, but the message was clear. Heroes made the nation proud, and nothing did that more emphatically than acts of extraordinary daring and bravery. Coming closer to the North Pole than explorers from any other country was as thrilling back then as what Lindbergh had recently done in crossing the Atlantic alone in the *Spirit of St. Louis*. Even though he had not personally set foot at this high latitude, Greely deserved this medal as the leader who had guided his men that far.

Like so many other nineteenth-century polar explorers, Adolphus Washington Greely had professed he was going to the ends of the earth to add to human knowledge. And like almost all of them, he had lied. His motives were purely selfish: he wanted to become famous, earn lots of money, and be proclaimed a hero. But, in order to have a chance at getting these rewards, he had to first pretend to have "higher" reasons for risking his life and enduring such hardship. Advancing the cause of "science" was what nations in his day had adopted as their rationale for expeditions to the Arctic and Antarctic, and so this was the purpose he and other explorers had to pretend they fully endorsed. If they didn't, they weren't funded. Roald Amundsen would learn this lesson two decades later. After returning from his maiden voyage on the *Belgica* to Antarctica, the twenty-seven-year-old Norwegian sat down to talk with his already-famous countryman, Fridtjof Nansen, in Oslo. Likely as a result of this encounter, Amundsen enlarged his agenda for his next expedition, realizing that it "must have a scientific purpose as well as the purpose of exploration. Otherwise I shall not be taken seriously and would not get backing."[12] He then visited a prominent German explorer and scientist (who was also a colleague of Karl Weyprecht's) and won his crucial support by declaring that locating the North Magnetic Pole was his real objective, not traversing the Northwest Passage.

One can liken this calculated embrace of science to an arranged marriage: it brought financial security by feigning genuine affection. The explorers' true passion was for breaking records and making a name for themselves. But this "mistress"—the bitch-goddess Success—had to be kept out of sight, since society frowned upon would-be heroes who displayed naked and unabashed egotism.[13] So the pursuit of the poles was a kind of fraud—a deception perpetrated by vainglorious men on the millions desirous of transcendent, self-sacrificing deeds, abetted by governments anxious to demonstrate their own superiority on the world stage. In this light, Weyprecht's dream of nations cooperating for mutual benefit seems like the exception that proves the rule: fierce competition in pursuing territorial conquests—much like being first to put a man on the moon—was the order of the day.

Explorers' jaundiced view of science was apparent from the early forays into the Arctic wilderness. Lieutenant George Back of the Royal Navy, Franklin's trusted, artistically talented companion on two land expeditions starting in 1819, had been handed the unenviable assignment of surveying the route northward to the Open Polar Sea—a mission that was both daunting and deadly. As a result of surprisingly cold winter weather and poor supply lines, half of his men died on the way. Each of them was weighted down by roughly eighty pounds of gear and provisions and had to carry these loads up and down steep mountains, around lakes, and across rivers. Often Back's party had to make time-consuming detours in order to map a curving coastline, at a time when their food was fast disappearing. Back's journal of this "unfortunate voyage" contained some caustic verses on the surveying job they were supposed to carry out at such a human cost:

Th' inhospitable regions are explored around—
and large tracts added to Science's name—
Unfortunately there—no sustenance is found
To crown our prospects and future fame—[14]

Even a trained naturalist like Elisha Kane, whose books glamorized his dramatic adventures purportedly in the name of science, made use of his treks in northern Canada and Greenland to look for desirable routes to the Open Polar Sea.[15] Being media-savvy and keenly aware of the need to give his readers the hero they wanted, he was careful to couch his real intentions as an ennobling quest.[16] When Kane departed for the Arctic on the *Advance* in June of 1853, he stressed that this voyage was being undertaken "for the double purpose of scientific discovery, and to learn of the fate of Sir John Franklin."[17] Kane was hardly the first or only explorer to use the missing and much-lamented English navigator as an excuse for investigating new territory. But his duplicity was craftier: the fact that Kane fell in love with a younger woman, Maggie Fox—who had convinced many people that she and her sisters were spiritual mediums capable of contacting the dead through séances—says a lot about his own character.[18] Possessing distinguished medical credentials made it plausible for him to claim that scientific curiosity was motivating his expeditions. Kane adroitly marketed himself as a hero of science through his vivid, dramatic writings and spellbinding public appearances.[19] On occasion, Kane would let his guard down and admit that the "agony" of taking outdoor measurements in midwinter seemed pointless. He had his men continue these tasks mostly to relieve their boredom and feelings of depression. Personally, Kane had no patience for this tedious, taxing work. He once described his observing the movement of a magnetometer at twenty below zero with evident sarcasm. Someday, he wrote, a "grateful nation" will doubtless appreciate the 480 weekly recordings made under these frightful conditions and "will never think of asking, '*Cui bono* all this?'"[20]

The turning of polar explorers into larger-than-life figures bearing the collectives hopes and dreams of their people toward the poles and bringing back knowledge that would make the world a better place had started—posthumously—with Sir John Franklin. Decades after he had disappeared into the Arctic, the "portly and sedentary" Englishman was remembered as a person who was "filled with that spirit which is even more national than the love of adventure, more English even than the passion for the 'great waters'—the thirst for the discovery of the unknown."[21] The American explorer Hall echoed these sentiment when he applauded Franklin as a "martyr to science," thus misconstruing what had actually been a quest to complete the Northwest Passage.[22] As was noted earlier, Hall himself was largely ignorant of scientific matters, and this deficiency proved problematic when he sought funds from Congress for his 1871 polar expedition. The lawmakers insisted on his having a scientific raison d'etre: in the post-Civil-War era, explorers had to be more than "frontiersmen."[23] In the end, he only got $50 thousand for his voyage by promising that he would bring along a scientific team—a condition that bothered him a great deal, since their presence might divert from his real goal, which was to stand on "that spot of this great and glorious orb of God's creation where there is no North, no East, no West . . . [on] the crowning jewel of the Arctic dome."[24] Hall also (rightly) concerned about dissension arising between him and these scientists.

Even Hall's competitor for funding, Isaac Hayes—like Kane a medical doctor—seems to have taken on a research mission only to satisfy his backers. After his first trip to the Arctic, accompanying Kane in 1855, Hayes had made clear his intention to trek as far north as possible the next time. However, after failing to attract money to search for the Open Polar Sea because many prospective donors regarded his proposal as too dangerous, Hayes then recast it, giving it a scientific purpose, and quickly won support from the recently established Smithsonian Institution and the

American Philosophical Society.[25] So when he sailed out of Boston Harbor on the deck of the schooner *United States*, in July 1860, he could boast of his voyage as being "purely a scientific one." But, in fact, Hayes spent most of his time searching for a passage to the Open Polar Sea and achieving a new Farthest North. (When temperatures plummeted that winter, Hayes was forced to face the fact that a polar sea free of ice was illogical. He felt "defeated," his hopes of becoming another "scientist hero" like Kane dashed, his chance for lasting fame gone.) Instead of immersing himself in scholarly articles about the Arctic at night in his cabin, he dipped into Marco Polo's tale of traveling along the Silk Road. Adding to Hayes's disappointment, his claim to having reached the latitude of 82.30 degrees north was later disproven: Hayes had overestimated how far he had gotten by 140 miles and made other untrue statements, including that he had come within sight of the ocean. But these reversals did not stop him from entitling his 1867 book on this expedition *The Open Polar Sea*.[26]

Pretending to put science first was common practice in the nineteenth century—another instance of the Victorian tendency to cover over what one really desired by what was socially acceptable. Even some Scandinavians evinced this predilection. Borchgrevink, who had constructed an image of himself as the only "real" scientist interested in exploring Antarctica, showed his true colors by his lack of skill in handling specimens and using scientific instruments properly. While stopping in Madeira on the way south he had riled the scientists on board by complaining that they were spending too much time doing research, and then, in Antarctica, he had insisted that the geologist Louis Bernacchi stop taking magnetic readings so that he could take a photograph of a seal instead.[27] Nansen, the dean of Norwegian polar explorers, was also wont to speak about his devotion to science, although with some equivocation. He had once affirmed that scientific study ought to be the "sole object of all explorations," while admitting that many explorers—himself included—were driven by an obsession with the "Holy Grail" of reaching the pole first. Once that had been accomplished, then doing "pure" science could come paramount.[28] In his youth, the Norwegian had been torn between doing what he had been trained to do as a PhD student in Oslo (then called "Christiana")—namely, devote his life to learning more about the nervous system of simple marine life forms—and satisfying his hunger for adventure, discovery, and fame. This conflict came to a head after the *Fram* had been drifting slowly for months, and the "coldly professional" Nansen secretly made up his mind to leave the ship and the rest of its crew behind to strike out overland for the pole with just one other man, Hjalmar Johansen.[29] Up until that point Nansen had waffled like Hamlet, at one point seemingly resigned to giving up his dream when the *Fram* kept pointing south. On New Year's Day in 1904, he wrote, "Perhaps the gain to science will be as great, and, after all, I suppose this desire to reach the North Pole is only a piece of vanity." As if needing to convince himself, he added that vanity was merely "a child's disease, got over long ago."[30]

But just two weeks later Nansen changed his mind: "It [a polar dash] might almost be called an easy expedition for two men," he would recall in his aptly named 1897 book *Farthest North*—a plan that he had actually been weighing for months. As he added, in a moment of awkward psychological justification: "Is the soul of man nothing but a succession of moods and feelings, shifting as incalculably as the changing winds?"[31] So on to the Pole it would be, with the prospect of achieving an historic "first" ending all his prevarication and high-minded pretense about the vital importance of science.[32] Science could now wait. For descendants of adventuresome Norsemen like Nansen and Amundsen, this was an inescapable choice. The Far North was their birthright—and where destiny beckoned them. No matter how "rational" they might sound about their motives and plans, in the crunch being the first to stand at the top of the world was what they dreamed about before falling asleep and the first thing they thought about when they woke up.

If an emphasis on scientific research can be gauged by how frequently expedition findings were put to practical use, then it was the British, and not the Scandinavians, who paid the least heed. English polar parties seemed almost constitutionally incapable of changing their methods in light of what their predecessors had learned. To some degree, this clinging to old ways spoke to their steadfast belief that mind was superior to matter: British sailors and their officers possessed sufficient character, wisdom, and time-tested tradition to deal with whatever obstacles they happen upon while crossing the polar ice. In their role of explorers, they would change the world, not let the world change them. For example, nearly a century after James Cook and his men espied the continent of Antarctica for the first time, in 1774, British naval crews were still wearing virtually the same uniforms—blue woolen jackets and flannel pants. Even the likelihood that many in the Franklin party had frozen to death did not persuade the Admiralty to switch to the fur-lined parkas favored by local Inuit.

When Captain Francis Leopold McClintock accepted Lady Franklin's invitation to head an expedition to find "relics" of her presumed dead husband in 1857, he went to great lengths to refit the yacht *Fox* for Arctic service, but he took no steps to provide his men with clothing and provisions more suited to the Far North than those his missing predecessor had taken along. Winter coats and other garments were, instead, selected from "an ample supply ... which had remained in store from former expeditions." The food staple McClintock had procured for the *Fox*— some 6,682 pounds of pemmican—was essentially the same as what the Royal Navy had been requisitioning from the same vendor for the past dozen years.[33] However, McClintock and his men did show some innovative thought in putting out nets to catch seals and whales. They also shot and killed bears. After the *Fox* became stuck on an ice floe in mid-November and the crew settled into their winter quarters, the lieutenant had them experiment (successfully) with hauling sledges over the ice—an exhausting, back-breaking practice that would subsequently remain *de rigueur* for the British Navy up until Scott's day.[34] It was left to Norwegian and some American polar explorers to study Inuit ways and adopt their dress, diet, shelters, and means of transportation so that they would have a better chance of surviving in this brutal environment. Tradition-minded commanders like McClintock did conduct scientific experiments: the observant leader of the *Fox* expedition would go so far as to measure the smile of an Inuit man he had met in Greenland. McClintock also tested the level of ozone in the Arctic atmosphere and learned to use instruments purchased by the Royal Society to help him locate the North Magnetic Pole. But such pursuits were subordinate to his primary objective—to find any signs of the vanished Franklin party and learn what had happened to them. Yet, as much as scientific curiosity and investigation were part of his nature, McClintock was also compelled to penetrate the northern mists by ambitions that had little to do with better understanding the natural world. Charles Darwin he was not.

While they made a point of publicly emphasizing their commitment to science, in private polar explorers were often disparaging or dismissive of what they considered unnecessary "distractions." The British, the Americans, and the Scandinavians were equally culpable of this hypocrisy. In seeking funds for his Arctic expedition between 1907 and 1909, Roald Amundsen shrewdly tailored his appeals to the Royal Geographical Society and the Norwegian government so that they stressed his planned magnetic and anthropological research and made no mention of his intention to get to the North Pole first. Around the same time, Ernest Shackleton made known his interest in reaching the South Magnetic Pole—a major objective of British Antarctic science since the 1830s. But Shackleton brought only two scientists on the *Nimrod* and declined to take Mawson along as a geologist, worried that the Australian's interest in exploring the Antarctic coast would only take away resources Shackleton needed for his planned dash to the pole.[35] It was only after he had failed to reach this goal in 1907 that the Irish explorer pursued the magnetic pole with anything approaching ardor: he had decided to garner whatever acclaim that might come with achieving this "first." When Shackleton had sailed south with Scott a few years before, on the *Discovery*, both men found the scientific observations they were supposed to make en route a waste of precious time, as they were anxious get to Antarctic before the winter season set in. Shackleton vented his disdain for these tasks in these mocking verses inserted in the ship's journal:

> To be aroused from slumber from the deadest of the night,
> To take an observation, gives us all a morbid blight,
> How in the name of all that's blank, can temperatures down here,
> Concern these scientific men at home from year to year?
> To us alone they matter, for it's cold enough, Alas!
> To freeze the tail and fingers off of a monkey made of brass.[36]

Shackleton's candor here contrasts sharply with his deception when he insisted to Scott, in a February 21, 1910, letter that his proposed Antarctic expedition was going to be "purely scientific."[37] Not all polar explorers may have been so disingenuous, but the ones in charge usually were. And often there were good reasons for being so. Planning, organizing, promoting, and financing an expedition to the top or bottom of the world was a complex logistical—and political—process, which required leaders to pull off a tricky balancing act between their personal aspirations and their scientific and governmental sponsors' interest in getting a good return on their investment.[38] At times, this inherent conflict forced explorers like Greely, Amundsen, Nansen, Shackleton, and Scott to make compromises that undermined their effectiveness. The most prominent example of this was Scott's agreeing to let Wilson, Bowers, and Cherry-Garrard set out for Cape Crozier when he really needed them in top shape for the grueling trek to the South Pole and back that lay just a few months ahead.[39] Scott could not bring himself to veto this excursion, for several reasons.

First of all, he felt obligated to carry out scientific tasks with which he had been entrusted. For a navy officer, orders were, after all, orders. (Members of his party had already made two geological outings in 1911, to survey glaciers to the west of their base camp and bring back mineral samples.) Scott may have regarded these side trips as a means of alleviating the interminable boredom of an Antarctic winter and therefore worthwhile. (Most of his men did not think very highly of science *per se*. According to one historian, "The philosophy of the tenement dwellers [in the hut] was 'Down with Science, Sentiment and the Fair Sex.'"[40]) Secondly, he did not have the heart to turn Wilson down: he respected him too much. He envied Wilson's innocence, passion, and focus in carrying out tasks that mattered so much to him, without having to deal with competing demands as he did. Furthermore, Scott admired the selfless dedication of men like "Uncle Bill," who meticulously applied the scientific method to solve practical problems and took a "keen avocational interest" in their work.[41] Unlike Wilson, he considered research to be an important, if secondary, aspect of his mission.[42] Lastly, Scott may have seen in Wilson's seemingly absurd quest to bring back penguin eggs from Cape Crozier parallels with his own romantic impulse to "go for broke" in order to beat Amundsen to the pole.

Devastated by finding the Norwegians' tent at the South Pole, Scott quickly shifted gears and made science his new top priority, with hopes of salvaging some small triumph on the way back after this crushing defeat. Taking time to gather rocks containing fossils millions of years old and haul them back to Cape Evans was his way of giving his companions a goal they *could* accomplish. The fossils' scientific value was not the issue: he wanted to show his men were not defeated and could still muster the courage and forbearance that a watching world had expected of them.[43] When the news of the deaths of Scott, Bowers, and Wilson reached England, newspapers there were quick to grasp this saving grace. An editorial in the *Times* published after their memorial service praised Scott and his men for gallantly withstanding the "remorseless forces of Nature, clinging in ever increasing peril and weakness to the scientific records and geological specimens that it was the primary object of their expedition to secure. It is thus that they snatched victory out of the jaws of defeat." Through the explorers' sacrifice for this higher cause, the English people had regained their "emotional birthright" and could offer up a "song of thankfulness" to these lost men, who had demonstrated that "the unconquerable will can carry them through, loyal to the last to the charge they have undertaken."[44]

This glorifying of science following the Scott tragedy was an ironic twist in the longstanding clash between territorial and scientific reasons for exploring the Arctic and Antarctic. Science carried the day, but only by default. The reality, that these two missions had so often been at loggerheads, was quietly overlooked. But it was still true that trying to accomplish two conflicting objectives at the same time could be highly problematic. For many of the men who served on these expeditions, similar tension between their leaders' declared (scientific) purpose and concealed (territorial) ambitions could be equally debilitating. They could easily lose confidence in commanders who were not forthright with them or who needlessly endangered their lives. Any perceived breach of trust could destroy morale. For instance, when Nansen declared his intention to quit the *Fram* and strike out for the North Pole, his crew was shocked because he had always treated them as equals and openly discussed his plans. Now they could see that there were two sides to his personality: Nansen could be either withdrawn or gregarious. And they weren't sure what kind of man he really was. Officers noted in their diaries how glad they were to be getting rid of such an unpredictable, mercurial leader. Many men on board resented his self-serving abandonment.[45]

Elisha Kane evoked the same hostile reaction when he arbitrarily reversed his position and decided he was not going to turn his ship around and head south—as he had promised his homesick men he would—when ice was building up around the *Advance* in late August of 1853. Instead they would stay where they were for the winter so that he would be in a better position to launch a sledge excursion toward the pole when spring arrived. A chronically malcontented William Godfrey might not be the most reliable source, but his observation that "chance or Providence seldom favors those who expose themselves to unnecessary hazards for unattainable objects" expresses his disdain for a commander who had put his ambitiousness ahead of the well-being of his men.[46] Likewise, when

Adrien de Gerlache deliberately steered the *Belgica* further south into the Antarctic pack in February 1898, without first telling his crew that he had intended all along to winter in the ice so that he could set a new Farthest South record, his men gave in to "melancholy and depression," and some of them temporarily lost their reason. To give them something to do, de Gerlache promptly ordered that hourly weather observations be carried out, and that hundreds of marine creatures and plants be collected.[47] But these tasks were only busy work, and the men knew that. Afterward, de Gerlache would try to justify his decision to spend the winter locked in the ice as stemming from an irresistible impulse to "wrest a few of its jealously guarded secrets from the pristine Antarctic" and praised his voyage's scientific achievements as an inspiration to the Belgian people. These statements didn't fool anyone.[48]

Although some deception may have been necessary to recruit crews for long and dangerous voyages to the Far North or Far South, such dishonesty would invariably emerge and weaken a leader's standing. Men who signed up under one set of assumptions and then found out they had been misled could be forgiven for feeling betrayed. They had been tricked into risking their lives for another man's glory, and now there was no turning back.

CHAPTER NINE

NO MAN IS AN ISLAND

There is no way of telling if Richard Evelyn Byrd entitled his book about the five lonely winter months he had spent in a prefabricated hut near Antarctica's Ross Ice Barrier in 1934 *Alone* as a sly, veiled reference to Charles Lindbergh's better known *We*, which chronicled the aviator's historic solo flight across the Atlantic. If he did, this would have been Byrd's subtle way of linking his extraordinary feat to what the world's most famous and admired man had accomplished seven years earlier. A highly experienced naval aviator, Byrd had competed against Lindbergh in the race to become the first to reach Paris by air, but while landing after a test flight his plane had flipped over, injuring Byrd and his copilot Floyd Bennett and taking them temporarily out of the running. Byrd could thus only glance up as Lindbergh's *Spirit of St. Louis* soared into the early morning sky over Long Island's Roosevelt Field. (With Bennett and another companion, he would make his own successful transatlantic flight just over a month later, ditching his plane in the ocean near the Normandy coast.) Lindbergh had chosen the plural pronoun to pay tribute to his plane. Man and machine—melded together like horse and rider—had pulled this off. The factory workers who had built it had etched the words "We are all with you" on the propeller spinner, so the young, shy hero was implicitly giving them credit, too. But Lindbergh didn't really believe in "we." At heart he was a loner. Flying was a way for him to get away from everyone else. In a much later book of his, *The Spirit of St. Louis*, the aviator would recall, "What advantages there are in flying alone! . . . By flying alone I've gained in range, in time, in flexibility; and above all, I've gained in freedom. I haven't had to keep a crew member acquainted with my plans. My movements weren't restricted by someone else's temperament, health, or knowledge. My decisions aren't weighted by responsibility for another's life."[1] Indeed, "Lucky Lindy" had been all alone during his harrowing flight, but it had lasted only thirty-three-and-a-half hours, whereas Byrd had been by himself at the bottom of the world, with the next closest person 123 miles away, for nearly half a year. Few have ever experienced such isolation—and loneliness—before or since. In the modern era, the most well-known instance was that of the shipwrecked Scottish sailor Alexander Selkirk, who had survived for four years on an uninhabited island in the Pacific, becoming the putative model for Daniel Defoe's Robinson Crusoe. But for sheer length of solitude, few have surpassed the Native American woman Juana Maria, who lived without any human company on one of the Channel Islands off the coast of California for eighteen years before being rescued.

The thought of being so completely cut off from companionship triggers a primal anxiety. Humans are social creatures, and prolonged aloneness can be the most depressing fate one can suffer, as prisoners in solitary confinement can well attest. So it seemed, in particular, during the Age of Discovery, when adventure-seeking Europeans and Americans found themselves utterly alone in an untrodden wilderness, or washed up on a tropical island, with no one else anywhere near. Over time, the fictional Crusoe came to feel that he was "as one whom Heaven thought not worthy to be number'd among the living, or to appear among the rest of His creatures."[2] Life without fellowship was a kind of death, and the only way Crusoe could escape from this existential funk and truly be alive again was to find a companion, as he eventually did in Friday. To *choose* to be all alone, even for a short while, struck most of Defoe's contemporaries as inviting madness. And yet, as nineteenth-century explorers ventured further into the unknown, they inevitably became isolated from civilization—if not completely by themselves, then in small groups. For those daring to enter the remote and uninhabited polar regions, these journeys involved experiencing profound loneliness. Staying there for long was courting not only great physical peril, but also psychological trauma.

Byrd later claimed his solitary sojourn in the Antarctic interior had been the unintended consequence of a spur-of-the-moment change of plans: the plane bringing him from Little America had been delayed in taking off so there hadn't enough time left, with winter coming on fast, for it to go back and pick up enough supplies for three men. So he impulsively opted to remain at "Advance Base" by himself, angering his wife, who was dismayed by his cable abruptly announcing this decision. But it is hard to not to conclude that Byrd had intended this all along: a career naval officer, he was not used to taking spontaneous actions. Indeed, he admitted in *Alone* that choosing to live by himself in the one-room shack was not a "reckless whim."[3] A proud and strong-willed descendant of one of Virginia's first families, he had never shied away from daunting challenges, in the air or on the ice. At this point in his life, at the age of forty six, having been named the youngest admiral in US Navy history some five years before, Byrd may have wanted to tackle one more physical challenge before he became too old for such grueling tests. Fed up—like Lindbergh—with the constant "hullabaloo" of modern life, the highly decorated Byrd likely thought of Advance Base as a welcome retreat— much as medieval monks had withdrawn into caves to enjoy a state of pure repose and contemplation. Byrd, too, was undisturbed by external obligations—his only link to the outside world being three radio calls each week.

There so sequestered, he could be true to his own self, be his own master, allow his mind to roam freely and widely by reading and listening to phonograph records, subject to "no man's laws but my own"—even if physically he was completely captive, with no relief party expected for at least half a year. If something went wrong down there, there would be no possibility of rescue. Byrd was totally self-reliant—a modern-day Crusoe. His world was what he would create. He professed to have no worries about that. He could cope. His only regret was not having a cookbook.

Like others who had been drawn to this frigid frontier, he saw his retreat as returning him to a nobler age, when more elemental virtues had prevailed. Its mantra echoed Polonius's advice about being true to one's self. But Byrd's so secluding himself was also an act of colossal egoism: by following his own dictates he was thumbing his nose at those who cared for him most—notably, his wife of nearly twenty years and their four children. In his life he cast a shadow so long that none of them could ever escape it. (His only son, also Richard E., was so burdened by his father's fame that he ended his days as an alcoholic derelict, dying alone in an abandoned Baltimore warehouse at the age of sixty-eight.) The admiral made up his mind to stay there alone without telling any of his friends either, knowing they would try to stop him.

Still, for a man who had spent most of his life in the air and in the glare of publicity, it was a peculiar choice. Temperamentally, he was certainly not another "Lone Eagle"—quite the opposite, in fact. Whereas Lindbergh had sought seclusion (again) after he had become world famous in 1927, Byrd had never shied away from the limelight. He had sought out rich men to bankroll his explorations and courted the media to ensure they would be well publicized. He had cultivated a public persona as America's "lone adventurer and last explorer" as assiduously as Lindbergh guarded his privacy.[4] During his previous trip to Antarctica he had brought more men with him than any other explorer of his day. He seemed to enjoy such a large entourage. So why did he choose to go alone this time? Was it some kind of self-imposed punishment? Was he simply tired of his fame and wanted a break from the adulation? Or, conversely, was this act of "foolish, glory-seeking indulgence"—as one biographer has surmised—merely a "stunt," an aging explorer's last shot at stealing the spotlight?[5] Byrd publicly justified staying through the winter so he could carry out meteorological observations impossible to make during other seasons—and thus learn more about Antarctic weather. But in his memoir, he was blunt about his reasons: "I really wanted to go for the experience's sake."[6] Here was another compulsively driven man who cloaked his naked ambitions in scientific garb. By midwinter Byrd had dropped this research pretense, wondering if the weather-related figures were even worth the rolls of paper he had used to record them.

Isolation unhinged him. For long hours he lay in his cot, crying, facing the blank wall.[7] Only a month into his stay, Byrd wrote that he now fully understood the "brain-crackling loneliness of solitary confinement."[8] (According to one source, the explorer had brought a dozen straitjackets and two coffins on the plane to Advance Base.[9]) The uninterrupted silence around him was like that of the grave: there was no way out of it. Two times each day he would slip out through a trapdoor to take weather readings—and maintain a semblance of purpose by keeping up this routine. His existence was devoid of any human contact, except the intermittent radio calls, and during those sessions he hid his growing depression, out of vanity, perhaps: why should he let them know? Like many polar explorers before him, Byrd had to accept that he had orchestrated his own predicament, but failed to anticipate all of its aspects. He could not tear down this prison; he was not God. His shack resembled a dilapidated railroad refrigerator car. Out of fear of being buried alive in it, Byrd left the trap door open all the time, and so temperatures inside ranged from ten to forty degrees below zero. Once in deep snow he nearly lost his way back to the hut, and for months he inadvertently poisoned himself with carbon monoxide fumes that were seeping out of his stove. This and other mishaps strained his mental state, and when the generator conked out in early July, preventing him from sending messages to the outside world, he came to the "brink of death and madness."[10] Finally, Byrd broke down and conceded defeat: on the phone he practically begged for someone to come as soon as possible. The snow tractors that lumbered over the drifts in August of 1934 to reach his hut found inside, amid the frozen vomit, the discarded tin cans, and the odiferous squalor, a broken, sick, old man—not the same person who had brusquely waved them off five months before. And he would never really be that person again.

Isolation in the Arctic and Antarctic crushed the spirit as well as the body. There, hell was the absence of other people. Sensing this, few men dared to enter these cold, indifferent domains without companionship. Otherwise it was a death sentence. The words "all alone" sent a chill down their spines—caused more anxiety than an approaching polar bear. Facing an unyielding Nature, human company was the only compensation. This was really why Byrd came with so many men on his other expeditions, making sure these comrades were "kept warm and enthusiastic and in absolutely united fellowship by this principle of always thinking of the other man first and with constantly increasing personal devotion to their leaders."[11] This was the wisdom Ernest Shackleton had practiced with singular adroitness, conveying consistently by his actions that he was always prepared to suffer more than his men, thereby making them always willing to die for him— and for each other. *In extremis* explorers cared for their fellows as lovingly as their mothers had cared for them when they were little boys. The need for companionship was that intimate, and that great, for they were helpless without it. But who would look after a man on his own? This was the question none dared to raise, and none dared to find out.

Up until Byrd's sojourn at Advance Base, being alone near the poles was not a realistic option. For one thing, prior to the advent of airplanes, it was impossible to get to a location in the Arctic or Antarctic where there were no other humans close by: one simply couldn't travel that far into the interior without help. To set out on one's own would be as suicidal as Lawrence ("No Surrender") Oates's stepping outside his tent in the dark when he wanted the others to go ahead without him. In the history of polar exploration up to the twentieth century almost no one ever willingly entered this frozen wilderness by himself or chose to remain there alone. Aside from Byrd, only the English explorer Augustine Courtauld voluntarily agreed in 1930 to submit to solitary duty, also to carry out weather-related readings. The twenty-six-year-old stockbroker and yachtsman had lived in an igloo deep in Greenland, 112 miles from his base, for five months. His food was almost exhausted when he was rescued. Near the midpoint in his stay Courtauld confided in his diary, "If I ever get back to the Base nothing will induce me to go on the Ice Cap again."[12] (In our day the British army officer Henry Worsley astonished the world by nearly completing a one-man trek across the Antarctic continent, only stopped by fatigue—not apparently by loneliness—from completing the last thirty miles of his journey. But like Byrd, he had a phone link to the outside world.)

Prior to Byrd's stay at Advance Base, one of the few explorers who had experienced such devastating solitude was Frederick Cook, left alone on Smith Sound (between Greenland and Canada's northernmost island) when his companion, Rudolph Franke, departed to lay down a cache for their spring trek in January 1908. Writing in his diary, the man who had already spent a winter icebound in Antarctica lamented, "If a man were to select a place to frustrate evildoers artificially he could find no more appropriate place than to place an individual isolated in this land of torment with its cold wind to be feared [more] than the fire of hell and its darkness more degenerating than the influence of the devil."[13] But Cook's loneliness had lasted only four days. The closest to Byrd's in terms of length was when the explorer Knud Rasmussen, son of a Danish missionary and an Inuit-Danish mother, had crossed northern Canada in sixteen months by dog sled—a journey of some twenty thousand miles, making it the longest ever of its kind—in the early 1920s.[14] But Rasmussen had been accompanied by two Inuit hunters.

If it ever happened that a man ended up totally alone—say, as the sole survivor of an ill-fated expedition—his fate was sealed. In more recent history, there was only one notable exception to this rule—the Anglo-Australian explorer and geologist Douglas Mawson. In November 1912, Mawson began a journey with two companions—Xavier Mertz and Belgrave Ninnis—to map King George V Land, near the eastern coast of Antarctica. During the course of this eight-week trek, Mawson avoided physical injury but had to ward off loneliness and despair after Ninnis vanished down a crevasse and Mertz died of malnutrition (and distress over having to eat his beloved dogs).[15] Up until the moment when Mertz slipped into unconsciousness, the two surviving men had clung to each other as to life rafts in a turbulent sea. Still grieving over the sudden death of Ninnis, for whom he had developed a deep, motherly affection, Mertz had recorded in his diary, "Mawson and I have a long way to go, and we must stick together and be good comrades to reach winter quarters."[16] But that was not to be. After having nursed Mertz—undressing him after he had fouled his trousers and trying vainly to feed him some broth and hot chocolate—Mawson could only watch helplessly as his companion died in the early morning hours and then, the next evening, drag his frozen body outside, covering it with blocks of snow and a cross made of sledge runners. With his base camp some one hundred miles away, his hopes for getting there were fading fast: "I am afraid it [staying put while Mertz was dying] has cooked my chances altogether," he intimated, with a hint of recrimination, in his diary.[17] Their ship, the *Aurora*, was due to leave Cape Denison for Australia in a month, and, sitting alone in the wind-ripped tent, Mawson could not conceive of making it back by then. He had self-lessly stayed with his friend to the bitter end, but now that decision was going to cost him his own life.

By a series of miracles, Mawson did make it back. He survived falling into an abyss and dangling by a rope over a fourteen-foot deep crevasse. He traveled one hundred miles overland, his body literally falling apart at each step—the soles of his feet peeling off like strips of bacon—and his food running out. It was an amazing story of solo survival. Oddly, his account of this extraordinary trip back is dry and matter-of-fact—possibly because Mawson could not bring himself to recall his emotions at that time, or because he simply did not want to reveal them in print, or because he hadn't experienced the feelings that most people would have under such circumstances. Ever more strangely, he makes no mention of his dead companions or of his own state of mind. Apparently it was not in Mawson's nature to bare his soul. Mertz and others had commented on his aloofness, and this quality seems to have stuck to him even in the most trying of situations. It may have done him some good. In any event, Mawson's story of that long, lonely trip back leaves much to the imagination, inviting some to speculate that he was covering something up, or had something to be ashamed of. But we will never know. His survival has to speak for itself. And yet it doesn't tell us what we really want to know. So we are left to scour Richard Byrd's *Alone* for some inkling of what the exquisite torture of polar isolation felt like. Alas, it, too, leaves much out.

To avoid ending up alone, expedition leaders had to pick men who would hold up under the extreme conditions at the top and bottom of the world. They had to look for candidates with the range of traits needed to stay alive there. Not just any strapping young sailor or soldier would do. Physical stamina was only important up to a point. Above and beyond it were qualities that were hard to define. One had to go on intuition—by sizing up a man's inner fiber. For, in the end, survival depended on human chemistry. On the ice, a band of explorers had to function like a closely knit family, highly attuned to the needs of all its members and yet willing to put them aside, if need be, for the good of all. In their capacity for selfless attentiveness and interdependence, polar expeditions resembled small military units under war. To cite one example of this behavior, when one of George Back's men arrived from another Canadian outpost during the exceptionally cold winter of 1820–1821, the seamen who welcomed this near-frozen messenger "spent time rubbing warmth into him, giving him change of clothes and some warm soup... [and] nursed him with the greatest kindness, and the desire of restoring him to health seemed to absorb all regard for their own situation."[18]

If the leader made a bad choice and brought along someone who did not subscribe to this philosophy, if the bonding did not take place, the results could be as catastrophic as finding one's self all alone. In the Arctic and Antarctic, no man could be an island. All had to hang together, or die. The closeness forced upon expedition members went further than the quasi-homoerotic bonding during combat because, at the poles, there was no raging battle (only the occasional polar bear) to divert their attention. They lived like Siamese twins, aware that any moment one of them might do or say something that could grievously wound another or drive him mad. To keep from each other's throats under such sustained stress, they all had to speak softly and tread lightly.

The lesson that abrasive personalities could destroy esprit was not overlooked by latter-day explorers like Byrd, whose original plan for wintering on the Ross Ice Barrier with *two* other men had been based on keen psychological insight: whereas a pair would soon tire of "hearing one voice everlastingly and seeing one face and being confronted with one set of habits and idiosyncrasies," the presence of a third would mitigate against this inevitable antagonism.[19] In Byrd's view, leadership was all about creating cohesion and compatibility. When the then-navy captain made public that he was embarking on his first expedition to Antarctica in 1928, he received some twenty thousand applications from eager young men—much as legions of able-bodied Englishmen had besieged Ernest Shackleton with letters fourteen years before, after the much admired Irishman had announced his intention to cross the same continent.[20] Thanks to his experiences as a naval officer and pilot, Byrd had a good idea of the attributes he was looking for. First of all, his men had to be able to cope with fear and danger over a long period of time. In addition, he wanted young men who possessed imagination and flexibility. Preferably, they should be of medium height (since big men ate more and their bodies did not hold up as well in cold climates).

Loyalty was also important. Team members had to have temperaments that fit in and thus diminished the friction resulting from living in close quarters. They further needed a "crusading spirit" and had to be free of personal vices, such as a fondness for drink.[21] Beyond that, Byrd didn't really care much what his team members looked like or where they came from. (Early in the organizing stage, he had toyed with including several Inuit men from Greenland.) Those externals were inconsequential.[22] But evaluating candidates for polar service was a tricky business, since few of them had ever been to that part of the world before. Byrd had to count on his hunches. He ended up selecting forty-two men to go with him on this trip. Unfortunately, they didn't all live up to his expectations: many were insubordinate and got drunk (as did their commander), and an insecure Byrd had to worry about a mutiny breaking out. But he may have been his own worst problem: his need to puff up his own image made him too controlling, and some of the men came to regard him as constitutionally dishonest—lying about having flown over the North Pole, for instance.[23] Stuck indoors for the long winter, many lapsed into depression or sullenness, and Byrd's therapy of "medicinal" alcohol didn't do much to alleviate this. Little in the admiral's past had prepared him for the peculiar challenges of handling men in such a static, claustrophobic environment, and his leadership deficiencies soon became obvious for all to see. Many of Byrd's men ended up ruing their decisions to accompany him to Antarctica.

The "Little America" expedition of 1928–30 was not the first, nor the last, to be riven by personality clashes—fueled by constant proximity, boredom, and physical discomfort. Keeping a party reasonably harmonious and in good spirits under these conditions was as daunting a task as steering around hidden crevasses, and only a handful of expedition heads had the ability to do both well. Most leaders sought to build a compatible team by picking men like themselves—men they could relate to. Career officers like John Franklin, George De Long, Adolphus Greely, and Robert Scott felt most comfortable with soldiers and sailors accustomed to discipline and standard procedures, men who would follow orders, no matter what.[24] For these commanders, the "military mind" was also the sign of a dependable, predictable character. In the pressure-cooker polar environment, personal traits such as stoic perseverance, pluck, and cheerfulness could be more important than physical strength because psychological resilience was essential. Some commanders were influenced by racial bias: De Long, for one, rejected "point blank" French, Italian, and Spanish candidates for his *Jeannette* voyage, and tried to avoid English, Irish, and Scottish ones if at all possible. Next to Americans, he preferred

Scandinavians.[25] Experience in the Arctic or Antarctic also counted for a great deal, especially when it came to choosing the civilian scientists, but qualified persons with this background were scarce.

With the right group of men, with shared values and backgrounds, an expedition could set sail with bonds already established. Later on, stuck in the ice for a year or more, officers and men could still feel connected— "at home" with one another. This reassuring connection could help offset the strangeness and perils of their situation. This was certainly the hope, at least. To achieve this effect, naval commanders from the days of Cook, Parry, Ross, and Franklin onward tried as much as possible to recreate on board the conditions under which their crews normally lived. Carrying on this way also enhanced morale. Maintaining routines created the illusion that life was continuing normally and tended to make the crew feel positive about their missions.

But on military expeditions, strict adherence to hierarchy was obligatory, and this need divided crews into two camps—officers and men. This was, of course, accepted tradition. Below decks, officers had separate quarters from the sailors and soldiers, and the two groups had different amenities, diets, and off-duty pastimes. For example, on his ships *Erebus* and *Terror*, Franklin and his fellow officers enjoyed fresh eggs for breakfast and dined on beef tongue, as befitted their higher social (and military) status. The ordinary sailors ate well, but not as sumptuously. Officers and men did not socialize, except on special occasions, and they generally pursued their leisure activities in separate spaces like a proper Victorian couple. (They did come together now and then to compete in games on the snow, like soccer, when they were icebound.)

Other suspensions of this shipboard segregation occurred on holidays such as Christmas and New Year's, when ordinary sailors were permitted to enter the officers' quarters to extend their good wishes (but not to stay for dinner), or when theatrical skits or other frivolous entertainments were staged. But even though the responsibilities for these were allocated according to rank, the ship's company could strengthen their camaraderie during such special occasions. For example, when *Erebus* and *Terror* were under the command of Sir James Clark Ross in 1840 and became trapped in the ice together in the Antarctic pack around Christmas, the officers and men on both ships joined forces to stage an elaborate masquerade. The sailors constructed a mock tavern, while the twenty-two-year-old surgeon and naturalist Joseph Dalton Hooker (son of the renowned botanist William Hooker) and the second master of *Terror* carved a statue of Venus de Medici out of ice. Captain Crozier of *Terror* entered this elaborately decorated space wearing his dress blues and escorting a bewigged "Miss Ross" on his arm. The couple was greeted with a loud volley of rifle shots. To resounding cheers the two officers then danced a quadrille. More dancing ensued, until an abundance of alcohol caused the festivities to deteriorate into hijinks, with some officers mischievously slipping ice cubes down the backs of "ladies fainting with cigars in their mouths," and tipsy sailors staggering out on to the ice for a snowball fight.[26] Raucous shipboard parties like these relieved the daily tedium, raised morale, and temporarily broke down the barriers between officers and men. Such bonding events prepared them for leaner times ahead, when it would become essential to share what little they had left.[27]

On civilian expeditions, maintaining solidarity required other strategies. Men who had not spent their lives obeying orders without question had a harder time dealing with the dangers and deprivations of extended polar voyages and were less willing to put their lives in the hands of men just because they held a higher position. Some crew members were stubborn individualists, such as the Yankee sailor William Godfrey, who bedeviled Kane's 1853 Arctic expedition by defying orders and then deserting the ship. Kane himself despised military discipline, having witnessed seamen brutally flogged when he was a surgeon in the navy. Revulsion over these incidents prevented him from being as strict with his men as he might—and should—have been.[28] Like his American contemporaries Charles Hall and Isaac Hayes, as well as Norwegians like Nansen and Amundsen, Kane wanted to establish an egalitarian attitude among members of his party, giving the men more leeway to think and act on their own. If they were shown respect, he reasoned, crew members would treat each other—and Kane—the same way, and thus the group as a whole would function better. Likewise, on the *Fram*, Nansen had men of all ranks share the same quarters. He thought that "living together in the one salon, with everything in common" improved morale. The men wore no insignia and performed the same duties.[29] However, Nansen's interest in breaking down barriers had its cultural limits: as was pointed out, for most of their journey toward the North Pole he and his companion Johansen stuck to the formal "you" when addressing each other.

Naïve expectations that shipmates would treat each other like brothers and thus enhance their odds of surviving ran afoul of the stubborn realities of Arctic navigation. Bent upon reaching the fabled Open Polar Sea in 1860, Isaac Israel Hayes had to sift through a horde of applicants— "enough to have fitted out a respectable squadron," he complained—all eager to make history at his side. Unfortunately, few of the ones he selected had ever been to sea, let alone to the Far North. En route there, the Penn-trained physician, who had served under Kane during an earlier search for this fabled body of water, informed his crew that "mutual dependence" was the virtue that would sustain them in this quest. Living together on the recently renamed *United States*—what he called "our little world"— was remarkably harmonious, until the ship was driven onto an iceberg and trapped in encroaching ice. With temperatures plunging and no way out escaping their predicament, his crew complained loudly and bitterly. To mollify them, Hayes established daily routines that he hoped would "cultivate the social relations and usages of home," convinced that such "little formal observances promote happiness and peace." These included holding weekly inspections, printing a newspaper, and having the officers put on their gray dress uniforms and the men show up "very neat and creditable" for Sunday services. Sounding more like a preacher than a medical doctor, Hayes observed in his journal that "true politeness is so great a blessing." But the deepening polar darkness took its toll: the newspaper and other "distractions" were forgotten, and the men on board the *United States* languished in a stupor, unable to muster the "cheerful laugh and the merry jest" of their sunny days. Only the dismal clanging of the ship's bell now denoted the passage of time. Against the interminable night and its silence, "pluck, and manly resolution, and mental resources" were as useless as masts without sails, or engines without fuel. When the first signs of spring appeared, Hayes impetuously took a sledge party out over freshly fallen snow, only to tire quickly after a winter without exercise and halt in their tracks, exhausted: "The men are completely used up, broken down, dejected, to the last degree," Hayes had to admit. "Human nature cannot stand it." In his growing despair, he blamed the extreme circumstances they were in, not his approach to it, complaining that "human beings were never before so beset with difficulties and so inextricably tangled in a wilderness. . . . They are brave and spirited men enough, lack not courage nor perseverance; but it does seem as if one must own that there are some difficulties that cannot be surmounted." Ultimately, this party did reach what Hayes could proclaim as a new Farthest North—close to eighty-two degrees of latitude—providing him a great triumph, albeit not the one he had set out to attain.[30] And even this accomplishment would not stand up to close scrutiny: Hayes apparently overestimated by about one hundred miles how close to the pole he had come—a mistake he never conceded. What he did acknowledge to himself was that treating his men decently and maintaining some semblance of normal, convivial life was no guarantee of success in the Arctic. Nature was the one who determined that.

Charles Hall, a loner and outsider in the States, lived among the Inuit for four years, starting in the summer of 1864, and developed a deep affection for these "children of nature," even though his original intent had been to befriend them only in order that they would reveal details about the missing Franklin party's fate. Spending New Year's 1865 in a Greenland igloo, at a time when his countrymen had been slaughtering each other during nearly four years of civil war, Hall dined with his neighbors on frozen venison at 62 degrees below zero and then made a speech, in their language, thanking the Inuit for treating him as "a brother."[31] (Later, however, he would grow disillusioned with these natives after finding out they had not deigned to bring food to some starving English sailors.[32]) When he was about to depart on his third Arctic expedition, in 1871, the deeply religious Hall once again allowed his faith in others to blind him to reality. In remarks before the American Geographical Society, at New York's Cooper Union, Hall praised the officers, scientists, and crew members who had signed up for this trip and predicted—ironically—that "Though we may be surrounded by innumerable icebergs, and though our vessel may be crushed like an egg-shell, I believe they will stand by me to the last."[33] In fact, almost from the start, the German scientists on board refused to bow to Hall's authority. His party was split into hostile factions, several men were chronically intoxicated, and the ship's physician was accused of having poisoned Hall with arsenic. The *Polaris* expedition ended in disaster, with the ship sinking and the survivors then being forced to drift on an ice floe for six months before they were brought to safety.

In many cases, what an expedition leader professed to believe in dealing with his men conflicted with his own (hidden) ambitions. His focus was setting a new geographical record, and keeping his crew happy was only a means to that end. In the crunch, that could become all too apparent. On the *Fram*, Nansen made sure that all the men enjoyed the same healthy diet, exercised together, and had plenty of opportunities to amuse themselves: so "arranging things sensibly" made them genuinely happier.[34] But his concern for his crew's well-being did not stop him from leaving them to their own devices when he and Johansen departed for the North Pole. Amundsen treated his companions with more consistent fairness during their march to the South Pole in 1911. When they finally reached it, he made sure that they planted their flag together. For, as Amundsen later wrote: "It was not for one man to do this; it was for all who had staked their lives in the struggle, and held together through thick and thin."[35] But this sensible philosophy did not stop him from keeping his plans a secret.

Because their parties had to contend with a harsh and volatile climate and the ever-present threat of disaster, enlightened expedition leaders tried to make life at the ends of the earth as pleasant as possible. Establishing strong friendships was vital to sustaining a positive attitude and the will to live. But solidarity was not all that was needed. Like soldiers under fire, members of polar expeditions had to respect their leaders and obey their orders. Nor could leaders play favorites. Sequestered in an igloo or on a ship at forty below, explorers had to strike a balance between looking out for each other and doing what was necessary for the group as a whole, even if that meant neglecting a friend in desperate need. During the *Terra Nova* expedition, twenty-four-year-old Raymond E. Priestley, a veteran of Shackleton's record-breaking trip south a few years before, served as a geologist and meteorologist with the so-called Northern Party, which was given the task of mapping territory between Cape Evans and Cape Adare early in 1912.[36] Due to unusual amounts of sea ice that winter, the *Terra Nova* was not able to pick up this party after the eight weeks allotted to geological research was over, and the six men had to spend the winter inside a twelve-by-nine-foot snow cave they had dug out by hand. All told, they endured nearly seven months in this makeshift shelter, surviving off their original supply of rations, supplemented by occasional penguin and seal meat. This "imprisonment" was trying physically—the men suffered chronically from gastrointestinal ailments—but also psychologically.

Priestley, who published an account of this prolonged isolation a few years afterward, recalled that a "wave of depression" had swept over him and his fellow explorers early in their confinement, and that they had come close to going mad, packed into their tiny subterranean cubicles. They had grated on each other's nerves, tempers had flared like runaway rockets, and when the six of them were finally able to toss aside their sleeping bags and escape on sledges from this gloomy, fetid Antarctic igloo, they were as sullenly estranged from each other as spouses who have lost a child and blame each other for this tragedy. As the second of eight children and son of a Gloucestershire headmaster, Priestley all too well understood the claustrophobic and contradictory dynamics of tightly knit groups. He grasped that hibernating in the essentially static polar winter demanded a high degree of order, even though the intimate experience tended to efface all arbitrary distinctions between the men, putting officer and enlisted man on "common footing." This leveling would undermine the social structure on which discipline depended.[37]

As a rule, the job of reconciling order and fellowship fell, inevitably, to the party's leader. For better or for worse, his personality and decision-making skills shaped the group's mood and its cohesiveness and thus—up to a point—how well it would hold up. Military commanders should have had an advantage over their civilian counterparts because they were used to giving unilateral commands. But, in the unpredictable and unfamiliar polar domain, these officers were prone to making bad decisions, and these could easily lead to disaster. Military men were also wont to put too much emphasis on maintaining discipline and too little on attending to group morale. Enforcing rules could become self-defeating if the men came to regard such practices as hopelessly out of touch with reality and therefore absurd. Then they might rise up in rebellion.

This had been the case at Fort Conger—trapped in total darkness and winter ice eleven hundred miles above the Arctic Circle—when Lieutenant Greely had asked several soldiers to wash the officers' laundry. (They had flatly refused.) Greely had previously revealed his martinet tendencies when he had demanded that all crew members attend Sunday services even if they weren't Christians, banned card playing on the Sabbath, forced the men to undergo humiliating physical exams regularly, and chewed out two lieutenants for sleeping late. To many of the crew, it seemed that Greely's obsession with such trivial matters masked an underlying insecurity about what they should do next. When he suddenly announced that the party was going to abandon the relative safe and comfortable quarters and take to boats to reach food supplies further south, his fellow officers and many of the soldiers privately grumbled that he was leading them to their deaths. Greely antagonized the scientists in his party and could not prevent other relationships from souring. The physician Pavy considered him "full of vanity" and unfit to command.[38] There were numerous threats of mutiny. Burdened by so much dissension and distrust, the small expedition party nearly fell apart. As it was, in the end only seven men survived. Well into the twentieth century, leaders who tried to uphold military discipline under extreme conditions similarly faced resistance. For instance, the leader of Scott's Northern Party, Lieutenant Victor Campbell, seemed incapable of easing naval regulations in light of the extraordinary deprivations his party faced during the Antarctic winter they spent in an ice cave. Like Greely, Campbell insisted on formally reprimanding men for the smallest infractions at a time when they had been reduced to living like animals.[39]

On the other hand, a leader like Robert Scott could not hide his misgivings and mood swings; his Sphinx-like aloofness, brooding secrecy, and unpredictable actions created an unsettling atmosphere. Scott had a soft, "feminine" side to his character, which somewhat offset his Royal Navy "stiffness."[40] But his go-by-the-book mentality inclined him to stick to timeworn procedures, and this tendency did not serve him well in the Antarctic, where one had to improvise or perish. At times Scott could be kindly, solicitous, and charming, like an older brother: Cherry remarked that he had "never known anybody, man or woman, who could be so attractive when he chose."[41] But more often he chose to be otherwise— shy, morose, introspective, and seemingly content in the evenings at Cape Evans to read novels by Galsworthy and Hardy or scribble in his journal. He was not the sort of man who would cheerfully make the rounds, stopping by bunks with an impish grin on his face to ask how the others were doing. (He was certainly not an Ernest Shackleton, who inspired genuine love and devotion among his men. When his thoroughly exhausted party had finally reached Elephant Island after seven hellish days in open boats, he remained the indefatigable cheerleader. As the geologist James Wordie noted, "The Boss is wonderful, cheering everyone and far more active than any other person in the camp."[42]) According to Cherry, Scott cried easily—over the deaths of ponies as well as other misfortunes. Inexplicably he would also lapse into a melancholic funk for weeks on end. His mercurial moodiness made for a dark, impenetrable enigma at the heart of the *Terra Nova* party. Most of his men came to care for him, but from a distance. At his core, they sensed Scott was intellectually dishonest— evident in his refusal to admit he was in a race with Amundsen.

A civilian expedition leader started out with his status ill-defined. He had to solidify it early on, when the men were receptive to his guidance and positively disposed toward him. He had to woo and win over his charges as adroitly and ardently as a suitor. He had to cement his authority when the sun was shining, when food was still plentiful, and when his crew did not yet pine for home. For when the situation worsened—when rations had to be cut, or after a vessel had been icebound for many months—the men responded to their leaders based on the judgement they had already formed. If there were no reservoir of trust, they would rebel. The wise commanders cultivated loyalty from the start. Amundsen selected his team members largely on the basis of that one trait. So did Peary. When he made his "successful" dash to the North Pole in the spring of 1909, the nearly toeless naval engineer traveled with four support parties. One by one they were ordered to turn back, denying them any share in the glory of this historic achievement—ostensibly to save time, but really to turn this into Peary's triumph. Even the veteran Arctic explorer and loyal friend Robert Bartlett, who had carefully steered the *Roosevelt* far into the ice and then broken trail for the handicapped lieutenant to within one-hundred-and-fifty miles of his goal, was curtly told to turn back. Yet, except for Bartlett, these men did not feel Peary had destroyed their trust in him. Only his longtime African-American companion Matthew Henson, who did make it to the pole (or thereabouts) with him, would later castigate Peary as a "selfish man" who thought only about his "own glory and that of nobody else."[43] As the eminently self-satisfied explorer saw it, his subordinates had been as "perfect beyond my most sanguine dreams . . . as loyal and responsive to my will as the fingers of my right hand."[44]

Nansen wanted strong, healthy Norwegian sailors who shared his hunger to reach new frontiers. This shared motivation—not personal allegiance—tended to hold them together when the chips were down, when the usual protocols no longer seemed to make any sense. When the goals of a leader and those of his men were at odds, a falling out—if not worse—was apt to occur. This was most likely to happen when the head of the expedition tipped his hand and revealed—as Peary and, before him, Kane and Nansen did—that his desire for personal fame was paramount. Much like "glory hounds" in combat—zealous, brash, and ambitious infantry lieutenants who order their troops to "go over the top" so that these officers can afterward win medals—selfish expedition leaders invited disaffection, wrath, and even mutiny by breaking faith with their men. Such was the case with the Second Grinnell Expedition in 1854. Elisha Kane wanted to spend another winter locked in ice on board the ironically named *Advance* so that this would put him in a good position to push on to the Open Polar Sea in the spring. But many of his men and officers were desperate to get back home and felt—rightly—that Kane was putting his wishes ahead of their well-being. With little left to eat, they were "wretchedly prepared" for another long confinement on the ship. When staying was first put to a vote, only one of the seventeen men favored remaining in the Arctic. After a second vote, a party of nine left for an Inuit outpost at Upernavik, Greenland, in what Kane considered an act of mutiny.[45] The rest reluctantly stayed with him.

Charles Hall, equally obsessed with getting to the pole, likewise faced an apparent uprising in 1868 when some of his men began to doubt that their vessel would ever be freed from the ice. Hall had to shoot and kill the ringleader—an unarmed sailor named Patrick Coleman—to quell this revolt-in-the-making, although it remains unclear that he was justified in doing so. (Some historians believe Hall was beside himself because of his party's failure to make any significant progress toward reaching the North Pole.[46] A group of whalers he had recruited to guide his ship to the North Pole had quit, leaving him without skilled navigators.) And then, during the infamous *Polaris* voyage a few years later, Hall—a poor leader and judge of character—had gotten into acrimonious arguments with the ship's medical officer, several other scientists, and members of the crew, resulting in acts of insubordination and, possibly, Hall's murder. A major source of his problems was that his men were not personally loyal to him: they had joined the expeditions for reasons of their own—either for the money or to do scientific work, not to complete Hall's territorial quests.

Another liability on the *Polaris* expedition was its binational nature. Soon after the ship had sailed from the Brooklyn Navy Yard, the German scientists formed their own clique in opposition to Hall's authority. The German crew members, who accounted for most of the sailors, sided with them, fracturing the party along national lines and making it impossible to reach consensus. Such divisiveness was even more pronounced on the later voyage of the *Belgica*: the plethora of languages spoken on board turned it into a floating Tower of Babel. Growing anxiety and adversity during polar expeditions induced those with a common language and background to draw together, to the exclusion of all the others. But, instead of allaying fears, this bonding tended to reinforce them. Increased isolation only made crews feel more alone and helpless. Miscommunication and suspicion could easily arise when there were language barriers—as frequently existed between Western explorers and their Inuit and other indigenous contacts. Trust could be broken, and unity of purpose could be lost. Intensifying alienation could weaken one's hold on reality. Inevitably, members of multinational parties could be more susceptible to mental and emotional breakdowns.

Conversely, homogeneous bands of explorers—men from the same country who celebrated the same holidays, who loved the same dishes, who knew by heart the same bawdy songs, who grew misty-eyed at the hoisting of the same flag, and who longed for the same home thousands of miles away tended to stick together. When the going got tough, they could find comfort in these communal ties. Love of country also gave men stranded in the polar realms greater reason for enduring their ordeal. As Alexander Armstrong, surgeon on HMS *Investigator* during its 1848 search for the Franklin party, wrote of its crew, their "noble spirit and patriotic feeling" helped them overcome hunger-induced weakness to carry supplies off the slowly sinking ship. He hailed this feat as "one of the brightest pages in the history of our country."[47] While sailing south to Antarctica on the *Discovery* in 1901, Scott's men dropped off postcards at ports of call along the way to call attention to their expedition. These messages conveyed that they understood the connection between their mission and their nation's renown, as did these lines of Kipling's:

What is the flag of England? Ye have but my bergs to dare,
Ye have but my drifts to conquer, Go forth for it is there.[48]

Such chauvinism sustained many polar expeditions, during a time when European powers were competing against one another around the world. When a band of Italians from the beset *Polar Star* were trekking toward the North Pole on sledges at the turn of the century, they concluded their Sunday prayers with shouts of "Long Live the King!"[49] And sailors who followed Nansen and Amundsen to the ends of the earth were buoyed by similar sentiments. To mark their national independence day, on May 18, 1894, the crew of the *Fram* (they were all Norwegians) breakfasted on smoked salmon and ox tongues, after having affixed blue-white-and-red ribbon bows to their shirts. Then, having raised a Norwegian flag to the top of the mast, they marched out onto the ice holding pennants, stepping smartly to patriotic songs played by Johansen on his accordion. Followed by more men bearing rifles and harpoons, this "stately cortege" strode twice around the icebound ship and then gave her a hearty cheer before returning for more raucous festivities on board.[50]

Careful selection of crew members, a mutually agreed-upon purpose, wise planning, an astute, honest, and unselfish leader, and cohesiveness made for a successful expedition. But all these advantages could prove insufficient if the polar world conspired against the explorers. Lack of food and extreme cold, helplessness and desperation, a crushed hull or an early winter could not be surmounted by even the wisest of commanders and the most dedicated of crews. An unforeseen catastrophe could wreck an expedition in a minute. In the end, Nature still reigned in this hyperborean realm, and the best any party could do was to prepare as much as possible and then respond wisely to the circumstances it had to deal with. Survival had to be a collective effort. With very, very few exceptions, no man could stave off disaster by himself.

Chapter Ten

"WE HAVE MET THE ENEMY, AND HE IS US"

A self-professed "romantic" with an "unconquerable love of adventure," William Godfrey jumped at the chance to go north with Elisha Kane in search of Sir John Franklin in the spring of 1853. When the *Advance* slipped loose of her tarred mooring lines in New York harbor, bands blared "The Star-Spangled Banner," crowds on the docks roared, horns in the bay tooted, and Godfrey and the rest of the excited crew experienced "a feeling of expansion . . . as though we had all been suddenly enlarged to heroic dimensions," with tears of joy rolling down their cheeks. It felt, he would later write, that "our voyage was all romance and unalloyed pleasure," as if this they were commencing a blissful marriage. But this Arctic honeymoon would not last very long. From the start, Godfrey noticed that the brig was not adequately equipped for a long stay in the Far North. Like a bridegroom eloping in haste, Kane had not planned well, and all on board would suffer for his impetuousness later on. On the way to Newfoundland, many of the men became violently seasick. Continuing on toward Baffin Bay, the *Advance* was besieged by huge ice floes and then became stuck fast. The men were spent and homesick and fearful of dying like Franklin's crew, but Kane insisted on pressing ahead, overland. Later, a party he led, determined to locate the Open Polar Sea, nearly starved and froze to death during twenty-seven consecutive days in the open. Temperatures as low as forty below made some of the men go temporarily mad—chanting strange ditties, howling like animals, and making wild, spastic gestures. After that, they were never the same again. The chill settled permanently in their bones. With the arrival of winter, depression set in. As Godfrey would recall, the "very soul of man seems to be suffocated by the oppressive gloom, the horrid silence, the changeless appearance of surrounding objects, among which no signs of animated nature can be discerned; for all that the eye can compass is fixed and still, like a sad and dreary picture, or some magnificent piece of sculpture, representing a scene of utter desolation."[1] Hostility and insubordination festered in the dark bowels of the imprisoned ship. The second winter it was worse—all eighteen men packed into a single room, many stricken with scurvy, the others sullen, gaunt, hollow-eyed, and ready to explode. One time, an irate Kane took a belaying pin and smashed it over the head of one sailor who had disobeyed his orders and laid the other—Godfrey—out flat. Sailors punched each other with the ferocity of dogs locked up in a metal cage. When Kane caught Godfrey trying to abandon the ship, he pummeled him with a slug of lead hidden inside his mitten. He then fired a shot at the fleeing sailor, but missed. Godfrey disappeared into the snowdrifts.[2] At that point, the men on the *Advance* had another four months of this hell to get through before they could escape to the south.

Anyone who has ever lived in close quarters with a group of strangers will not be surprised that polar explorers readily got on each other's nerves, grew testy, turned hostile, lashed out in anger, and even became violent. Much as expeditions to the Arctic and Antarctic may have started out cheerfully like the *Advance*, all too often simmering resentment below decks destroyed this camaraderie. To some extent, this fraying of nerves can be chalked up to the perils of their mission: sailing into uncharted, ice-choked waters, plodding through untrustworthy, hip-deep snow, running out of food, encountering fierce storms and vertical pressure ridges, sleeping in bags on shifting floes, remaining for months and even years in cheerless outposts devoid of all life—this relentless struggle against the polar elements tried men's souls more than any other endeavor at this point in human history, an era still innocent of mass slaughter by machine gun.

It is thus no wonder that so many explorers "broke" under these conditions, as Godfrey's shipmates did, and railed at each another. *Someone* was to blame for the disaster that had befallen them—and *someone* had to be held accountable. Screaming at an approaching iceberg or baying at the moon like Inuit dogs didn't help: unless one was deeply religious, there could be no hope that God would respond and part the ice. Cursing the wind would not make it stop blowing. Nature would not relent or show any mercy. So, looking for scapegoats, men like those on the *Advance* turned on each other. The fellowship that had been an antidote against isolation and despondency became the locus of discontent. Welling, ugly emotions that they could no longer be contained erupted with a fury. Those among them who represented "the Other" were the first targets of their wrath.

Differences in class, country of origin, and status set them apart. Diverse crews on vessels like the *Southern Cross* and the *Belgica* soon thus splintered into national cliques. The men on the Belgian ship spoke French in the main cabin, German and English in the scientific quarters, and a hybrid of English, Norwegian, French, and German in the forecastle—a linguistic stew that Frederick Cook professed to find salubrious, making the *Belgica* feel like a "well-regulated family." But using so many different languages did not bring them closer. Once fears of having winter in the Antarctic arose, the crew slipped into a "disgruntled" funk, "hopelessly oppressed by the sense of utter desertion and loneliness." Retreating inward, the men tried not to provoke each other, but under these circumstances that could hardly be avoided. As a medical doctor, Cook reasoned that tension was common on long voyages like theirs—one of those dirty little secrets that never left the ship or made it into print. Boredom bred a "monotonous discontent" since men were forced to stare at the same faces, listen to the same jokes, and put up with the same annoying personality quirks day after day without interruption.[3] But, being new to these conditions, Cook underestimated how much linguistic and cultural barriers could stoke this smoldering anger.

On the doomed *Polaris*, the German scientists agreed from the start to speak only their own language, and this decision only increased their disaffection from Charles Hall and his cockamamie scheme to strike out in blinding snow to notch a new Farthest North. For his part, Hall had even more reason to distrust these foreigners, whose presence on board he had only grudgingly accepted. How could he not interpret their animated conversations below decks as signs of plotting against him? Complaints by the chief scientist Emil Bessels and his compatriots about having to blindly follow Hall's orders bubbled over into talk of quitting the ship. The German deckhands—only one member of the crew was American—sided with their countrymen, raising the specter of a mass mutiny off the west coast of Greenland. Hall considered reaching for his revolver to squelch this threatened uprising. In the end, it did not come off, but shortly before Hall died under mysterious circumstances in his stateroom on November 8, 1871, he accused Bessels of having poisoned his coffee.[4] Even Hall's death, which Bessels would later describe as "the best thing that could have happened for this expedition," did not end the rancor. Instead, the German scientists formed an even tighter and more secretive circle. Later on, in December, when the crippled *Polaris* abruptly sailed off, the Germans left behind adamantly refused navigator George Tyson's order to take up pursuit: they insisted he had no authority over them. All the highly experienced whaler could do was fume in his journal that the German sailors were "determined to control their destiny. They want to be masters here. They go swaggering about with their pistols and rifles . . ."[5] Tyson also had to worry that the rebellious crew members might shoot him or one or more of the Inuit in their party and then commit the ultimate barbarity of eating their flesh.

As was noted earlier, Adolphus Greely had his own share of troubles with a quasi-foreigner who had come with him to Lady Franklin Bay. His nemesis was the French-educated and French-speaking Dr. Octave Pavy, whose disdain for military protocol was as repellent to his commanding officer as his dubious character and purportedly "Bohemian" lifestyle.[6]

Greely wrote his wife that he considered Pavy "a tricky double-faced man, idle, unfit for any Arctic work except doctoring & sledge travel & not first class in the latter." The feisty physician gave as good as he got, agreeing with Lieutenant Kislingbury that Greely was a self-absorbed martinet unfit for this mission and scribbling similarly derogatory comments in his journal.[7] These two strong egos openly clashed when Pavy refused to obey Greely's written order that he hand over his notes on the various species he had observed and collected at Fort Conger, along with his personal diary. Greely then had the physician put under guard—an indignity that a defiant Pavy accepted "physically, but not morally."[8] Given the deteriorating conditions at their isolated Arctic outpost, Greely's response to Pavy's noncompliance (as to that of his good friend and second-in-command, Kislingbury) comes across as excessive and counterproductive. It certainly did not increase his expedition's chances of surviving. In Pavy's case, what it revealed was the incompatibility of the military and civilian approaches to such a precarious situation.

Conflicts like these arose from more than differences in language and background. As was evident on the Greely expedition, temperament could also create disharmony. But national differences could easily become personal. The lone Norwegian who accompanied Scott, twenty-three-year-old champion skier Tryggve Gran, found himself in an awkward position knowing that his English party was in a tight race to the South Pole against his countrymen. The aristocratic Oates at first would have nothing to do with him and disparaged Gran "as both dirty and lazy" simply because he wasn't British and thus presumed to be hostile.[9] Gran made no secret of his hope that Amundsen would get to the pole first: he proudly tacked up a Norwegian flag over his bunk. Ironically, it was Gran who would later be told to bring the Union Jack to Scott's Southern Party, which had forgotten it in their haste to get started from Hut Point. This "irony of fate" made Gran feel that he was, indeed, part of this "mixed brotherhood." Later, returning from the site where he and the others had just discovered the frozen bodies of Scott, Bowers, and Wilson, the young Norwegian reflected that being with these men had taught him the true meaning of friendship—a bond that could, at times, transcend patriotism.[10] It was this same sense of a deeper bond among kindred spirits that allowed ordinary Germans to express concern about the fate of Ernest Shackleton and his largely English party when they were attempting to cross Antarctica in 1914—at a time when their two countries had just declared war on each other.

Just as potentially injurious to an expedition's success as nationalistic feelings were disagreements over its purpose, its priorities, and its strategies. Some of these conflicts were inevitable: expeditions were sometimes funded and organized for a variety of reasons and then expected to carry out these different missions. For example, the reporters whom *New York Herald* publisher James Gordon Bennett Jr. had assigned to go along as "seamen for special service" on the *Jeannette* in 1879—to publish sensational scoops about reaching the pole—clashed frequently with the naval officers who were trying to run the ship according to military regulations. The journalists' annoyance over having to toe the line "hardened into outright rebellion" once the ship became icebound.[11] On one occasion, Jerome Collins, one of the two of them on board, refused to comply with De Long's orders and was promptly relieved of his duties. When the other, Raymond Newcomb, challenged the commander's authority, he was placed under arrest. More importantly, the goals of scientific investigation and territorial discovery were frequently incompatible. This was the case regardless of the nationalities involved. In conflict from the start, these disagreements over purpose only intensified at sea. This was certainly the case on the *Southern Cross*: en route south, in Madeira, the scientists had tarried to collect specimens, exasperating the expedition's leader, Borchgrevink, who was focused on getting to Antarctica before winter set in.

Likewise, the normally congenial Shackleton could not stomach having scientists tag along on his 1907 *Nimrod* voyage to Antarctica: like Borchgrevink, he didn't want anyone getting in the way of his territorial objective—reaching the South Pole. Shackleton's single-mindedness created friction between him and the other officers—notably, with Lieutenant Rupert England, whose insistence on being cautious and taking extra time to unload the ship in McMurdo Sound caused Shackleton's to fire him and send him back to England. Such clashes occurred often, especially when the chain of command was not well established. Charles Hall tried to prevent questioning of his authority by making sure that his official orders spelled out that everyone else on the expedition was under his command and subject to "the rules, regulations, and laws governing the discipline of the Navy."[12] But then he had all but assured that conflict would arise if he were to die, by naming both his sailing master, Sidney Budington, and the chief scientist, Bessels, his successors. Before Hall's death, Budington had voiced his low opinion of the explorer, confiding to Tyson that he did not like being commanded by "a man not of the sea." He and others in the party also took umbrage at the civilian Hall being called "Captain." (Budington's animus seems to have stemmed, in part, from his having been caught stealing chocolate and sugar and then being reamed out by Hall for this theft.) Hall and Budington constantly locked horns—mainly, over the question of whether or not they should steer further into the ice with winter already coming on in late August 1870. Since the opinion of the landlubber Hall (who wanted to proceed) was not given much credence, the German scientists sided with Budington, increasing the ill-feelings on the ship. When the sailing master refused to go on after they had dropped anchor in a bay they would aptly name "Thank God Harbor," Hall finally gave in. Tyson was appalled that the head of an expedition could tolerate such "insolence and incompetence," but kept his own counsel. Still, the divisions on the *Polaris* only grew deeper—and more ominous.[13]

When rival explorers ended up in the same party, sparks were bound to fly. Among such contentious relationships that of Shackleton and Scott stands out. The middle-class Anglo-Irish Shackleton, the second of ten children, had grown up with dreams of going to sea, devouring books like *20,000 Leagues under the Sea* and Charles Hall's *Life with the Esquimaux* while neglecting his schoolbooks. Restless and bored by life at home, he managed to obtain a post on a Merchant Marine vessel bound for Cape Horn and the Pacific when he was only sixteen, in the spring of 1890. Gregarious, hard-working, headstrong, preternaturally ambitious, and supremely self-confident, Shackleton soon set his sights on more glorious adventures. Antarctica seemed a good place for him to make a name for himself: England was then focusing its attention on achieving territorial firsts there. But he soon ran into a formidable obstacle—Robert Falcon Scott. As leader of the National Antarctic Expedition, Scott got to pick the men he would take with him, and the application of the twenty-seven-year-old-Shackleton did not particularly impress him. However, because of his experience on sailing schooners, Shackleton was eventually offered the position of third officer on the *Discovery* in the midsummer of 1901. Scott, six years his elder and more reserved by nature, liked Shackleton's obvious enthusiasm, even though Scott's preference for an all-Royal-Navy crew caused him to have some misgivings about the easygoing, outspoken, and willful merchant mariner, who struck him as a "maverick."[14] Nonetheless, Scott showed his confidence in Shackleton by selecting him to go with him to attain a new Farthest South the following November, even though Shackleton had no prior experience in the polar regions. However, Shackleton's collapse on the way back, due largely to a heart condition (which he had concealed), prompted Scott to reassess him—and order Shackleton to return to England by relief ship—an unexpected decision that left the Irishman angry and reeling. He harbored suspicions that Scott was sending him back for ulterior reasons, out of fear that Shackleton might one day upstage him.

This incident foreshadowed clashes between the two explorers later in their careers. Both were bent on going down in the history books for achieving geographical milestones in Antarctica, and having this same goal put them on a collision course. Scott was wont to look at life through a Darwinian lens, and it was clear that he felt he and Shackleton were in a winner-take-all struggle for dominance.[15] His experiences with Shackleton during the *Discovery* expedition bore this out. After recovering in

New Zealand, touring the United States and returning to England to marry, Shackleton made plans to undertake another Antarctic land expedition, only to discover—to his surprise and dismay—that Scott intended to set out on one of his own. This put them in direct competition for funding from the Royal Geographical Society. The two rivals then became embroiled in a petty territorial spat: Scott insisted the desirable winter anchorage at McMurdo Sound was his and warned Shackleton in a tart letter to stay away from it. If the Irish explorer didn't, he would be standing in the way of Scott's completing his "life's work."[16] Taking a diplomatic tack, Shackleton then agreed to spend the winter elsewhere, but, in the end, heavy ice conditions forced him to point the *Nimrod* toward this Antarctic base in January 1908. Privately, Scott seethed over what he perceived as a duplicitous attempt to beat him to the South Pole.[17] During a subsequent sledge trip, Shackleton savored the immense satisfaction of besting Scott's Farthest South record, even though he had to turn back when the pole itself was tantalizingly close—only 112 miles away. A year and a half later, he tried to patch things up with Scott, writing that he would not interfere with Scott's next—and final—expedition, but would instead wait to embark on another journey until after Scott had completed his.[18] But their relationship remained badly strained. In November 1911, it was with the two goals of upstaging his rival and beating the Norwegians that Scott departed from Cape Evans for the South Pole, only to perish tragically on the way back. In death, as in life, Shackleton—the leader who miraculously brought every last member of his incredible *Endurance* expedition back alive—appears to have bested his challenger, whose martyrdom could not erase the fact that he had failed to reach the pole first. In the words of English polar historian Max Jones, "Today the stiff and indecisive Scott lies in Shackleton's towering shadow."[19] As Scott had foreseen, there could only be one winner in this titanic Antarctic struggle.

The fierce rivalry between Frederick Cook and Robert Peary is also well known, but it is often forgotten that the two men started out as congenial, mutually admiring companions: Peary invited the twenty-six-year-old Cook to come along as surgeon on an 1891 trek across northern Greenland after he had favorably sized up the doctor in his Philadelphia apartment. When Peary became incapacitated after breaking a leg, Cook skillfully set it and assumed command. But after that reasonably happy pairing, the explorers became locked in an epic race to be the first man to set foot at the North Pole. Cook kept the details of his forthcoming dash secret, and after his sensational claim to have made it to ninety degrees north made headlines around the world, the two became bitter enemies—and remained so for the rest of their lives.

Antagonism between competing explorers was unavoidable, given the high stakes involved. But conflicts between leaders and their men could be assuaged if the person in charge showed genuine concern for their welfare and made decisions that did not lead to unnecessary risks. Unfortunately, that was not always the case. Elisha Kane's contretemps with the sailor Godfrey on the Second Grinnell Expedition of 1853 is the most well-known of these confrontations—chiefly because the explorer's death freed Godfrey to tell his own version of what happened between them in the Arctic. (Before they sailed from the Brooklyn Navy Yard, Kane had required his officers and men to sign a document promising not to publish accounts of the expedition.) But Godfrey was not the only member of that expedition to skirmish with Kane. When the *Advance* reached a bay off the northern coast of Greenland in late August, Kane was bent upon continuing further north, to make it easier for him to make a dash for the pole in the spring. But all but one of his officers and crew thought this would be foolhardy: they wanted to head south to safety. They did not trust Kane's judgment, as he had never had command of a ship before, let alone one in these waters. Godfrey would later write that he felt their surviving a winter in Greenland was as unlikely as "a salamander's supposed ability to live in fire."[20] None of the men thought the *Advance* had the slightest chance of reaching the North Pole. (The expedition's professed goal of locating the Franklin party was all but forgotten at this point.)

Kane reluctantly compromised and agreed to look for a winter anchorage at the next possible opportunity. He later claimed that the others "received this decision in a manner that was most gratifying"—an innocuous statement that scarcely does justice to their angry reaction.[21] In fact, Kane's unilateral decision to go on belied his professed intention to treat his crew fairly and take their wishes into account. The men now clearly saw that their best interests would always come second to those of the doctor and his officers. The seeds for future disagreements and confrontations were thus sown. Indeed, reduced to "near desperation" that first winter, this Grinnell expedition would be torn apart by dissension and outright defiance of Kane's vacillating leadership. This peaked when all but five men voted to quit the ship the following summer and seek haven at the Danish outpost of Upernavik. After suffering through a horrific second winter on the ship, several on board openly disobeyed Kane's orders by skipping weekly prayers and made no secret of the fact they loathed him for his arrogance and indifference to their plight.[22]

The interminable, inky-black polar winters were often an unsparing test of an expedition's cohesiveness. Unable to leave their crowded quarters, the men would grow intolerant of each other's quirks and their leader's dominant personality. The four officers on the Greely party found that being packed into a fifteen-by-seventeen foot room at Fort Conger during the winter of 1881–1882 was like putting them inside a pressure cooker and slowly turning up the gas. A "mordant" Pavy and a "sarcastic" Kislingbury were easily irritated by Greely's vain and overbearing manner, and his unavoidable proximity only magnified these flaws.[23] Few leaders still enjoyed admiration when things went badly. They were the ones who got blamed. Weaknesses and inconsistencies in their personalities were magnified. Robert Scott galled his officers on the *Terra Nova* expedition by his shifting moods. At times he could be empathetic, but at others his insecurities would cause him to demand "rigid unquestioning literal obedience to orders." He had no ability to see himself critically, or with humor. In the mornings he could be "peevish," thus setting a bad tone for the rest of the day. Scott's mercurial nature kept the others at a distance, which made them feel ill-at-ease and more lonely. (In a letter to his mother before leaving for the South Pole, "Titus" Oates had complained that Scott always thought about himself first, and "the rest nowhere." Because of this selfishness, and Scott's inability to be "straight" with him, the veteran soldier had developed an intense dislike for his leader.[24]) Cherry-Garrard, who was much more admiring of Scott, also considered him temperamentally "weak" and reserved, someone who suffered depressions that could last for weeks—and then abruptly turn into an "irritable autocrat."[25] Scott's nickname on his final expedition was "The Owner"— a term devoid of the casual affection of "Boss"—which is what Shackleton's men called him.[26] No doubt, Scott suffered by comparison with a saintly, stable figure like "Bill" Wilson, whose faith kept him grounded and forward looking. (In his journal, Wilson, too, made derogatory comments about Scott and his leadership.[27]) It was also Scott's fate to have to deal with predicaments for which he was constitutionally ill-prepared, and his reactions under the ensuring stress did not show him at his best. Having none of the reassuring wit and charm that Shackleton possessed almost to a fault, Scott could not rally his companions to handle the crises that arose on the march south. His impromptu changes of plan did not sit well with them, and some historians have judged him harshly for the choices he made en route. Of course, failure makes all actions look suspect. We can only speculate how differently Scott might be viewed today if his Southern Party had beaten the Norwegians to the pole, and he had returned to tell the tale.

It is perfectly understandable that heated friction would develop among men under these most trying and desperate of circumstances, when their lives were on the line and there was little they could do to help themselves. In such existential plights, many human beings put aside worries about their companions and concentrate on their own survival needs. In withdrawing, they wrestle alone with mounting despair and fear, unable to share these feelings and gain comfort from doing so. The sense of fellowship they may have treasured in happier days now comes fraught with resentment: they have no way of retreating into their own thoughts and finding solace there, for others are invariably present, an annoying reminder of their common plight. There is no space for their souls to find peace. The group becomes the oppressor and the tormentor. Under such conditions, always being together can be just as harmful as always being alone. To ward off the ill-effects of others' presence, polar explorers put up psychological barriers between each other, such as remaining silent, averting eyes, staring blankly into space, showing no emotion, or becoming angry. Studies have found small groups are particularly prone to such antisocial reactions. The strains of close quarters irked the men on the *Discovery* expedition even before they reached Antarctica. The day their vessel crossed the equator, in late August of 1901, they staged the traditional seawater dunking for those making their maiden crossing into the Southern Hemisphere. In a foul mood from having been penned up below decks in tropical temperatures, with navy men quartered unhappily with merchant mariners, the neophytes did not take kindly to this ritual, and downing too much whisky afterward turned the festivities into an ugly brawl, with Scott fecklessly trying to restore discipline among his motley crew. This shipboard fight was a harbinger of things to come, when group tensions would be compounded by an adverse Nature.[28]

The Arctic and Antarctic regions had a way of bringing out the worst in those who dared to go there. Unremittingly unpleasant conditions oppressed the explorers and kept them feeling peevish. This state of mind made them hypersensitive to the slightest aggravation—spilling a soup dish or misplacing a pouch of tobacco. When minor incidents like these took place, they were all too quick to blame one of their companions and further sour the mood. Geologist Raymond Priestley was clearly being too sanguine when he predicted, early in his sojourn with the Northern Party at Cape Adare, that "the days when the Polar winter under normal conditions was a thing to be dreaded are past now, for good and all."[29] He had no idea what lay in store for him. By the time Priestley and the

237

rest of his six-man sledge party were finally able to emerge from the ice cave where they had been forced to hibernate for the austral winter, in February 1912, his outlook had changed dramatically: "I do not for a moment say that any of us would care to repeat that winter; indeed, I believe that another similar experience would kill most of us, or drive us mad." What it had certainly done was to tear them apart. With the cave only about five-and-a-half-feet high, none of them had been able to stand up straight except when they went out to hunt for seals or penguins, or haul their bloody carcasses back inside. They had worn the same ragged, blackened garments for eight months, with only a change of socks every third one. The filth, the foul air, the inadequate lighting, the tight spaces, the disgusting hooch they had to spoon into their mouths day after day, month after month, the oppressive cold, the even colder latrine—all these conditions had turned them into sullen recluses. Over half a year of this "inert vegetating existence" had reduced them to long periods of silence, interrupted now and then by "threadbare" conversation, along with evening singing of "chorus songs." Tensions between the easily annoyed career naval officer Victor Campbell ("a shy, steely Old Etonian in flight from a troubled marriage") and several other men had been bottled up, but barely concealed.[30] With only three well-worn books at their disposal—the New Testament, *David Copperfield*, and Boccaccio's *Decameron*—their only imaginative escape for this wintry prison was via their daydreams, or while they slept, when the visions always revolved around food, rescue—or disaster. Normally active young men, capable of filling idle time by carrying out weather-related experiments, repairing gear, reading, listening to music, playing board games, and enjoying other pastimes, this "dirty, unwashed, and unkempt" band remained in a stupor for five months. When they were finally able to go out of their frozen cave and see the sunlight overhead, the men of this Northern Party silently congratulated themselves for having endured this "almost unparalleled strain" without once losing their tempers. They had come to know one other better than most persons ever do, but this knowledge was not something they had wanted or sought. Indeed, so much minute awareness of another human had been unbearable. They needed to get away and put this experience behind them. On the trip back the men found it hard to talk. They were afraid to say anything that might provoke a negative reaction, and so they limited their remarks to the weather, the sledges, and the snowy terrain they were crossing. They stayed away from any more controversial subjects "as you would the devil."[31] To an observer, Priestley and his team members would have appeared as total strangers, like those one comes upon in a train compartment in a foreign country—all happily lost in silence, all happily oblivious to each other's company.

In the nineteenth and early twentieth centuries, the psychological damage done by polar explorations was usually overlooked: during that Victorian Age particularly, it wasn't the sort of thing one talked about. Suffering of that sort was a weakness at odds with the public image of the explorer as stoic, manly hero. Frederick Cook's describing how his shipmates on the *Belgica* grew isolated and depressed is a rare revelation. So was Jean-Baptiste Charcot's account of the voyage of the *Pourquoi-Pas? IV*, a three-masted French barque he had had built to chart sections of the Antarctic coastline starting in 1908. Even on this splendidly outfitted vessel, replete with three laboratories and a scientific library, disaster could not be averted. (Years later, in 1936, his ship would be struck by a violent storm near Iceland and wrecked on reefs. All but one of her thirty-one crew members, including Charcot, would perish.) The stately ship ran aground and then was quickly encircled by thickening ice. The men had to hastily put together igloos for the winter. Largely inexperienced in polar conditions, they grew despondent in the gathering darkness and fell victim to a variety of ailments, ranging from scurvy to swollen limbs to shortness of breath. Their anxiety about being cut off indefinitely from the rest of the world was magnified by their communal confinement. With considerable understatement, Charcot would later note that his men, increasingly aware that their life together "with no possibility of finding distraction from temporary failure of nerves, with no hope of being able to take a meal alone or in other company, has its painful moments."[32] Neither on the ship nor on the ice was there a single place where they could "shut themselves in" alone. Contact with others became insufferable not because they had changed, but because their "weaknesses or defects [were] no longer under the mask by which . . . one hides them in ordinary social life." Fascinated as well as perplexed by this phenomenon, Charcot—both a physician and an explorer—pondered making a study of the "psychology of the restricted community."

But it would take nearly a century for social scientists to investigate how constant companionship during polar explorations can be as devastating as isolation. What should provide comfort can end up only making a long imprisonment worse. In writing about these deleterious effects in 2008, anthropologist Lawrence Palinkas and psychologist Peter Suedfeld pointed out that being forced to live together for many months without interruption in the Arctic and Antarctic can make individuals suspicious of their mates to the point of paranoia.[33] They come to believe that others are hoarding food, not doing their share of the work, or plotting against them.[34] During one of the expeditions led by Charles Hall, a carpenter named Nathaniel Coffin became so obsessively fearful that he imagined other crew members were trying to drill a hole into his quarters so that they could spray carbonic acid on him and kill him.[35] (It was later established that Coffin had been wounded in the head during the Civil War and subsequently discharged from the Union Army, and that it was this old injury that had caused him to go insane.[36])

Not all commanders were unmindful of this lurking danger. Amundsen, for one, recognized that conflicts between the expedition leader and the ship's captain had often been the undoing of voyages to the Arctic, producing "incessant friction, divided counsels, and a lowered morale" among the crew. To avoid such outcomes, the Norwegian explorer had resolved to learn how to pilot a ship himself, so that all the decision-making would lie in his hands.[37] Amundsen and some other leaders also tried to minimize resentment by treating their men more democratically—as Kane had given his Grinnell party a chance to vote on whether or not they should stay on for the Arctic winter. But, as Kane had discovered, loosening the reins of power sometimes only invited more dissension. Leaders could not reassure their men that all would be well. They, too, were helpless. All they could do was maintain the pretense of being in control. For that to happen, commanders needed opportunities to be by themselves and reflect. This helped to keep them from losing their sanity. As much as he worried about his men's deteriorating morale on the ice-bound *Jeannette*, George De Long also knew that he had to get away from this depressing situation now and then in order not to succumb to it. So, on many a night, he would slip away from the ship unnoticed, enjoying this precious solitude to absorb new energy and see the world differently. And this interlude worked its magic. From a hundred yards away, his ship looked like it had been "dropped out of fairyland," while the Arctic sky took on the "grandest, wildest and most awful beauty."[38] Amid this nocturnal splendor, De Long could also understand more clearly what was happening to his party—how the "melancholy of the polar darkness, the claustrophobic dread that could set in while one was living under conditions of near imprisonment—the whole Arctic experience was a perfect incubator for insanity."[39]

For the men back on the *Jeannette*, fitfully sleeping on their damp bunks below decks in total silence and darkness—aware that when they awoke many hours later the silence and darkness would not have gone away, that their breakfast would be the same that they had been eating for months, that everything they would do during their waking hours would be the same as it had been the day before and the day before that and the day before that, stretching back further in time than they cared to recall—acutely aware that their shipboard life would unfold in this totally predictable and unchanging way for months come, as if it were the script of a play they had been ordered to perform, always playing the same roles and delivering the same lines, for no apparent reason and for no apparent audience—for them, there were no such restorative respites as De Long could occasionally enjoy. For these trapped souls and for the thousands of others who had already faced the same fate in the polar world, and the thousands more yet to come here, there would be no such reprieve. Here they lived outside of time and outside of space. They had no past and seemingly no future. There were not dead, but they were not truly alive either. Their existence was a pointless absurdity, and they had no way out of it. No wonder they turned on each other. At least that provoked some sort of change—the only way to shatter the frozen sea inside their heads.

Chapter Eleven

IN THE END WAS THE WORD

In the end, all he had left was the blunt stub of a pencil and a blank sheet of paper. The other two—Wilson and Bowers—lay still in their bags and likely close to death if not already dead, and so Scott was all alone with his thoughts and his flickering hopes that some modicum of redemption could be salvaged at the end of his life from what must have felt like a horrible cascade of failure. First, they had failed to beat the Norwegians to the Pole; then—with the bitterly cold wind barreling into the tent like an inept cat burglar—they had failed to make it back to One Ton Depot; after that, they had failed to take the more "natural" and ambitious step of setting out in that direction in a blizzard so that they could at least die nobly "in their tracks"; and finally they had even failed to spare themselves this final ignominy by swallowing the morphine tablets and slipping peacefully into unconsciousness. (Suicide was considered "against the code" by which they had lived.[1] Still, Oates had made that choice—by walking out of the tent to die in the snow—and they had admired him for doing so.) So here they were, so close to getting back, but fading away helplessly in this hellish spot, not going out like medieval knights charging on horseback with leveled silvery lances, but flat on their backs, incapacitated by hunger and weakness as their faint, misty breaths gradually ebbed into nothingness.

Mindful of his imminent demise and all that it implied, Scott found some consolation—as he so often did—in words. For him, it was poignantly fitting that the end of his physical existence and the end of his journal-keeping would coincide. One was only fulfilled through the other. His elegant, evocative prose expressed all that his life had striven to be but never succeeded in fully becoming: with these words—*his* lance—he would transcend the cruel and unjust fate he had been handed and achieve another kind of victory. The pencil and paper would record how his code of honor and willingness to sacrifice his life for a greater cause had not faltered at the end and would thus lay down a legacy for generations to come. Death be not proud, indeed. In extremis, Scott did not summon up Donne's defiant words, but instead scratched out a long farewell that blended acceptance with stern admonition—the parting words of a father about to go over the trenches and hurl himself against the hot steel pouring from the machine guns, of a brave man who realizes his message for posterity lies not in what he is going to accomplish but in the fact that he will end his life nobly. (In one of his last letters, he would make this explicit: "But we have been to the pole and we shall die as gentlemen."[2]) This they will long remember. Holding the paper firmly, with his numb fingers still exercising enough control, he first scribbled, "It seems a pity but I do not think I can write more—R Scott." Then, seemingly overwhelmed by despair and a welling sense of finality, he added, "For God's sake look after our people."[3]

And then, presumably, he closed his eyes to await his death, snugly cushioned by his two loyal companions, flinging an arm protectively across Wilson's frozen body, which was leaning against the tent pole. "The Owner," this shy and complex man who had led this British Antarctic Expedition all the way to the South Pole as he had vowed he would—but arrived too late to grab the brass ring—was now hoping for better luck in his afterlife. If nothing else, his words would ensure that—words that flowed from his pencil with a felicity and grace that belied this sorry ending, in this godforsaken place, and thus would be remembered long after any of the errors or miscalculations on his part would be forgotten. Words would extract triumph out of the maw of defeat and death: "Once short sleep past, we wake eternally / And death shall be no more," as the "Holy Sonnet" penned over three centuries before by the ailing Dean of St. Paul's had prophesied.[4] In life, words had served him as a soothing balm against the slings and arrows of outrageous fortune that his kindred spirit, Hamlet, had so eloquently rued. In his writings—in the main, the journals he kept during his two Antarctic journeys—Scott had attained a degree of power and mastery denied him during his journeys across unpredictable, treacherous ice and snow, and in the face of much misfortune. Alone at his desk, hunched intently over his desk in his winter quarters at Hut Point, with pencil in one hand, smoldering pipe in the other—with photos of his wife, Kathleen, and two-year-old son Peter arrayed on the wall to his left and a jumble of books and gear behind him—Scott entered into a kingdom of his own making—a splendidly constructed place where the heroic spirit he had admired since his Victorian childhood could flourish, where each stroke of the pencil expanded its dominion a little farther, soaring above and beyond unforeseeable mishaps and unpleasant setbacks as a black, funeral veil would drape and conceal a pained face beneath.[5] It was this thirst for the lofty and the ethereal that had made Scott insist—foolishly, because he was the expedition leader—on being the first person to ascend in a balloon over what he had just named "King Edward VII Land" during his penultimate *Discovery* expedition. The diminutive and occasionally indolent "Con," whom a bemused father had dubbed "Old Mooney" for his tendency to lose himself in dreams, had first envisioned a glorious life of adventure by burrowing into the rosy yarns popular among English boys in his day. Later, as commander of the *Terra Nova* party, he had stocked the ship's library with volumes by his good friend J. M. Barrie (author of *Peter Pan, or The Boy Who Never Grow Up*—the impish free spirit for whom Scott would name his son), Charles Dickens, Charlotte Brontë, Rudyard Kipling, Edward Bulwer-Lytton, and Thomas Hardy (*Tess of the d'Urbervilles* was a particular favorite), preferring these fictional diversions to the musty, dog-eared volumes on polar expeditions entrusted to him by his mentor and fellow Royal Navy officer, Clements Markham.[6] (Scott read Darwin, too, but one senses he was more dismayed than enlightened by the naturalist's depiction of the base impulses driving humankind.[7])

As a writer, one of Scott's greatest gifts was his ability to express empathy and compassion during times of great adversity. Unlike so many of his naval predecessors, who tended to stick dutifully to the facts, he was not uncomfortable registering his feelings. This was certainly so when it came to the hardships suffered by the animals that he had brought south— the ponies ("wretched creatures") who had stood stoically and mutely for weeks on board a violently rocking *Terra Nova* as it had plowed through heavy seas south of New Zealand, and the shivering shipboard dogs, whose "pathetic attitude, deeply significant of cold and misery" apparently touched him more than the suffering of his men.[8] Another strength was his capacity for hope. Despite being unsure of himself at times, Scott came across in his journals as a blithe optimist, someone who was always surprised when things went wrong. (The first published version of his journal was redacted to omit any incidents that showed Scott in an unfavorable light.[9]) Trials and tribulations in Antarctica were treated lightly. At one point, stuck in the coastal pack, with icebergs swarming around the ship like ravenous polar bears, threatening at any instant to crash headlong into the ship, disaster may have loomed, but in Scott's telling this incident was only a lark: "Everyone is wonderfully cheerful; there is laughter and song all day long," he noted on December 17, 1910. Still trapped in the ice on Christmas Day, he added: "In spite of the unpropitious prospects everyone on board is cheerful and one foresees a merry dinner to-night."[10]

In describing their hauling supplies ashore in early January, Scott seemed so caught up in this happy turn of events—"It's splendid to see at last the effect of all the months of preparation and organisation"—that the disaster that ensued (the sinking of a motorized tractor) seemed to have caught him blindsided, like a man gazing so reverently at the sunset that he fails to notice that his house is on fire. His descriptions of setting up camp read like the brochure for a guided tour. The hut the men hastily erected was not just adequate, but the "most perfectly comfortable habitation," the finest ever built on the continent, and they were "simply overwhelmed with its comfort." In spite of the plunging temperatures outside, the men carried out their tasks "indefatigably": each was "in his way a treasure." Scott's praise knew no bounds: "For here and now I must record the splendid manner in which these men are working. I find it difficult to express my admiration for the manner in which the ship is handled and worked under these very trying circumstances." As the Antarctic darkness deepened that May, Scott expressed none of the gloomy thoughts of earlier explorers during this grim, seasonal transition. Instead, he saluted the esprit d'corps that prevailed inside their quarters: "With me there is no need to draw a veil; there is nothing to cover. There are no strained relationships in this hut, and nothing more emphatically evident than the universally amicable spirit which is shown on all occasions."[11]

Like a proud father hovering over his boys, Scott could not decide which one he loved the most. Of Wilson, he wrote: "There is no member of our party so universally esteemed." Bowers was singled out for his "indefatigable zeal, his unselfishness, and his inextinguishable good humour." When Bowers, Cherry, and Wilson staggered back to Hut Point from Cape Crozier, barely recognizable with faces and clothes blackened by blubber, Scott saw only knights whose heroism was attested by their having made it back alive. Typically, he viewed their extraordinary excursion as raw material for a motivational narrative: "It makes a tale for our generation which I hope may not be lost in the telling," he noted, with just a tinge of authorial envy.[12]

After Scott's diaries were readied for the presses, all derogatory comments about his men having been expunged, the journals projected an image of the Southern Party as a band of jovial, pluckish English gentlemen who had remained coolheaded under tremendous stress and then embraced their martyrdom gallantly and without complaint.[13] (Such editorial "cleansing" was often done before expedition journals were published.[14]) Even taking this pruning into account, Scott's optimism comes across as hopelessly naïve—a fatal character defect. As the months went by, and things did not go smoothly for the *Terra Nova* party, he was slow to adjust his outlook. A dismaying series of setbacks—drowned ponies, the sunken tractor, roaring blizzards caused by Antarctica's "mysterious" weather—were recounted like sudden, unexpected thunderstorms that temporarily keep boys inside and postpone their fun, not as hints of lurking doom. These incidents could not put a dent in what he really relied on, and that was the fiber of the men at his side. This remained unbending until the end. As reality sunk in on the way back from the pole, Scott's words of praise turned into pity: it was "poor" Oates and "poor" Wilson who were now suffering helplessly, much as the ponies had on board ship.

Still, in his last letters to their friends and family members, Scott went out of his way to hallow these men who had put their trust in him, finding the right phrases to soothe the anguish of his recipients. Writing to Oates's devoted mother, Caroline, who had persisted in calling her son "Baby Boy" for several years after his birth, and who would worship at the altar of his memory for the rest of her life, Scott offered spiritual consolation, although he was an agnostic: "The ways of Providence are inscrutable, but there must be some reason why such a young, vigorous and promising life is taken," he jotted inside the indifferent tent. In a letter to Barrie, Scott obliquely referred to Oates's decision to commit suicide as another noble gesture: "we have done everything possible, even to sacrificing ourselves in order to save sick companions." But, here, too, his praise was calculated. Scott coupled his wish that this selfless act set "an example for Englishmen of the future," with the more pragmatic admonition that "the country ought to help those who are left behind to mourn us."[15] In a flattering postscript aimed at eliciting Barrie's financial help for Scott's widow and son, the explorer wrote: "I never met a man in my life whom I admired and loved more than you but I never could show you how much your friendship meant to me—for you had much to give and I nothing."[16]

At the end of his life Scott could not stop himself from deploying well-chosen words for ulterior motives. Nor had he lost his elevating eloquence in the blackness of that tent. In his "Message to the Public," penciled on the back of his last notebook, he again stressed the example that he and the others had set, by demonstrating that modern-day Englishmen "can endure hardship, help one another and meet death with as great a fortitude as ever in the past." These sentences alone were sufficient to guarantee him a prominent niche in the pantheon of his country's heroes.[17] The inspirational power of his larger opus was recognized immediately by his contemporaries. In *The Independent Weekly*, for instance, Scott's last journal was lauded for adding "an imperishable page to English literature, more valuable than any of the manuscripts of poetry and fiction treasured in the British Museum, for it reveals the very heart of a noble man, written in his dire extremity and defeat, yet courageous, patriotic, uncomplaining, unselfish, sincere."[18]

Not that Scott was alone among explorers in using the written word to sing his own praises and thereby enshrine his reputation. Writing and publishing a hagiographical book about a polar expedition was the leader's prerogative and his testament. It was practically a sure-fire way to acquire fame and considerable income—vital, in cases where outside funding was lacking or insufficient, for financing future expeditions.[19] Scott had certainly had that goal firmly in mind. His first book, *The Voyage of Discovery*, published in 1905, had earned a chronically penurious Scott nearly eight times what the Royal Navy paid him in a year—and made him a household name.[20] Yet when he was organizing his *Terra Nova* expedition five years later, during an economic downturn in England when the Admiralty was no longer in a position to fund polar expeditions, he had to solicit donations of products from manufacturers and even shilling contributions from schoolboys (to help pay for dogs and equipment).[21] Even with this help, Scott was still so short of cash that he could not afford to spend two years in Antarctica and therefore had to head south from New Zealand in November 1910 even though it was then already late in the season.[22] For him, reaching the South Pole first was a huge roll of the dice: if he succeeded he would be "made for life," but if he failed, he would not likely get funding for another expedition.[23]

Anticipating that he would be the first to get there (still unaware of Amundsen's plans when the *Terra Nova* left London in June of that year), Scott could see his book becoming a huge bestseller, and he started keeping his journal with that eventuality in mind. It did turn out that way, but, of course, Scott did not live to reap the benefits. After Kathleen Scott received the three notebooks her husband had beside him in Antarctica at the time of his death, she first sold the serial rights to *Strand* magazine for £2 thousand (roughly £170 thousand or $250 thousand today) and then negotiated a contract with the London publisher Smith, Elder, giving her the bulk of the proceeds from book sales. The two-volume *Scott's Last Expedition* came out toward the end of 1913. Within two months the profits exceeded £9 thousand (approximately $1 million today). Several other editions subsequently came out, with sales remaining steady until the 1950s. So by the time she died, in July of 1947, Kathleen Scott, an accomplished sculptor whose second husband was a baron, could rightly be considered a wealthy woman.[24] Robert Falcon Scott had done his duty by her.

He thus joined a long line of explorers who had turned ill fortune in the Arctic and Antarctic into good fortune at the bank. During the first decades of the nineteenth century, British navigators William Parry and John Ross had capitalized on the public's insatiable appetite for tales of heroic adventure and discovery by publishing accounts of their quests for the Northwest Passage. Even though these were plainly written (as befitted reports originally intended for the Admiralty), they sold well and made their authors famous. (The young Brontë sisters, Charlotte and Emily, were so enamored of these two dashing naval officers that they renamed a pair of toy soldiers for them.) Because Parry and other naval commanders of that day had exclusive rights to publish narratives about their expeditions, they were assured of the profits. Parry, for example, negotiated a contract with the eminent London publisher John Murray giving him a thousand guineas for the rights to Parry's journal about his second Arctic voyage—an amount more than ten times his yearly lieutenant's salary. Later on, well-known British polar explorers like John Franklin could make a tidy sum from their stories even if—as in Franklin's case—they did not include glowing successes. After coming back to England and being celebrated as the "man who ate his boots," Franklin signed a lucrative deal with Murray to write a book detailing his harrowing ordeal in the Canadian wilderness. This was a huge success, turning Franklin—despite his blunders and the expedition's calamities—into a national hero. The book's descriptions of near starvation and hints of cannibalism doubtless drove up sales: this first book of Franklin's—over eight hundred pages long, in two volumes—went into four British editions in the year and a half after it first came out, while the narrative of his second, far less gripping overland expedition only came out in one edition.[25]

The huge popularity of books about polar explorers did not escape the notice of an "anxious, driven, sickly, brilliant, adventurous, and insecure young man" named Elisha Kent Kane.[26] As his biographers have pointed out and his letters reveal, Kane epitomized the "culture of fame" in midcentury America. With the help of his brother, Tom, Kane created a persona that was tailor-made to fit the needs of his countrymen for a resourceful hero who, struggling gamely against an implacable Nature, triumphed over great odds, and brought them great glory. To captivate his readers, Kane embellished his improbable tales with grand language and a heightened, Romantic sensibility. It helped that Kane had not previously read any books about the Arctic, so that his imagination was not constrained by the more realistic style of storytelling then practiced: instead, he could write about it *de novo*, with an artist's framing eye and a novelist's flair for drama.[27]

Mailed back to his brother and father in Philadelphia, Kane's vivid, on-the-spot impressions during the first Grinnell expedition were given a "final polish" and his "pretty fancies" reshaped for publication, giving Tom confidence that Elisha's forthcoming book would "make more sensation than any thing written by a Navy man in our day."[28] Its success was all but guaranteed since articles of Elisha's had already appeared in print, putting the "public mind . . . in beautiful order for its reception." Tom Kane was dead-right: his brother's second book—the massive, two-volume *Arctic Explorations*—was reportedly read by as many as three million people. Its author's grasp of the melodramatic style was on full display. For instance, in describing what he considered to be the "continent" of Greenland, Kane wrote:

> Imagine, now, the centre of such a continent, occupied through nearly its whole extent by a deep, unbroken sea of ice, that gathers perennial increase from the water-shed of vast snow-covered mountains and all the precipitations of the atmosphere upon its own surface. Imagine this, moving onward like a great glacial river, seeking outlets at every fjord and valley, rolling icy cataracts into the Atlantic and Greenland seas; and having at last reached the northern limit of the land that has borne it up, pouring out a mighty frozen torrent into unknown Arctic space.[29]

These two publications made the Kane family rich.[30] (His second—and last—book alone netted $75 thousand in royalties—or $2.2 million in today's terms.) Like other expedition leaders, Kane left out the mistakes he had made and their tragic consequences, including the avoidable deaths (due to hypothermia) of three of the two dozen men who had gone with him. After his party finally returned to New York Harbor in the fall of 1854, Kane was relieved that, during the welcoming reception, no crew members uttered a single word that contradicted his version of a harmonious, well-led expedition. In constructing his narratives with an eye to fulfilling his armchair audience's hunger for vicarious adventure, adversity, danger, suffering, forbearance, and heroism, Elisha Kane created a model for polar books that would be imitated—not always successfully—by many later explorers, up to Scott and beyond. What Kane had astutely sensed was that Americans were in desperate need of heroes.

In the decade before the Civil War, the United States was virtually bereft of living great men. The nation had not been at war since 1814, and the opportunities for young men to demonstrate courage and fortitude had since diminished. For a time, adventures in the Western wilderness filled the void that had been created by a lasting peace. Early settlement of the Ohio Valley had given rise to mythical figures like Daniel Boone, but once the empty spaces on the map were filled in and Native American tribes driven out, the potential for conquest and glory there evaporated. The remote, exotic, and forbidding Far North then presented itself as the next frontier for the restless and expansive national spirit. As the United States was transitioning from an agricultural to an industrial nation, a longing to return to this earlier era, to escape the confines of civilization, became evident—the urge captured in Huck Finn's eagerness to "light out for the Territory." If settled Americans were unable or unwilling to do this, they could at least satisfy their curiosity by reading about what others had done. As the literary critic William E. Lenz has written (in regard to Antarctica), nineteenth-century exploration furthered cultural renewal and affirmation—a process in which many Americans took great pride. Books by explorers reinforced belief in the country's initiative, determination, scientific know-how, and manly virtues.[31] At the same time, greater affluence, combined with the mass production of books, was turning the United States into a nation of readers. The number and circulation of major newspapers were growing exponentially, spearheaded by publishers like James Gordon Bennett Sr., Horace Greeley, and Henry Jarvis Raymond (founder of the *New York Times* in 1851). National readership more than doubled between 1828 and 1840, from 60 million to 168 million. As part of this trend, the monetary value of books that sold well was apparent: Nathaniel Hawthorne's *Scarlet Letter* sold four thousand copies in its first ten days, but two years later, in 1852, a million persons purchased *Uncle Tom's Cabin*.

So what Kane tapped into was a newly discovered goldmine. In England, the commercializing of explorers as carriers of national values and aspirations had a longer history. As early as the 1820s John Franklin had sensed he could make a fortune by turning humdrum naval journals into bestsellers: therefore he refined the narrative style and language of his second book to attract a general audience.[32] The popularity of his Canadian narratives convinced later British explorers to write as compellingly so that they, too, could appeal to this burgeoning market. Then the mysterious disappearance of the Franklin party created intense interest in the search to find traces of the missing men. After Francis Leopold McClintock had returned to England with sensational news about the fate of these sailors, he could count on his book selling well—as it did. Copies of the first edition sold out within a few weeks.[33] Press barons and government officials seeking to promote polar exploration also fueled public fascination with stories of heroic achievement at the ends of the earth.

A leading player in this effort was Clements Markham, the personification of British imperial aspirations at the poles. As a scarcely twenty-year-old Royal Navy cadet, Markham had participated in one of the Franklin search missions and contracted a bad case of Arctic fever. In his forties he had returned, rekindling a love for voyages of discovery, courageous young explorers, and the patriotic glory that attended them. While serving as president of the Royal Geographical Society he had almost single-handedly revived British interest in polar expeditions. Markham marshalled his formidable personality and writing talents to convince his countrymen that England should once again rule the Arctic seas. He publicized the lure of polar adventure and discovery most effectively in *The Threshold of the Unknown Region*, published in 1873. In his introduction to this book, Markham declared his purpose was to "recall the stories of earlier adventurers, to narrate the recent efforts of gallant adventurers of various nationalities to cross the threshold [into the unknown], to set forth the arguments in favour of a renewal of Arctic exploration by England, and to enumerate, in detail, the valuable and important results to be derived from North Polar discovery." True to his word, Markham larded his descriptions of earlier expeditions with homage to Franklin's "gallant crews," the "remarkable success" of Charles Hall's *Polaris* expedition, the "steady determination" and "pluck" of Leigh Smith (another pioneering Arctic voyager), and Kane's important discoveries and selfless care of his crew members when they were stricken by scurvy. So enumerating this "glorious roll of Arctic worthies" gave latter-day British officers and men illustrious examples to emulate, so that their country could complete the conquest of the still-uncharted Far North.[34]

Books like *The Threshold of the Unknown* and Kane's *Arctic Explorations* raised the bar for future accounts of polar adventures. The enormous commercial success of such volumes convinced other explorers they needed to write equally dramatic and self-aggrandizing narratives. (Publishers, naturally, encouraged them.) But telling their stories compellingly could be an even greater challenge than trekking for weeks through ice and snow. (A recent biographer of Frederick Cook's has speculated that the Brooklyn physician "may have reasoned that to be able to write the account of such a journey [to the North Pole] without actually having done it . . . would be a greater accomplishment than the journey itself."[35]) Explorers felt pressures to exaggerate or even fabricate what they had accomplished in order to make their books more exciting. The public's craving for sensationalism—to ratchet up polar narratives as Kane had done—pushed them in that direction. Each new tale had to deliver on these greater expectations or else disappoint readers. In this hyperbolic climate, there was a temptation for explorers to claim feats they had not actually accomplished. The telling of the story became detached from the actual truth. But so falsifying their stories put these explorer-writers in a morally dubious position: they had to live with the awareness that they had not been completely honest. Usually they were protected from having their distortions or lies revealed by agreements that no other versions of their expeditions could be published. Thus the explorer's story became *the* official account, but often at the expense of his integrity. There was still always a chance that someday he would be found out. But many found the risk well worth taking. The rewards were simply too enticing to resist.

This tendency to subjectify historical writing and infuse it with hortatory messages became common during the second half of the nineteenth century, when nations like England and the United States sought to revitalize patriotic values as they competed for prestige and stature around the world. To celebrate masculine virtues of courage and self-sacrifice, they needed books that captured not only the great deeds of the past but also the enduring national spirit that made these so admirable. Charles Kingsley's 1855 novel *Westward Ho! or the Voyages and Adventures of Sir Amyas Leigh, Knight, of Burrough, in the county of Devon, in the Reign of Her Most Glorious Majesty, Queen Elizabeth* illustrates this trend in England, where an infatuation with medieval and Renaissance chivalry acted as an antidote for what was seen as a morally depleted and materialistic modern world. In his dedication to this tale of storied victories over the Spanish, a chauvinistic Kingsley extolled "that type of English virtue, at once manful and godly, practical and enthusiastic, prudent and self-sacrificing" that was exemplified by his characters.[36] For nineteenth-century readers, Arctic and Antarctic explorers filled a void formerly occupied by saints, Arthurian knights, and other legendary figures of the distant past. They were regarded in equally reverent and adoring terms well into the next century. For instance, in his 1910 *Heroes of the Polar Seas*, J. Kennedy Maclean hailed the superior virtue of these "lion-hearts," and the "fortitude and heroism" that have distinguished their efforts to reach the poles. No other human endeavor could claim "the same glamour and romance" or match the "wonderful heroism" of those men who have "laid their all upon the altar of duty."[37] Private organizations and governments that sponsored polar expeditions similarly glorified their participants in order to justify the investments made in them. The medals handed out by organizations like the Royal Geographical Society elevated what might appear to some to be rather modest accomplishments.[38] Because they had so much riding on a successful outcome, sponsors like the Explorers Club were loath to question the claims of historic firsts made by expeditions they had financed, such as Robert Peary's assertion in 1909 that he had reached the North Pole.[39]

During this period, there was a gradual shift away from celebrating genuine geographical milestones to acknowledging noble, self-sacrificing effort. This change came in light of the dismal record of disappointment, disaster, and defeat compiled by expedition after expedition attempting to blaze new routes through the ice or conquer the poles. This litany of failure dated back to the lost Franklin party and the dozens of relief and search vessels that had been dispatched to find survivors. In death, Franklin was deified for his "gallantry," even though it was not clear what he had done to deserve this honor. After it was confirmed that he and all of his 128 officers and men had perished—from cold, scurvy, disease, starvation, lead poisoning, or despair—without having sailed through the fabled Northwest Passage, some members of the British public were perplexed: how could the leader of such a disastrous voyage be considered heroic? The best answer Alfred, Lord Tennyson, could come up with when he was composing an epitaph for Franklin in Westminster Abbey was to contrast the explorer's earthly failure with his heavenly "success":

NOT here! the white North has thy bones; and thou
Heroic sailor-soul,
Art passing on thine happier voyage now
Toward no earthly pole.

To the left of these verses and a marble bust of Franklin in the Chapel of St. John the Evangelist was placed an inscription commemorating him and his "gallant crews" for "completing the discovery of the North-West Passage." But here, too, a flowery phrase was stretching the truth. One of Franklin's ships had, indeed, entered a passage that would have taken them in a northwesterly direction to the Arctic Ocean, but had gotten stuck there, on the vestibule of that journey. After Franklin's death, surviving crew members had pushed ahead over the ice and established that a channel ran further westward, but to call this "completing the discovery" of a route to Asia overstates what they actually achieved (even in light of what we know since *Terror* was located in 2016). But the British public back then was not particularly interested in getting the facts right: they wanted something to cheer.

In fact, Franklin was declared a hero merely because he had *tried* to accomplish something grand and noble. Later polar explorers whose lives also came to a tragic end were similarly exalted. George De Long and his men on the *Jeannette* and—to a lesser degree—Charles Hall on the *Polaris* were notable examples of explorers whose death in the frozen Far North led to their apotheosis. The premature death of Elisha Kent Kane—in Cuba, only in his thirties—had brought him a similar veneration. But Robert Falcon Scott would surpass them all, thanks to the stirring words he left behind in his tent—sanctifying words that put him out of reach, "beyond our poor power to add or detract," as Lincoln had said about the dead at Gettysburg. Those who survived their expeditions would face a more arduous path to immortality—one littered with the inconsistencies and imperfections of long, complicated lives. As they aged, once idolized explorers would not always measure up to their own graven images, no matter how hard they and their admirers sought to merge them. In lasting so long they displaced their own legends. If Scott had somehow made it back to Hut Point and then spent the rest of his life explaining why he had gotten to the pole after Amundsen, his contemporaries would have thought of him as an indecisive, inadequate, and deeply flawed leader. If his unexpurgated journals had been published during his lifetime, the halo over his head might have been removed a long time ago. But in early death he found a sheltering shroud. No one was going to parse Scott's own epitaph. He would have the last word.

In Edwardian England, printing the legend took priority over revealing the bald facts. After Scott's death, some of his companions who did return home recalled him as a kind of demigod. They were already cementing his heroic, self-deprecating image. In his book on the *Terra Nova* expedition, the photographer Herbert Ponting recalled asking Scott, at the outset of their voyage south, what kind of reception he expected he would receive if he returned to England as the conqueror of the South Pole: "He replied that he cared nothing for this sort of thing; that he would willingly forgo all acclamation both now and later; that all he desired was to complete the work begun on our first expedition seven years ago, reach the goal of his hopes, and get back to his work in the Navy again. This reply was characteristic of the man. Ambitious, yet modest and assuming, he was disdainful of the plaudits of the crowd, and show and ostentation were foreign to his nature."[40] Writing about "our Leader" later in this book, Ponting curiously described him a man of "splendid physique," whose face was a "faithful index to the resolution and courage that dominated his soul," a man who was "Sound in his judgment, and just in his criticisms . . . always quick to appreciate and generous in praise." Scott's one admitted defect—his occasional moody silence—was justified by his "sense of obligation to his country to push the venture to success."

Such elevation of polar explorers was representative of their times: biographies of great men and women were supposed to highlight their admirable qualities, not dwell upon the warts and other blemishes that fascinate our own, more skeptical and inquisitive age. But romanticizing the deeds of figures like Scott also modeled the courage and selflessness that countries like England, Norway, Italy, Germany, France, and the United States wanted revived to spur national regeneration. Not long after Scott's death, the London *Times* opined that his sacrifice showed that "in an age of depressing materialism men can still be found to face unknown hardship, heavy risk, and even death, in pursuit of an idea, and that the unconquerable will can carry them through, loyal to the last to the charge they have undertaken." Scott and his men had snatched "victory out of the jaws of death" by upholding the "temper of men who build empires."[41] This was a nationalist cause Scott had consciously made his own, and one that he repeatedly called attention to in his journal—particularly when he was close to death and could perceive that his importance as a living, breathing human being was giving way to symbolic value.

For Arctic and Antarctic explorers who lacked Scott's literary gifts or who did not regard their expeditions as having such emblematic meaning, telling and selling their stories had more pragmatic consequences: they paid the bills and made future expeditions possible. Charles Hall, for one, was able to finance his second voyage north in 1864 with a boost from the publicity and profits generated by a book on his first expedition, *Arctic Researches and Life among the Esquimaux*. During his disastrous last voyage, on the *Polaris*, Hall had planned on confiscating all the diaries, journals, and similar records written by his officers and crew members so that he could cannibalize them in putting together his own account to fund future trips. For Roald Amundsen, who could not count on backing from the Norwegian government, producing books was an essential component of his fundraising. Unfortunately, he wasn't very good at this. He was hamstrung by his disinterest in writing, as well as by his innate, Scandinavian modesty. So his books failed to deliver what readers wanted from polar narratives. In his diary of the *Belgica* voyage, Amundsen stuck to recounting the facts, shying away from the psychological insights that would make Frederick Cook's account of this expedition so absorbing.

His Canadian biographer, Stephen Bown, has put a positive spin on this understated approach: "Amundsen wrote about his exploits with a wry, self-deprecating sense of humour free of the nationalist bombast and pedantic cereal-box philosophy, the fake moralizing and shallow introspection, that was so common in the pronouncements of many other explorers of the era."[42] The ultimate pragmatist, Amundsen had no interest in exaggerating his accomplishments: they could speak for themselves. It wasn't until he found himself some seventy thousand kroner (roughly $10 thousand) short when about to leave for the Northwest Passage in the spring of 1903 that Amundsen was convinced by a Norwegian chemist and part-time journalist to write a newspaper article outlining his plans. This front-page spread caught the eye of two wealthy ship owners, whose generous donations then enabled Amundsen to set sail. Henceforth, he never again neglected publicity.[43] Even still, the Norwegian never really warmed to what he considered a necessary evil. After he and his men made it to the South Pole in 1911, newspaper editors and publishers besieged Amundsen with lucrative offers.[44] But the winner in this bidding war—John Murray in England—ended up with a less-than-scintillating book:[45] Amundsen made this thrilling adventure sound like "an amusing ski outing," undertaken by a "jolly group going about their tasks without a care in the world."[46] His description of their arrival at their goal could not have been more leaden, or more unlike Scott's: "We reckoned now that we were at the Pole."[47] Reviews of *The South Pole* were generally unfavorable and sales poor.[48]

In sum, writing about the poles could be as demanding as going there: one set out into uncharted territory with grand hopes—for fame and fortune. As authors as well as explorers, some possessed the skills required for success, had some good luck along the way, and afterward accomplished what they had set out to do, becoming rich and famous. Others did not fare as well. The urge to conquer new frontiers and the urge to write about these polar adventures could go hand in hand: one could sustain the other. The ability to tell their stories well could enhance their reputations and make them rich. Pressures to perform both "journeys" successfully were enormous, for much was riding on these outcomes. In writing their stories, explorers could easily succumb to the temptation to embellish here and there in order to make their deeds appear more heroic and make their books more popular. For no one could dispute what they asserted. Over time, as the goal of Arctic and Antarctic exploration narrowed to making it first to the poles, the men undertaking these grueling treks would be likewise tempted to lie about what they had accomplished. Cheating—altering entries in a logbook or putting down the wrong coordinates on a map—was also fairly easy and almost impossible to detect. Truth at the poles was highly subjective—it was what the explorer said it was. In the frozen wastes at the ends of the earth, as on the written page, he exercised the unchallenged dominion of a god, and it was solely up to him to determine how he would use this. Whether to falsely claim a triumph or openly admit a defeat was often the choice that had to be made. He could choose to live with fame, or with himself. Only he would know for sure what kind of man he was.

CHAPTER TWELVE

PRINTING THE LEGEND

T hroughout most of the Victorian era, determined young men headed
north and south in ships looking for validation. True, they were
hoping to make geographical discoveries like the Northwest Passage,
the Open Polar Sea, and the two poles, but their voyages into the vast,
blinding whiteness at the top and bottom of the world were really tests
of who they were and what they could achieve when the odds were
hopelessly stacked against them. Aside from the battlefield, there were
no other places that provided such proving grounds. But progress was
frustratingly slow: expeditions had to hole up for months if not years in
the darkness, inside makeshift huts or ice-shrouded ships, to await the
day when they could finally move on, and often it never came. Too often
they were pushed back by relentlessly advancing ice like soldiers under
an overwhelming counterattack. Too often the heavy wooden hulls were
crumpled like orange crates, lifted high and groaning like beasts in great
pain into the vast twinkling vault of the polar night and then released to
slowly slip back and then slide beneath the inky surface, leaving the men
utterly helpless, thousands of miles from home, with only a few blankets,
cans of pemmican, and bags of biscuits—and no idea which way to go.

Because they could not win this war against the polar elements, it was
hard to say what counted as success. At times, the best they could do was
to pile up stones on a windswept promontory, plant a flag on some previously unknown coastline, or take a reading with a sextant to document
that they had come farther north or south than any other human beings.
Thus they left their marks. But these too would quickly disappear: the

snow would cover everything over, and it would look as if they had never been there. So their last moments staring silently up at the stars before turning around and pointing their strides toward home were bittersweet. It was not at all like winning a race and then shouting and throwing their hats into the air. It felt more like leaving a church after the last hymn had been sung, and there was nothing more to be said. There was no feeling of exuberance. They were deeply humbled. The ice kingdom had worn them down, day after day, month after month, making them feel they were just some intrusive feature of the landscape that had had the impudence to stand out above the rest, and now the wind and the ice and the snow were conspiring to wipe away all their traces. If the cold and bad food, the scurvy and the loneliness, hadn't killed them, or driven them mad, or reduced them to a shivering bundle of rags with frostbitten toes and hundred-yard stares, then one could call that a victory, perhaps. But the men didn't use words like that. Mostly they were just glad to be getting out of there alive.

Over time, the point of going so far for so little gain was lost on most of these men, but others kept coming, raw recruits ignorant of what lay in store for them. They, too, had their tests to pass and journeys to complete. There were always more men who longed to find out how well they would hold up. But fewer came now, since the Franklin disaster had shown the folly of sending large groups far into the Arctic and Antarctic. Too many might become trapped and die, all together at one place, and governments didn't want that on their consciences or in the newspapers. Those who still arrived, on stately tall ships with iron-sheathed bows, had added reason for believing that what they were trying to do was important. Here, in this frozen wasteland, they were not only showing their own mettle, but their country's, too. They were competing against men from other countries, battling the same elements, suffering the same deprivations, vying to set new records, to show the world who was best. It was like fighting a war. Only one could emerge the victor. As this century was drawing to a close, a nation's prowess was measured more by the extent of its territorial reach than by the might of its armies. Acquiring new land was a symbolic stand-in for triumphing on the battlefield. But in this land grab, there were only a precious few prizes left to be claimed.

The two poles—deep within the icy, forbidding lands at the ends of the earth—were the ultimate ones. They had no intrinsic value: these were not places to establish colonies or extract resources. They, too, were only symbols. The poles were earthly oddities, geographically precise locations without any physical reality. They were merely abstractions on a map. As Robert Peary would put it, the North Pole was "a theoretical point, without length, breadth or thickness."[1] The author of a recent book on the Cook-Peary controversy has defined it more philosophically as "a spot in the mind of man where even the concepts of the mind—time and direction—are no longer valid . . . a place whose location can be determined only by other concepts of the mind—numbers and letters manipulated in abstract formulae."[2] In short, it was an illusion. The North Pole only mattered, as George Leigh Mallory would say of Everest, because it was there.[3] But, even for only that reason, these two dots where all longitudinal lines came together had taken on great significance.

The country whose emissaries first set foot there would attest to its supremacy, just as, in the twentieth century, landing on the moon first would. Having rebuffed human advances for so long, the poles had become even more irresistible, like a woman who has spurned unwanted suitors for years. Getting there had become a grim obsession, for nothing less would do. The world's attention was riveted by the expeditions dispatched there. Millions of ordinary citizens avidly followed the explorers' every step in the newspapers—cheered on these small bands of fur-clad, shivering men carrying their tiny, tattered flags, realizing that their progress through ice floes and blizzards lent meaning to their own lives. For it was their struggle, too, and they badly wanted their share of the spoils.

In a larger sense, the race to the poles was a test for the entire species. In the ice, it might be Englishmen against Norwegians, expedition against expedition, as they gamely plodded on, but subliminally at least what was driving these intrepid bands forward was their belief that finally reaching these two imaginary places—the last terrestrial frontiers—would prove something important to all of them. They were suffering to show what humans were still capable of doing, in an age dominated by machines, in which *Homo sapiens* seemed diminished. They were going to affirm that no goal was out of reach, so long as one tried hard enough and long enough to reach it. They would prove that humankind held sway over the entire planet, even in its most remote corners. Like the explorers' courage, the march of civilization would not accept any limits.

For their leaders, it was about something else. Their ambitions were monomaniacal and self-centered. Becoming the first to plant a foot at the poles would be the fulfillment of *their* lives, what *they* had striven for all these years. It would bring them the fame and adulation they had sought since childhood and enshrine their names in the annals of human endeavor forever. Their pursuit of the poles, while couched in language that might appear self-effacing, was anything but: it was all about them. And they would go to any lengths to prevail. However, the abstract nature of the poles made "discovering" them fiendishly complicated. Explorers could approach these locations with the help of compasses, sextants, and dead reckoning— the latter highly inaccurate because of the uneven polar terrain. But in the end, as they got very close, it came down to guesswork. There were no maps to guide them, no landmarks, no tracks in the snow pointing the way, no striped barber pole rising above the pressure ridges to tell them where to stop. Making it to ninety degrees north or south and knowing when that had been accomplished presented extraordinary challenges, particularly after enduring the most arduous trekking in the world. Expeditions aiming for the North Pole had to travel for over two weeks from their northern-most depot or staging area, covering between fifteen and twenty-five miles a day with little food and less sleep, and in temperatures that rarely rose above minus thirty degrees, even in midsummer. In Antarctica, the journey across the Great Ice Barrier (also known as the Ross Ice Shelf), up the steep side of the Beardsmore Glacier, and then over the high-altitude polar plateau, in even more brutal conditions, took longer—over three weeks for Scott's and Amundsen's parties in 1911 and 1912.

Moreover, because the sites of the poles were not obvious, explorers had to take great pains to determine their positions so that they could substantiate their claims to having reached them. In their attempting to do so, the earth's magnetic fields and polar topography worked against them. At the top and bottom of the earth, compasses aren't of much use: they continue to point toward the magnetic—not geographical—poles, and near the North Pole that means to the south. Taking accurate sextant readings requires a true horizon—something nearly impossible to find with jutting ice blocking the line of sight. The sun also has to be visible—at least briefly—so that the exact angle of its elevation can be measured. But at the poles the sky is rarely clear. Furthering complicating this task was the fact that the North Pole is not situated at a fixed location but sits atop a frozen sea made up of constantly moving ice: where the pole is one day is not where it will be the next.[4] On the stationary Antarctic continent, locating the pole was thus somewhat easier, especially for Scott and his men, as the Norwegians had left their tent standing, along with its deflating greeting ("Welcome to 90 Degrees"), to mark the spot or, as Amundsen realistically put it, "as near the pole as humanly possible with the instruments at our disposal."[5] Knowing the British were hot on his heels, the Norwegian had hastily done his level best to confirm he had reached the right place, first with a jury-rigged sextant, then by having his men fan out for twelve miles in all four directions like prospectors stacking out a claim so large that they would never have to worry about anyone challenging it. When Scott's party came upon this forlorn campsite thirty three days later they were so despondent that they gave no thought to contesting what their rivals had apparently achieved. Besides, English gentlemen did not accuse other gentlemen of lying. They brooded and stared disconsolately at the camera and let that image do the talking for them.[6]

In the extreme north, the situation had been different, and so had the men contesting the pole. First of all, this was not really a "race": Peary made his dash to the top nearly a full year after his competitor, Cook, asserted he had gotten there. Furthermore, Peary did not hear about Cook's startling announcement until after the navy commander had returned to New York on the SS *Roosevelt*, convinced *he* had been the first to get to the pole, in 1909. Secondly, the competition to "discover" the North Pole was strictly personal—Cook and Peary were both Americans—so national pride was not on the line, as it would be in Antarctica. Without doubt, Amundsen and Scott had their own selfish motives—as usual, fame and money topped the list—for sledging to the South Pole, but these were glossed over by a patriotic veneer; both parties wanted to bring honor to their countries by arriving there ahead of the other. For Peary and Cook, wrapping themselves in the Stars and Stripes was incidental: the victory would belong to one of them, not to their country. So far the two American explorers had failed in every attempt to reach the pole. This would be their last shot at glory. The other difference in these two quests was that Cook and Peary were chasing a phantom. There was no *there* there. At the top of the world, no hard, irrefutable facts could be established, no measurements verified, no claims proven or disproven. Truth hinged almost entirely on the explorer's word. And with these two men that was a slender reed, indeed. Given these circumstances and their enormous ambitions, the temptation to fudge the facts and cheat was irrepressible.

Making dubious claims had been part of polar exploration since the first ships had come upon a strange, unknown land, given it a name, and boasted of their "discovery." In the modern era, a notable case involved the then Lieutenant Commander Richard E. Byrd. In the spring of 1926, he and his copilot, Floyd Bennett, had taken off from an airfield on the island of Spitsbergen (now Svalbard), Norway, in a three-engine, Dutch-made Fokker F.VII with plans to fly over the North Pole—some 1,535 miles away—for the first time. After a nearly sixteen-hour flight, the two men returned safely, declaring they had reached their destination. Byrd was hailed as a great national hero, awarded the Congressional Medal of Honor, received by President Calvin Coolidge at the White House, and feted by several hundred thousand persons during a ticker-tape parade up Broadway.[7] A year ahead of Lindbergh's solo flight across the Atlantic, America had its first hero of the skies. The following year Byrd would capitalize upon his newfound stardom to finance a similar flight over the South Pole. But, decades later, questions were raised about his first record-setting one. In 1996, Byrd's diary—long kept under lock and key by family members—was made public, revealing sextant readings that differed from what he had originally stated in his official report to the National Geographic Society. It appeared that Byrd—or someone else—had erased the solar altitude he had first recorded in his flight log to make it look as if he had flown as far as the pole. In fact, he had turned back some fifty or more miles short of his objective, purportedly due to an engine oil leak. Even at the time, some had argued that Byrd's plane, the *Josephine Ford*, could not possibly have covered the distance to the pole and back in the time he and Bennett had been in the cockpit. Skepticism about the flight's course had reemerged after Byrd's death in 1957, with various published accounts suggesting that the explorer had confessed to not having reached the pole. But, to this day, there is no conclusive proof, one way or the other.[8] With Cook and Peary, the compulsion to alter, distort, or misrepresent the facts appears to have been just as great, if not greater.

Over a century after he claimed to have reached the North Pole in 1908, Cook remains the more complex figure, whose motives and personality cannot easily be discerned. He did experience a series of life-changing events that seem to have made him susceptible to stretching the truth. After losing his first wife, Libby, and their only child in 1890, Cook had sought solace, escape, and adventure by signing on as a physician on two earlier polar expeditions—first to the Arctic, with Peary, then to the Antarctic, on board the *Belgica*. Subsequently he led two parties through Alaska's Denali range. In later years, he would recall being first drawn to the polar world after hearing about Peary's plans in 1891, at a time when Cook was still struggling to get his medical career started: "It was as if a door to a prison cell had opened. I felt the first indomitable, commanding call of the Northland. To invade the Unknown, to assail the fastness of the white, frozen North—all that was latent in me, the impetus of that ambition born in childhood, perhaps before birth, and which had been stifled and starved, surged up tumultuously within me."[9] The "spell" of the Arctic had taken hold of him and would not let go. After showing compassion for others while providing medical care on these first expeditions (setting Peary's broken leg, helping men on the *Belgica* ward off scurvy), Cook seemed to become more self-centered. From then on, he focused on making a name for himself (and earning money) by accomplishing—or, rather, claiming to have accomplished—historic exploratory feats.[10]

One can only speculate what brought about this change in Cook's temperament and ambitions. Most likely it was his (not unreasonable) realization that only spectacular "firsts" would bring him the fame and the income he needed to continue exploring.[11] The first of these was his 1906 climb to the top of what was then known at Mount McKinley, making him the first person to scale this highest (over twenty thousand foot) peak in North America. However, shortly after the North Pole controversy erupted, doubt was cast on this earlier claim of Cook's, as none of his photographs of the summit matched what subsequent climbers saw when they reached that point. Suspicions about his dishonesty would dog the New York physician for the rest of his life. Once he stopped exploring, his odd behavior only deepened this mistrust.[12] In retrospect, it seems that Cook had come to the conclusion that if he could not accomplish what he had set out to do then he would have to settle for convincing others that he had.

Cook's rival was driven to succeed by deep-seated insecurities. After his father had died when he was barely three years old, Peary had moved with his mother from Pennsylvania back to coastal Maine, where he would become the center of her small universe—much the way that dominant mothers of other famous men of his era (Franklin Roosevelt and Douglas MacArthur, to name two) would act after they were widowed.[13] This included doting on them, being excessively protective, and dressing them as little girls (as was common practice then). Considering him fragile, Peary's mother, Mary, kept him from roughhousing with other Portland boys his age, which gave young "Bertie" the label of sissy, as well as a lifelong lisp.[14] Her sheltering ways continued when she accompanied seventeen-year-old Robert to nearby Brunswick, to enroll in Bowdoin in the fall of 1873.[15] For the rest of his life, Peary was seemingly bent on erasing this childhood coddling and proving that he could more than hold his own against all others.[16] As one biographer has put it, "He was determined to be inferior to no man and obligated to none."[17] Early on, the unconquered and largely unexplored Far North beckoned to him as the place where he would demonstrate his worthiness. As a boy, Peary had read Elisha Kane's *Arctic Explorations* and first felt that region's tug on his imagination. In 1885, four years after joining the navy as a lieutenant in civil engineering, the twenty-nine-year-old Peary wrote down on a piece of paper his secret ambition to be the first man to make it to the top of the world. The following year he signed on with a whaler bound for Greenland and got his first look at the vast white expanse where his destiny lay. Practically from that day forward, Peary devoted his life to achieving that goal with almost superhuman singlemindedness.

In a broader cultural context, Cook and Peary represented the American ideal of the self-made man—a notion not as deeply rooted in the European psyche. They both were fiercely determined to rise to the top and set themselves apart from others through their own unflagging efforts, rather than depend upon personal connections, as many other explorers could. Theirs was a winner-take-all, Hobbesian view of life as ceaseless struggle, as exemplified by contemporaries like Jack London and John D. Rockefeller and fictional characters like Horatio Alger. Being self-reliant was central to their aspirations, and it thus was no coincidence that American polar explorers like Peary and Cook showed little interest in establishing friendships with their peers or subordinates. In the annals of Arctic and Antarctic exploration, there are few American equivalents to Amundsen's easygoing camaraderie with his fellow Norwegians on their way to the South Pole or Shackleton's almost maternal devotion to his men during the *Endurance* ordeal. Being first at all costs was a lonely, isolating quest. Hence, Peary felt no pangs of remorse when he told his loyal companion Bob Bartlett to turn back before the final push to the North Pole so that Peary would not have to share his triumph with another white man. Bartlett shed tears over this devastating decision, but Peary did not.[18]

Because they (like Scott Fitzgerald's fictional Gatsby) were creatures of their own invention, governed by their own rules, desperate for personal redemption, these two American explorers could more easily slip free of the moral coils that constrained others and could keep them from fulfilling *their* dreams. Cook and Peary would not let anything stop them, not even the need to tell the truth. Indeed, both took various steps to prevent that from being revealed. Neither man brought along any independent, reliable witnesses on their final dashes to the pole. After waving goodbye to the New York millionaire John R. Bradley (who had accompanied Cook to the Arctic, ostensibly to hunt for bear and walrus) at the far northern Greenland settlement of Annoatok in early September 1907, the Brooklyn explorer was—save for a German named Rudolph Franke—the only white person within hundreds of miles. Cook proceeded north toward the pole the following spring with only two sleds, twenty-six dogs, and two Inuit sledders. After dismissing Bartlett, the sole remaining white man in his party, when his goal was within his grasp, Peary went ahead with only his devoted companion of many years, the African-American Matthew Henson, and four Inuit sledders. Due to Henson's unwavering loyalty and lack of experience with navigational instruments, the explorer could count on any claim of his not being disputed.

Because of the small size and makeup of their entourages, Cook and Peary controlled the geographical data that were recorded along the way and then released to the press (and, later, to skeptical observers) about how far they had traveled. But neither man was particularly adept at determining their positions. This deficiency made it easier for them to get the figures wrong or inaccurately calculate the point they had reached. The pole itself was too protean to be precisely located—by them or by anyone else. So Cook and Peary could get away with admitting that, even though they had made their best, good-faith efforts to verify their "discovery," they could not be absolutely certain of it. In the first of three articles he published in *Hampton's Magazine* in 1911, the upstate New York doctor portrayed the Arctic as a "region of insanity, where one cannot believe the evidence gathered by one's eyes."[19] This peculiar state of mind had made it impossible for him to say exactly where he had been. Yet in this same article Cook asserted that he had, indeed, reached the pole. He was, in effect, taking his readers with him down the rabbit hole that lay at the top of the world. In his book-length account of his epic journey, Cook would reiterate that he could not be completely sure that he had made it to the top of the world. All he could state with certainty was that he had been the first person to reach "that spot known as the North Pole as far as it is, or ever will be, humanly possible to ascertain the location of that spot."[20] This vagueness and uncertainty plagued Peary as well. In fact, after he had returned to civilization, the explorer did not immediately issue a statement attesting that he had reached the pole.[21] It wasn't until he had heard about Cook's claim after arriving back in New York that Peary became convinced that he had gotten there first.[22]

Finally, aside from the quicksilver nature of their destination, any need to be sure of having reached ninety degrees north was trumped by their greater need to win this race. Peary had pursued the North Pole with ruthless tenacity for twenty-three years, neglecting family, friends, and a secure naval career in doing so.[23] (He spent only three of his first twenty-three years of marriage with his wife and their two children, and two of those with Josephine were in the Arctic.) When he left Greenland for the pole in the spring of 1909, he was fifty-three years old—nearly as superannuated as John Franklin had been when he had disappeared into the Arctic mists. Peary knew time was running out: this would be his last hurrah, his final bid for immortality. Likening his long quest to a chess game, he realized that "It was win this time or be forever defeated."[24] He fully knew that Americans only loved winners: his book about failing to reach his elusive goal during a previous (1906–1907) expedition had not sold well at all, even though Peary had managed to set a new Farthest North record.[25] In financing this next trip, he had cobbled together just enough money from the Peary Arctic Club to pay for necessary repairs of the *Roosevelt* and then gotten last-minute contributions from the widow of his philanthropist friend Morris K. Jesup, as well as from other donors, to cover the remaining expenses so that the ship could sail. But if Peary failed this time it was not likely they would help him again.

Cook was a younger man, still in his early forties, but also near the end of his rope. To sustain his checkered career, he, too, badly needed cash, and only reaching the North Pole would keep the funds flowing into his shrinking Brooklyn bank account. The son of German immigrants of modest means, Cook had never made a profitable living as a doctor (he was largely reliant on his second wife's assets) and had few of the wealthy, well-connected friends Peary could count upon—not to mention an influential admirer like President Theodore Roosevelt.[26] (Bradley, the big-game hunter from New York, was his only major benefactor.) Cook's ascent of Mount McKinley a few years before had been motivated by a shortage of money, and Cook was not in much better financial shape in 1908. In short, for both men, winning the "dash" to the pole was not only an abiding dream but an essential outcome for their psychological and material well-being.

Because getting there first was so vitally important to both men, it was almost inevitable that a bitter, interminable, and perhaps unresolvable dispute would arise over which one really deserved the laurels. Initially, the world wasn't quite sure what to make of this unprecedented and unsightly spectacle of two explorers arguing publicly over who had won what has been called the "most prized jewel in the crown of human exploration."[27] It was as if two dapper gentlemen in tails had showed up at the Metropolitan Opera house holding a ticket to the same front-row orchestra seat and then would not stop fighting over it when the curtain went up. The nasty squabble was embarrassing and demeaning. In the opinion of one contemporary author, even Peary's jubilant telegram announcing that he had "Nailed the Stars and Stripes to the Pole" was in bad taste, totally out of character for a "dignified naval officer."[28] Reflecting this general consternation, the first books written about the controversy diplomatically sought to stay above the fray. Opined another observer, "There is glory enough in it for both the daring explorers."[29] But clearly that was an unsustainable position: either one or the other had to be declared the winner.

The problem was that neither explorer had definitive proof. So, to secure this prize, they had to fight it out in the court of public opinion as doggedly as they had fought the elements in the unforgiving Arctic. Cook won the first round with his stunning announcement of success in September 1909. At first, he was wildly celebrated around the world and rapturously welcomed in Copenhagen as the greatest hero of the day. But then, after he failed to produce any documents to back up his word, doubt and skepticism crept in. In the professional and social circles that mattered, the little-known doctor did not enjoy the same stature and credibility as Peary to lend credibility to his claim. Enraged by his rival's claim and apparent attempt to steal his glory, the navy captain then launched a venomous verbal barrage, denouncing Cook as a liar and a fraud. (In 1911, Peary would snarl "What a consummate cur he is!"[30]) A legion of eminent scientists and explorers, including Ernest Shackleton, quickly rallied to Peary's side, having concluded that Cook could not possibly have arrived at ninety degrees north in the time period he had specified.[31] At first taken aback by this ferocious attack, Cook soon fired off his own salvo, insisting he had gotten to the pole first and calling Peary not only a liar, but a murderer and adulterer as well. (Peary had taken Inuit "wives" and fathered children by them.)

It turned out that Cook had left his papers behind in Greenland, and then, after Peary refused to allow them to be taken on board the *Roos-*

evelt, they had been lost. Peary's own records were locked up for decades in the vault of the National Geographic Society, which had sponsored him. Not being white, the only other witnesses to these alleged conquests of the North Pole were considered unreliable, and so their testimony was disregarded—an outcome both explorers could have expected.[32] Further disparaging of Cook was stoked by powerful, partisan institutions like the Explorers Club and newspapers like the *New York Times* (which had given Peary a significant advance on his book).[33] For example, in a September 1909 article, the *Times* crowed that London papers were all lining up behind Peary, adding that it was because of his "high reputation as a man and an explorer that the world accepts his word without a shadow of hesitation."[34] The Mainer was hailed as a genuine American hero, a man who had demonstrated tremendous courage and resolve in achieving this historic milestone. At the same time, the vicious nature of Peary's personal attacks on Cook and his refusal to have anything to do with his rival cost him considerable public support. Newspaper polls found that overwhelming majorities rejected the naval engineer's assertions because, as one article put it, "he had treated ungraciously a man who was trying to rob him of his glory."[35] It seemed that character, not written records, was to be arbiter of truth.

But graver doubts about Cook's own credibility arose after reports of his having apparently lied about having scaled Mount McKinley surfaced later in 1909. In short order he was tossed out of the Arctic Club of America, the Explorers Club, and similar organizations. He became a pariah. Cook's case was further weakened when a review of Peary's available records by "independent" experts (chosen by the National Geographic Society) ended with an endorsement of Peary's claim. When he testified before a congressional committee investigating the polar controversy, Peary was treated with respect, and the lawmakers ultimately concluded, in January 1911, that he had, indeed, made it to the North Pole.[36] Meanwhile, Cook's lobbying efforts in Washington to gain official recognition and a gold medal went nowhere. He was brusquely rebuffed.

In the searing words of Ohio congressman Simeon D. Fess, Cook now stood exposed as the "chief imposter of the age."[37] The explorer's 1923 conviction for mail fraud drove the final nail in his coffin, by seemingly confirming that he was an untrustworthy, dishonest character.

Over the ensuing years, most of those who studied the then-available documentation concurred that Peary had likely made it all the way to the top, and Cook had not. Public opinion accepted this verdict until the early 1970s, when a closer examination of a document of Peary's in the National Archives indicated that he had only gotten to within 121 miles of the North Pole—and that he had known this. Dennis Rawlins, the independent scholar who located this long-lost document, declared that it exposed "one of the greatest scientific frauds of this century."[38] This written record confirmed doubts that the explorer could have possibly covered the distance to the North Pole and back as quickly as he had asserted. (Peary had ridden most of the way on top of a sledge.) Furthermore, Rawlins and other researchers have questioned how Peary could have marched due north for some five hundred miles and ended up at the exact location of the pole with only a compass to guide him (and without a qualified navigator). Rawlins memorably dubbed this implausible feat a "413-mile Pole-in-one."[39] This paper, combined with other suspicious findings—such as clean pages apparently inserted in his diary after the fact—convinced the *Times* in 1997 to retract its longstanding advocacy of Peary's claim. Once cheered as a great American hero, he was now scorned as a megalomaniacal and mendacious cheat.

At the same time as Peary's reputation was plummeting, Cook's stock was rising. He came to be seen as the victim of a vicious vendetta, or, in the words of another historian, as "neither a liar nor a con man, but a unique and valuable hero, who, at the minimum, is not simply one of the greater victims in America's history, but the all-time champion"—a man who, in Cook's own words, had suffered "so bitterly and so inexpressibly" for defending his claim to have been the first person to make it to the North Pole.[40] Most recent scholars have come around to believing that both men lied and that neither actually got there.[41] One historian, Roger Launius at the Smithsonian Institution, has recently chimed in, "I have no doubt from what I have learned about both that they would willingly alter the truth for their benefit. They did so many other times that it is impossible not believe them capable of it here."[42]

The fact that this controversy has gone on for so long, with little sign of ever being laid to rest, says a great deal about Cook and Peary, their unbridled ambitions, and their disregard for facts when victory was all that mattered. For, even if neither man had deliberately lied about what they had accomplished, their failure to adequately document their journeys leaves them open to second-guessing and censure. But the ebb and flow in this long-running feud between backers of Cook and those of Peary says more about how American society has changed since these two larger-than-life figures dominated the headlines more than a century ago. Before then, a man's word was the measure of his character—and his deeds. To be a successful explorer one had to be an honorable person, because coping with the extraordinary challenges of surviving in an inhospitable environment, enduring prolonged isolation and hardship, and overcoming the constant dangers that came with such territory required more than physical stamina and courage; it called for moral strength. The notion that a person who made it to the North Pole could also be a liar and a cheat was tantamount to saying that a star football player could also be a paraplegic.[43] They were both equally contradictions in terms. The very public Cook-Peary spat confounded this assumption that ability and integrity were inseparable, if not virtually synonymous. No matter which of the two men had tried to deceive the world in order to win glory—or if they both had—blind admiration for heroic figures was called into question.

But such a change in outlook did not come easily: we like to look up at our heroes, not down on them. We don't want to go rummaging through their closets, discovering unpleasant facts. Thus, in the wake of the Cook-Peary dispute, a new yearning for genuinely selfless, uplifting, and uncomplicated heroes returned. In the polar realm, men like Scott and Shackleton amply filled this bill, their careers and reputations (seemingly) unblemished by any hint of moral failing. So did—especially for Americans—Charles Lindbergh, whose youthful innocence, naiveté, humility, and quiet courage revived the nineteenth-century notion that bona fide virtue undergirds great achievement. In the United States, belief in this truism persisted through World War II and into the 1960s. But then the country became embroiled in a war in Vietnam that put this to a severe test. As that conflict dragged on and tore the country apart, the discrepancy between honorable intentions and sordid deeds became all too apparent. The reason given by President Lyndon Johnson for going to war—an attack by North Vietnamese torpedo boats on an American destroyer in the Gulf of Tonkin—turned out to be a fabrication. Then lies to the public and Congress about the conduct, progress, scope, and likely outcome of the Vietnam War were exposed by the publication of the "Pentagon Papers" in the *New York Times*. Concurrently, President Richard Nixon's dishonesty and criminality were revealed during the Watergate scandal and the subsequent congressional investigation that resulted in his impeachment. Millions of Americans were compelled to acknowledge the previously inconceivable fact that the leader of their country had deceived them, broken the law, and used government agencies to discredit his political opponents.

It is hardly coincidental that several books exposing the apparent lies and deceptions of Robert E. Peary were researched, written, and published during that turbulent period of American history, when belief and trust in authorities reached an all-time low. After assuming that men and women of great stature were above such behavior, many Americans began to reexamine what they had previously been told about their leaders as well as their heroes—past and present. No longer could the aura of fame protect them from close scrutiny. In light of these altered circumstances and a more critical perspective, the long-dormant Cook-Peary case, once apparently settled on the basis of flimsy evidence, was reopened. This time Peary's words would be weighed against his actions, and a more objective sense of what had really happened would emerge. The past would now be reassessed using a new epistemology: facts would be determined independently of the person or persons who reported them. This re-examination of historical events inevitably extended to other explorers and their claims. Men like John Franklin, Elisha Kent Kane, George De Long, and Robert Falcon Scott would no longer be wrapped in hagiographic phrases like "tragic martyr" or "gallant hero." One prominent example of this change in approach was Roland Huntford's 1979 book detailing Scott's poor planning and numerous mistakes made on the way to the South Pole, comparing the English explorer unfavorably with Amundsen, and deflating his heretofore mythical status. Huntford's later book on these two competitors, *The Race for the South Pole* (2010), further diminished Scott's image by including unflattering sections from his journals that had been left out of earlier published versions. In this book, Huntford concluded that the explorer's words reveal him as "a man given to blaming his colleagues for his own failings; a man with a strong sense—quite early in the expedition— that his preparations have been inadequate; a man who describes one of his dying colleagues as stupid; a man who, on realising he has missed out on being the first to the pole, writes that he can still salvage his reputation if he can get the news to the outside world before Amundsen. A man eager to mask his failure by playing up his mission's scientific endeavour. A man who at one point writes his expedition is a shambles."[44]

For Peary, a similarly damning verdict was delivered by Robert M. Bryce's encyclopedic (nearly one thousand pages of text alone) *Cook & Peary: The Polar Controversy, Resolved,* which appeared in 1979. Yet, despite its title (and exhaustive research) Bryce's book does not definitively "resolve" this dispute for all time—only, perhaps, for our own. Future historians will pore over all the records as well as dissect the characters of the two men in a different light, under the influence of their own cultural values and perspectives, and quite possibly arrive at different conclusions. This constant process of revisiting and revising the past is already evident in more recent books that have defended Scott against

Huntford's attacks—notably, Susan Solomon's *The Coldest March* (2001) and Ranulf Fiennes's *Captain Scott* (2003).[45]

There are three major problems that frustrate attempts to verify who had first reached the North Pole. First, as was noted earlier, there are no visible, permanent landmarks to indicate where Cook or Peary may have been. (At the South Pole, the Norwegians' tent is now estimated to be covered by more than fifty feet of snow and ice.[46]) Secondly, there were not sufficient geographic measurements to establish their precise locations. Early in the twentieth century there were no orbiting satellites that could pinpoint a spot on the ice. Ironically, in an age that put much emphasis on exact measurement, the North Pole stubbornly resisted such spatial definition—and, in fact, exposed its limitations, much as quantum mechanics would reveal inadequacies in Newtonian physics. Thirdly, the expedition leader's monopoly over what was reported to the outside world eliminated the possibility of any independent verification of his claims. And objective observations were not always in the explorer's best interests, especially when they might not bear out what he had asserted. This was certainly true for both Cook and Peary. Indeed, if one accepts the current consensus that neither man actually set foot at the North Pole, then the lack of accurate geographic coordinates made their false claims hard to refute. Each explorer could concentrate on destroying his rival's reputation, confident that the other could not produce compelling evidence that these damning allegations were untrue. In the end, it would come down to one man's word against the other's, and which one the public chose to believe. Certainty could never be firmly established, and so the outcome remains shrouded by doubt. To this day, the reputations of Cook and Peary are mired in a kind of no man's land, somewhere between truth and falsehood, between hero and charlatan.

By becoming the determiners of truth at the poles, explorers risked becoming further alienated from "the real world." They had already physically removed themselves from it by venturing so far into the barren ice caps and becoming utterly isolated from civilization. If a commander then gave in to the impulse to distort, exaggerate, or lie about what he had accomplished, he would have to live with the secret of this deception. In public, he would always be concealing the truth—hiding behind his heroic image, a man divided against himself. He might have gained fame, but he also lost his soul in the process. For Cook and Peary, this Faustian bargain was a price well worth paying. If they needed to assuage their consciences about their lies, they could always find ways to rationalize them. Perhaps they had made an inaccurate calculation, but who could say for sure? Even if they had fallen a bit short of their goal, hadn't they accomplished enough to deserve the accolades? There was little risk of their ever being challenged on these points. For the people back home badly wanted their explorers to succeed. This need took precedence over insisting they stick to the facts. One could even say that the public and the explorers were colluding to assure that great patriotic achievements would be celebrated, even if they never took place. Both the teller of the tale and his audience longed for glorious deeds. As the polar historian Beau Riffenburgh has written, "Those involved in the business of exploration knew that it often bore little resemblance to the accounts that were presented to the public, but the depiction of exploration was rarely changed once formats were discovered that were not only mutually beneficial to the explorers and the newspapers, but popular with the hero-seeking public."[47] This was the lesson taken to heart by fame-hungry predecessors like Elisha Kent Kane, who wielded his pen more adroitly than a dogsled. Long before Cook and Peary, other polar explorers had played loose with the facts, embellishing their adventures to sell more books. The public was captivated by these hyperbolic accounts. Polar fabrication fulfilled their need for the kind of grandiose gesture that was missing in their humdrum, civilized lives. Cook's and Peary's stretching the truth about reaching the North Pole was the outgrowth of this well-established polar tradition of amplifying reality. Back then, Americans needed to see these two men as singularly courageous figures surmounting unimaginable obstacles to reach a goal that had evaded conquest for centuries. That they were also self-absorbed scoundrels who cheated and then tried to hoodwink the world would take decades to be conceded, during an age with different needs and a different view of human nature.

This bifurcation of the explorer into public and private selves has numerous parallels in our own day. Politics is the most obvious example. To succeed in such a highly visible career, one has to become adept at compartmentalizing and pretending to tell the truth. Today we assume that what public figures have to say is self-serving: the dichotomy of inner and outer truth is a necessary evil. But during the nineteenth century, there was no such assumption. On the contrary, words and deeds were supposed to flow from the same source—one's integrity—and any inconsistency between them was a serious moral defect. Since then facts have come to count for more than character, and truth to be based on more than belief. Our view of men like Cook and Peary stems from a twenty-first-century recognition that heroes are not always what they seem to be, much as we might wish they were.

Thus we have learned to wrestle with questions that seem impervious to definite answers. We live in an age of ambiguity—the age of "Rashomon," the uncertainty principle, and persistent conspiracy theories, when truth seems ultimately subjective. This fact can be frustrating (as when some Americans persist in believing that the first moon landing was staged in a movie studio), but also liberating. It expands our possibilities. Yet, this same freedom to shape reality comes with its own psychological costs—the loss of a clear sense of who we are and what is real. Before 1900, facts were seemingly fixed and irrefutable: they anchored us in the world. After Cook and Peary had strutted across the world stage, this changed. Since then, we are forced to live with doubts. Did they torment these explorers as well? Did they lie awake at night ruing the lies they had told so that they could uphold their reputations? Did they suffer from some form of madness? We can only wonder.

ACKNOWLEDGMENTS

Researching a book on polar explorers is another kind of expedition—a long, hard slog through archives and libraries instead of around ice floes and across expanses of windswept snow. While this journey of mine has been far less perilous and far more comfortable, it has had its own share of challenges, which might have proved more daunting without the help I received along the way. I have been fortunate in receiving gracious guidance and good tips from a number of librarians and archivists in tracking down important books and documents I might otherwise have missed. In particular, I would like to thank Naomi Boneham, archivist at the Scott Polar Research Institute in Cambridge, England; Lacey Flint, archivist and curator of Research Collections at the Explorers Club in New York City; Susan Kaplan, director of the Peary-MacMillan Arctic Museum and the Arctic Studies Center at Bowdoin College; Morgan Swan, outreach librarian at the Rauner Library, Dartmouth College; staff at the Archival Center of the Newburyport (Massachusetts) Public Library; and librarians at the American Philosophical Society Library in Philadelphia, as well as the Rare Book and Manuscript Library of Columbia University.

In addition, I would like to thank Beau Riffenburgh, for advice and encouragement along the way; Steven Mitchell and his production staff at Prometheus Books, for shepherding my manuscript into its present form; and my agent, Eric Myers, for being daring enough to take on this work and patient enough to see it through to publication.

Salisbury, Connecticut
March 2018

NOTES

INTRODUCTION

1. "Into the Land of Mystery," *Boston Transcript*, August 7, 1897.

2. Adrien de Gerlache, *Fifteen Months in the Antarctic*, trans. Maurice Raraty (Norfolk: Bluntisham, 1998), p. 68.

3. Frederick A. Cook, *Through the First Antarctic Night, 1898–1899: A Narrative of the Voyage of the "Belgica" among Newly Discovered Lands and over an Unknown Sea about the South Pole* (London: Heinemann, 1900), p. 50.

4. Hugo Decleir, introduction to *Roald Amundsen's "Belgica" Diary: The First Scientific Expedition to the Antarctic*, ed. Hugo Decleir (Norfolk: Bluntisham, 1999), p. 7.

5. For a sampling of Racoviţă's humorous drawings of other scientists acting like buffoons, see Geir O. Klover, ed., *Antarctic Pioneers: The Voyage of the "Belgica," 1897–99* (Oslo: Fram Museum, 2010), pp. 62–72.

6. The Belgian government awarded the expedition subsidies that covered a third of the total cost of outfitting it. The rest was raised from private donors. Adrien de Gerlache, *The Belgian Antarctic Expedition under the Command of A. de Gerlache de Gomery* (Brussels: Hayez, 1904), p. 7.

7. Henryk Arctowski, "The Antarctic Voyage of the *Belgica* during the Years 1897, 1898, and 1899," *Annual Report of the Board of Regents of the Smithsonian Institute, 1901* (Washington: Government Printing Office, 1902), p. 378.

8. Maurice Raraty, introduction to *Fifteen Months in the Antarctic*, by de Gerlache, p. xvi.

9. All told, five members of the *Belgica* crew were fired for not obeying orders or displaying incompetence. Four others quit at various points, for reasons of their own. Even though some of these men were replaced, the ship was undermanned during its voyage to Antarctica.

10. De Gerlache, *Fifteen Months*, pp. 42, 81–82. Cook, *First Antarctic Night*, pp. 65–66, 125.

11. Sarah Moss, *Scott's Last Biscuit: The Literature of Polar Travel* (Oxford: Signal Books, 2006), p. 18.

12. Cook, *First Antarctic Night*, pp. 131, 172–73.
13. De Gerlache, *Fifteen Months*, p.108.
14. De Gerlache, *Belgian Antarctic Expedition*, p. 29.
15. Ibid., p. 30.
16. Cook, *First Antarctic Night*, pp. 250, 252.
17. Ibid., p. 282.

CHAPTER ONE: TRAILING CLOUDS OF GLORY

1. William Elder, *Biography of Elisha Kent Kane* (Philadelphia: Childs and Peterson, 1859), p. 301.

2. David Chapin, "'Science Weeps, America Weeps, the World Weeps': America Mourns Elisha Kent Kane," *Pennsylvania Magazine of History and Biography* 123, no. 4 (October 1999): 281.

3. Remarks of Andrew J. Holman, Philadelphia Common Council, February 26, 1859, quoted in Elder, *Elisha Kent Kane*, p. 290.

4. E. W. Andrews, *Memoir and Eulogy of Dr. Elisha Kent Kane* (New York: Masonic Grand Lodge, 1857), p. 52.

5. Use of the plural form continued even after the Civil War. Adopted in 1865, the Thirteenth Amendment read as follows: "Neither slavery nor involuntary servitude, except as a punishment for crime whereof the party shall have been duly convicted, shall exist within *the United States*, or any place subject to *their* [italics added] jurisdiction."

6. Even as late as the 1840s, the idea that the top and bottom of the earth enjoyed warm temperatures still enjoyed some credence. Edgar Allan Poe described such a tropical island paradise in the Antarctic in his 1838 *Narrative of Arthur Gordon Pym of Nantucket*. This novella was so convincing that some readers felt world maps should be revised to reflect this "discovery."

7. In peacetime, the British navy's fleet was reduced from 700 to 120 vessels. The number of ordinary seamen on active duty dropped from 140,000 to 20,000.

8. Pierre Berton, *The Arctic Grail: The Quest for the Northwest Passage and the North Pole, 1818–1909* (New York: Viking, 1988), p. 20.

9. It turned out that this thaw was only a temporary aberration, indirectly caused by a huge volcanic eruption in present-day Indonesia in 1815.

10. Anonymous, "Continental Travelling and Residence Abroad," *Quarterly Review* 38 (July/October 1828): 152.

11. John Barrow, *A Chronological History of Voyages into the Arctic Regions* (London: John Murray, 1818), p. 379. For a discussion of this pattern of glorifying explorers, see Beau Riffenburgh, *The Myth of the Explorer: The Press, Sensationalism, and Geographical Discovery* (London: Belhaven, 1993).

12. Quoted in Frances Trevelyan Miller, *Byrd's Great Adventure: The Fight to Conquer the Ends of the Earth* (Chicago: Winston, 1930), p. 124.

13. William E. Parry, *Journal of a Voyage for the Discovery of a North-West Passage from the Atlantic to the Pacific* (London: John Murray, 1821), p. xiv.

14. Riffenburgh, *Myth of the Explorer*, p. 16.

15. See Gillen D'Arcy Wood, *Tambora: The Eruption That Changed the World* (Princeton: Princeton University Press, 2014), p. 148.

16. Erika Behrisch Elce, introduction to *As Affecting the Fate of My Absent Husband: Selected Letters of Lady Franklin Concerning the Search for the Lost Franklin Expedition, 1848–1860*, ed. Erika Behrisch Elce (Montreal: McGill-Queen's University Press, 2009), p. 17.

17. "At an early point, public fascination with the polar quest became untethered from any worldly measure of success. Instead, the enterprise took on the characteristics of a neo-Arthurian cult, to which Britain's finest knights would naturally be sacrificed in search of the elusive grail" (Wood, *Tambora*, p. 148).

18. Quoted in Sarah Knowles Bolton, *Famous Voyagers and Explorers* (New York: T. Y. Crowell, 1893), p. 247.

19. Stefan Petrow, "Public Opinion, Private Remonstrance, and the Law: Protecting Animals in Australia, 1803–1914," in *Past Law, Present Histories*, ed. Diane Kirkby (Canberra: Australian National University E Press, 2012), p. 64.

20. Bolton, *Famous Voyagers*, p. 268.

21. George Back, *Narrative of the Arctic Land Expedition to the Mouth of the Great Fish River* (London: John Murray, 1836), p. 180.

22. See "Progress of the Land Arctic Expedition, under Lieut. John Franklin, RN," *Times* (London), November 21, 1821; Franklin, journal, June 1820–April 1821, Scott Polar Research Institute (SPRI), Cambridge; Paul Nanton, *Arctic Breakthrough: Franklin's Expeditions, 1818–1847* (Toronto: Clarke, Irwin, 1970), p. 115.

23. Midshipman George Back, in charge of a separate party to map territory near Hudson's Bay in 1822, lost half of his twenty two men to hunger. Afterward he composed these haunting lines:

Fell famine then with pestilential breath
Rudely assaulted our too feeble crew—

some weep—some rave—and meet immediate death—
Whilst some prepare fresh horrors to review—

See Back, "Recollections of our Unfortunate Voyage to Discover the Country between the Mouth of the Coppermine River and Hudson's Bay," quoted in George Back, *Arctic Artist: The Journals and Paintings of George Back, Midshipman, with Franklin, 1819-1822*, ed. C. Stuart Houston (Montreal: McGill-Queen's University Press, 1994), p. 321.

24. Nanton, *Arctic Breakthrough*, p. 220.

25. Berton, *Arctic Grail*, p. 336.

26. Elce, introduction, p. 18.

27. "Arrival of the 'Caledonia' Fourteen Days Later from London," *Gloucester Telegram* (Gloucester, MA), September 6, 1845.

28. See, for example, "By the 'Britannia.' Thirteen Days Later from England," *Commercial Advertiser* (New York), November 22, 1845.

29. "Foreign: The Arctic Expedition," *New Hampshire Sentinel*, June 11, 1845.

30. "The Arctic Expedition," *Boston Recorder*, July 29, 1847.

31. Elce, introduction, p. 12.

32. Nanton, *Arctic Breakthrough*, p. 235.

33. Ibid., pp.231–33. Nanton points out, "Never before or since have the Arctic wastes seen such a variety of ships."

34. Chauncey C. Loomis, *Weird and Tragic Shores: The Story of Charles Francis Hall, Explorer* (Lincoln: University of Nebraska Press, 1971), p. 21. During their second winter, the Franklin party encountered the most ice to clog Arctic waters in seven hundred years.

35. John Cleves Symmes, an infantry officer and veteran of the War of 1812, had revived the theory that the earth was hollow and "habitable within." A proposal to send an expedition to test this hypothesis was tabled after Andrew Jackson became president. This notion had been largely met with ridicule and questions about Symmes's sanity. For more details on his theory, see Duane A. Griffin, "Hollow and Habitable Within: Symmes's Theory of Earth's Internal Structure and Polar Geography," *Physical Geography* 25, no. 5 (2004): 382–97.

36. When he was president, Lincoln noted that the Bible, John Bunyan's *The Pilgrim's Progress*, and Riley's book had contributed the most to shaping his political views.

37. John Franklin, *Narrative of a Second Expedition to the Shores of the Polar Sea, in the Years 1825, 1826, and 1827* (London: John Murray, 1828), p. 36.

38. Quoted in Bolton, *Famous Voyagers*, p. 264.

39. Quoted in Francis Spufford, *I May Be Some Time: Ice and the English Imagination* (London: Faber and Faber, 1996), p. 87.

40. William E. Parry, *Journal of the Third Voyage for the Discovery of a North-West Passage* (London: Cassel, 1889), p. 32.

41. Iain McCalman, *Darwin's Armada: Four Voyagers to the Southern Oceans and Their Battle for the Theory of Evolution* (New York: Simon and Shuster, 2009), p. 134.

42. Berton, *Arctic Grail*, p. 334.

43. Clements Markham, *The Threshold of the Unknown Region* (London: Sampson Low, Marston, Low and Seale, 1873), pp. 1–2.

44. Franklin preferred to have "quiet steady persons" of "exceptional character" travel with him. (Letter of Franklin to William McDonald, March 29, 1824; "Franklin, John" folder, Bassett Jones Collection, Rare Book and Manuscript Library, Columbia University.) Similarly, the American Arctic explorer Lieutenant George Washington De Long selected his crew for the *Jeannette* on the basis of character as well as health and marital status (single) (Hampton Sides, *In the Kingdom of Ice: The Grand and Terrible Polar Voyage of the USS* "Jeannette" [New York: Random House, 2014], p. 80). It is interesting to note that having a "bad character" is apparently not always a liability under conditions of great deprivation. So found the psychologist Bruno Bettelheim during his stay in Nazi concentration camps. (See Wilfrid Noyce, *They Survived: A Study of the Will to Live* [New York: Dutton, 1963], p. 4.)

45. For a study of how leaders can help others stay alive in situations like those regularly encountered in the polar regions, see John Leach, *Survival Psychology* (London: Macmillan, 1994).

46. Caroline Alexander, *The Endurance: Shackleton's Legendary Antarctic Expedition* (New York: Knopf, 1999), p. 68.

47. Back, *Narrative of the Arctic Land Expedition*, p. 42.

48. Franklin, *Narrative of a Second Expedition*, p. 162.

49. J. Kennedy Maclean, *Heroes of the Polar Seas: A Record of Exploration in the Arctic and Antarctic Seas* (London: W. and R. Chambers, 1910), pp. 263, 9.

50. Ernest Shackleton, "Proposed Trans-Antarctic Expedition," undated typescript, pp. 8, 1. North Star Rare Book Store, Great Barrington, MA. Previously, Shackleton had earned some £20 thousand by charging visitors to go on board his ship *Nimrod*, after its return from Antarctica in 1909 (Roland Huntford, *Shackleton* [London: Atheneum, 1986], p. 316).

51. Sides, *In the Kingdom of Ice*, p. 32. Sides claims that Bennett's target had been a grand piano in the living room, but other sources insist it was the fireplace.

52. Raymond Lee Newcomb, *Our Lost Explorers: The Narrative of the Jeannette Arctic Expedition: As Related by the Survivors, and in the Records and Last Journals of Lieutenant De Long* (Hartford: American Publishing, 1883), p. 17.

53. George W. De Long, *The Voyage of the Jeannette: The Ship and Ice Journals of George W. De Long*, ed. Emma De Long, vol. 1 (Boston: Houghton Mifflin, 1884), pp. 24, 39.

54. Leonard F. Guttridge, *Icebound: The Jeannette Expedition's Quest for the North Pole* (Annapolis: Naval Institute Press, 1986), pp. 3–4. This quotation is from the *Watertown Times*, July 7, 1879.

55. De Long, *Voyage of the Jeannette*, vol. 1, pp. 38, 57, 74, 153, 378, 382, 404. Some of these comments are from De Long's widow, Emma, who edited his journal. This document was retrieved from the ice by a rescue party.

56. Elce, introduction, p. 18.

57. Nanton, *Arctic Breakthrough*, p. 110.

CHAPTER TWO: HAIL THE CONQUERED HERO!

1. Arthur Conan Doyle, "Life on a Greenland Whaler," *Strand Magazine*, March 1897, Project Gutenberg Australia, http://gutenberg.net.au/ebooks13/1306971h.html (accessed April 5, 2015).

2. Felix Driver, *Geography Militant: Cultures of Exploration and Empire* (Malden, MA: Blackwell, 2001), pp. 93, 103–104.

3. Arthur Conan Doyle, *Dangerous Work: Diary of an Arctic Adventure*, ed. Jon Lellenberg and Daniel Stashower (Chicago: University of Chicago Press, 2012), p. 236.

4. Doyle, "Captain of the *Pole-Star*," in *Dangerous Work*, pp. 340, 341, 345, 350.

5. "Sir John Franklin's Expedition," *Daily News* (London), November 10, 1849.

6. "Rescue of Sir John Franklin," *Morning Post* (London), November 10, 1849.

7. "Novel Proposition for the Discovery of Sir John Franklin," *The Era* (London), October 28, 1849.

8. Letter of Lady Jane Franklin to Frederick W. Beechey, November 14, 1849, Box 1, Franklin, Jane folder, Bassett Jones Collection, Rare Book and Manuscript Library, Columbia University.

9. Writing to Lady Franklin, Grinnell noted that all the "pounds sterling of olde [*sic*] England, the dollars of this country, including the gold dust of California, would be nothing" compared with finding Franklin's men alive. Letter of Grinnell to

Jane Franklin, October 25, 1850, MS 248/412/2-112, Scott Polar Research Institute (SPRI), Cambridge.

10. Robert Randolph Carter, *Searching for the Franklin Expedition; The Arctic Journal of Robert Randolph Carter*, ed. Harold B. Gill Jr. and Joanne Young (Annapolis: Naval Institute Press, 1998), p. 26.

11. Ibid., pp. 20, 21, 28–29, 35, 46, 57.

12. Mark M. Sawin, *Raising Kane: Elisha Kent Kane and the Culture of Fame in Antebellum America* (Philadelphia: American Philosophical Society, 2008), p. 75.

13. See, for example, Sherard Osborn, *Stray Leaves from an Arctic Journal; or, Eighteen Months in the Polar Regions in Search of Sir John Franklin's Expedition, in the Years 1850–51* (London: Longman, Brown, Green, and Longmans, 1852). For details on the debate in British naval circles about which route they should take, see John Brown, *The North-West Passage and the Plans for the Search for Sir John Franklin* (Cambridge: Cambridge University Press, 2014).

14. Fergus Fleming, *Ninety Degrees North: The Quest for the North Pole* (London: Granta, 2001), p. 11.

15. William C. Godfrey, *Godfrey's Narrative of the Last Grinnell Arctic Exploring Party in Search of Sir John Franklin, 1853-4-5* (Philadelphia: J. T. Lloyd, 1857), pp. 74, 77, 79, 94, 96, 99, 100.

16. "*Arctic Explorations: The Second Grinnell Expedition, in Search of Sir John Franklin, 1853, '54, '55,*" *New London Daily Star* (CT), March 16, 1857.

17. Elisha Kent Kane, *Arctic Explorations: The Second Grinnell Expedition in Search of Sir John Franklin, 1853, '54, '55*, vol. 1 (Philadelphia: Childs and Peterson, 1857), p. 196.

18. David Chapin, *Exploring Other Worlds: Margaret Fox, Elisha Kent Kane, and the Antebellum Culture of Curiosity* (Amherst: University of Massachusetts Press, 2004), pp. 56, 59.

19. Sawin, *Raising Kane*, pp. 80, 83, 86, 92, 93, 96.

20. Godfrey, *Godfrey's Narrative*, pp. 134, 139, 197, 201, 204, 216, 228, 229, 134. Interestingly, another published account of the Second Grinnell Expedition makes no mention of this incident or any other controversial episode. Purportedly written by the expedition's astronomer, this book—August Sonntag, *Professor Sonntag's Thrilling Narrative of the Grinnell Exploring Expedition to the Arctic Ocean 1853–1855, In Search of Sir John Franklin* (Philadelphia: J. T. Lloyd, 1857)—was actually fabricated by an unknown writer and published together with Godfrey's critical account of Kane's behavior, to undercut what the sailor had maintained (Sawin, *Raising Kane*, p. 338).

21. Godfrey, *Godfrey's Narrative*, p. 21.

22. Chapin, *Exploring Other Worlds*, p. 197.

23. While Scott recorded in his journal that Oates had left the tent willingly, saying "I am going outside and may be some time," Edward Wilson, who was also keeping a journal, did not record that this comment had ever been made. Scott had given the other three men with him morphine doses, noting that it might be better for Oates—a "terrible hindrance"—to commit suicide. For a discussion of this incident, see Sarah Moss, *The Frozen Ship: The Histories and Tales of Polar Exploration* (New York: Blue Book, 2006), pp. 210–11.

24. In a 1999 review of Roland Huntford's book *The Last Place on Earth*, author Caroline Alexander claimed this statement came from Scott, citing as her source the "explorer father" of a friend of hers, but it does not appear in any other published work by or about Scott. Nonetheless, it contains more than a grain of truth. (See Alexander, "The Race to the Bottom," *New York Times*, October 31, 1999.) However, during his fateful last expedition, Scott did have his men practice skiing and manhauling prior to starting their push to the South Pole.

25. George W. De Long, *The Voyage of the Jeannette: The Ship and Ice Journals of George W. De Long*, ed. Emma De Long, vol. 1 (Boston: Houghton Mifflin, 1884), p. 92. See also Leonard F. Guttridge, *Icebound: The Jeannette Expedition's Quest for the North Pole* (Annapolis: Naval Institute Press, 1986), p. 85.

26. Richard W. Bliss, ed., *Our Lost Explorers: The Narrative of the Jeannette Arctic Expedition: As Related by the Survivors, and in the Records and Last Journals of Lieutenant De Long* (Hartford: American Publishing, 1883), p. 180.

27. Guttridge, *Icebound*, pp. 120, 122, 129, 147, 149.

28. Hampton Sides, *In the Kingdom of Ice: The Grand and Terrible Polar Voyage of the USS Jeannette* (New York: Random House, 2014), p. 191.

29. Ibid., p. 188.

30. Guttridge, *Icebound*, pp. 112, 122, 129, 147, 149, 151, 157, 179.

31. John W. Danenhower, "Lieutenant Danenhower's Narrative (Cont.)," *Our Lost Explorers*, p. 207.

32. Guttridge, *Icebound*, p. 109.

33. De Long, *Voyage of the Jeannette*, p. 383.

34. Ibid., p. 374.

35. "Lieutenant De Long's Diary," entry for October 10, 1881, *Our Lost Explorers*, p. 390.

36. Hjalmar Johansen, *With Nansen in the North: A Record of the Fram Expedition in 1893–96*, trans. H. L. Braekstad (New York: Ward, Lock, 1886), p. 290.

When they finally got back to civilization, Nansen reverted to using the formal form of address.

37. Diana Preston, *A First Rate Tragedy: Captain Scott's Antarctic Expeditions* (London; Constable, 1997), p. 21. His Antarctic companion Apsley Cherry-Garrard wrote that Scott was afflicted by bouts of depression that sometimes lasted for week. (Cherry-Garrard, *The Worst Journey in the World* [1922; New York: Carroll and Graf, 1989], p. 206).

38. For the impact of Scott's upbringing on his personality and naval career, see David Crane, *Scott of Antarctica: A Life of Courage and Tragedy in the Extreme South* (New York: HarperCollins, 2005), pp. 16–54 passim.

39. Michael Smith, *I Am Just Going Outside: Captain Oates—Antarctic Tragedy* (Staplehurst, UK: Spellmount, 2002), p. 116; Crane, *Scott of Antarctica*, p. 468.

40. Michael Smith, *Shackleton: By Endurance We Conquer* (London: Collins Press, 2014), p. 43.

41. T. H. Baughman, *Before the Heroes Came: Antarctica in the 1890s* (Lincoln: University of Nebraska Press, 1994), pp. 94–5, 105, 111, 113.

42. Despite all this corrosive dissension during the *Southern Cross* expedition, it did produce important scientific findings and set a new Farthest South mark of 78.50 degrees south. All but one man returned home safely.

43. Cook made a lifelong friend of Roald Amundsen as a result of his kindness and life-saving actions on the *Belgica*. Years later, the famed Norwegian explorer visited Cook several times in prison in the United States (where he was serving a seven-year sentence for mail fraud), demonstrating that this youthful bond remained strong.

44. Fleming, *Ninety Degrees North*, p. 246.

45. Nansen had vacillated between staying on the ship and striking out for the North Pole, even though "his conscience tugged at him" for considering the latter course of action. Charles W. Johnson, *Ice Ship: The Epic Voyages of the Polar Adventurer "Fram"* (Lebanon, NH: University Press of New England, 2014), p. 69.

46. It was felt that the expedition had enough provisions to last more than three years, but this proved not to be the case. See US Congress, *Proceedings of the "Proteus" Court of Inquiry on the Greely Relief Expedition of 1883* (Cambridge: Cambridge University Press, 2012), p. 281.

47. Leonard F. Guttridge, *Ghosts of Cape Sabine: The Harrowing True Story of the Greely Expedition* (New York: G. P. Putnam's Sons, 2000), p. 54.

48. The two men had previously wintered together in Greenland, and Clay had come to despise the doctor. Ibid., p. 6.

49. Adolphus W. Greely, *Three Years of Arctic Service: An Account of the Lady*

Franklin Bay Expedition of 1881–1884 and the Attainment of the Farthest North, vol. 1 (London: Richard Bentley and Sons, 1886), p. 63.

50. See, for example, "Proceedings of a Board of Survey, convened at Ft. Conger, Jan. 10th, 1882," Folder 3:12, Series V, Collection of the Lady Franklin Bay Expedition, 1881–1884, Research Collections, Explorers Club, New York.

51. David L. Brainard, *The Outpost of the Lost: An Arctic Adventure* (Indianapolis: Bobbs Merrill, 1929), pp. 16, 17.

52. Ibid., pp. 20, 21.

53. Journal of C. B. Henry, December 26, 1881–August 8, 1882, Folder 3:5, Series V, Collection of the Lady Franklin Bay Expedition.

54. Greely, *Three Years of Arctic Service*, p. 312.

55. Guttridge, *Ghosts of Sabine*, p. 106.

56. Brainard, *Outpost of the Lost*, p. 42.

57. Guttridge, *Ghosts of Sabine*, pp. 163, 198.

58. Greeley, *Three Years of Arctic Service*, vol. 2 (London: Richard Bentley and Sons, 1886), p. 684.

59. Several others were observed taking extra portions of food, tobacco, tea, or alcohol, but none of them suffered any consequences other than being banned from preparing meals. (See diary of David L. Brainard, March 1–June 21, 1884, Folder 6, Box 2, Papers from the Lady Franklin Bay Expedition, Papers of David L. Brainard, Rauner Special Collections, Dartmouth College Library, Hanover, NH.) But Brainard omitted mention of these thefts in his books about the Lady Franklin Bay Expedition.

60. Brainard, *Outpost of the Lost*, p. 130.

61. Brainard, diary entry of May 12, 1884.

62. Letter of Adolphus Greely to Bassett Jones, April 15, 1931, Bassett Jones Papers, 1818–1938, Rare Book and Manuscript Library, Columbia University.

CHAPTER THREE: BY NATURE POSSESSED

1. James Cook, *The Three Voyages of Captain Cook Round the World*, vol. 3 (London: J. Limbird, 1824), pp. 51–2; George Young, *The Life and Voyages of Captain James Cook* (London: Whittaker, Treacher, 1836), p. 168.

2. Even Irish philosopher Edmund Burke's concept of the "sublime" did not suffice to enable them to comprehend what they saw on their journeys into these frozen and vacant kingdoms. See Robert G. David, *The Arctic in the British Imagination, 1818–1914* (Manchester: Manchester University Press, 2000), p. 12.

3. Eric Wilson, *The Spiritual History of Ice: Romanticism, Science, and the Imagination* (New York: Palgrave Macmillan, 2003), p. 4.

4. Cook, *Three Voyages*, pp. 22, 47.

5. The English-born American sealer John Davis first landed on the Antarctic coast in 1821.

6. Carsten Borchgrevink, *First on the Antarctic Continent; Being an Account of the British Antarctic Expedition, 1898–1900* (London: George Newnes, 1901), pp. 105, 116.

7. John Franklin, *Narrative of a Second Expedition to the Shores of the Polar Sea, in the Years 1825, 1826, and 1827* (London: John Murray, 1828), p. 46.

8. William E. Parry, *Journal of a Voyage for the Discovery of a North-West Passage from the Atlantic to the Pacific: Performed in the Years 1819–1820, in His Majesty's Ships Hecla and Griper, under the Orders of William Edward Parry* (London: John Murray, 1821), p. 117.

9. For a discussion of how preconceptions shape what we see and how we respond to new environments, see Paul Simpson-Housley, *Antarctica: Exploration, Perception, and Metaphor* (London: Routledge, 1992).

10. Mark M. Sawin, *Raising Kane: Elisha Kent Kane and the Culture of Fame in Antebellum America* (Philadelphia: American Philosophical Society, 2008), p. 94.

11. So he wrote in his 1823 novel *Wilhelm Meister*. See Wilson, *Spiritual History of Ice*, p. 73. The German philosopher believed that these huge frozen formations had shifted and shaped land masses elsewhere on earth during a great ice age.

12. William E. Parry, prayer, May 27, 1827, "Prayers used on *Hecla*, 1827, Voyage to North Pole" MS 438/44, Scott Polar Research Institute (SPRI), Cambridge.

13. George Back, *Narrative of the Arctic Land Expedition to the Mouth of the Great Fish River* (London: John Murray, 1836), pp. 71, 117, 120, 179, 181.

14. Charles F. Hall, *Arctic Researches and Life among the Esquimaux: Being the Narrative of an Expedition in Search of Sir John Franklin, the Years 1860, 1861 and 1862* (New York: Harper & Brothers, 1865), p. 34.

15. Max Jones, *The Last Great Quest: Captain Scott's Antarctic Sacrifice* (Oxford: Oxford University Press, 2003), p. 65.

16. Wilfrid Noyce, *The Springs of Adventure* (Cleveland: World Publishing, 1958), p. 87.

17. Jean-Baptiste Charcot, *The Voyage of the "Why Not?" in the Antarctic*, trans. Philip Walsh (New York: Hodder and Stoughton, 1911), p. 294.

18. Apsley Cherry-Garrard, *The Worst Journey in the World* (New York: Carroll and Graf, 1989), p. 62.

19. Alexander Armstrong, *A Personal Narrative of the North-West Passage, with Numerous Incidents of Travel and Adventure during Nearly Five Years' Continuous Service in the Arctic Regions while in Search of the Expedition under Sir John Franklin* (London: Hurst and Blackett, 1857), p. 209.

20. Elisha Kent Kane, *The United States Grinnell Expedition in Search of Sir John Franklin: A Personal Narrative* (New York: Sheldon, Blakeman, 1857), p. 59.

21. Sara Wheeler, *Terra Incognita: Travels in Antarctica* (London: Jonathan Cape, 1996), p. 141.

22. Martin Conway, *With Ski and Sledge over Arctic Glaciers* (London: J. M. Dent, 1898), pp. 105–106.

23. Wheeler, *Terra Incognita*, p. 51.

24. Ibid., pp. 84–85.

25. Ibid., p. 141.

26. Elisha Kent Kane, Greenland Notebook, Correspondence, Elisha Kent Kane Collection, American Philosophical Society (APS), Philadelphia.

27. Elisha K. Kane, *Arctic Explorations: The Second Grinnell Expedition in Search of Sir John Franklin, 1853, '54, '55*, vol. 2 (Philadelphia: Childs and Petersen, 1857), pp. 14, 15, 34, 44, 52, 53.

28. W. Parker Snow, *Voyage of the Prince Albert in Search of Sir John Franklin: A Narrative of Every-Day Life in the Arctic Seas* (London: Longman, Brown, Green, and Longmans, 1851), p. 70.

29. Louis Bernacchi, "Landfall," in *The Ends of the Earth: An Anthology of the Finest Writing on the Arctic*, ed. Elizabeth Kolbert (New York: Bloomsbury, 2007), p. 31.

30. Kane, *Grinnell Expedition*, pp. 26, 67, 388.

31. Clements Markham, *The Lands of Silence: A History of Arctic and Antarctic Exploration* (Cambridge: Cambridge University Press, 1921), pp. 10–11.

32. William H. Gilder, *Schwatka's Search: Sledging in the Arctic in Quest of the Franklin Records* (New York: Echo, 2007), p. 7.

33. Kane felt that the scale of these massive icebergs dwarfed what humans had built. See Kane, *Grinnell Expedition*, p. 67.

34. Quoted in Iain McCalman, *Darwin's Armada: Four Voyagers to the Southern Oceans and Their Battle for the Theory of Evolution* (New York: Simon and Schuster, 2009), p. 134.

35. George W. De Long, *The Voyage of the Jeannette: The Ship and Ice Journals of George W. De Long*, ed. Emma De Long, vol. 2 (Boston: Houghton Mifflin, 1883), pp. 448, 472.

36. Parry, *Journal of a Voyage*, pp. 115, 123–26.

37. Catherine Delmas, Christine Vandamme, and Donna Spalding Andreolle, eds., introduction to *Science and Empire in the Nineteenth Century: A Journey of Imperial Conquest and Scientific Progress* (Newcastle on Tyne: Cambridge Scholars, 2010), p. vii.

38. William Wordsworth, "The Tables Turned" (1798).

39. Bernacchi, "Landfall," p. 40.

40. Fridtjof Nansen, introduction to Roald Amundsen, *The South Pole: An Account of the Norwegian Expedition in the "Fram," 1910–1912*, trans. A. G. Chater, vol. 1 (London: John Murray 1913), pp. xxix–xxx.

41. The English poet William Blake had used the phrase "Minute Particulars" in his "prophetic" poem *Jerusalem* (1804–1820) to describe all of Creation being present in its smallest forms:

> He who would do good to another must do it in Minute Particulars.
> General Good is the plea of the scoundrel, hypocrite, and flatterer;
> For Art and Science cannot exist but in minutely organized Particulars . . .

42. Michael Friendly, "The Golden Age of Statistical Graphics," *Statistical Science* 23, no. 4 (2008): 4, https://arxiv.org/pdf/0906.3979.pdf (accessed May 7, 2015).

43. Parry, *Journal of a Voyage*, p. vii.

44. Back, *Narrative of the Arctic Land Expedition*, pp. 218, 222, 224.

45. Kane, *Arctic Explorations*, pp. 152, 153.

46. Francis Leopold McClintock, *The Voyage of the "Fox" in the Arctic Seas: A Narrative of the Discovery of the Fate of Sir John Franklin and His Companions* (London: John Murray, 1859), p. 218.

47. The Scott party was so dedicated to gathering scientific specimens that they lugged thirty-five pounds of plant fossils back from the South Pole. These were found inside the tent next to the bodies of Scott, Wilson, and Bowers.

48. Cherry-Garrard, *Worst Journey in the World*, p. 582.

CHAPTER FOUR: "LA BELLE DAME SANS MERCI"

1. Ralph M. Myerson, "Isaac Israel Hayes," *Polar Priorities* 20 (September 2000), Elisha Kent Kane Historical Society, http://archive.is/S6EU (accessed October 20, 2015). Cf. Douglas W. Wamsley, *Polar Hayes: The Life and Contributions of Isaac Israel Hayes, MD* (Philadelphia: American Philosophical Society, 2009), p. 73.

2. Isaac I. Hayes, *An Arctic Boat Journey in the Autumn of 1854* (Boston: Brown, Taggard, and Chase, 1860), pp. 3-4.

3. Ibid., pp. 10–11.

4. Quoted from Hayes's journal, in Chauncey C. Loomis, *Weird and Tragic Shores: The Story of Charles Francis Hall, Explorer* (Lincoln: University of Nebraska Press, 1971), p. 265.

5. One of the more famous paintings capturing the Arctic's otherworldly beauty is based on a sketch made by Hayes during his subsequent voyage there, in 1861. This is Frederic Church's *Aurora Borealis*. Hayes described what he had seen with this painterly language: "The light grew by degrees more and more intense, and from irregular bursts it settled into an almost steady sheet of brightness. . . . The exhibition, at first tame and quiet, became in the end startling in its brilliancy. The broad dome above me is all ablaze. . . . The colour of the light was chiefly red, but this was not constant, and every hue mingled in the fierce display. Blue and yellow streamers were playing in the lurid fire; and, sometimes starting side by side from the wide expanse of the illuminated arch, they melt into each other, and throw a ghostly glare of green into the face and over the landscape. Again this green overrides the red; blue and orange clasp each other in their rapid flight; violet darts tear through a broad flush of yellow, and countless tongues of white flame, formed of these uniting streams, rush aloft and lick the skies" (Hayes, *The Open Polar Sea: A Narrative of a Voyage of Discovery towards the North Pole, in the Schooner "United States"* [New York: Hurd and Houghton, 1867], p. 194). Some contend this painting expresses the bittersweet mood in the United States following the Union victory in the Civil War.

6. Wamsley, *Polar Hayes*, p. 351. Wamsley notes that little is known about Hayes's tutelage under Church. Most likely the explorer would have studied with him after Church's return to New York from South America in 1857. The two met probably met when Hayes was lecturing about the Arctic and raising funds to return there. Church had a keen interest in painting the polar world. They became good friends, subsequently occupying studios in the same Greenwich Village location, the Tenth Street Studio Building.

7. Hayes, *Arctic Boat Journey*, p. 97.

8. Ibid., pp. 110, 147, 286.

9. Hayes, *Open Polar Sea*, p. 24.

10. Hayes, *Open Polar Sea*, p. 25.

11. Loomis, prologue to *Weird and Tragic Shores*, p. 3.

12. Barry Lopez, introduction to *Arctic Dreams: Imagination and Desire in a Northern Landscape* (New York: Charles Scribner's Sons, 1986), p. xxviii.

13. Quoted in Francis Spufford, *I May Be Some Time: Ice and the English Imagination* (London: Faber and Faber, 1996), p. 93.

14. Hayes, *Arctic Boat Journey*, p. 331.

15. See Beau Riffenburgh, *The Myth of the Explorer: The Press, Sensationalism, and Geographical Discovery* (London: Belhaven, 1993), pp. 5–6.

16. Lopez, *Arctic Dreams*, p. 12.

17. Quoted in Spufford, *I May Be Some Time*, p. 6.

18. In the eight years prior to departure of the *Jeannette*, thirty-three whaling ships, carrying a total of over six hundred men, had vanished in the ice guarding the Bering Strait. Leonard F. Guttridge, *Icebound: The Jeannette Expedition's Quest for the North Pole* (Annapolis: Naval Institute Press, 1986), p. 161.

19. Lopez, *Arctic Dreams*, pp. 217–8.

20. Jean-Baptiste Charcot, *The Voyage of the "Why Not?" in the Antarctic*, trans. Philip Walsh (New York: Hodder and Stoughton, 1911), p. 63.

21. Anthony Fiala, *Fighting the Polar Ice* (New York: Doubleday, 1906), pp. 63, 4, 6, 25, 28, 82, 86. Fiala noted, "The spirit of the Age will never be satisfied until the command given to Adam in the beginning—the command to subdue the earth—has been obeyed, and the ends of the earth have revealed their secrets to the eye of man."

22. Jeannette Mirsky, *To the Arctic! The Story of Arctic Exploration from Earliest Times to the Present* (New York: Viking, 1934), p. 7.

23. Elisha Kent Kane, *Arctic Explorations: The Second Grinnell Expedition in Search of Sir John Franklin, 1853, '54, '55* (Bedford, MA: Applewood, 1856), pp. 347, 385.

24. Hayes, *Open Polar Sea*, p. 301.

25. George W. De Long, *The Voyage of the Jeannette: The Ship and Ice Journals of George W. De Long*, ed. Emma De Long, vol. 2 (Boston: Houghton Mifflin, 1883), p. 484.

26. Hampton Sides, *In the Kingdom of Ice: The Grand and Terrible Polar Voyage of the USS Jeannette* (New York: Random House, 2014), p. 177.

27. Elisha Kent Kane, *Adrift in the Arctic Ice Pack: From the History of the First US Grinnell Expedition in Search of Sir John Franklin* (New York: Outing, 1915), pp. 202–203.

28. Hayes, *Open Polar Sea*, p. 223.

29. George Back, *Narrative of an Expedition in HMS Terror, Undertaken with a View to Geographical Discovery of the Arctic Shores in the Years 1836–7* (London: John Murray, 1838), pp. 94–95.

30. Elisha Kent Kane, *The United States Grinnell Expedition in Search of Sir John Franklin: A Personal Narrative* (New York: Sheldon, Blakeman, 1857), p. 379.

31. Kane, *Adrift in the Arctic Ice Pack*, p. 330.

32. Isaac I. Hayes, "Twice Alone: A Tale of the Labrador," *Century Magazine* (November 1870): 82, https://ia601008.us.archive.org/7/items/TwiceAloneATaleOfTheLabrador/Twice%20Alone-A%20Tale%20of%20The%20Labrador.pdf (accessed May 28, 2015).

33. Quoted in Iain McCalman, *Darwin's Armada: Four Voyagers to the Southern Oceans and Their Battle for the Theory of Evolution* (New York: Simon and Schuster), p. 134.

34. Jacob Wassermann, *Bula Matari: Stanley, Conqueror of a Continent*, trans. Eden and Cedar Paul (New York: Liveright, 1933), p. 134.

35. Mirsky, *To the Arctic!* p. 9.

36. For a discussion of this medieval revival, see Robert Girouard, *The Return to Camelot: Chivalry and the English Gentleman* (New Haven: Yale University Press, 1981). See also Diana Preston, *A First Rate Tragedy: Captain Scott's Antarctic Expeditions* (London: Constable, 1997), p. 39.

37. Quoted in Wilfrid Noyce, *The Springs of Adventure* (Cleveland: World Publishing, 1958), p. 87.

38. "He seemed to keep a mental finger on each man's pulse.... At all times he inspired men with a feeling, often illogical, that, even if things got worse, he could devise some means of easing their hardships" (Frank A. Worsley, *Shackleton's Boat Journey* [New York: Norton, 1977], p. 170).

39. Quoted in Roland Huntford, *Shackleton* (New York: Atheneum, 1986), p. 559.

40. Ernest Shackleton, *South! The Story of Shackleton's Last Expedition, 1914–1917* (London: Heinemann, 1970), p. 179.

41. Ibid., p. 174.

42. Worsley, *Shackleton's Boat Journey*, pp. 187–88.

43. Apsley Cherry-Garrard, introduction to *The Worst Journey in the World* (New York: Carroll and Graf, 1989), p. vii.

44. George Seaver, foreword to *Worst Journey in the World*, by Cherry-Garrard, p. lxxxiii.

45. Robert Scott, quoted in Cherry-Garrard, *Worst Journey in the World*, p. 132.

46. Cherry-Garrard, *Worst Journey in the World*, pp. 62, 231, 242.

47. Ibid., pp. 254, 267, 281, 252.

48. Ibid., p. 597.

49. Robert F. Scott, *Scott's Last Expedition: The Personal Journals of Captain R. F. Scott, RN, CVO, on His Journey to the South Pole* (New York: Dodd, Mead, 1923), pp. 395, 414, 424.

50. Cherry-Garrard, *Worst Journey in the World*, p. 525.

51. Biographer Roland Huntford claimed that Scott impregnated a young woman in 1889—after which there was an inexplicable hiatus in his career. (Roland Huntford, *The Last Place on Earth: Scott and Amundsen's Race to the South Pole* [New York: Random House, 1999], pp. 113–14.) But this allegation has not been substantiated.

52. Robert F. Scott, "Sledging Problem in the Antarctic: Men versus Motors," (typescript), British National Antarctic Expedition, vol. 2, 1901–1904, Scott Polar Research Institute (SPRI), Cambridge.

53. Scott, *Last Expedition*, pp. 28, 22, 242.

54. Preston, *First Rate Tragedy*, p. 161.

55. T. H. Baughman, *Pilgrims on Ice: Robert Falcon Scott's First Antarctic Expedition* (Lincoln: University of Nebraska Press, 199), p. 144.

56. David Crane, *Scott of Antarctica: A Life of Courage and Tragedy in the Extreme South* (New York: HarperCollins, 2005), pp. 140, 143.

57. In one of his final letters, to Wilson's wife Oriana ("Ory"), Scott wrote: "His [Wilson's] eyes have a comfortable blue look of hope and his mind is peaceful with the satisfaction of his faith in regarding himself as part of the great scheme of the Almighty." (Scott, *Last Expedition*, p. 472.)

58. Quoted in Crane, *Scott of Antarctica*, p. 565.

CHAPTER FIVE: KEEPING THE BRUTES AT BAY

1. John Wilson, *John Franklin: Traveller on Undiscovered Seas* (Montreal: XYZ, 2001), p. 121.

2. John Franklin, journal entry of July 11, 1845, in H. D. Traill, *The Life of Sir John Franklin, RN* (London: John Murray, 1896), p. 344. With its nearly fourteen tons of canned food (in 29,000 cans), 58,800 gallons of beer, 4,500-plus gallons of West Indian rum, 3,588 pounds of tobacco, five tons of oatmeal, and one ton of East Indian tea (among other items), the expedition was the most "lavishly provisioned" of all Arctic voyages. (Scott Cookman, *Ice Blink: The Tragic Fate of Sir John Franklin's Lost Polar Expedition* [New York: John Wiley and Sons, 2000], pp. 47, 49.)

3. Quoted in Sarah K. Bolton, *Famous Voyagers and Explorers* (New York: T. Y. Crowell, 1893), p. 264.

4. William Kennedy, *A Short Narrative of the Second Voyage of the Prince Albert in Search of Sir John Franklin* (London: W. H. Dalton, 1853), pp. 33, 52.

5. Robert McClure, *The Discovery of a Northwest Passage* (London: Longman, Brown, Green, and Longmans, 1856), pp. 149, 222–23.

6. Elisha K. Kane, *Arctic Explorations: The Second Grinnell Expedition in Search of Sir John Franklin, 1853, '54, '55* (Bedford, MA: Applewood, 1856), pp. 443–45.

7. Wilson, *John Franklin*, p. 71.

8. John Hobhouse, *Travels in Albania and Other Provinces of Turkey*, vol. 1 (London: John Murray, 1838), pp. 20–21.

9. There were notable exceptions to this rigid class divide. James Cook, for example, rose from able seaman to become a captain and his country's most illustrious explorer of the eighteenth century.

10. William E. Parry, *Journal of a Voyage for the Discovery of a North-West Passage from the Atlantic to the Pacific: Performed in the Years 1819–1820, in His Majesty's Ships Hecla and Griper, under the Orders of William Edward Parry* (London: John Murray, 1821), p. 126.

11. Katherine Lambert, *The Longest Winter: The Incredible Survival of Scott's Lost Party* (Washington: Smithsonian Institution, 2004), pp. 142–43.

12. George W. Stockard Jr., *Victorian Anthropology* (New York: Free Press, 1987), p. 3.

13. Quoted in Pierre Berton, *Arctic Grail: The Quest for the Northwest Passage and the North Pole, 1818–1909* (New York: Viking, 1988), p. 115.

14. Parry, *Journal of a Voyage*, p. 287.

15. William E. Parry, *Journal of the Third Voyage for the Discovery of a North-West Passage* (London: Cassell, 1889), p. 170.

16. George Back, *Narrative of an Expedition in HMS Terror, Undertaken with a View to Geographical Discovery of the Arctic Shores in the Years 1836–7* (London: John Murray, 1838), p. 38.

17. William C. Godfrey, *Godfrey's Narrative of the Last Grinnell Arctic Exploring Party in Search of Sir John Franklin, 1853-4-5* (London: J. T. Lloyd, 1857), p. 45.

18. Quoted in Paul Nanton, *Arctic Breakthrough: Franklin's Expeditions, 1818–1847* (Toronto: Clarke, Irwin, 1970), p. 45.

19. John Franklin, *Narrative of a Second Expedition to the Shores of the Polar Sea, in the Years 1825, 1826, and 1827* (London: John Murray, 1828), p. 58.

20. Elisha Kane, *The United States Grinnell Expedition in Search of Sir John Franklin: A Personal Narrative* (New York: Sheldon, Blakeman, 1857), pp. 38–39.

21. Kane, *Arctic Explorations*, p. 354.

22. Quoted from Kane, "First Lessons from the Eskimos," in *Polar Secrets: A Treasury of the Arctic and Antarctic*, ed. Seon Manley and Gogo Lewis (Garden City, NY: Doubleday, 1968), p. 164.

23. In his biography of Hall, Chauncey C. Loomis wrote that Kane regarded the Eskimo way of life "as a temptation to be resisted when he and his men were in trouble; it was better to die a civilized man than to imitate the brutish savage" (Chauncey C. Loomis, *Weird and Tragic Shores: The Story of Charles Francis Hall, Explorer* [Lincoln: University of Nebraska Press, 1971], p. 25).

24. "A New Arctic Expedition," *New York Times*, June 1, 1860.

25. Charles F. Hall, *Arctic Researches, and Life among the Esquimaux: Being the Narrative of an Expedition in Search of Sir John Franklin, in the Years 1860, 1861, and 1862* (New York: Harper and Brothers, 1865), pp. 78, 137.

26. Loomis, *Weird and Tragic Shores*, p. 99.

27. all, *Arctic Researches*, pp. 79, 114, 123, 132, 133, 160, 219.

28. Hall's enthusiasm for the potential of the Inuit people knew no bounds. When an indigenous woman who had spent nearly two years in England complained to him that explorers swore too much, he turned rhapsodic in his admiration for her exceptionally civilized ways: "Here, one of the iron daughters of the rocky, ice-ribbed North, standing like an angel, pleading the cause of the true God, weeping for the sad havoc made and making among her people by those of my countrymen who have been, and ever should be, the glorious representatives of freedom, civilization, and Christianity!" (Hall, *Arctic Researches*, p. 162).

29. Ibid., p. 522.

30. Fridtjof Nansen, preface to *Eskimo Life*, trans. William Archer (London: Longman, Green, and Company, 1893), pp. viii–ix.

31. Ibid., p. 302.

32. Vilhjalmur Stefansson, *My Life with the Eskimo* (New York: Macmillan, 1913), p. 32.

33. Ibid., p. 154.

34. Stefansson, *The Friendly Arctic: The Story of Five Years in Polar Regions* (New York: Macmillan, 1921), pp. 24–25, 89.

35. Jonathan M. Karpoff, "Private versus Public Initiative in Arctic Exploration: The Effects of Incentives and Organizational Structure," *Journal of Political Economy* 109, no. 1 (2001): 40.

36. John Maxtone-Graham, *Safe Return Doubtful: The Heroic Age of Polar Exploration* (New York: Charles Scribner's Sons, 1988), pp. 45, 17.

37. Parry, *Journal of the Third Voyage*, p. 29.

38. Adolphus Greely, *Three Years of Arctic Service: An Account of the Lady Franklin Bay Expedition of 1881–1884 and the Attainment of the Farthest North*, vol. 1 (London: Richard Bentley and Sons, 1894), p. 208.

39. David Crane, *Scott of Antarctica: A Life of Courage and Tragedy in the Extreme South* (New York: HarperCollins, 2005), p. 182.

40. Michael Smith, *An Unsung Hero: Tom Crean, Antarctic Survivor* (London: Headline, 2000), p. 26.

41. Robert F. Scott, *The Voyage of the "Discovery,"* vol. 1 (Cambridge: Cambridge University Press, 2014), p. 467.

42. Bruce also thought getting to the pole had no real value. Antarctica mattered to him only because of its putative natural resources and the scientific discoveries to be made there. See William S. Bruce, *Polar Exploration* (New York: Henry Holt, 1911), pp. 238–39.

43. Markham had an aversion to skiing, largely because Borchgrevink, with whom he had a falling out, favored it. Scott initially hewed to this position in the Antarctic. (T. H. Baughman, *Pilgrims on Ice: Robert Falcon Scott's First Antarctic Expedition* [Lincoln: University of Nebraska Press, 1999], pp. 96, 108.) After some experimentation with skis during the *Terra Nova* expedition, he reverted to his belief that nothing could "equal the honest and customary use of one's own legs" (Quoted in Crane, *Scott of Antarctica*, p. 160).

44. See Clements Markham, *The Threshold of the Unknown Region* (London: Sampson Low, Marston, Low and Seale, 1873), p. 316, and Parry, *Journal of a Voyage*, p. 287.

45. Letter of Elisha Kent Kane to Henry Grinnell, May 7, 1852. Folder 1, Series 1: Correspondence, Elisha Kent Kane Papers, American Philosophical Society, Philadelphia.

46. Jakob Wassermann, *Bula Matari: Stanley, Conqueror of a Continent*, trans. Eden and Cedar Paul (New York: Liveright, 1933), p. 117.

47. Quoted in Manley and Lewis, *Polar Secrets*, p. 161.

CHAPTER SIX: DOG EAT DOG, MAN EAT DOG, MAN EAT MAN

1. Roald Amundsen, *The Northwest Passage: Being the Record of a Voyage of Exploration of the Ship "Gjøa" during the Years 1903–1907*, vol. 1 (New York: Dutton, 1908), p. 126.

2. Adolphus Greely, *Three Years of Arctic Service: An Account of the Lady Franklin Bay Expedition of 1881–1884 and the Attainment of the Farthest North*, vol. 1 (New York: Charles Scribner's Sons, 1886), pp. 115–16, 159.

3. Other explorers found slaying dogs equally distasteful and upsetting. Matthew

Henson, who accompanied Peary on several polar expeditions, grew so attached to these indispensable creatures because of their endurance and intelligence that when he and Peary were forced to kill one to feed the other dogs, Henson pronounced this act "such a horrible matter that I will not describe it" (Matthew Henson, *A Negro Explorer at the North Pole* [New York: Frederick A. Stokes, 1912], p. 120).

4. Fridtjof Nansen, *Farthest North*, vol. 1 (Westminster, MD: Constable, 1897), pp. 83, 115, 118, 123, 134, 137, 201; vol. 2, pp. 6, 120, 242, 270, 279, 289, 292, 341, 350. See also Hjalmar Johansen, *With Nansen in the North: A Record of the "Fram" Expedition in 1893–96*, trans. H. L. Braekstad (New York: Ward, Lock, 1899), pp. 20, 160–61, 168, 201, 202, 225, 236.

5. Robert F. Scott, *Scott's Last Expedition: The Personal Journals of Captain R. F. Scott, RN, CVO, on His Journey to the South Pole*, vol. 1 (New York: Dodd, Mead, 1923), pp. 162, 312.

6. So did Amundsen's men on their voyage to Antarctica. See Roald Amundsen, *The South Pole: An Account of the Norwegian Antarctic Expedition in the "Fram," 1910–1912*, vol. 1, trans. A. G. Chater (London: John Murray, 1913), photo facing p. 149.

7. Stephen R. Bown, *The Last Viking: The Life of Roald Amundsen* (Da Capo: New York, 2012), p. 128.

8. Roland Huntford, *The Last Place on Earth: Scott and Amundsen's Race to the South Pole* (New York: Random House, 1999), pp. 204–205, 329. In his diary, Amundsen noted that he considered the dogs his "children."

9. Sara Wheeler, *Terra Incognita: Travels in Antarctica* (London: Jonathan Cape, 1996), p. 104.

10. Louis Bernacchi, *To the South Polar Regions: Expedition of 1898–1900* (London: Hurst and Blackett, 1901), p. 165.

11. Huntford, *Last Place on Earth*, p. 365.

12. Some sources contend that this first person to approach him, Frank Bickerton, actually uttered these words, but it is more likely that this was only what Bickerton was wondering. See David Roberts, *Alone on the Ice: The Greatest Survival Story in the History of Exploration* (New York: Norton, 2013), p. 245.

13. In 1915, the *New York Evening Globe* ran a story quoting Mawson as saying that he had contemplated eating part of Metz's body, but then rejected this idea because it would have left a "bad taste" in his mouth if had done so. Mawson subsequently denied that he had made this remark.

14. Theodore Bickel, *Mawson's Will: The Greatest Survival Story Ever Written* (New York: Stein and Day, 1997), pp. 114, 119, 123, 131, 146, 160, 163; Wheeler, *Terra Incognita*, pp. 129, 130; Douglas Mawson, *The Home of the Blizzard: Being the*

Story of the Australasian Antarctic Expedition, 1911–1914, vol. 1 (Oxford: Benediction Classics, 2008), pp. 196–97, 206.

Many years after the fact, an Australian told the British travel writer Sara Wheeler that Mawson had confessed during a subsequent overland trek in his adopted country that he had eaten part of Mertz's corpse to stay alive. See Wheeler, *Terra Incognita,* p. 130. More recently, the Australian historian David Day has contended, in a book entitled *Flaws in the Ice: In Search of Douglas Mawson* (London: Scribe, 2013), that Mawson deliberately reduced Mertz's rations to hasten the latter's death, so that Mawson could survive by eating his friend's flesh. But Day has no real evidence to back up this highly controversial claim.

15. See, for example, Frazer, *The Golden Bough,* 3rd ed. (Cambridge: Cambridge University Press, 2012), pp. 19–20.

16. Amy Mitchell-Cook, *A Sea of Misadventures: Shipwreck and Survival in Early America* (Columbia: University of South Carolina Press, 2013), p. 112.

17. Nathaniel Philbrick, *In the Heart of the Sea: The Tragedy of the Whaleship Essex* (New York: Viking, 2000), pp. 164, 167. Five of the six sailors eaten on these boats were African American.

18. When the captain of the *Essex,* George Pollard Jr., returned to Nantucket, a crowd of some one thousand turned out on the docks to see him, knowing full well what he and the other whalers had done to survive. There were no cheers, only silent stares. However, Pollard was never charged with a crime and went on to assume command of another ship. (Philbrick, *In the Heart of the Sea,* p. 202.)

However, in 1884, when four survivors of an English yacht that had sunk in the South Atlantic drew lots to see which one of them would be sacrificed for the others, this incident eventually led to a charge of murder against two of the men, Tom Dudley and Edwin Stephens. They were convicted and sentenced to death, but ended up serving only a six-month sentence. This case established the legal precedent that necessity could not justify murder.

19. As the Canadian businessman who helped finance the recent successful search for Franklin's ships told Adam Gopnik of *The New Yorker,* "It always had to be somebody else doing the eating. British gentlemen in the service to Queen and country don't eat each other. Eskimos and polar bears do." Adam Gopnik, "The Franklin Ship Myth, Verified," *New Yorker,* October 1, 2014, p. 6.

20. Erika Behrisch Elce, introduction to *As Affecting the Fate of My Absent Husband: Selected Letters of Lady Franklin Concerning the Search for the Lost Franklin Expedition, 1848–1860,* ed. Erika Behrisch Elce (Montreal: McGill-Queens University, 2009), p. 23.

21. "The Arctic Expedition," *Times* (London), October 23, 1854.

22. Ken McGoogan, foreword to *John Rae's Arctic Correspondence, 1844–1855*, by John Rae (Victoria, BC: TouchWood, 2014), p. 79.

23. Elce, *As Affecting the Fate*, p. 24.

24. The *Times* also denounced the Inuit as "liars" in an October 27 editorial, saying that they might have been "tempted by the emaciation and weakness of the white men to attack them." The *Sun* stood up patriotically for Franklin's "noble band of adventurers," by arguing that they could not possibly have "resorted to such horrors." When Rae returned to London, Lady Franklin received him coldly, telling him his assertions about her husband's party were "shameful." She vowed that he would pay a high price for trusting the word of "savages" in writing his report. (Ken McGoogan, *Fatal Passage: The Story of John Rae, the Arctic Hero Time Forgot* [New York: Carroll and Graf, 2001], pp. 210–11.)

25. Richard King, *The Franklin Expedition from First to Last* (London: John Churchill, 1855), p. 105.

26. Charles Dickens, "The Lost Arctic Explorers," *Household Words: A Weekly Journal* 10 (December 1854): 433–37.

27. A. Keenleyside, M. Bertulli, and H. C. Fricke, "The Final Days of the Franklin Expedition: New Skeletal Evidence," *Arctic* 50, no. 1 (March 1997): 36–46. Previously, during an 1879 search on King William Island, more bones believed to be from the Franklin party had been found, with signs that the flesh on them had been eaten.

28. Letter of Francis Leopold McClintock to Lady Jane Franklin, September 27, 1859, MS 248/439/22, Scott Polar Research Institute (SPRI), Cambridge.

29. Quoted in Bruce Henderson, *Fatal North: Murder and Survival Aboard the USS* Polaris, *the First US Expedition to the North Pole* (New York: New American Library, 2001), pp. 168, 171.

30. Leonard F. Guttridge, *Ghosts of Cape Sabine: The True Story of the Greely Expedition* (New York: G. P. Putnam's Sons, 2000), pp. 275, 296–97.

31. Beau Riffenburgh, *The Myth of the Explorer: The Press, Sensationalism, and Geographical Discovery* (London: Belhaven Press, 1993), p. 107.

32. George F. Shrady, "The Rescue of Lieutenant Greely, the Effects of the Arctic Climate, and Cannibalism," *Medical Record* 26, no. 8 (August 23, 1884): 207.

33. Riffenburgh, *Myth of the Explorer*, p. 109.

34. J. Kennedy MacLean, *Heroes of the Polar Seas: A Record of Exploration in the Arctic and Antarctic Seas* (London: W. and R. Chambers, 1910), pp. 91–92. Throughout the nineteenth century, doubts persisted in print about whether the Franklin crew had actually practiced cannibalism—or, if they had, if this was morally inexcusable. In an

1881 book, William Henry Gilder, a survivor of the Battle of Gettysburg, a *New York Herald* reporter, and second-in-command of an 1878–1880 polar expedition seeking to locate Franklin-related documents, relics, and remains, quoted a letter to him from Rae, exculpating the doomed party: "I considered it no reproach, when suffering the agony to which extreme hunger subjects some men, for them to do what the Esquimaux tell us was done. Men so placed are no more responsible for their actions than a madman who commits a great crime." In the same book, Gilder theorized that it been the Inuit who had cut up the flesh and consumed it. William H. Gilder, *Schwatka's Search: Sledging in the Arctic in Quest of the Franklin Records* (New York: Charles Scribner's Sons, 1881), pp. x–xi.

35. McGoogan, *Fatal Passage*, p. 216.

36. Riffenburgh, *Myth of the Explorer*, p. 31.

37. Quoted in Pierre Berton, *The Arctic Grail: The Quest for the Northwest Passage and the North Pole, 1818–1909* (New York: Viking, 1988), p. 145. Franklin changed his mind after nearly starving to death in the Canadian Arctic.

38. David Crane, *Scott of Antarctica: A Life of Courage and Tragedy in the Extreme South* (New York: HarperCollins, 2005), p. 30.

39. Scott, *Scott's Last Expedition*, p. 60.

40. Scott referred to Oates this way in a March 6, 1912, entry in his journal.

41. Quoted in Apsley Cherry-Garrard, *The Worst Journey in the World* (New York: Carroll and Graf, 1989), p. 554.

42. Since there is no record of these parting words in Wilson's diary, some have speculated that Scott made them up, to obscure that he had encouraged Oates to commit suicide.

CHAPTER SEVEN: MORE NOBLE THAN THE "GREED FOR DISCOVERY"

1. David Thomas Murphy, *German Exploration of the Polar World: A History, 1870–1940* (Lincoln: University of Nebraska Press, 2002), p. 18.

2. Mindful of the fate of the Franklin party, Weyprecht had issued ammunition to his officers, instructing them to shoot themselves (and tell the crew to commit suicide) rather than resort to cannibalism.

3. Letter of Charles P. Daly, *New York Tribune*, January 17, 1886, quoted in Karen M. Morin, *Civic Discipline: Geography in America, 1860–1890* (Farnham, UK: Ashgate, 2011), p. 127.

4. Fergus Fleming, *Ninety Degrees North: The Quest for the North Pole* (London: Granta Books, 2001), p. 82.

5. Christopher Carter, "Going Global in Polar Exploration: Nineteenth-Century British and American Nationalism and Peacetime Science," in *Globalizing Polar Science: Reconsidering the International Polar Years and Geophysical Year*, ed. Roger D. Launius, James R. Fleming, and David H. DeVorkin (New York: Palgrave MacMillan, 2010), p. 97.

6. Cornelia Luedecke, "The First International Polar Year (1882–1883): A Big Science Experiment with Small Science Equipment," *Proceedings of the International Commission on History of Meteorology* 1, no. 1 (2014): 58.

7. Ironically, given the spirit of international cooperation, scientific reports written in Dutch, Russian, Swedish, and other languages were not translated, so that findings were not widely shared. Roger. D. Launius, "Toward the Poles: A Historiography of Scientific Exploration during the International Polar Years and the International Geophysical Year," in *Globalizing Polar Science*," p. 64.

8. Marc Rothenburg, "Making Science Global? Coordinated Enterprises in Nineteenth-Century Science," in *Globalizing Polar Science*, p. 25.

9. George W. Stocking Jr., *Victorian Anthropology* (New York: Free Press, 1987), p. 3.

10. Felix Driver, *Geography Militant: Cultures of Exploration and Empire* (Malden, MA: Blackwell, 2001), p. 4.

11. Jeannette Mirsky, *To the Arctic! The Story of Arctic Exploration from Earliest Times to the Present* (New York: Viking, 1934), p. 8. Cf. Robert G. David, *The Arctic in the British Imagination, 1818–1914* (Manchester: Manchester University Press, 2000), p. 16.

12. Erika Elce, introduction to *As Affecting the Fate of My Absent Husband: Selected Letters of Lady Franklin Concerning the Search for the Lost Franklin Expedition, 1848–1860* (Montreal: McGill-Queens University Press, 2009), p. 16.

13. Edward J. Larson, *An Empire of Ice: Scott, Shackleton, and the Heroic Age of Antarctic Science* (New Haven: Yale University Press, 2011), pp. 62, 75.

14. David Day, *Antarctica: A Biography* (Oxford: Oxford University Press, 2013), p. 20. See also David J. Cantrill, *The Vegetation of Antarctica through Geological Time* (Cambridge: Cambridge University Press, 2013), pp. 2–3.

15. John Franklin, *Narrative of a Second Expedition to the Shores of the Polar Sea, in the Years 1825, 1826, and 1827* (London: John Murray, 1828), p. 319.

16. George Back, *Narrative of the Arctic Land Expedition to the Mouth of the Great Fish River* (London: John Murray, 1836), p. 16.

17. Max Jones, *The Last Great Quest: Captain Scott's Antarctic Sacrifice* (Oxford: Oxford University Press, 2003), p. 29.

18. Quoted in T. H. Baughman, *Before the Heroes Came: Antarctica in the 1890s* (Lincoln: University of Nebraska Press, 1994), p. 53.

19. Kane's dissertation, published in 1842, was entitled *Experiments on Kiesteine, with Remarks on Its Application to the Diagnosis of Pregnancy* (Philadelphia: University of Pennsylvania, 1842).

20. Elisha Kent Kane, *Adrift in the Arctic Ice Pack: From the History of the First US Grinnell Expedition in Search of Sir John Franklin* (New York: Outing, 1915), pp. 29, 39. See also Kane, *The United States Grinnell Expedition in Search of Sir John Franklin: A Personal Narrative* (New York: Sheldon, Blakeman, 1857), p. 27.

21. In a letter dated April 21, 1851, Thomas Kane wrote to his brother: "A flood of glory [underlined] has rushed in at the doors and windows, that could not fail to carry everything before it. . . . You are expected home to be the biggest kind of Sion that has reared here [in Philadelphia] since the redoubtable Stephen Decatur of the War of 1812." (Elisha Kent Kane Papers, American Philosophical Society, Philadelphia.)

22. Elisha Kent Kane, *Arctic Explorations: The Second Grinnell Expedition in Search of Sir John Franklin, 1853, '54, '55* (Bedford, MA: Applewood 1856), pp. 153, 165, 166.

23. For a thorough treatment of this scientific quest, see Granville A. Mawer, *South by Northwest: The Magnetic Crusade and the Contest for Antarctica* (Edinburgh: Birlinn, 2006).

24. "Arctic Explorations: The Second Expedition, in Search of Sir John Franklin, 1853, '54, '55," *New London Daily Star*, March 16, 1857. By comparison, the top-selling book in the United States during the nineteenth century—Harriet Beecher Stowe's *Uncle Tom's Cabin*—sold three hundred thousand copies the year it first appeared, in 1853.

25. Francis Leopold McClintock, *The Voyage of the "Fox" in the Arctic Seas: A Narrative of the Discovery of the Fate of Sir John Franklin and His Companions* (London: John Murray, 1859), p. 44. McClintock noted that this study should be of particular value in case his voyage otherwise might be "altogether barren of results." By the 1860s, the Royal Geographical Society was supplying ordinary travelers with scientific instruments so they could conduct on-site measurements all around the world. (Jones, *Last Great Quest*, p. 34.)

26. Ibid., p. 174.

27. Day, *Antarctica*, p. 99.

28. Quoted in Baughman, *Before the Heroes Came*, p. 52.

29. Murphy, *German Exploration of the Polar World*, p. 1.

30. Initially, the congressional committee considering Hall's request for funding had turned him down, on the grounds that he did not "possess any of the qualifications

necessary to carry out an expedition that should be thought of only in connection with scientific discovery." (See "Expedition to the North Pole: Unseemly Conduct of Captain Hall," *Philadelphia Inquirer*, April 12, 1870.) Hall had irritated members of this committee by attacking Isaac Israel Hayes—a rival for government funding with impressive scientific qualifications—during his own presentation.

31. Michael F. Robinson, *The Coldest Crucible: Arctic Exploration and American Culture* (Chicago: University of Chicago Press, 2006), p. 79.

32. Excitement surrounding the De Long expedition was intense. Many thought the *Jeannette* might actually reach the North Pole, while others expressed grandiose hopes that this voyage might "determine laws of meteorology, hydrography, astronomy and gravitation, reveal ocean currents, develop new fisheries, discover lands and peoples hitherto unknown, and by extending the world's knowledge of such fundamental principles of earth-life as magnetism and electricity and the various collateral branches of atmospheric science, solve great problems important to humanity" (*Watertown* [New York] *Daily Times*, July 7, 1879, quoted in Leonard F. Guttridge, *Icebound: The "Jeannette" Expedition's Quest for the North Pole* [Annapolis: Naval Institute Press, 1986], p. 3).

33. De Long had preferred an all-military crew so that he could count on their respecting his authority at all times. (Hampton Sides, *In the Kingdom of Ice: The Grand and Terrible Polar Voyage of the USS* Jeannette [New York: Random House, 2014], p. 80.)

34. Sarah Moss, *Scott's Last Biscuit: The Literature of Polar Travel* (Oxford: Signal Books, 2006), p. 93.

35. Scientific records of the expedition took up eighty-five pages in the second volume of Greely's account of this expedition. He boasted that his team had collected more extensive data on these phenomena than any other International Polar Year party. (Adolphus W. Greely, *Three Years of Arctic Service: An Account of the Lady Franklin Bay Expedition of 1881–1884 and the Attainment of the Farthest North*, vol. 1 [New York: Charles Scribner's Sons, 1886], p. v.)

36. Leonard F. Guttridge, *Ghosts of Cape Sabine: The True Story of the Greely Expedition* (New York: G. P. Putnam's Sons, 2000), p. 108.

37. However, it was discovered during their second year in the Arctic that some records had not been diligently kept, or specimens properly labelled. (Adolphus W. Greely, *Three Years of Arctic Service*, vol. 2 [London: Richard Bentley and Sons, 1886], p. 65.)

38. See "Means of the Meteorological Observations Made at Fort Conger, 1881–1883," Appendix 1, Greely, *Three Years of Arctic Service*, vol. 2, p. 342.

39. Quoted in Jones, *Last Great Quest*, p. 41.

40. Quoted in Morin, *Civic Geography*, p. 127.

41. Jones, *Last Great Quest*, pp. 62–63.

42. Letter of Wilson to Dr. Edward T. Wilson, September 16, 1909, quoted in David Crane, *Scott of Antarctica: A Life of Courage and Tragedy in the Extreme South* (New York: HarperCollins, 2005), p. 398.

43. Scott, journal entry of July 13, 1911. Quoted in Larson, *An Empire of Ice*, p. 274.

44. Wilson had studied the migration of Emperor penguins during the *Discovery* expedition and subsequently published a monograph on the life cycle of these birds.

45. Crane, *Scott of Antarctica*, pp. 427, 500.

46. Robert F. Scott, *Scott's Last Expedition: The Personal Journals of Captain R. F. Scott, RN, CVO, on His Journey to the South Pole*, vol. 1 (New York: Dodd, Mead, 1923), p. 253.

47. Tryggve Gran, *The Norwegian with Scott: Tryggve Gran's Antarctic Diary, 1910–1913*, trans. G. Hattersley-Smith (Greenwich: National Maritime Museum, 1984), p. 114.

48. Scott, *Scott's Last Expedition*, pp. 287, 311.

49. Apsley Cherry-Garrard, *The Worst Journey in the World* (New York: Carroll and Graf, 1989), pp. 231–32.

50. Ibid., pp. 254, 267, 270, 274.

51. British explorers did participate in an expedition led by Douglas Mawson in 1929–31, and a privately funded mission took place later in the 1930s, but by then the English public had lost its fascination with this part of the world.

52. Quoted in Jones, *Last Great Quest*, p. 165.

CHAPTER EIGHT: "DOWN WITH SCIENCE, SENTIMENT, AND THE FAIR SEX"

1. Winfield S. Schley and James R. Solely, *The Rescue of Greely* (New York: Charles Scribner's Sons, 1885), pp. 222–23. Other accounts have challenged what Schley recollected, claiming that Greely had simply asked for food or told his rescuers to let him and the others die in peace. See, for example, Michael F. Robinson, *The Coldest Crucible: Arctic Exploration and American Culture* (Chicago: University of Chicago Press, 2006), p. 84. See also Charles H. Harlow, "Greely at Cape Sabine: Notes by a Member of the Relief Expedition," *Century Illustrated Monthly Magazine* 30, no. 1 (May 1885): 83. Harlow had been the photographer on the rescue mission and took pictures on site shortly after Greely and the other survivors had been discovered.

2. Greely's instructions from the War Department had included a sledge outing to nearby Cape Joseph Henry, but this was actually somewhat south of the Fort Conger base camp. Adolphus W. Greely, *Three Years of Arctic Service: An Account of the Lady Franklin Bay Expedition of 1881–1884 and the Attainment of the Farthest North*, vol. 1 (London: Richard Bentley and Sons, 1886), p. xii.

3. Leonard F. Guttridge, *Ghosts of Cape Sabine: The True Story of the Greely Expedition* (New York: G. P. Putnam's Sons, 2000), p. 109.

4. David L. Brainard, letter to Maria L. Brainard, [various dates, 1882], Folder 24, Box 7, Series V, "Personal or Private Letters and Notes," Collection of the Lady Franklin Bay Expedition, Research Collections, Explorers Club, New York.

5. To go on the Lady Franklin Bay Expedition, which was also an Army operation, Pavy had to be temporarily given the rank of captain—a designation that irked him as he was decidedly unmilitary and despised how this appointment restricted his freedom.

6. Greely, *Three Years of Arctic Service*, vol. 2, p. 310, and vol. 1, p. 180. Chartering the *Proteus* to bring the party to Ellesmere Island had used up three fourths of Greely's $24 thousand budget, so that he was forced to buy supplies, including scientific equipment, at the cheapest possible price, thus sacrificing quality. Greely, *Arctic Service*, vol. 1, p. 38.

7. Guttridge, *Ghosts of Cape Sabine*, p. 62. Thermometers designed to measure solar and earthly radiation turned out to have too small a scale to be of use so far north, and crucial winter readings were therefore abandoned. (Greely, *Arctic Service*, vol. 1, p. 127.) The Greely party had also arrived in the Arctic without sufficient winter clothing, and the men had to stitch together coats and other garments from blankets. (See "Medical Report of Hospital Steward Biederbeck," in Adolphus W. Greely, *Report on the Proceedings of the United States Expedition to Lady Franklin Bay, Grinnell Land*, vol. 1 [Washington: Government Printing Office, 1888], p. 335.)

8. Sergeant George W. Rice and Dr. Pavy went on the first exploratory excursion from Fort Conger just over a week after the Greely party had moved into its winter quarters in late August. Other depot-laying trips took place early the next month. (See journal of C. B. Henry, Folder 3:5, Series V, Collection of the Lady Franklin Bay Expedition, Explorers Club.)

9. Greely, *Arctic Service*, vol. 1, pp. 238, 296, 297.

10. Ibid., p. 335.

11. "Adolphus Greely, Arctic Explorer of 1882, Recipient of Congressional Medal of Honor," *Cornell Daily Sun* (Ithaca, NY), March 28, 1935.

12. Roald Amundsen, *My Life as an Explorer* (Garden City: Doubleday, 1927), pp. 32–34.

13. In a 1906 letter to H. G. Wells, William James described pursuit of the "bitch-goddess Success" as our "national disease."

14. George Back, "Recollections of our Unfortunate Voyage to Discover the Country between the Mouth of the Coppermine River and Hudson's Bay," entry of January 10, 1822, Back, "Miscellaneous Items" folder, Scott Polar Research Institute (SPRI), Cambridge.

15. See, for example, letter of Elisha Kent Kane to Henry Grinnell, May 10, 1855. Henry Grinnell Correspondence, Elisha Kent Kane Collection, American Philosophical Society, Philadelphia. In this letter Kane explained that his surveying of Smith Sound was primarily for that purpose.

16. David Chapin, "'Science Weeps, the World Weeps, Humanity Weeps': America Mourns Elisha Kent Kane," *Pennsylvania Magazine of History and Biography* 123, no. 4 (October 1999): 277.

17. "Arctic Expedition," *Constitution* (Middletown, CT), June 8, 1853.

18. Kane recognized the exploitative parallels between his lectures and Maggie Fox's communing with the dead. As he once wrote to her, "just as you have your wearisome round of daily money-making, I have my own sad vanities to pursue." (Undated letter of Kane to Maggie Fox, quoted in *The Love Life of Dr. Kane: Containing the Correspondence, and a History of the Acquaintance, Engagement, and Secret Marriage between Elisha K. Kane and Margaret Fox* [Whitefish, MT: Kessinger, 1999], p. 49.)

19. When Kane died he was celebrated for his scientific discoveries, which had made him "the greatest hero" of his day. (Chapin, "'Science Weeps,'" p. 275.)

20. Elisha K. Kane, *Arctic Explorations: The Second Grinnell Expedition in Search of Sir John Franklin, 1853, '54, '55* (Bedford, MA: Applewood, 1856), pp. 146, 165.

21. H. D. Traill, *The Life of Sir John Franklin, RN* (London: John Murray, 1896), p. 444.

22. Charles F. Hall, introduction to *Arctic Researches and Life among the Esquimaux: Being the Narrative of an Expedition in Search of Sir John Franklin, in the Years 1860, 1861, and 1862* (New York: Harper and Brothers, 1865), p. xix.

23. Robinson, *Coldest Crucible*, p. 81. When Hall had first appeared before the House Appropriations Committee in April 1870, his gratuitous attacks on Isaac Hayes riled its members, who concluded that Hall did not "possess any of the qualifications necessary to carry out an expedition that should be thought of only in connection with scientific discovery" and voted against giving him any money. ("Expedition to the North Pole: Unseemly Conduct of Captain Hall," *Philadelphia Inquirer*, April 12, 1870.)

24. Quoted in Charles F. Hall, *Narrative of the North Polar Expedition: US Ship*

Polaris, Captain Charles Francis Hall Commanding, ed. G. M. Robeson (Washington: Government Printing Office, 1876), pp. 18–19.

25. Whereas members of Congress were loath to "squander" money on someone as unqualified for this polar mission as they thought Hall was, they were persuaded by scientific organizations to back Hayes. For example, officials at the Geographical Society of New York wrote lawmakers, stating that Hayes—the recipient of several medals for his contributions to polar science—was considered "the most able, eminent, and experienced of living American Arctic explorers." ("An Expedition to the Polar Seas," *Philadelphia Inquirer*, April 13, 1870.)

26. Isaac I. Hayes, *The Open Polar Sea: A Narrative of a Voyage of Discovery towards the North Pole, in the Schooner "United States"* (New York: Hurd and Houghton, 1867), pp. vii, 164, 182, 317, 355. In the spring of 1861, Hayes would have renewed hopes of finding open water to the north, based upon theories of Humboldt and others that higher latitudes did not necessarily correlate with lower temperatures. But testing this theory would be beyond his capabilities. After escaping the ice and returning to Halifax, Hayes realized he now had to "sacrifice all the hopes and all the ambitions which had encouraged me through toil and danger, with the promise of fame to follow the successful completion of a great object; to abandon an enterprise in which I had aspired to win for myself an honorable place among the men who have illustrated their country's history and shed lustre upon their country's flag."

27. T. H. Baughman, *Before the Heroes Came: Antarctica in the 1890s* (Lincoln: University of Nebraska Press, 1994), pp. 95, 105.

28. Quoted in J. Kennedy Maclean, *Heroes of the Polar Seas: A Record of Exploration in the Arctic and Antarctic Seas* (London: W. and R. Chambers, 1910), p. 13.

29. Beau Riffenburgh, *The Myth of the Explorer: The Press, Sensationalism, and Geographical Discovery* (London: Belhaven, 1993), p. 142.

30. Fridtjof Nansen, *Farthest North: Being the Record of an Voyage of Exploration of the Ship "Fram" (1893–1896) and of a Fifteen Months' Sleigh Journey by Dr. Nansen and Lieut. Johansen*, vol. 1 (Westminster, MD: Constable, 1897), pp. 325–26.

31. Ibid., pp. 330, 331.

32. This abrupt decision did not change Nansen's public image as a man of science, however. For example, in a review of his book *Farthest North*, which appeared in the *Saturday Review*, the Norwegian explorer was described as being before "everything else . . . a man of science." Nansen had not left behind his wife and child and traveled so far north "that he might write a book of adventure, or gain the barren laurels of having reached a more northerly point on the surface of the earth than any other human being since human history," but rather to gather a "richer harvest of

scientific data than any other expedition that has ever entered the Arctic circle." ("The Story of the *Fram*," *Saturday Review of Books* 83, no. 2156 [February 20, 1897]: 199.)

33. Francis Leopold McClintock, *The Voyage of the "Fox" in the Arctic Seas: A Narrative of Discovery of the Fate of Sir John Franklin and His Companions* (Cologne: Konemann, 1998), pp. 25, 28.

34. McClintock also felt that dogs might also be used for this purpose.

35. David Day, *Antarctica: A Biography* (Oxford: Oxford University Press), pp. 133, 143.

36. Edward J. Larson, *An Empire of Ice: Scott, Shackleton, and the Heroic Age of Antarctic Science* (New Haven: Yale University Press, 2011), pp. 18, 58, 121.

37. Letter of Shackleton to Scott, February 21, 1910, quoted in Elsbeth Huxley, *Scott of the Antarctic* (Lincoln: University of Nebraska Press, 1977), p. 187.

38. The British inclusion of scientific work in their Antarctic expeditions was not popular with the public, which was "anxious to have a race to the South Pole and to read of the triumph of English courage and endurance over their continental rivals." (Day, *Antarctica*, p. 143.) As was pointed out in an article in the British medical journal *Lancet* in 1910, "The cultivation of an adventurous spirit is of vital importance to a nation having such extensive maritime interests as those of Great Britain, and the national sense of patriotism is thrilled when British navigators show themselves as ready in the present day as in the past to run great risks and to suffer hardships in traveling the Polar [*sic*] ice fields." ("Captain Scott's Antarctic Expedition," *Lancet* 175, no. 4506 [January 8, 1910]: 120.)

39. Before the three men left, Scott took Wilson aside and stressed to him that he needed to have Cherry-Garrard and Bowers return in good shape for the polar trek. (Susan Solomon, *The Coldest March: Scott's Fatal Antarctic Expedition* (New Haven: Yale University Press, 2001), p. 135.)

40. Diana Preston, *A First Rate Tragedy: Captain Scott's Antarctic Expeditions* (London: Constable, 1997), p. 150.

41. Larson, *Empire of Ice*, p. 115.

42. In September 1909, Scott wrote in his journal that "the scientific exploration of a considerable extent of the Antarctic continent" was a secondary objective of his *Terra Nova* expedition. (Entry of September 16, 1909, quoted in Wilfrid Noyce, *The Springs of Adventure* [Cleveland: World, 1958], p. 159.)

43. Francis Spufford has argued that collecting these fossils, with their clues to early life on the planet, was "among the most forward-looking things Scott ever did." But it is not at all clear that the explorer himself would have seen it that way. (Spufford, introduction to *The Ends of the Earth: An Anthology of the Finest Writing on the Arctic*, ed. Elizabeth Kolbert [New York: Bloomsbury, 2007], p. 6.)

44. Crane, *Scott of Antarctica*, pp. 5–6. However, in his journal entries made during the trip back, Scott made no mention of scientific accomplishments and only praised the endurance of his companions.

45. Charles W. Johnson, *Ice Ship: The Epic Voyages of the Polar Adventurer Fram* (Lebanon, NH: University Press of New England, 2014), pp. 82–83.

46. William C. Godfrey, *Godfrey's Narrative of the Last Grinnell Arctic Exploring Party in Search of Sir John Franklin, 1853-4-5* (Philadelphia: J. T. Lloyd, 1857), p. 71.

47. Adrien de Gerlache, *The Belgian Antarctic Expedition under the Command of A. de Gerlache de Gomery* (Brussels: Hayez, 1904), p. 43.

48. Adrien de Gerlache, *Fifteen Months in the Antarctic*, trans. Maurice Raraty (Norfolk: Bluntisham, 1998), p. 104.

CHAPTER NINE: NO MAN IS AN ISLAND

1. Quoted in Wilfrid Noyce, *The Springs of Adventure* (Cleveland: World, 1958), p. 81.

2. Daniel Defoe, *Robinson Crusoe* (London: Macmillan, 1868), p. 158.

3. Richard E. Byrd, *Alone* (New York: G. P. Putnam's Sons, 1938), p. 11. He wrote to his wife, Marie, that she should not be concerned since he had "planned the whole thing." (Lisle A. Rose, *Explorer: The Life of Richard E. Byrd* [Columbia: University of Missouri Press, 2008], p. 34.)

4. Warren R. Hofstra, "Richard E. Byrd and the Legacy of Polar Exploration," *Virginia Magazine of History and Biography* 110, no. 2 (2002): 147.

5. Lisle A. Rose, "Exploring a Secret Land: The Literary and Technological Legacies of Richard E. Byrd," *Virginia Magazine of History and Biography* 110, no. 2 (2002): 191.

6. Byrd, *Alone*, p. 3.

7. Gabrielle Walker, *Antarctic: An Intimate Portrait of a Mysterious Continent* (Boston: Houghton, Mifflin, Harcourt, 2013), p. 335.

8. Quoted in Rose, *Explorer*, p. 352.

9. Esther D. Rothblum, "Psychological Factors in the Antarctic," *Journal of Psychology* 124, no. 3 (1990): 257. Rothblum cited as her source an article by Charles S. Mullin Jr.: "Some Psychological Aspects of Isolated Antarctic Living," *American Journal of Psychiatry* 117, no. 4 (October 1960): 323–25.

10. Rose, *Explorer*, p. 360.

11. Henry Fairfield Osborn, foreword to *Byrd's Great Adventure: The Fight to*

Conquer the Ends of the Earth, by Francis Trevelyan Miller (Chicago: Winston, 1930), p. 15.

12. Quoted in Noyce, *Springs of Adventure*, p. 83.

13. Robert M. Bryce, *Cook & Peary: The Polar Controversy, Resolved* (Mechanicsburg, PA: Stackpole, 1997), p. 319. Cook had suffered from feelings of isolation on the way to the pole, even though he was accompanied by two Inuit men. He later would write, "We were alone—all alone in a lifeless world. . . . With eager eyes we searched the dusky plains of frost, but there was no speck of life to grace the purple run of death." (Cook, "The Conquest of the North Pole," *New York Herald*, October 1, 1909, quoted in Bryce, *Cook & Peary*, p. 409.)

14. For an account of this truly amazing journey, see Stephen R. Bown, *White Eskimo: Knud Rasmussen's Fearless Journey into the Heart of the Arctic* (New York: Da Capo, 2015), pp. 223–51.

15. Mertz was also a vegetarian, so it was difficult for him to digest meat. For this psychological explanation for his death, see D. Carrington-Smith, "Mawson and Mertz: A Re-Evaluation of Their Ill-Fated Mapping Journey during the 1911–1914 Australasian Antarctic Expedition," *Medical Journal of Australia* 183, nos. 11–12 (December 5–19, 2005): 638–41.

16. Lennard Bickel, *Mawson's Will: The Greatest Survival Story Ever Written* (New York: Stein and Day, 1997), p. 125. See also Charles F. Laseron, *South with Mawson: Reminiscences of the Australasian Antarctic Expedition, 1911–1914* (Sydney: Australasian Publishing, 1947), pp. 212–13.

17. But this expression of regret did not find its way into his book *Home of the Blizzard*.

18. Quoted from the journal of John Richardson, in Seon Manley and Gogo Lewis Garden, ed., *Polar Secrets: A Treasury of the Arctic and Antarctic* (New York: Doubleday, 1968), p. 144.

19. Byrd, *Alone*, pp. 15–16.

20. Rose, *Explorer*, p. 220. Some five thousand men had volunteered for this earlier expedition of Shackleton's.

21. Nansen also looked for men who were as ambitious as he was—who possessed "the same thirst for achievement, the same craving to get beyond the limits of the known which inspired this people in the Saga times." (Fridtjof Nansen, *Farthest North: Being the Record of a Voyage of Exploration of the Ship "Fram" (1893–1896) and of a Fifteen Months' Sleigh Journey by Dr. Nansen and Lieut. Johansen*, vol. 1 [Westminster, MD: Constable, 1897], p. 93.)

22. Ibid., p. 222. See also Eugene Rodgers, preface to *Beyond the Barrier: The*

Story of Byrd's First Antarctic Expedition (Annapolis: Naval Institute Press, 1990), p. ix.

23. When he was researching a book on this expedition, Eugene Rodgers found that many surviving veterans did not want to talk to him about Byrd. (Rodgers, *Beyond the Barrier*, p. vi.)

24. Scott biographer Roland Huntford points out that Scott lacked confidence around nonmilitary types. (Huntford, *The Last Place on Earth: Scott and Amundsen's Race to the South Pole* [New York: Random House, 1999], p. 137.)

25. George W. De Long, *The Voyage of the "Jeannette": The Ship and Ice Journals of George W. De Long*, ed. Emma De Long, vol.1 (Boston: Houghton Mifflin, 1884), p. 68.

26. Iain McCalman, *Darwin's Armada: Four Voyagers to the Southern Oceans and Their Battle for the Theory of Evolution* (New York: Simon and Schuster, 2009), p. 141.

27. Sherard Osborn, *Stray Leaves from an Arctic Journal; or, Eighteen Months in the Polar Regions in Search of Sir John Franklin's Expedition, in the Years 1850–51* (London: Longman, Brown, Green, and Longmans, 1852), p. 152.

28. Mark M. Sawin, *Raising Kane: Elisha Kent Kane and the Culture of Fame in Antebellum America* (Philadelphia: American Philosophical Society, 2008), p. 168.

29. Nansen, *Farthest North*, vol. 1, p. 144.

30. Isaac I. Hayes, *The Open Polar Sea: A Narrative of a Voyage of Discovery towards the North Pole, in the Schooner "United States"* (New York: Hurd and Houghton, 1867), pp. 16, 162, 167, 168, 203, 222, 316, 317.

31. Charles F. Hall, *Narrative of the Second Arctic Expedition Made by Charles F. Hall: His Voyage to Repulse Bay, Sledge Journeys to the Straits of Fury and Hecla and to King William's Land* (Washington: Government Printing Office, 1879), p. 130.

32. Quoted from Hall's journal, in Chauncey C. Loomis, *Weird and Tragic Shores: The Story of Charles Francis Hall, Explorer* (Lincoln: University of Nebraska Press, 1971), p. 130.

33. Ibid., p. 259.

34. Nansen, *Farthest North*, vol. 1, p. 144.

35. Roald Amundsen, *The South Pole: An Account of the Norwegian Antarctic Expedition in the* Fram, *1910–1912*, trans. A. G. Chater, vol. 2(London: John Murray, 1913), p. 445.

36. Members referred to this outing by its original name, the "Eastern Party."

37. Raymond E. Priestley, *Antarctic Adventure: Scott's Northern Party* (New York: E. P. Dutton, 1915), pp. 232, 249, 279, 30.

38. Quoted in Leonard F. Guttridge, *Ghosts of Cape Sabine: The True Story of the Greely Expedition* (New York: G. P. Putnam's Sons, 2000), p. 81.

39. Katherine Lambert, *The Longest Winter: The Incredible Survival of Scott's Lost Party* (Washington: Smithsonian Institution, 2004), p. 145.

40. David Crane, *Scott of Antarctica: A Life of Courage and Tragedy in the Extreme South* (New York: HarperCollins, 2005), p. 119.

41. Apsley Cherry-Garrard, *The Worst Journey in the World* (New York: Carroll and Graf, 1989), p. 204.

42. Quoted in Caroline Alexander, *The Endurance: Shackleton's Legendary Antarctic Expedition* (New York: Knopf, 1999), p. 131.

43. "Peary as His Friends Portray Him," *Current Literature* 48, no. 5 (May 1910): 496.

44. Robert E. Peary, *The North Pole: Its Discovery in 1909 under the Auspices of the Peary Arctic Club* (New York: Frederick A. Stokes, 1910), pp. 270–71.

45. Elisha K. Kane, *Arctic Explorations: The Second Grinnell Expedition in Search of Sir John Franklin, 1853, '54, '55* (Bedford, MA: Applewood, 1856), p. 83.

46. See, for example, Loomis, *Weird and Tragic Shores*, p. 219.

47. Alexander Armstrong, *A Personal Narrative of the North-West Passage, with Numerous Incidents of Travel and Adventure during Nearly Five Years' Continuous Service in the Arctic Regions while in Search of the Expedition under Sir John Franklin* (London: Hurst and Blackett, 1857), p. 575.

48. From Kipling's poem "The English Flag," quoted in T. H. Baughman, *Pilgrims on Ice: Robert Falcon Scott's First Antarctic Expedition* (Lincoln: University of Nebraska Press, 1999), p. 89.

49. Luigi di Amedeo, *On the "Polar Star" in the Arctic Sea*, trans. William Le Queu, vol. 1 (London: Hutchinson, 1903), p. 89.

50. Nansen, *Farthest North*, vol. 1, p. 196.

CHAPTER TEN: "WE HAVE MET THE ENEMY, AND HE IS US"

1. William C. Godfrey, *Godfrey's Narrative of the Last Grinnell Arctic Exploring Party in Search of Sir John Franklin, 1853-4-5* (Philadelphia: J. T. Lloyd, 1857), pp. 19, 20, 32, 35, 66, 77, 78, 98, 107–108.

2. Pierre Berton, *The Arctic Grail: The Quest for the Northwest Passage and the North Pole, 1818–1909* (New York: Viking, 1988), pp. 288, 290.

3. Frederick A. Cook, *Through the First Antarctic Night, 1898–1899: A Narrative of the Voyage of the "Belgica" among Newly Discovered Lands and over an Unknown Sea about the South Pole* (London: Heinemann, 1900), pp. 58, 277, 282, 290.

4. This charge was never conclusively substantiated, although an exhuming of Hall's corpse in 1968 determined that he had ingested an unusual amount of arsenic during the final weeks of his life. (See Chauncey C. Loomis, *Weird and Tragic Shores: The Story of Charles Francis Hall, Explorer* (Lincoln: University of Nebraska Press, 1971), p. 345.) To this day, it remains unclear if he had consumed this willingly, to commit suicide, or been murdered.

5. Bruce Henderson, *Fatal North: Adventure and Survival aboard USS "Polaris," the First US Expedition to the North Pole* (New York: New American Library, 2001), pp. 94, 115, 151, 169.

6. Adolphus W. Greely, *Three Years of Arctic Service: An Account of the Lady Franklin Bay Expedition of 1881–1884 and the Attainment of the Farthest North*, vol. 1 (London: Richard Bentley and Sons, 1886), pp. 94, 62.

7. Berton, *Arctic Grail*, p. 443.

8. Adolphus W. Greely, untitled ms., July 19, 1883, Folder 28, Box 3, Series II, "Official Orders and Narratives," Collection of the Lady Franklin Bay Expedition, 1881–1884, Research Collections, Explorers Club, New York.

9. Diana Preston, *A First Rate Tragedy: Captain Scott's Antarctic Expeditions* (London: Constable, 1997), p. 143.

10. Tryggve Gran, *The Norwegian with Scott: Tryggve Gran's Antarctic Diary, 1910–1913*, trans. G. Hattersley-Smith (Greenwich: National Maritime Museum, 1984), pp. 138–39, 156, 219.

11. Fergus Fleming, *Ninety Degrees North: The Quest for the North Pole* (London: Granta, 2001), p. 215.

12. Quoted in Loomis, *Weird and Tragic Shores*, p. 267.

13. Henderson, *Fatal North*, pp. 55–56, 62, 63.

14. David Crane, *Scott of Antarctica: A Life of Courage and Tragedy in the Extreme South* (New York: HarperCollins, 2005), p. 171.

15. Scott once wrote to his wife Kathleen that he regarded life as a constant struggle to survive. See Francis Spufford, *I May Be Some Time: Ice and the English Imagination* (London: Faber and Faber, 1996), p. 317.

16. Quoted in Michael Smith, *Shackleton: By Endurance We Conquer* (London: Oneworld, 2014), p. 128.

17. Scott told his wife that he believed Shackleton had intended all along to break his promise. (Crane, *Scott of Antarctica*, p. 390.)

18. Letter of Ernest Shackleton to Robert Scott, July 6, 1909, MS 367/17/1, Scott Polar Research Institute (SPRI), Cambridge. Six months later, Shackleton wrote again, explaining that any forthcoming expedition of his would be "purely scientific"

and not make any effort to reach the South Pole. (Letter of Shackleton to Scott, February 21, 1910, MS 367/17/2, SPRI.)

19. Max Jones, *The Last Great Quest: Captain Scott's Antarctic Sacrifice* (New York: Oxford University Press, 2000), p. 8.

20. Godfrey, *Godfrey's Narrative*, p. 57.

21. Elisha K. Kane, *Arctic Explorations: The Second Grinnell Expedition in Search of Sir John Franklin, 1853, '54, '55* (Philadelphia: Childs and Peterson, 1856), p. 84.

22. Mark M. Sawin, *Raising Kane: Elisha Kent Kane and the Culture of Fame in Antebellum America* (Philadelphia: American Philosophical Society, 2008), pp. 204, 273.

23. Berton, *Arctic Grail*, pp. 441–42, 254.

24. Roland Huntford, *The Last Place on Earth: Scott and Amundsen's Race to the South Pole* (New York: Random House, 1999), pp. 321, 401–402.

25. Apsley Cherry-Garrard, *The Worst Journey in the World* (New York: Carroll and Graf, 1989), p. 205.

26. Preston, *First Rate Tragedy*, p. 127.

27. Crane, *Scott of Antarctica*, p. 220.

28. Ibid., p. 123.

29. Raymond E. Priestley, *Antarctic Adventure: Scott's Northern Party* (New York: E. F. Dutton, 1915), p. 77.

30. Sara Wheeler, *Cherry: A Life of Apsley Cherry-Garrard* (London: Jonathan Cape, 2001), p. 76. "At the end of the day, Campbell's word was law." (Victor Campbell, *The Wicked Mate: The Antarctic Diary of Victor Campbell*, ed. H. G. R. King [Bluntisham, Huntington: Erskine, 2001], p. 129.)

31. Priestley, *Antarctic Adventure*, pp. 278, 279, 295, 353–54.

32. Jean-Baptiste Charcot, *The Voyage of the "Why Not?" in the Antarctic*, trans. Philip Walsh (New York: Hodder and Stoughton, 1911), pp. 199, 209, 210.

33. In his study of how to improve the chances of survival after a disaster, John Leach has also concluded that "crowding" increases stress, although being alone can quickly bring a survivor "to his knees in a surprisingly short time, quicker indeed than many physical or physiological factors." See John Leach, *Survival Psychology* (London: Macmillan 1994), pp. 116, 107.

34. Lawrence A. Palinkas and Peter Suedfeld, "Psychological Effects of Polar Expeditions" *Lancet* 371, no. 9607 (January 12, 2008): 158.

35. Sarah Moss, *The Frozen Ship: The Histories and Tales of Polar Exploration* (New York: Blue Bridge, 2006), p. 166.

36. See "Report from the Committee on Invalid Pensions," January 9, 1877, report no. 79, House of Representatives, 44th Congress, 2nd Session, *Index of Reports*

*of Committees of the House of Representatives for the Second Session of the 44th Congress,
1886–87*, vol. 1 (Washington: Government Printing Office, 1877).

37. Roald Amundsen, *My Life as an Explorer* (Garden City, NY: Doubleday,
1927), p. 19.

38. Quoted in Hampton Sides, *In the Kingdom of Ice: The Grand and Terrible
Polar Voyage of the USS* Jeannette (New York: Random House, 2014), p. 176. See also
De Long, *The Voyage of the Jeannette: The Ship and Ice Journals of George W. De Long*,
vol. 1, ed. Emma De Long (Boston: Houghton Mifflin, 1883), p. 472.

39. Quoted in Sides, *In the Kingdom of Ice*, p. 177.

CHAPTER ELEVEN: IN THE END WAS THE WORD

1. Elsbeth Huxley, *Scott of the Antarctic* (Lincoln: University of Nebraska Press,
1977), p. 254.

2. Letter of Scott to Sir Edgar Speyer, March 16, 1912, quoted in Robert F.
Scott, *Scott's Last Expedition: The Personal Journals of Captain R. F. Scott, RN, CVO,
on His Journey to the South Pole* (New York: Dodd, Mead, 1923), p. 461.

3. Scott was granted his wish: after some ten thousand persons attended the
memorial service for him and the other lost explorers in London, some £74 thousand—
or roughly £3.5 million (or over $5 million) in today's currency—was donated to their
families. (Katherine Lambert, *The Longest Winter: The Incredible Survival of Captain
Scott's Lost Party* [Washington: Smithsonian Institution, 2004], p. 201.)

4. Appropriately enough, during the memorial service for Scott at St. Paul's, on
February 14, 1913, the dean read similar lines from 1 Corinthians: "O death, where is
thy sting? O grave, where is thy victory?"

5. That Scott has achieved such last fame primarily because of his literary
achievement is an argument advanced in a recent biography of the explorer—David
Crane's *Scott of Antarctica. A Life of Courage and Tragedy in the Extreme South* (New
York: HarperCollins, 2005).

6. Apsley Cherry-Garrard, *The Worst Journey in the World* (New York: Carroll
and Graf, 1989), p. 202. See also J. M. Barrie, introduction to *Scott's Last Expedition*,
p. xiii. Barrie's Peter Pan declares that "Dreams do come true, if we only wish hard
enough. You can have anything in life if you will sacrifice everything else for it."

7. In a short paper written between Antarctic expeditions, Scott voiced his
disdain for the existing European model, "with all its hideous inequalities of condition
and opportunity," and preference for those who quested for a "new and nobler

social order" based on moral principle. (Robert F. Scott, "Note on the Social Order," undated, handwritten manuscript, British National Antarctic Expedition [BNAE], vol. 2, 1901–1904, Scott Polar Research Institute (SPRI), Cambridge.)

8. Scott, *Scott's Last Expedition*, pp 11, 7.

9. Stephen R. Bown, *The Last Viking: The Life of Roald Amundsen* (New York: Da Capo, 2012), p. 195.

10. Scott, *Scott's Last Expedition*, pp. 15, 44.

11. Ibid., pp. 73, 87, 100, 214.

12. Ibid., pp. 230, 338, 287.

13. Max Jones, introduction to *Journals: Captain Scott's Last Expedition*, by Robert F. Scott (Oxford: Oxford University Press, 2006), p. xxxiv. Cf. Francis Spufford, *I May Be Some Time: Ice and the English Imagination* (London: Faber and Faber, 1996), p. 322. One example was Scott's critical reaction to discovering the state in which Shackleton had abandoned Hut Point, leaving the window open so that the space inside was full of snow as well as boxes overflowing with excrement. (Diana Preston, *A First Rate Tragedy: Captain Scott's Antarctic Expeditions* [London: Constable, 1997], p. 139.)

14. For example, George De Long's widow, Emma, undertook a similar pruning of harsh comments he had written about his fellow officers on the *Jeannette*. (See Leonard F. Guttridge, *Icebound: The "Jeannette" Expedition's Quest for the North Pole* [Annapolis: Naval Institute Press, 1986], p. 307.)

15. Scott, *Last Expedition*, p. 471.

16. Ibid., pp. 412–13.

17. It has been pointed out that Scott's observation, in his letter to Barrie that "We are showing that Englishmen can still die with a bold spirit, fighting it out to the end," echoes the words uttered by Wendy at the end of *Peter Pan*: "We hope our sons will die as English gentlemen." See Jones, introduction to *Journals*, p. xxxv.

18. "A Triumphant Failure" [review of *Scott's Last Expedition*], *Independent Weekly* (New York) 76 (January 27, 1913): 408.

19. Scott was also in need of more money to support his wife. The couple had initially put off marriage because Scott did not feel he and Kathleen would have enough to live off. (Preston, *First Rate Tragedy*, p. 95.)

20. David Crane, *Scott of Antarctica: A Life of Courage and Tragedy in the Extreme South* (New York: HarperCollins, 2005), p. 322. Scott's book was well received: the London *Spectator* called it the "ablest and most interesting record of travel to which the present century has yet given birth." (Quoted in Max Jones, *The Last Great Quest: Captain Scott's Antarctic Sacrifice* [Oxford: Oxford University Press, 2003], p. 69.)

21. Preston, *First Rate Tragedy*, p. 171.

22. Crane, *Scott of Antarctica*, p. 503.

23. Preston, *First Rate Tragedy*, p. 61.

24. Jones, introduction to *Journals*, pp. xxiv, xliv–xlviii.

25. Richard Davis, "History or His/story? The Explorer *cum* Author," *Studies in Canadian Literature / Études en littérature canadienne* 16, no. 2 (1991): 96, https://journals.lib.unb.ca/index.php/scl/article/view/8143/9200 (accessed November 12, 2015).

26. Mark M. Sawin, *Raising Kane: Elisha Kent Kane and the Culture of Fame in Antebellum America* (Philadelphia: American Philosophical Society, 2008), p. 2.

27. On his second polar expedition, starting in 1853, Kane brought along his own large "well-chosen" library. "The Arctic Exploration," *Plattsburgh* (NY) *Republican*, June 11, 1853. Cf. Kane, *Arctic Explorations: The Second Grinnell Expedition in Search of Sir John Franklin, 1853, '54, '55* (Bedford, MA: Applewood, 1853), p. 14.

28. Letter of Thomas Kane to Elisha Kent Kane, January 26, 1851, Elisha Kent Kane Collection, American Philosophical Society, Philadelphia.

29. Kane, *Arctic Explorations*, p. 133. A passage such as this one recalls Shelley's description of the Arve in his 1817 poem "Mount Blanc":

Thus thou, Ravine of Arve—dark, deep Ravine—
Thou many-colored, many-voiced vale, Over whose pines, and crags, and caverns sail
Fast cloud-shadows, and sunbeams! Awful scene, Where Power in likeness of the Arve
comes down
From the ice-gulfs that gird his secret throne, Bursting through these dark mountains
like the flame
Of lightning through the tempest!

30. Pierre Berton, *The Arctic Grail: The Quest for the Northwest Passage and the North Pole, 1818–1909* (New York: Viking, 1988), p. 303. Cf. "*Arctic Explorations: The Second Expedition in Search of Sir John Franklin, 1853, '54, '55*," *Daily Star* (New London), March 16, 1857.

31. William E. Lenz, introduction to *The Poetics of the Antarctic: A Study in Nineteenth-Century American Cultural Perceptions* (New York: Garland, 1995), pp. xxii, xxiv.

32. Davis, "History, or His/story?" p. 101.

33. McClintock initially sold some seven thousand copies of his 1858 book *The Voyage of the "Fox."* Beau Riffenburgh, *The Myth of the Explorer: The Press,*

Sensationalism, and Geographical Discovery (London: Belhaven, 1993), p. 43. See also Shelagh D. Grant, foreword to *The Voyage of the "Fox" in the Arctic Seas*, by Francis Leopold McClintock (Victoria, BC: Touchwood, 2012), p. 2.

34. Clements Markham, *The Threshold of the Unknown Region* (London: Sampson Low, Marston, Low, and Searle, 1873), pp. vi–vii, 271, 195, 123, 190.

35. Robert M. Bryce, *Cook & Peary: The Polar Controversy, Resolved* (Mechanicsburg, PA: Stackpole, 1997), p. 901.

36. Charles Kingsley, *Westward Ho! Or the Voyages and Adventures of Sir Amyas Leigh, Knight, of Burrough, in the County of Devon, in the Reign of Her Most Glorious Majesty, Queen Elizabeth* (London: Macmillan, 1878), dedication page.

37. J. Kennedy Maclean, *Heroes of the Polar Seas: A Record of Exploration in the Arctic and Antarctic Seas* (London: W. and R. Chambers, 1910), pp. 2, 13, 14.

38. Like explorers' speaking tours and meetings with royalty and presidents, medals "certified their stories of success." Dennis Rawlins, *Peary at the North Pole: Fact or Fiction?* (Washington: Robert E. Luce, 1973), p. 61.

39. Conversely, these organizations were quick to discredit explorers whose purported achievements diminished those of the expeditions they had financed. The Arctic Club of America, for instance, led the attack against Frederick Cook, since it had funded Peary: fourteen members of that organization had each donated $4 thousand to finance the latter's bid to be the first person to get to the North Pole. (Wally Herbert, *The Noose of Laurels: The Discovery of the North Pole* [London: Hoddard and Stoughton, 1989], p. 144.)

40. Herbert Ponting, *The Great White South or with Scott in the Antarctic* (New York: Robert M. McBride, 1923), pp. 60, 128, 165.

41. Quoted in Crane, *Scott of Antarctica*, p. 6.

42. Stephen R. Bown, prologue to *The Last Viking: The Life of Roald Amundsen* (New York: Da Capo, 2012), p. xvii.

43. Roland Huntford, *The Last Place on Earth: Scott and Amundsen's Race to the South Pole* (New York: Random House, 1999), p. 76.

44. After his return from the South Pole, Amundsen negotiated a contract giving the London *Daily Chronicle* exclusive newspaper rights outside Scandinavia to his story for £2,000. In Norway, his brother Leon hammered out a deal that earned Amundsen a record amount of 111,000 kroner for the book rights. (Tor Bomann-Larsen, *Roald Amundsen*, trans. Ingrid Christophersen [Stroud, Gloucestershire: History Press, 2014], pp. 113–14.)

45. The English publisher Heinemann had sought to secure publication rights, but withdrew from the competition after deciding the manuscript was lacking in

marketable qualities. (Chris Turner, *1912: The Year the World Discovered Antarctica* [Berkeley: Counterpoint, 2012], p. 136.)

46. Bown, *Last Viking*, pp. 95, 190.

47. Roald Amundsen, *The South Pole: An Account of the Norwegian Antarctic Expedition in the Fram, 1910–1912* (Paderborn: Salzwasser Verlag, 2010), pp. 243, 302.

48. Turner, *1912*, p. 137.

CHAPTER TWELVE: PRINTING THE LEGEND

1. Bruce Henderson, *True North: Peary, Cook, and the Race to the Pole* (New York: Norton, 2005), p. 257.

2. Robert M. Bryce, prologue to *Cook & Peary: The Polar Controversy, Resolved* (Mechanicsburg, PA: Stackpole, 1997), p. xi.

3. Some associate this remark with Edmund Hillary, the first man to climb to the top of Everest. But, in fact, Mallory uttered it just before he set out on his ill-fated climb in 1924.

4. Even in Antarctica, the ice covering its surface moves, at an estimated rate of thirty-three feet per year, in the direction of the Weddell Sea. See Dale Mole, "In Search of Amundsen's Tent," Geographic South Pole, June 3, 2012, https://southpoledoc.wordpress.com/2012/06/03/in-search-of-amundsens-tent/#content (accessed June 3, 2015).

5. Roald Amundsen, *The South Pole: An Account of the Norwegian Antarctic Expedition in the "Fram,"* trans. A. G. Chater (London: John Murray, 1913), pp. xvii–xviii.

6. Scott did think that the tent was not at the pole, but a mile-and-a-half distant from it. (See Robert F. Scott, diary entry of January 18, 1912, quoted in Roland Huntford, *Race for the South Pole: The Expedition Diaries of Scott and Amundsen* [London: Continuum, 2010], p. 249.)

7. "City, State and Nation Welcome Byrd," *New York Times*, June 24, 1926.

8. Before his death in 1928, Bennett reportedly admitted that Byrd had ordered him to go back to Spitsbergen when the leak was discovered. (See, for example, Shelton Bart, *Race to the Top of the World: Richard Byrd and the First Flight to the North Pole* [Washington: Regnery History, 2013], pp. 364–65.) However, Bart and some other historians have concluded that Byrd actually did reach the North Pole. (See, for example, Lisle A. Rose, *Explorer: The Life of Richard E. Byrd* [Columbia: University of Missouri Press, 2008], p. 142.)

9. Frederick A. Cook, *My Attainment of the Pole: Being the Record of the Expedition That First Reached the Boreal Center, 1907–1909* (New York: Kennerly, 1912), p. 27.

10. At least one author (and noted polar explorer) has speculated that Cook's hunger for fame was aroused by his experiences in the Antarctic while serving as physician on the *Belgica*. (Wally Herbert, *The Noose of Laurels: The Discovery of the North Pole* [London: Hodder and Stoughton, 1989], p. 24.) Herbert's book debunking the claims of Cook and Peary was self-serving, in that he and his party had unequivocally arrived at the North Pole in 1969. By undermining the contentions of these two earlier explorers Herbert therefore stood to go into the history books as the first to attain this milestone.

11. For his second attempt at climbing Denali, Cook had received contributions from several patrons, including a saw manufacturer who promised him $10 thousand—or nearly $300 thousand today—if Cook would go hunting with him in Alaska after the climb.

12. Cook's conviction and seven-year prison sentence for promoting a fraudulent oil company in Texas destroyed much of his remaining credibility.

13. Roosevelt's father died when he was twelve, and MacArthur's when Douglas was sixteen.

14. Henderson, *True North*, p. 34.

15. Douglas MacArthur's mother would similarly follow him to West Point when he enrolled there in 1899.

16. In 1887, after his first Arctic expedition, Peary had written, "Remember, mother I *must* have fame, and I cannot reconcile myself to years of commonplace drudgery and a name late in life when I see an opportunity to gain it now and sip the delicious draughts while yet I have youth and strength and capacity to enjoy it to the utmost. And I am not entirely selfish, mother. I want my fame *now* while you can enjoy it too." (Quoted in Herbert, *Noose of Laurels*, p. 65.)

17. John Edward Reems, *Peary: The Explorer and the Man* (Boston: Houghton, Mifflin, 1967), p. 52.

18. Henderson, *True North*, p. 221.

19. "Dr. Cook Admits He Guessed," *Eugene Register-Guardian* (OR), November 30, 1910.

20. Cook, *My Attainment of the Pole*, pp. 3–4.

21. Harold Horwood, *Bartlett: The Great Canadian Explorer* (Garden City, NY: Doubleday, 1977), p. 93.

22. In his diary, Peary did not record that he had arrived at the pole or what he had done during the thirty hours spent there. (Herbert, *Noose of Laurels*, p. 18.)

23. Peary was granted a long-term leave of absence with full pay so that he could focus exclusively on polar exploration.

24. Robert E. Peary, *The North Pole: Its Discovery in 1909 under the Auspices of the Peary Arctic Club* (New York: Greenwood, 1910), pp. 9–10.

25. Henderson, *True North*, p. 186.

26. A typical New York City physician earned $1500 in 1909. Cook earned twice this amount that same year for giving a single lecture on his "discovery" of the North Pole at Carnegie Hall. (Bryce, *Cook & Peary*, p. 956.)

27. Ibid., p. 11.

28. Charles Morris, *Finding the North Pole: Dr. Cook's Own Story of His Discovery, April 21, 1908; The Story of Commander Peary's Discovery, April 6, 1909* (Washington: W. E. Scull, 1909), p. 48.

29. J. Martin Miller, editor's preface, *Discovery of the North Pole: Dr. Frederick A. Cook's Own Story of How He Reached the North Pole, April 21st, 1908, and the Story of Commander Robert E. Peary's Discovery, April 6th, 1909* (Philadelphia: G. A. Parker, 1909), [unpaginated].

30. Letter of Robert E. Peary to Thomas H. Hubbard, January 26, 1911, quoted in Bryce, *Cook & Peary*, p. 525.

31. Even Cook's old friend from the *Belgica* expedition, Roald Amundsen, withdrew his support of the doctor's claim after taking a close look at the evidence.

32. Rebecca M. Herzig, *Suffering for Science: Reason and Sacrifice in Modern America* (New Brunswick: Rutgers University Press, 2005), p. 78.

33. The *Times* paid $4000 for the rights to serialize Peary's account of his polar trek. (Bryce, *Cook & Peary*, p. 377.)

34. "London Applauds Peary's Exploit," *New York Times*, September 7, 1901.

35. *Pittsburgh Press*, September 26, 1909, quoted in Reems, *Peary*, p. 282.

36. The actual finding was that Peary had gotten with 1.6 miles of the pole. This was close enough for him to be named its "discoverer" and be awarded a retirement rank of rear admiral. But Peary still had his detractors, who felt he did not deserve this honor. After the House Committee on Naval Affairs had first rejected promoting Peary, the secretary of the Arctic Club (and staunch supporter of Cook), Captain Bradley S. Osbon, wrote to its members saying that to "have given this selfish egotist, this frigid braggart, the trite rank of Rear Admiral would have been a foul blot on the records of Congress and an insult to the navy of the United States. It would have disgusted millions of our citizens who have no confidence in this alleged pole hunter and arctic fur trader and story teller." ("Osbon Denounces Peary," *New York Times*, February 15, 1910.)

37. "The North Pole Aftermath," remarks of Honorable S. D. Fess, House of

Representatives, March 4, 1915," available online at: http://www.polarcontroversy
.com/fess.htm (accessed April 4, 2016).

38. John Noble Wilford, "Peary Notes Said to Imply He Failed to Reach Pole,"
New York Times, October 13, 1988.

39. Dennis Rawlins, *Peary at the North Pole: Fact or Fiction?* (Washington:
Robert E. Luce, 1973), pp. 144–45. Rawlins caustically noted that "Peary's unique
aiming ability is equalled only by his intuition for gauging distance." The explorer's
"whole claim on precise distance estimation is preposterous, as his own figures show."

40. Hugh Eames, *Winner Lose All: Dr. Cook and the Theft of the North Pole*
(Boston: Little, Brown, 1973), pp. 5, 313.

41. A leading advocate of this conclusion is Robert M. Bryce, in his monumental
Cook & Peary: The Polar Controversy, Resolved (1997).

42. Roger Launius, "Recalling a Century Old Controversy: Did Cook or Peary
Reach the Pole First?" Roger Launius's Blog, September 28, 2015, https://launiusr
.wordpress.com/2015/09/28/recalling-a-century-old-controversy-did-cook-or-peary
-reach-the-north-pole-first/ (accessed January 31, 2016).

43. Norwegian explorer Roald Amundsen would face similar condemnation for
initially concealing from Robert Scott his intent to make for the South Pole.

44. John Crace, "Captain Scott: A Second-Rate Hero?" *Guardian*, September 27,
2010, http://www.theguardian.com/world/2010/sep/27/captain-scott-antarctic
-amundsen-south-pole (accessed February 7, 2016).

45. Solomon has pointed out that unusually cold weather prevented Scott and
his companions from returning to their base camp more speedily.

46. Mole, "In Search of Amundsen's Tent."

47. Beau Riffenburgh, *The Myth of the Explorer: The Press, Sensationalism, and
Geographical Discovery* (London: Belhaven, 1993), p. 3.

INDEX

Tierra del Fuego, 14–15
Tollefsen, Adam, 11
Tyson, George, 156, 228, 231

United States (ship), 193, 214–15
Upernavik (Greenland), 95, 98, 221, 235

Wandel Island, 101
weather, polar, 12, 30, 52, 81, 87, 102, 116, 125, 146, 167, 170, 171, 184–86, 190, 200, 204, 205–206, 238, 239, 248, 332n45
Weyprecht, Karl, 163–66, 173, 190, 310n2

whaling, 11, 25, 28, 32, 48, 101, 165, 177, 195, 301n18
Wilson, Edward A., 62, 78–79, 109, 111–12, 114–15, 117, 125, 160–61, 178–80, 197–98, 229, 236, 243–44, 247–48, 294n23, 299n47, 303n57, 310n42, 314n44, 318n39
Wordie, James, 220
World War I, 18, 100, 113, 165, 177, 182
Worsley, Frank, 41, 111
Worsley, Henry, 207